Taste of TORAH

(a little nosh of d'rash)

Edited by
Rabbi Marshal Klaven

Cover Design and All Illustrations by
Christina Mattison Ebert-Klaven

Goldring/Woldenberg Institute of Southern Jewish Life
P.O. Box 16528 · Jackson, MS 39236 · www.isjl.org

Taste of Torah:
A Little Nosh of D'rash

2013 Paperback, First Printing
© 2013 Goldring/Woldenberg Institute of Southern Jewish Life

Edited by Rabbi Marshal Klaven
Cover Design and All Illustrations by C. Mattison Art & Illustration

ISBN 978-0-9703885-1-3
Manufactured in the United States of America

Published by the Museum of the Southern Jewish Experience,
A Project of Goldring/Woldenberg Institute of Southern Jewish Life
P.O. Box 16528
Jackson, MS 39236
Tel: (601) 362-6357   Fax: (601) 366-6293
www.isjl.org

For our communities, with whom we are blessed to work,
as we strive to sustain and strengthen
Jewish identities and Jewish values in the South.

MENU

THE FIRST COURSE: B'REISHIT • GENESIS

THE SECOND COURSE: SH'MOT • EXODUS

Foreword

This book that you are holding represents not only the latest accomplishment of the Goldring/Woldenberg Institute of Southern Jewish Life, but also the completion of a major milestone in this young organization's life. 2013 is the celebration of the ISJL's "B'nai Mitzvah" year, marking 13 years of our existence. The ISJL was formed with intention and with a very specific purpose. By partnering with communities, congregations, and organizations, the ISJL promotes shared resources, creating a larger pool of resources from which small and middle sized communities can partake. We look toward larger congregations, communities, leaders, funders, agencies, talents, scholars, and others to assist in our outreach to isolated, or underserved, or even neglected communities. As we well know, children from small communities often become leaders in larger communities.

The realization that so much of the growth of the larger urban Jewish populations stems from the outward migration from all corners is still taking a long time to grasp. It behooves all of us to create a new paradigm, informed by the knowledge that reaching the underserved is so critical. Somehow, the Jewish community got focused on Jewish "outreach" referring only to the "un-churched," the unaffiliated, and the intermarried. For decades, we focused on that sort of outreach, neglecting to deliver education and rabbinic services, stimulating arts and culture, and community engagement opportunities to Jews in smaller communities. Instilling an expectation of this Jewish communal life in all of our children, not just those in the biggest cities, can establish a baseline expectation, and when they move from their hometowns to any new location they will already be looking to participate in Jewish life, not because "now they can" but because "they always have and always will."

When the ISJL opened its doors, there was a great deal of optimism coming forth from the Southern Diaspora. Actually, the ISJL is not a "Southern solution" – it is a model for what can be in every section of the U.S. That has always been the vision, and we remain even more committed to this model now, in our second decade of existence. Every day, we are proving the efficacy of this model as we offer more programs, more partnerships, and ultimately a more interrelated Jewish community. Ours is an approach that stretches across the sometimes impenetrable theological boundaries.

Rabbi Marshal Klaven, our current ISJL "itinerant rabbi," has spearheaded the effort to bring this book to fruition. He is a wonderful example of the tremendous impact the ISJL rabbinic program has on the communities we serve. The bar of excellence was first set by Rabbi Debra Kassoff, continued by Rabbi Batsheva Appel, and is now continuing to reach new heights with Rabbi Klaven. My gratitude and praise go to all three of our rabbinic leaders. The ISJL rabbinic program puts our rabbis on the road, but they cannot be everywhere at once. The weekly *Taste of Torah* emails were originally conceived as a way for us to deliver rabbinic support in the form of a share-able *d'var Torah*, accessible from anywhere. Our goal with this, as with so many of our initiatives, is to address the realities of the learners and potential learners we serve, in communities near and far, large and small. The response has been tremendous, ever since we first launched the weekly emails; and now it is our hope that this book will reach and inspire an ever-growing community of learners, across many geographic territories.

I would like to express my gratitude and a hearty mazel tov to Rabbi Marshal Klaven, on the completion of this book. He has overseen the entire process, involved his wonderful staff colleagues, and even secured a generous donor, the Lewis Bear Family Foundation, to provide the funding needed to allow this first publication – and he did all of this while overseeing 94 rabbinic and clergy appearances in 54 communities in the calendar year of 2012. He was unwavering.

As I thought about my writing of this forward, I was reminded that this publication is the passage into adolescence for the ISJL. Every single department within the ISJL has produced significant, thoughtful, practical, stimulating, and much needed opportunities of inclusion for Jewish communities of all sizes. The ISJL's delivery system has been a meaningful partner as well, as our Jewish communities welcome their neighbors who are not, into our spaces. The ISJL continues cultivating our connections, programs, and partnerships, and we are able to proudly witness our neighborhood growing larger.

I hope you enjoy this book, and also hope you will be inspired to learn more about the ISJL– and, of course, sign up for the weekly *Taste of Torah* emails, which are ongoing, so you can continue to be numbered among our neighbors, as well.

Macy B. Hart
ISJL Founder and President

Preface: 13 Years of the ISJL

The idea for the Institute of Southern Jewish Life grew out of the experience of its founder, Macy B. Hart. Raised in Winona, Mississippi, where his was the only Jewish family, Macy learned first-hand the challenges that Jews often face when they live in isolated and remote communities. His parents, Ellis and Reva Hart, drove Macy and his three siblings more than seventy miles to religious school – for several years, this meant a trip to Greenwood, Mississippi; later, when Greenwood's religious school closed, the Harts traveled instead to Cleveland, Mississippi. In addition to religious school, the Hart children attended youth group events at Temple Adath Israel in Cleveland; Macy was extremely active in the youth group, eventually becoming the president of the National Federation of Temple Youth when he was in college. This personal connection to the small-town southern experience and his commitment to fostering Jewish community shaped Macy's career.

In 1970, at age 22, Macy was hired to be the administrator for the newly established Henry S. Jacobs Camp in Utica, Mississippi. A part of the national network of summer camps owned by the Reform Movement's Union of American Hebrew Congregations, Jacobs Camp was built by the Jewish families of Mississippi, Arkansas, Louisiana and west Tennessee, with each congregation in the region raising money to build it. While the UAHC initially discouraged this effort, since the region it would serve had such a small Jewish population, the Jews of the region built it anyway, and donated it to the Union, who agreed to add it to the Reform Movement's national network. For these parents, such a camp would be an essential tool in transmitting Judaism to the next generation in a region where many of their children had little or no Jewish peer-group.

The following year, Macy became the director of Jacobs Camp and traveled throughout Mississippi, Arkansas, Louisiana, and western Tennessee to recruit Jewish children for the summer. Since it was one of the only non-congregational Jewish institutions in the region, Jacobs Camp, under Macy's leadership, became more than just a summer camp for children. It served as a hub for Jewish religious and cultural life in the region, with special programs and scholar-in-residence weekends during the off-season. It became a center of Jewish life in the region, especially for those living in small communities.

By the 1970s, many of these small Jewish communities were shrinking as children moved away to larger cities after college in search of greater social and economic opportunities. Since the 19th century, Jews had formed an important part of the merchant class in many of these small towns. But the economic decline of areas like the Mississippi Delta, structural changes in the retail industry, and the movement of Jews into the professional ranks drained the South's small towns of their Jewish population. One could witness these changes at Jacobs Camp, where in its early years a sizable minority of campers came from small communities. Over time, the number of Jewish children in these communities shrank. By the 1980s, several of the smaller congregations in the region were disbanding, and the camp became the repository for much of the Judaica that once graced the sanctuaries of synagogues that were now closed.

The impulse to preserve these physical artifacts as well as the stories of these dying communities led Macy to create the Museum of the Southern Jewish Experience in 1986. From the beginning, the museum was designed to be integrated into Jacobs Camp. Located on the camp grounds in Utica, the building would serve as both a museum and an indoor worship space for the camp. In May, 1986, the Plough Foundation of Memphis donated the money to build the museum. Julian and Kathryn Wiener, two leaders of the Jewish community in Jackson, Mississippi, agreed to serve as founding co-chairs of the museum. Vicki Reikes, a native of Hattiesburg, Mississippi, was brought in to help plan the museum, serving as its first project director, while Al Hopton and Melanie Dann were the architects of the building. In 1989, the Museum of the Southern Jewish Experience was dedicated in a ceremony featuring former Mississippi Governor William Winter and Rabbi Alexander Schindler, president of the UAHC.

The museum quickly began to document Jewish life in the region, especially in those places where the Jewish community was shrinking. The museum commissioned noted photographer Bill Aron to travel the Deep South taking pictures of contemporary Jewish life and vestiges of Jewish history in the region. The collection of photographs he produced, "Images of Southern Jewish Life," traveled around the country in addition to becoming the museum's first permanent exhibit. In 1991, the museum hired Marcie Cohen as its project director, who continued to travel with Aron to document Jewish life. Under Marcie's leadership, the museum continued its outreach to Jewish communities in the Deep South, collecting artifacts and oral histories. That same year, the museum also began to produce a regular newsletter, *Circa*. Herman Kohlmeyer was elected chairman of the board in 1991, a position he held for the next nine years.

In 1992, the museum entered into an unprecedented preservation agreement with Temple B'nai Israel in Natchez, Mississippi. The dwindling congregation owned a beautiful synagogue, built in 1905, and feared that it would be unable to maintain the building into the future. The Museum of the Southern Jewish Experience agreed to take ownership of the building. As long as the congregation remained active, they would maintain and operate the building; but once the congregation disbanded, the museum would preserve and operate the synagogue as a satellite branch of the MSJE. After the agreement, Marcie put together a series of exhibit panels telling the history of the Natchez Jewish community, entitled "The Natchez Jewish Experience," which was installed in the basement of the building. In 1994, the museum organized a Natchez Homecoming event, which brought in guest speakers and musicians to celebrate the history of Mississippi's oldest Jewish community. The documentary produced for this event, *The Natchez Jewish Experience*, won the 1994 Muse Award. Marcie Cohen left the museum in 1995 to pursue a successful academic career in the history of southern Jews and foodways.

The next major project of the museum was centered around the blockbuster "Splendors of Versailles" French art exhibit scheduled for Jackson, Mississippi in the summer of 1998. Macy had the idea to put together a satellite exhibit about the immigration of Alsatian Jews to the South that would capitalize on the large number of tourists that would be drawn to Jackson. In preparation for this major undertaking, the museum hired Dr. Mark Greenberg, the first historian on its staff, who worked on the research for the exhibit. By the fall of 1997, the MSJE had five staff members, who focused most of their efforts on putting together the exhibit. "Alsace to America," the museum's first major public exhibit was housed in downtown Jackson, not far from the "Splendors of Versailles" exhibit. In an effort to encourage visitors to spend multiple nights in the area, museum staff prepared a free guidebook to Jewish sites along the Mississippi River between Memphis and New Orleans entitled "Cultural Corridors." Exhibit-goers were also encouraged to visit the MSJE locations in Utica and Natchez. During the summer of 1998, over 26,000 people visited one of these MSJE exhibits. "Alsace to America" won several awards, including the Travel Attraction of the Year from the Mississippi Tourism Association, as well as awards from the Mississippi Arts Commission, Mississippi Heritage Trust, and the Mississippi Historical Society. After the summer, a smaller version of "Alsace to America" was installed in the Utica site as the new permanent exhibit.

During its first thirteen years of existence, the MSJE was focused on preserving, documenting, and interpreting the history of Jews in the South. After the great success of the Alsace exhibit, the museum continued its efforts to highlight southern Jewish history. Historian Mark Greenberg was honored as the Scholar of the Year in 2000 by the Mississippi Humanities Council for this work. But Macy's ambitions transcended the museum and its preservation of the past.

By the mid-1980s, Macy had the idea to create an institute of southern Jewish life, which would serve the current needs of southern Jewish communities in addition to preserving their histories. Macy envisioned a circuit-riding rabbi, who would travel to congregations in the region who did not have rabbinic leadership, as well as a traveling educator, who would work with the small religious schools in the region. In his initial formulation, the institute would also incorporate Jacobs Camp and would operate under the auspices of the UAHC. Macy proposed a new regional system for the Reform Movement, with each region having its own Institute that would serve the needs of all of its member congregations. When the national leaders of the UAHC did not support this new approach, Macy decided to move forward anyway with an institute for the Deep South region. In 1999, Macy secured grants from the Goldring Family Foundation, the Woldenberg Foundation, Steven Spielberg's Righteous Persons Foundation, the Samuel Bronfman Foundation, Soref-

Breslauer Foundation and others to support the expansion of the MSJE's mission. He also received a $250,000 challenge grant from various donors, which he supplemented by raising $216,000 in new gifts. These donations provided the seed money for the newly expanded organization.

In January of 2000, the Museum of the Southern Jewish Experience officially changed its name to the Institute of Southern Jewish Life with an explicit mission to serve the small, isolated Jewish communities of the region that had long been overlooked by national Jewish organizations and the Movements. According to the founding statement printed in *Circa*, the ISJL planned to employ a circuit-riding rabbi and educator to serve these communities, to preserve and maintain Jewish cemeteries and historic sites in the region, to record oral histories, and to develop a genealogy center. The Institute also planned to become an advocate for these small and isolated communities. Since the UAHC was not interested in supporting the work of the Institute, Macy left his position as director of Jacobs Camp, which he had held for thirty years, in order to devote all of his energy to the ISJL. Sylvia Goodman became the first board chairman for the ISJL in 2000. In September of that year, the ISJL held a gala event in New Orleans to officially launch the newly expanded organization. During the event, Bill Goldring announced a $3 million naming gift to the ISJL from the Goldring Family Foundation and the Woldenberg Foundation. With this important funding secured, the Goldring/Woldenberg Institute of Southern Jewish Life moved forward with its new expanded mission.

One of the first areas the ISJL expanded into was cultural programming. Lynette Allen came to the ISJL in 2000 to organize cultural events and bring touring artists and scholars to the region. The following year, Lynette created Jewish Cinema South, partnering with various local Jewish communities to create a network of film festivals that highlighted Jewish themes. During the program's first year, film festivals were held in Mobile, Montgomery, and Nashville. Historians Clive Webb and Lawrence Powell took part in the ISJL's Southern States Jewish Literary Series, traveling to various southern cities to speak about their books on southern Jewish history. In 2001, the ISJL organized "From Spanish Roots: A Jewish Cultural Expo," a weeklong series of events highlighting the heritage of Sephardic Jews in the South. Ellen Kushner, of National Public Radio's "Sound & Spirit" performed a concert during the celebration. Mark Greenberg and oral historian David Sampliner put together a new "Cultural Corridors" travel guidebook, giving the histories of eighteen different Jewish communities along the I-20 corridor in Texas, Louisiana, Mississippi, and Alabama. Greenberg left the ISJL in 2001, and was replaced by Dr. Stuart Rockoff the following year.

During 2002, the ISJL worked on a strategic plan that mapped out the organization's proposed expansion throughout the South over the following decade. To help fund these ambitious goals, Macy initiated a challenge in which a few individual donors pledged to give $500,000 if the Institute could raise another $1 million. With the help of his small staff, Macy reached the $1 million dollar goal by the October 31 deadline. The successful challenge campaign enabled the ISJL to hire new programmatic staff, including a rabbi, oral historian, educator, two education fellows, and seven summer interns. In 2003, Jay Tanenbaum became the chairman of the ISJL board.

That same year, the ISJL hired its first rabbi, Debra Kassoff, a recent graduate of Hebrew Union College in Cincinnati. Rabbi Kassoff was charged with serving the 34% of southern Jewish congregations that did not have a full-time rabbi. The idea of a circuit-riding rabbi was not new – such itinerant rabbis had been visiting small Jewish communities as far back as the 19th century. In this sense, the ISJL Rabbinic Department was reviving a "bold, old idea." The Rabbinic Department also hoped to bring visiting rabbis from other regions to serve small communities in the South. Even before Rabbi Kassoff officially started her new position in the summer of 2003, the ISJL's new rabbinic position received public recognition. The State of Mississippi asked the ISJL rabbi to give the benediction at the rededication of the Mississippi State Capitol in honor of the building's 100th anniversary.

The Education Department evolved significantly during its early years. By 2000, the ISJL was seeking to hire a professional Jewish educator, though it would take a few years to achieve this goal. Initially, the idea was to hire a credentialed educator with a graduate degree who would hold training sessions for religious school teachers in the Deep South, focusing on those from small congregations that did not have a full-time educator. The plan was to eventually hire five of these educators who would cover the entire South. The Education Department would create a standardized curriculum with carefully prepared lesson plans to help Sunday School teachers. This educator would also organize adult education programs over the internet. By 2002, with the department still in the idea phase, Macy decided to use education fellows, recent college graduates, to work directly with the congregations in the region.

In 2003, the ISJL moved forward with its education program, hiring an interim educator who created the spiral design of the curriculum, and partnering with the Community Foundation for Jewish Education of Metropolitan Chicago, who helped consult on the curriculum. The plan, announced in the winter issue of *Circa* in 2003, was to write a detailed curriculum, with scripted lesson plans, and to hire a full-time educator and two education fellows. The concept behind the curriculum was to create a common body of Jewish knowledge for supplementary religious school instruction. The ISJL Education Program would be piloted in four states: Mississippi, Louisiana, Alabama, and Arkansas, with plans to eventually expand to cover the 13 states of the South. The ISJL planned to hold a "Jewish educational workshop" at the end of the summer during which the curriculum and lesson plans would be presented to religious schools participating in the program. During the summer of 2003, three interns, all of whom were graduate students in Jewish education (two from the Jewish Theological Seminary and one from Gratz College), wrote the first semester's lesson plans, along with the first education fellows hired, Beth Kander and Amanda Abrams. The first education conference was held in

August at the Duncan Gray Conference Center outside of Jackson. It drew 32 participants from fifteen different communities, who agreed to take part in the first-year pilot of the program. A second conference was held in January 2004 to give out the second semester's lesson plans.

A central part of the ISJL philosophy was to take programs into the field, reaching out to the isolated Jewish communities in the South. As Macy wrote in *Circa* in 2003, "our success will be built upon the road trips of our Education Fellows and our Rabbi." That year, the ISJL's program staff visited 36 different communities, most of which were in Louisiana, Mississippi, Alabama, and Arkansas. Over the next several years, the Institute would expand its reach, eventually encompassing all thirteen states of the region. The Institute has always been trans-denominational, working with Reform, Conservative, Reconstructionist, and unaffiliated congregations.

Promoting Jewish culture in the region has remained an important part of the ISJL's mission. In 2005, the Institute brought leading historians of American Jewish history, including Deborah Dash Moore, Jenna Joselit, Stephen Whitfield, and Eli Evans to speak in several different southern Jewish communities. The following year, Marcie Cohen Ferris, who had previously served as the Project Director for the Museum of the Southern Jewish Experience and was now a professor at the University of North Carolina, went on two different literary tours to talk about her book *Matzoh Ball Gumbo*. The Institute also co-sponsored artistic programs, including Claudia Stevens' one woman show "An Evening with Madame F" and an exhibit by noted Jewish ritual object artist Tobi Kahn. Music was also a focus of ISJL cultural programming. In 2008, the Institute organized two concerts by the Robyn Helzner trio in areas still suffering from the effects of Hurricane Katrina. These free concerts, which were funded by the Covenant Foundation, were designed to bring the communities together for healing and friendship. In 2010, the ISJL partnered with the Charles and Lynn Schusterman Family Foundation to bring in Amir Gwirtzman as a musician-in-residence. For four months, Amir, a celebrated Israeli musician who plays 26 different wind instruments, traveled around the South giving concerts to both Jewish and non-Jewish groups in eight different states. His travels in Alabama were featured in a television program broadcast by the state's public television station. Since Lynette Allen left in 2003, Beth Kander, Andy Muchin, and Ann Kimball have filled the position of Director of Cultural Programming.

Since arriving in 2002, Dr. Stuart Rockoff has served as Director of the History Department at the ISJL. Under his leadership, the department has worked to document, preserve, and interpret the history of Jews in the South. Stuart has spoken about the Southern Jewish Experience to congregations and groups around the country and has published numerous articles and essays about the subject. After Hurricane Katrina, the ISJL partnered with the Jewish Women's Archive in Boston to produce the "Katrina's Jewish Voices" Oral History Project. These 80 video oral histories document the impact and response to the cataclysmic storm by the Jewish communities of New Orleans, Baton Rouge, and the Mississippi Gulf Coast. In 2006, Rockoff launched the "Digital Archive," later renamed the "Encyclopedia of Southern Jewish Communities," designed to offer online histories of every organized Jewish community in the South. States were added to the website one-by-one as the research and writing were completed. Mississippi, the first state, went online in 2006. By the end of 2012, ten states were completed with almost 250 community histories available as the encyclopedia was attracting almost 10,000 page-views per month. The Encyclopedia of Southern Jewish Communities has become an essential resource for teachers, students, and anyone interested in the history of southern Jews. In 2010, the Mississippi Humanities Council gave Stuart its Preserver of Mississippi Culture award.

Oral history has long been central to the work of the ISJL. Over the years, various staff oral historians have interviewed important and elderly members of southern Jewish communities. By 2012, the ISJL had over 800 interviews in its collection. Portions of some of these interviews have been used to illustrate community histories in the Encyclopedia of Southern Jewish Communities. Since 2009, Josh Parshall has worked as the ISJL Oral Historian, capturing essential stories that would otherwise be lost to history. Over the last decade, the History Department has continued to pursue the original mission of the Museum of the Southern Jewish Experience, to record and share the rich heritage of southern Jews.

As the Institute expanded to meet its new mission, the Museum of the Southern Jewish Experience, operating under its auspices, continued to preserve and share the story of southern Jews. One important role played by the museum has been to help closing congregations make the difficult transition from active to inactive. The museum received a wealth of documents and records from Clarksdale, Mississippi's Congregation Beth Israel after it closed in 2003. In 2006, the museum received two Torahs from the Clarksdale congregation, gifts of Lawrence Magdovitz. These Magdovitz Torahs have been lent out to other congregations in the region who needed a scroll. Also in 2006, the Institute helped to close down the synagogue in Helena, Arkansas after the dwindling membership of Temple Beth El decided they could no longer maintain the congregation. Rabbi Kassoff led the final service at the Helena temple, while Stuart Rockoff spoke about the history of the Jewish community during the bittersweet homecoming weekend. The Institute also helped to find new homes for the temple's Judaica and other items, which were given to a new congregation in Bentonville, Arkansas, as well as Temple Israel in Memphis, which used the artifacts to decorate a new chapel at the congregation's cemetery. The museum became the repository of artifacts and documents from several defunct congregations, including those in Demopolis, Alabama, Port Gibson, Mississippi, Corsicana, Texas, and many others.

In 2009, the ISJL worked with the few remaining members of B'nai Sholom in Brookhaven, Mississippi to help them close their 113-year-old synagogue, which was donated to the local historical society for use as a museum. Afterward, the Museum of the Southern Jewish Experience developed a small exhibit in the old synagogue that became a part of the museum's permanent display. The museum has been involved with several other projects in recent years. Museum Projects Coordinator, Kate Lubarsky, worked with the Historic Natchez Foundation to bring the traveling Smithsonian Exhibit "Journey Stories" to Natchez in 2009. Her successor, Rachel Jarman, who had earlier been an Education Fellow, developed a traveling trunk program in 2011 that taught school children across Mississippi about the Jewish immigrant experience in the state. This project prompted the Mississippi Humanities Council to give Jarman its Educator of the Year Award in 2012. The museum also co-sponsored the "Beyond Swastika and Jim Crow" exhibit with Tougaloo College in Jackson, which told the story of Jewish refugees who taught at black colleges in the South. In conjunction with the exhibit, Jarman organized an anti-prejudice workshop led by the Anti-Defamation League for local teenagers as well as a Freedom Seder that brought together blacks and Jews for a celebration of liberation from bondage. Since its inception, the Museum has frequently collaborated with and supported other cultural institutions, from Millsaps College to the Mississippi Museum of Art, and many others. Even after the Utica site of the museum closed in 2012, the Museum of the Southern Jewish Experience remains a vital part of the organization, working to preserve and interpret the story of southern Jews.

No part at the ISJL has grown as much as the Education Department. In 2005, the number of education fellows grew from two to three. By 2007, their number had doubled to six. By 2009, the department had ten education fellows and two full-time educators. During the initial pilot period, congregations who attended the summer education conference received access to the curriculum along with three visits from an education fellow each year for no charge aside from travel expenses. While only fifteen congregations were part of the program in its first year, this number had more than doubled by 2006. By 2008, sixty different Jewish congregations used the ISJL education system. The following year, the department reached a milestone when congregations in each of the thirteen southern states were part of the ISJL education program, which now reached over 3000 students in seventy different congregations. The steady growth in the education program during these early years was testament to the crucial need that it served. In 2008, the curriculum came out of pilot and participating congregations began to pay a fee, based on their number of students, to take part in the program. The ISJL Education Department has worked with schools with as few as one student and with as many as 300.

This tremendous growth has been overseen by Rachel Stern, who became the full-time Director of Education in 2006 after previously serving as a part-time consultant for the ISJL. Under Rachel's leadership, the ISJL curriculum was retooled each year, as lesson plans were improved and new supplementary units added. Sometimes these new units have been inspired by popular demand. When some congregations expressed interest in a high school unit on cyber-bullying, the Education Department developed one in 2010. Most every weekend during the school year, ISJL education fellows rent cars or board airplanes to visit one of the many congregations using the curriculum. During their visits, fellows sometimes lead services, Torah study, family education programs, or whatever else the community desires. These fellow visits are the embodiment of the ISJL's founding philosophy to take programs out to the communities and foster the growth of Jewish cultural and religious life in the region.

These principles have also guided the work of the Rabbinic Department. Since the hiring of its first rabbi in 2003, the ISJL has served small congregations without rabbinic leadership. Three rabbis have led the department: Debra Kassoff, from 2003-2006; Batsheva Appel, from 2006-2009; and Marshal Klaven, 2009-present. Each of the ISJL rabbis performed the duties of regular congregational rabbis, officiating at life cycle events, leading Shabbat services, and teaching Torah to their congregants. The only difference is that the ISJL rabbi's congregation is scattered throughout the South. Most weekends, the ISJL rabbi drives to small congregations across the region. To reach this far-flung virtual congregation, in 2003 the Rabbinic Department started sending out "Taste of Torah," a weekly Torah commentary email that is sometimes read from the *bimah* as the sermon during lay-led Shabbat services. Although the Rabbinic Department has never had more than one rabbi, supplemented by rabbinic student interns over the summer, it has worked to cover more of the region. In 2010, Rabbi Klaven visited congregations in ten different states. During his 2011 Passover Pilgrimage, he visited nine different communities in four states over ten days. In 2011, with help from a student rabbinic intern and visiting rabbis, the department served 34 different congregations with 57 visits. And, in 2012, the rabbinic outreach increased to 52 congregations on 97 visits, reaching over 5000 individuals.

The ISJL's circuit-riding rabbi has received a lot of recognition and press attention. Stories about the rabbi have appeared in many local newspapers in addition to the *New York Times* and *the Economist* magazine as well as on National Public Radio and the History Channel. Inspired by the Institute's idea of serving small, isolated congregations, several rabbis across the country have volunteered their time through the ISJL's "Rabbis on the Road" program. In 2012, Central Synagogue in New York City partnered with the ISJL to serve small congregations in the South, modeling the true sense of community that can exist between congregations of all sizes. Five of their clergy, under the leadership of Senior Rabbi Peter Rubinstein, visited eighteen different congregations to lead religious services and community programs.

While the ISJL program staff has been the public face of the organization, a number of behind-the-scenes stalwarts have been essential to the Institute's success. Lynda Yule started working for Jacobs Camp and the Museum of the Southern Jewish Experience in 1992, moving to the Institute full-time in 2000 as an administrative assistant. Lynda is the "voice of the ISJL" who answers the telephone - quite rare in this age of automated phone systems. Betsy Samuels also worked for the camp and the museum before joining the ISJL in 2000 as Chief Financial Officer. Nonnie Campbell has worked with Macy since 1990, and has been involved with the museum and the Institute from the very beginning as Office Administrator. Shirley Eriksen has worked as an administrative assistant for the Rabbinic and Education Departments since 2007.

In 2005, the Institute raised over $500,000 in its annual campaign from 860 donors and also received major grants from several large Jewish foundations. In 2006, the ISJL was named as one of the most innovative Jewish organizations in the country by Slingshot. The Institute has remained on the Slingshot list ever since, being named one of the ten "standard bearers" for Jewish innovation in 2011 and 2012. As the Institute expanded, Michele Schipper was hired in 2007 to serve as Chief Operating Officer, running the day-to-day operations of the organization while Macy focused on raising money to support the Institute's programs. In 2008, the ISJL received major grants from the Jim Joseph Foundation, the Marcus Foundation, and the Natan Fund. Rayman Solomon replaced Jay Tanenbaum as chairman of the ISJL board in 2009.

In 2008, the ISJL sought to create a new department that would reach beyond the Jewish world into the larger community. In the fall of that year, with generous support from a major foundation, the ISJL received a three-year grant to start a Social Justice Department. In 2009, Malkie Schwartz, the founder of Footsteps, a New York-based non-profit that was also listed in Slingshot, was hired to head up this new department. Under Malkie's leadership, this new initiative, which was renamed the Department of Community Engagement, started a peer mediation program called "Talk about the Problems (TAP)" in Jackson schools. The department also started the "Read, Lead, Succeed" program that worked on child literacy. Starting in 2011, the ISJL partnered with AmeriCorps to support an AmeriCorps fellow to work in the Department of Community Engagement. In 2012, the ISJL's TAP program was honored as a Mississippi Kids Count Success Story, while Malkie was named a Repair the World Fellow, working to create effective and meaningful Jewish service opportunities.

In 2012, with six active departments and a staff of 22 full-time and two part-time employees, the ISJL has come a long way from 1986 when it was a fledgling museum that existed primarily on letterhead. Throughout its history, the Institute has remained focused on serving the Jewish communities of the South, preserving their histories and helping ensure their futures. While its mission has remained steady, the organization has changed with the times, creating an active presence on Facebook, Twitter, and blog hosted by myjewishlearning.com. Through all of this growth and change, the Institute enters its B'nai Mitzvah year committed to the original vision of its founder, Macy Hart: *k'lal Yisrael*; every Jewish life counts, no matter where they live. They deserve Jewish culture, education, rabbinic services, and having their legacy preserved long after they are gone.

Stuart Rockoff, Ph.D.
ISJL Director, History Department

Introduction

"Check Tire Pressure." The message lit-up on the dashboard of my rental car. I was driving through Arkansas, in November, early in my work as the ISJL Circuit-riding Rabbi. For many, thoughts of a punctured tire might enter the mind along with a concern for an impending blowout, leaving the would-be traveler stranded on some remote country road. But my mind carried no such worry. My dad was an auto-mechanic. And, I had learned long ago – under his tutelage – that in winter, as the air gets cold, it is natural for the tire to lose some pressure because the individual air molecules within it slow and condense. So, I continued to drive.

Passing cotton field after cotton field, I began to think about how this natural process applied to so many other things in life. That is to say, when the winter season of existence rolls around, most things seem to naturally slow and condense, saving what little energy they have left for when it really matters. But, what about our congregants in these small Southern towns; how are they weathering the winter season in the life of their congregations? Do these individual molecules that make for solid Jewish communities likewise slow and condense? Or, do they somehow respond differently?

I ask because many of the 100-plus congregations under the ISJL Rabbinic Department's care feel the chill of winter more and more acutely with the passing of each year. Or, more accurately, we could say that this blustery change in season for the congregation is felt more and more acutely with the passing of each member. For the greatest resource of any congregation is its membership and, when that membership decreases, especially within these small Jewish communities, an external pressure mounts, a pressure that frankly threatens to flatten the congregation.

Yet, in my travels, I've observed many of these congregations defying the natural process. In the face of dwindling membership and resources, their individual congregants actually increase their activity, exuding an internal pressure which keeps the mounting external one at bay. As one of these congregants told me, "The weight of maintaining our little community is mounting on our shoulders. We can shrug off our responsibility. But, then, our congregation will fall. Or, we can bulk up, embracing our responsibility to hold up our congregation as high as we can, for as long as we can."

That is where the ISJL comes in. We are the mechanics of the Jewish communal world, helping our people find innovative ways to maintain the vehicle of their sacred lives in America: the congregation. With our resources and expertise in Jewish history, education, culture, community engagement, and religion, we – day-in and day-out – lift souls up, energizing the batteries of their minds, filling the tanks of their hearts. And, in doing so, these congregants (who valiantly work under ever-increasing pressure) can continue to drive on, delivering our precious Jewish heritage to the next generation, who receive it as a priceless inheritance.

Taste of Torah: From a Tasty Treat to a Full Meal

One of the tools of our trade is Taste of Torah, produced by the ISJL's Rabbinic Department. Simply put, each weekly Taste of Torah is a modern reflection of our ancient textual traditions that allow their eternal guidance to be heard and weighed into today's challenges. Reflections, such as these, have been called: *d'var Torah* (a word of Torah), *parshat hashavuah* (weekly portion), and *d'rash* (commentary). Historically, these messages were delivered in person by some sage. In fact, many are the stories in our culture about *shtetl* folk (townspeople) who eagerly awaited the circuit-riding rabbi of their time – like the Baal Shem Tov – to inspire them with God's teachings.

Nowadays, thanks to the blessing of technology, people don't have to wait so long. With a click of the button, these insights can be sent directly from the sage (wherever he/she may reside) to the home of those who wish to continue to grow in mind, heart, and soul. As such, reflections on our weekly portions have become ubiquitous in the Jewish world, as everyone and their bubbie seems to send one out: The Union of Reform Judaism's *Ten Minutes of Torah*, Chabad's *Parasha in a Nutshell*, The United Synagogue of Conservative Judaism's *Torah Sparks*, The American Israel Public Affairs Committee's *Sermon Tidbits*, etc. etc. And, this does not account for the numerous blogs, posts, and tweets sent by inspired individuals.

But, that was not the case back in the early 2000s, when the ISJL hired their first full-time Circuit-riding Rabbi, Rabbi Debra Kassoff. Rabbi Kassoff was ordained by the Hebrew Union College-Jewish Institute of Religion (HUC-JIR) in Cincinnati in 2003. Before entering the seminary, Rabbi Kassoff earned degrees in English Literature and Women's Studies from Williams College as well as an M.A. in English from Indiana University. Her training, her innate talents, and her passion made Rabbi Kassoff the ideal person to kick-start this hugely successful service for our innovative organization, the communities we are blessed to serve, as well as so many others beyond our region.

But let's be clear. Like all new recipes, it was not certain that this Taste of Torah would pleasure the palates of our people. So, initially, the tasting stayed in-house, delivered as openings to weekly staff meetings. Almost entirely written and delivered by Rabbi Kassoff, these weekly words from our tradition guided and inspired the ISJL staff in their devotion to our Southern congregations, who strive to sustain and strengthen Jewish identities and values in their areas. "God's word brought our people together then," shared ISJL Founder and President Macy B. Hart, upon reflection of our existence in the wilderness, "and it did so in those early years of the ISJL."

Not wanting to horde these Torah treats, the ISJL set its sights on sharing them as soon as possible. There was, however, one caveat. We did not want our delectable creation to be greeted and treated like spam, quickly stored only to be later chucked into the waste basket. "Certainly, this would have happened if we sent it out blindly, signing up people regardless of whether or not they wanted it," remarked Hart. "So, its construction was commenced with great consideration. One, it would only be sent to those who signed up. Two, it would be free. The Taste of Torah would be one of our many contributions to the Jewish community, both here in the South and anyone else who wished to subscribe. The rest I left to my rabbis."

Indeed, all of the ISJL's circuit-riding rabbis left their mark on the Taste of Torah, crafting it into one of the most successful online commentaries in existence today. Beginning with Rabbi Kassoff, who not only got the service going, but she also built its readership one person at a time... literally. As there was no affordable email services for small non-profit agencies at the time, Rabbi Kassoff went about the pain-staking process of collecting emails of interested individuals along her travels and adding them to a list. This bulk email list constituted the first distribution system for this Southern voice on our sacred traditions, which – by the time Rabbi Kassoff's tenure was complete – could proudly boast of having a readership of over 500.

They came to dine on Torah's knowledge because of the intimate connection Rabbi Kassoff made with each and every reader. As she expressed at the opening of her first Taste of Torah in October of 2003: "Dear Friends, this is the first of what will be a weekly message that I am writing especially for communities on my circuit. For me, it will be a way to keep in touch, to continue to be with you in spirit when I cannot be physically present. For you, it will be a Taste of Torah, a brief insight into the weekly Torah portion for you to enjoy. It will also be an opportunity for a direct line of communication—I encourage you to write back whenever you have anything to share or ask."

And they did. Even when Rabbi Kassoff left, her readers remained. They understood that they had generated a relationship not just with one rabbi, but with an organization that had their interests at heart. They remained and many, many more joined in a pivotal period of growth for the ISJL and Taste of Torah, under the new spiritual leadership of Rabbi Batsheva Appel. Rabbi Appel was ordained from the HUC-JIR in New York in 1996. After serving Jewish communities in New Jersey, New York, and Pennsylvania, Rabbi Appel wished to invest her time and talents with our Southern congregations, who had long transmitted the values of Torah from one generation to the next through story telling.

"Stories are often the best way to transmit Jewish values," said Rabbi Appel in 2006, as she began her work with the ISJL. Rabbi Appel went about that transmission task brilliantly, using stories from our tradition, stories from her time on the road, stories from here and stories from there to teach Torah and inspire generations old and young, who considered themselves blessed to be part of her growing readership. In fact, through her promotional and creative writing efforts, the Taste of Torah readership doubled over the course of Rabbi Appel's service to our Southern congregations. "Her concise and clear delivery," responded one reader, "made me look forward to each week with hope and excitement."

Rabbi Appel's delivery was aided by an online distribution service called Constant Contact. Yes, finally, technology had caught up with our imaginations! Not only did Constant Contact allow individuals to sign up directly with them and receive a Taste of Torah in their email each week from us, it also allowed us – under the direction of Rabbi Appel – to take its previous list-serve style and transform it into a real online colomn. It was an appealing change, as it gave the Taste of Torah a whole new look with color, photos, and various ways the readership could – if they so chose – connect with the ISJL Rabbi, and take advantage of the ISJL's various other resources.

With appreciation and affection for both my predecessors – Rabbi Appel and Rabbi Kassoff – I came to the ISJL upon my ordination from the HUC-JIR in 2009 to continue their inspirational work and try to build upon it. This has certainly come to fruition with our community outreach, as the Rabbinic Department now visits 50 small Southern congregations without full-time clergy in all 13 states of our region each year. As our outreach has expanded, so has the Taste of Torah service... thanks to a group effort! From our Education Fellows to our Historians, from our Cultural Program Ambassadors to our Community Engagement Specialists, all have promoted this resource to our communities and beyond.

That collective recipe, which has made Taste of Torah so deliciously appealing to our readers, is not complete. We continue to grow and expand our Taste of Torah offering. In the future, we hope to provide audio and visual recordings of the reflections, giving the tonal flavor of the piece that is sometimes lost in its written form. Congregations could then elect to project the visual reading during services, making the Taste of Torah delivery more intimate than ever before. While we continue to look to the future, we celebrate our past with this Taste of Torah book. It is meant to mark our B'nai Mitzvah Anniversary, thirteen blessed years of serving our Southern congregations, as we work with them to strengthen Judaism in the South.

Consuming the Contents of Taste of Torah

Judaism is a smorgasbord, offering a variety of items to nourish the mind, heart, and soul of the individual Jew and his/her Jewish community. In no way, could just one bite satiate the spiritual hunger our members. Therefore, much of the book that follows presents three different "bites" (*divrei Torah*) for each of the weekly Torah portions. We chose three to reflect the traditional Jewish practice of reading the Torah on a triennial cycle. That is to say, there is a custom of breaking up each Torah portion into three sections – one read each year for three years – so that, by the end of the third year, the congregation will have heard every part of every portion of Torah.

These measured bites of Torah allow for better digestion of the spiritual substance contained therein. Similarly, we hope that the Taste of Torah "bites" will allow for better consumption of the meaningful messages reflected from the weekly portions crafted by our Circuit-riding Rabbis. Readers are advised not to read every bite, one right after the other, making their way through the entire five course meal of Torah (a.k.a. the five books of Genesis, Exodus, Leviticus, Numbers, and Deuteronomy) in one sitting. That would, as with any over-indulgent dining experience, leave one feeling full to the point of nausea.

Thus, the ideal intellectual diet-plan for reading *Taste of Torah: A Little Nosh of D'rash* is to follow the portion calendar, devouring one to two "bites" each week. In this way, their meaningful material may marinate on the mind, allowing a reader's thoughts to bubble to the surface of cognition. This is one of the secrets to our successful recipe. The Taste of Torah is not a one-way highway, by which the Circuit-riding Rabbi comes to deliver God's teaching to our readers' tables. Rather, the ISJL's Taste of Torah is a crossroads where reader and writer meet and together work to uncover the Divine in all things.

Like every good adventure, one needs road snacks. We've got you covered, as this book includes – along the reading course – traditional Jewish recipes with a Southern twist: sweet potato challah with a honey-cinnamon glaze for Shabbat, hush puppy latkes as well as *sufganiot* and strawberries (a.k.a. beignets and berries) for Chanukah, pecan pie *hamantaschen* for Purim, fried matza balls with a *t'shuvah* (a.k.a. comeback) dipping sauce for Passover, a sweet tea *kugel* as well as a pimento cheese potato *kugel* with a kick for Shavuot, and a challah bread pudding with apples and honey bourbon for Rosh HaShanah.

In a way, I suppose you could say that we took the Jewish idiom – "*ein keimach, ein Torah; ein Torah, ein keimach* // without flour, there's no Torah; and, without Torah, there's no flour" – literally. After all, this statement goes right to the heart of Judaism, acknowledging that our culture provides us with a variety of items to nourish our minds, hearts and souls, which are inextricably linked. Therefore, we hope the inclusion of these recipes with the commentaries will encourage readers to create these confections at home, giving just cause to bring more people around the table, as we dive into all the nutrition of our people: whether it's the words of our faith or the words shared in fellowship.

A Prayer of Thanks before Eating

Before we dine on *Taste of Torah: A Little Nosh of D'rash*, it's proper to offer thanks, for no one person produced this project. Like all things at the Goldring/Woldenberg Institute of Southern Jewish Life, the Taste of Torah is a collective effort. So, first and foremost, we express our appreciations for Stephen Goldring (*z"l*) and his family as well as Malcolm Woldenberg (*z"l*) and his family. Without them, the ISJL and all we do for the benefit of Southern Jewry would not have been possible.

This innovative Institute also would not exist without the passionate leadership and forward vision of ISJL Founder and President Macy B. Hart. Born in Winona, Mississippi, Macy was intimately aware of the challenges that face Jewish communities in small towns. Despite the challenges, Macy's parents – Ellis and Reva – raised him to value the faith culture of our ancestors, a commitment Macy demonstrated throughout his life, whether as the President of the North American Federation of Temple Youth or as Director of the Henry S. Jacobs Camp of the URJ in Utica, MS. For him, the Institute was the logical next step in a lifelong goal of ensuring Judaism's survival for generations to come. For this pillar of Southern Jewry, we offer thanks to God.

Additionally, with gratitude, we acknowledge the ISJL Rabbis and our Rabbinic Interns, who have supported our Southern congregations in countless ways, including this Taste of Torah book. Rabbi Kassoff contributed "Masks and Ashes" for *Tzav*, "Silence" for *Shmini*, "There Will Always be Needy" for *R'eih*, and "Finding Renewal in Days of Old" for *Ha'azinu*. Rabbi Appel shares "Out of Revenge" for *Mishpatim*, "A Tabernacle in Our Hearts" for *T'rumah*, and "Shattered Hearts and Souls" for *Ki Tavo*. Rabbi Jason Levine (HUC-JIR, Cincinnati) offered "The Ripple Effect" for *Balak* and "Sanctuary! Sanctuary!" for *Matot-Masei*. Rabbi Joseph Robinson (AJU, Los Angeles) presented "Deconstructive History, Constructive Memory" for *Korach*. And, Rabbi Lisa Kingston (HUC-JIR, New York) gave us "The Others" for *Balak*. Their reflections are included in this collection to acknowledge the mutual blessing felt by them and our congregations during their time in the South. All others are contributed by me, Rabbi Marshal Klaven.

In addition to the reflections of our ISJL Rabbis and Interns, this book also includes writings from a number of other individuals, who we would like to thank. Thank you to Macy B. Hart for sharing your personal reflections about the ISJL and its significant place in the Jewish world for the book's foreword. Thank you to Dr. Stuart Rockoff for writing the history of the ISJL in its first 13 years. Thank you to Alan Elbaum and Rabbi Lisa Kingston for providing the summaries for the portions in the book of Genesis, Student Rabbi Tina Hughes for those in the book of Exodus, Josh Satok for the summaries in the book of Leviticus, Ben Chaidell for those in the book of Numbers and Amanda Winer for the portion summaries for the book of Deuteronomy.

Even with these contributions, the process of making this one of the finest collections of commentaries on the Torah could not have been possible without the Taste of Torah team. Every week, ISJL's Chief Operating Officer Michele Schipper, Chief Administrator Nonnie Campbell (whose idea initiated this project), and Rabbinic Assistant Shirley Eriksen diligently reviewed, edited, and fine-tuned each reflection, making sure it was of the highest quality for consumption by our readers. With Beth Kander (ISJL Development and Communications Coordinator), whose all-around brilliance enriches us all, and my superbly talented wife, Christina Ebert-Klaven (whose presence in my life is a gift from God), we owe this exceptional team a debt of gratitude that could not be paid back in a thousand life-times. Thank you; your efforts are truly priceless.

A special thank you goes to The Lewis Bear Family Foundation, who provided the funding to turn this dream into a reality. Their generosity is an extension of a deep personal relationship first developed when I officiated the wedding of Lewis Bear III to Jenn Taylor. They not only invited me into this meaningful moment for their family; they welcomed me with open arms and loving hearts into their family. For that tremendous human and financial generosity, I will be eternally grateful. On behalf of all the congregations, who will be supported through the sale of this book (as 100% of the proceeds will go to fulfilling the mission of the ISJL), I thank you from the depths of my heart.

Of course, what would the Taste of Torah be without our readers? The answer: ramblings of a rabbi. That is why the Taste of Torah has and will always be more than one rabbi's words; it is an exchange of energies, thoughts, perspectives, and wisdom from different individuals, who are studying the written word and reflecting upon life's experiences. Thank you to all who have been part of this journey in the past; thank you to all who are just joining; and thank you to all who may yet wish to come along on this road of self-discovery, understanding our place within the dynamics of this world. Through this collective exploration we – the Jewish community – may arrive to a prosperous future, safe and sound. Until then, may we enjoy the ride!

Rabbi Marshal Klaven
ISJL Director of Rabbinic Services

SHABBAT:
Erin Kahal's Sweet Potato Challah[1]

Ingredients:
1 package (7g) yeast
$^2/_3$ cup warm water
1 teaspoon ground cinnamon
½ teaspoons ground cardamom
3¾ cups unbleached white flour (substitute up to 1¾ cup whole wheat flour)
$^1/_3$ cup sugar
½ cup mashed sweet potato
¼ cup canola oil
1 egg (+ 1 egg for glaze)
1½ teaspoons salt
½ tablespoon honey

Sprinkle yeast into a small bowl and pour the warm water on it. Let stand for 10 minutes, and then stir to dissolve. Mix flour, ½ teaspoon cinnamon, and cardamom in a large bowl. Make a well in the center and pour in yeast/water mixture.

In a separate bowl, whisk together the sugar, pumpkin, oil, egg, and salt. Add to the flour mixture and combine thoroughly.

Turn dough out onto a lightly floured surface and knead for 5-10 minutes until the dough is pliable. (If it's too wet, keep adding flour in small amounts.) Let dough rest 2-3 minutes. Meanwhile, lightly oil the bowl, put the dough in it and re-cover with the towel. Let dough rise in a warm place until it has tripled in size, 2-3 hours.

Punch down dough, knead it a bit more, and cut it into two equal pieces. Cut each of the two pieces into three equal pieces (you should have 6 pieces). Roll each piece into a straight rope. Braid three ropes together and repeat so that you end up with two braided loaves. Line baking sheets with foil or parchment paper.

In a small cup, mix half of an egg with ½ teaspoon cinnamon and honey to make the glaze. With a small brush, coat the *challot* with the glaze. Place loaves on the sheets, cover, and let rise until doubled in size, about 30 minutes at 375 degrees.

---

[1] Recipe adapted from a Pumpkin Challah from Kveller.com and a Blessing of Bread by Molly Glazer.

GENESIS

B'reishit

Portion 1:
B'reishit // In the Beginning
Torah Portion: Genesis 1:1-6:8

"IN THE BEGINNING…" At the beginning of time, God illuminates the chaotic, dark abyss with the dramatic utterance: "Let there be light!" For the first six Divine-days, God fashions the universe as we know it. After each new creation – light, sky, vegetation, celestial objects, sea-creatures, birds, mammals – God makes an observation: "It is good." Yet, it is not complete. As a final act of Creation, God imbues a clod of earth with the Divine image: man and later woman. Thereupon, God calls the work "very good," and rests on the seventh day. Now, we are charged to be God's hands in this world, forever engaging in the Divine act of Creation.

But, not all is so smooth. At the heart of the Garden grows the Tree of Knowledge of Good and Evil, of whose fruit Eve and Adam are forbidden to partake. The snake, the most cunning of animals, tempts Eve into eating a forbidden fruit. Adam, whose resolve is no stronger than Eve's, soon follows suit. Now possessing, for better or worse, the knowledge of good and evil, the two humans seek to cover their nakedness. God, not pleased, expels them from the Garden, lest they eat from the Tree of Life and become immortal.

Thus, life – as it should – continues. Eve bears two children: Cain, who becomes a farmer, and Abel, who becomes a shepherd. Cain grows envious of his younger brother, for God accepts Abel's offerings and ignores those of Cain, and he commits the first murder. The Torah proceeds with a detailed genealogy of the ten generations linking Adam to Noah, the Torah portion of Genesis/*B'reishit* to that of Noah/*Noach*, as it concludes with a condemnation of the terrible wickedness of that later generation.

B'reishit // In the Beginning
Bite 1 – *Managing Creative Risks with a Divine Partner*

"Enormous. Vicious. Voracious. Swim for your life… It's Frankenfish!"[1] These words, from a 2004 movie trailer, were meant to incite fear and encourage interest in a horror flick about a genetically engineered fish wreaking havoc in the bayou. One on-line reviewer called it "a mix between the great-white shark in *Jaws*, the monster from the movie *Tremors*, and the *Creature from the Black Lagoon*."[2] In other words, a classic! Although not as insidious, some will argue that these words could easily apply to news headlines regarding Atlantic salmon, which are now being modified with the genes of ocean pout.

Ignoring the prohibition against fish "cross-dressing," the Atlantic salmon – when putting on the genes of ocean pout – are able to maintain production of their growth hormone year-round.[3] And, as a result, this Atlantic salmon reaches full maturity for human consumption in 18-months, (rather than 30 months, when it would have naturally arrived at its edible age). According to an independent panel convened by the FDA, "There is a reasonable certainty [that] no harm [can come] from the consumption of this animal;"[4] an assessment met with great cynicism by acclaimed chef Rick Moonen, who warns: Swim for your life… "This Frankenfish is [now] one step closer to our tables!"[5]

Although over dramatized for effect, Moonen's words transmit a justifiable concern. Namely, in addition to considering Frankenfish's impact on our diets, on our businesses, and on our environment, we may also wonder how this human creation impacts God's creation. In other words, in the wake of this new fish, we may ask: "Where does God's role to 'create Heaven and earth' end and our mandate to 'fill the earth and master it' begin?" For, after completing the heavy lifting of transforming the *tohu vavohu* (the unformed and chaos) into a finely ordered world, we were commanded by God – in this first Torah portion – to "be fertile and increase, to fill the earth and master it, ruling every living thing: from the birds in the sky to the fish in the sea." (Genesis 1:28)

It is a commandment which later generations have identified as the Biblical basis for our contemporary Jewish value of *Shomrei Adamah*, a value which encourages us to see ourselves not necessarily as rulers of the world, but more so as its sacred guardians. Even so, this mandate extends far beyond guardianship, for the sages have commented that the world's security was only

---

[1] Simon Barrett and Scott Clevenger. *Frankenfish*. Columbia-TriStar: 2004
[2] "Good Stupid Fun!" *Frankenfish*. http://www.imdb.com/title/tt0384833/USercomments
[3] The Atlantic salmon 's growth hormone naturally goes dormant during the winter months.
[4] Kim Carollo. "Something Fishy? Genetically Modified Salmon to Go Before FDA." www.abcnews.go.com
[5] Rick Moonen. "Say No to Genetically Engineered Salmon." *CNN Opinion Page*: 15 September 2010. Moonen is a chef in Las Vegas at Mandalay Bay, he is the author of *Fish Without A Doubt: The Cook's Essential Companion*, and he is one of the leading advocates for the sustainable seafood movement.

the first of our Divine priorities. Through each successive generation from Abraham to Moses, from the prophets of our people to the sages of our society, the *Brit Olam* (the Eternal Covenant) has expanded. Thus, suggests Jewish educator and writer Gila Gevirtz, eventually we are to "see ourselves as partners with the Holy One, embracing our role as fellow creators."[6]

Further exploring this notion, American theologian Ernest Holmes once wrote: "We are in partnership with the Infinite Mind. The name of this partnership is 'God and Company.' The supreme Intelligence, the universal Creative Order, the dynamic Law and the all-perfect Presence – this is God, our Silent Partner."[7] While there are certainly catchier names for such a partnership, like 'G-Crew' for example, Holmes' exposé is nonetheless insightful. Because, for many people, God is not necessarily absent in their lives. Rather, God is understood as being a Silent Partner, transferring over time most, if not all, of the heavy lifting in this building project – we call, 'the world' – into human hands. It's a promotion, if you will, interpreted as Divine recognition for our successful growth: physically, mentally, emotionally, as well as spiritually.

And, there can be little doubt that our increased responsibility from this creative promotion has resulted in tangible benefits for our world. Not only have we found ways to add years to life, we have also managed to add life to our years. And, while exploring the inner-space of the human body, we have also applied our developed strengths to adventure into outer-space with its celestial bodies, bringing back both a better understanding of the natural world as well as a greater awareness of God. Even so, some knowledge remains elusive. Our growth has not been without pain. There have been moments when our intention to create good has ended in havoc for the world. For example:

> With both the need and ability – thus the responsibility – to create more crops to satiate the hunger of people worldwide, genetically modified crops are common in fields throughout the U.S. In North Dakota alone, roughly 90% of the 1 million acres of canola are genetically altered to be resistant to herbicides. Although proper precautions were in place to ensure that the genetically altered plants did not enter the natural environment, a recent study by Meredith Schafer found that 86% of wild canola were derivatives of the genetically altered versions; a finding which raised concerns that this genetic alteration may one day result in a super-weed that would be resistant to all herbicides.[8]

Now, in light of these concerns, we may be inclined to demand less of a Silent Partner, and more a God who micro-manages. This dramatic shift, dictated by

---

[6] Gila Gevirtz. *Living as Partners with God*. Behrman House, Inc.: New Jersey. 1997
[7] Ernest Holmes. *Your Invisible Power*. Institute of Religious Science: Los Angeles, CA. 1940
[8] Geoffrey Brumfiel. "Genetically Modified Canola 'Escapes' Farm Fields. *NPR*: Morning Edition, 6 August 2010.

dire situations, occurs regularly in our society: when a teenager's supposed invincibility is challenged, when a business person's confidence is shaken, when the unbreakable bond of love is shattered. In moments such as these we cry out to God. We pray, "Don't be Silent! Don't turn a deaf ear! Hear our plea, we who have little merit, we who were once full of ourselves, leaving little room for You. Return to us, O God. Reestablish that order You so closely oversaw in the world's creation. Establish, once again, those boundaries of each day. For, surely then, we – as You did – can call things good once more."

But, for how long? How long until once again we push those boundaries, knowing full well they'll push back. Because whether it's a condition of our creation or an adaptation to our environment, it seems that we see boundaries not as guidelines to healthy living, but as challenges to be conquered, obstacles to be overcome. The great Dalai Lama observed as much, stating that often "great achievements take great risk;" something of which the Jewish people are intimately aware ever since our forefather Abraham took great risk to adventure from his home to achieve a Divine promise in a land he did not know. But in all our endless wonderings, we have been encouraged to manage those risks.

Not by relinquishing our creative responsibilities to a Micro-manager, nor by creating with reckless abandonment in the presence of a Silent Partner, rather we manage the risk of our mandate "to fill the earth and master it" best by finding an Active Partner in God, who "created Heaven and earth." That is what we must remember as we begin another journey through our texts with this Torah portion. In essence, as we start at its beginning, we are encouraged to leave room for God. For by leaving room for God, we cannot become full of ourselves. And, with God as our co-creator in this project called 'the world,' there will be little chance that one day we'll have to swim, fly, or even run for our lives as some Frankenfish, Frankenbird, or potentially even Frankenstein (who may or may not be a Member of the Tribe) is one step closer to our tables.

B'reishit // In the Beginning
Bite 2 – The Genesis of Lying

Can you imagine a world without lying? Well, the writers of the movie, *The Invention of Lying*, sure did. In the film, humans are – by nature – incapable of distorting the facts. This unconditional truth even extends to advertising, as an ad on the side of a bus reads: "Pepsi: when they don't have Coke." However, to our surprise, this world is not a blissful paradise. Sure, people trust one another with absolute assurance. But, unadulterated honesty has a cost. In this "just the facts" world, people give expression to any and all moments without regard for how their words may be received. As such, people's feelings are constantly trampled upon when human imperfections are brought to verbal light.

In a way, the movie writers seem to advocate for lying or believe, minimally, it has a role to play in this world. To our disbelief, they may be right. In this portion of *B'reishit,* we learn that lying was written into the very fabric of human life. In Genesis 2:16-17, God commanded Adam, saying: "Of every tree of the garden you are free to eat; but as for the tree of knowledge of good and bad, you must not <u>eat</u> of it." But, that's not what Adam told Eve. According to Eve, Adam said that "we may eat of the fruit of all the other trees in the garden. It is only the fruit of the tree in the middle of the garden that God said: 'You shall not eat of it *or* <u>touch it</u>, lest you die.'" (Genesis 3:3)

"Or touch it?!" This is an obvious exaggeration of the facts, a fib that was not part of God's original command. Although some rabbis criticize Adam's fabrication, many other sages come to his defense. According to this latter group, Adam's lie is justifiable because it "creates a hedge (or fence) around the Torah."[9] See, to the rabbis, "Torah is a garden and its precepts are precious plants. Just as a garden must be fenced around for the purpose of obviating willful or even unintended damage, so too must the precepts of Torah be 'fenced' around with additional inhibitions in order to preserve the original commandments from trespass."[10]

Thus, from this account, we may come to understand that there are moments in life when distorting the truth may be the appropriate. How could this be?! Has it not been taught by the great dispenser of advice, Ann Landers, that "the naked truth is always better than the best dressed lie?!" Good advice, especially if one forgets the ninth commandment: "You shall not give false testimony."[11] In fact, to this commandment, one could add a plethora of other such Biblical injunctions which condemn lying. For example, the prophet Zechariah states that the most important thing we can do in our lives is to "[first] speak the truth to one another, [then] render justice and peace in your gates."[12]

Choosing our words wisely is taught to be the first of our actions for good reason. Because, once the words leave our lips, we forgo our ability to control their use or misuse thereafter. It is a point illustrated in the story of Adam and Eve. According to the story, the serpent goes over to Eve following Adam's lie. As the serpent most likely fondles one of the fruits from the tree, he says to her: "See, you're not going to die."[13] And, "upon seeing that the tree was indeed good, (i.e. the serpent did not die as a result of touching the fruit, as Adam had foretold), she took (i.e. she touched it) and [because she too did not die], she then ate."[14] Thus, one could argue that it was not Eve's actions, but Adam's lie which set the stage for their eventual expulsion from the Garden of Eden.

Why then would the sages continue to justify Adam's lie? To simply say, it's to preserve God's words is not good enough. For, as we see from the story of

---

[9] Pirkei Avot de-Rabbi Natan, ch. 1.
[10] J. Israelstam, Pirkei Avot 1:1, note 7.
[11] Exodus 20:13
[12] Zechariah 8:16
[13] Genesis 3:4
[14] Genesis 3:6

Adam and Eve, the fence does not always work. "It may," as the rabbis warned, "fall and destroy that which it was meant to protect."[15] Nor, do I believe it's adequate to justify lying through the principle of *Shalom Bayit*, which permits spouses to tell white lies to one another in order to preserve the peace in the home.[16] For, in my opinion, the best way to ensure that peace is through open and truthful dialogue. Nonetheless, the rabbis are compelled to justify lying. Why? Because, without lying – without distorting the facts – there would be no work of fiction, no story to stimulate or stir our souls, no movie or play to ignite our imaginations. And, it may be said that without these things we would not have the heart to endure the truth, especially when the truth becomes – as it so often did – unbearable in the course of Jewish history.

The poet William Blake once wrote: "A truth told with bad intent, beats all the lies you can invent." His poignant words remind us that the topic of lying cannot be as black and white as we often have made it. For the truth, as the movie *The Invention of Lying* has depicted, can be as damaging as a lie. And, for that matter, a lie may be as healing as the truth. What makes the difference, as Blake acknowledges, is intent. Therefore let us, as we engage in this topic henceforth, restrain ourselves from immediately condemning a lie as bad and extolling honesty as good. Instead, may we fulfill the Divine image in which we were created by being more thoughtful and discerning beings, taking both truth and lie and evolving them into healthy and productive roles within our lives.

B'reishit // In the Beginning
Bite 3 – *Judaism's Original Sin*

"Come on [guys], do you want to live forever?!" Though sanitized for civilian ears, a rougher form of these words was spoken by Sergeant Daniel Daly, as a Marine's motivation to his fellow troops before stepping into the bloody battle of Belleau Wood during WWI. And, amazingly, it's the same question that continues to be raised within each and every generation, whether it was by the 18th century Prussian King Frederick II, at the Battle of *Kolin,* or the future Federation Lieutenant Johnny Rico in Earth's battle against the Bug-planet Klendathu in the Sci-fi movie *Starship Troopers.* Each presents that same enduring question: "Come on [guys], do you really want to live forever?!"[17]

Although the expected answer is "no," as we charge cavalierly into life's battles, it's hard not to reply emphatically: "Yes! Yes! Yes! In fact, I *do* want to live forever!" For, according to this Torah portion of *B'reishit,* that desire seems engrained into our very souls. Having already transgressed the Divine

---

[15] B'reishit Rabbah 19:3
[16] B'reishit Rabbah 48:14
[17] Prussian King, Frederick II, said at the Battle of *Kolin: "Kerls, wollt ihr ewig leben //* [Come on] dogs, do you want to live forever." And, the future Federation Lieutenant, Johnny Rico precisely yelled: "Come on you apes, do you wanna live forever?" [Jon Davison and Alan Marshall. *Starship Troopers.* TriStar Pictures International: 1997.]

command not to eat of the Tree of Knowledge, God – in God's abundant mercy – does not immediately throw Adam and Eve out of the Garden of Eden. Rather, knowing man's nature, God merely grows concerned: "What if man should also stretch out his hand and take from the Tree of Life and eat?" Then, concluded God, "They would live forever!" Only upon this realization does "the Lord banish man from the Garden." (Genesis 3:22-23)

For, in man's quest for immortality, there is sin.[18] Not simply because it transgresses the Divine separation between the mortal and immortal spheres. Living forever, comments Rav Huna, also "leads to slothfulness, which is of no benefit to anyone," a waste of the Divine potential inherent within us all.[19] Paraphrasing Proverbs, Rav Huna adds, "For then the garden is worked by a lazy man, it's the vineyard of a man lacking sense, soon to be overgrown."[20] Because, ironically, death is life's greatest motivator, the instigator for getting things done. Thus, "God stationed *cherubim* with fiery swords to guard the way to the Tree of Life." (Genesis 3:24) For, in limiting his years, God wanted to motivate man to make each day count! [21]

Yet, the original sin of seeking immortality is hard to shake. Whether it's in the past with Ponce de Leon's journey to the Fountain of Youth or in our present attempts to maintain our youth in old age, many have been the hours of our lives spent in vain. Even this realization may not halt our efforts entirely. Although we may not live forever, we are comforted by a hope that our children may. Such was likely the hope nurtured by "the daughters of men [when they] cohabitated with the [lesser] divine beings," at the end of this Torah portion. Perhaps, in this unimaginable union, some offspring may inherit the gene of immortality, "becoming the mighty men of old, men of renown." (Genesis 6:4)

But, as the flood story goes, these hopes too were drowned out by the rushing waters of life that cleansed the whole world of sin. For, such a punishment was precipitated by "man's wickedness on earth, how the Lord saw every plan devised by him was nothing but evil all the time." (Genesis 6:5) But not just any evil; it was a specific sin: our relentless pursuit of immortality. For such pursuits rob us and the world of time, of energy, of resources that could have been used to make the days we do have better. No one knows this more intimately then innovator Steve Jobs, who shared these words with the graduating class of Stanford University in 2005.[22]

---

[18] Generally, "original sin" is a state of collective sin born to every human being as a result of Adam and Eve's initial transgression of eating from the Tree of Knowledge. Though this interpretation is absent in Jewish theology, I'm the first to say that Judaism has an original sin: the incessant desire to live forever. God recognizes this in Adam and Eve; it is the specific wickedness of man that precipitates the flood; and, it is the reason for the Tower of Babel. If the front door to eternity is blocked, then man is left to try the back door, building a tower to Heaven. (See Genesis 11:1-9)

[19] B'reshit Rabbah 22:1

[20] Proverbs 24:30-31

[21] Specifically, states Genesis 6:3, God limits man's life to 120 years.

[22] See http://news.stanford.edu/news/2005/june15/jobs-061505.html

Remembering that I'll be dead soon is the most important tool I've ever encountered to help me make the big choices in life. Because almost everything – all external expectations, all pride, all fear of embarrassment or failure – these things just fall away in the face of death, leaving only what is truly important...

[That being said,] no one wants to die. Even people who want to go to heaven don't want to die to get there. Yet, death is the destination we all share. No one has ever escaped it. And that is as it should be, because Death is very likely the single best invention of Life. It is Life's change agent. It clears out the old to make way for the new.

Right now the new is you...so don't waste it living someone else's life. Don't be trapped by dogma – which is the result of other people's thinking. Don't let the noise of others' opinions drown out your own inner voice. And, most importantly, have the courage to follow your heart and intuition. They already know what you want to become. Everything else is secondary.

So, come on! Do you really want to go on, attempting to live forever? Given our tradition, the answer should be emphatically "no!" For, in perceiving our death, our view on life comes into greater focus, for death – as Steve Jobs taught – is the fertile ground from which we are motivated to make a more meaningful, more productive, more fruitful life. And with this fruit (perhaps an apple), not only will our lives be nourished, so too – we pray – will the lives of our children, our children's children, and all the world. *V'zot habracha*, this is the blessing of our limited but no less important lives. May we live them well!

Portion 2:

Noach // Noah
Torah Portion: Genesis 6:9-11:32

"NOAH WAS A RIGHTEOUS MAN." This epitaph, which begins the portion, pins Noah as the only hope for a corrupted generation. As the sole survivor of a flood that will wipe out the first generation of God's creation, Noah – along with his family – builds an ark, encapsulates the seed of every type of life therein, so that he can – upon the recession of its waters – restart the process of creation, this time more in harmony with the will of the Creator.

The Biblical narrative reassures humankind that God will never again destroy the living beings of the world. The eternal reminder of this promise, the lasting symbol of this Covenant, is none other than the rainbow. Yet, when the waters subside, humankind once again faces the harsh challenges of a mortal existence. As soon as Noah leaves the ark, "He drank wine, and grew drunk." (Genesis 9:21) Noah's character typifies the great challenge of remaining "righteous" in spite of one's less-than-perfect surroundings.

A second narrative in this portion is the Tower of Babel, man's way to get into Heaven. This story reiterates the theme of humankind pushing the limits of what is acceptable and explains how humankind diversified after the flood. To preserve the Divine order of creation, God must confuse their speech and spread them apart. From this, we see a change in the Divine-mortal relationship. Rather than erasing the Eternal's creation, God maintains the Covenant; humankind is preserved even as it is punished.

Towards the end of this portion of Noah, a genealogical line is traced from him to the patriarch Abram. Thus, a universal forefather (Noah) leads us to a particular one (Abraham). Out of a newly re-established humankind comes a leader who will eventually share the revelation of monotheism to the world.

Noach // Noah
Bite 1 – *A True Prophet Makes No Profit*

Ladies and gentlemen, please allow me to introduce you to a friend of mine: Angie. Her online list helps thousands make daily distinctions and decisions on everything from effective mechanics to defective ones, from productive movers to destructive ones, from responsive doctors to insensitive ones, and even true prophets from false ones (should you be in the market). Okay, to really find that difference one must turn to the Bible. There, succinctly written, are the words: "If a prophet speaks in the name of the Lord and the oracle does not come true, then that oracle was not spoken by the Lord and the prophet is false."[23]

Clearly, then, if a prophet receives words from the Lord and those words come true, it stands to reason that the prophet was likewise true. Yet, Noah – by most accounts – is not considered a true prophet, despite the fact that – in this Torah portion of *Noach* – God tells him: "I have decided to put an end to all flesh, for the earth is filled with lawlessness because of them. I am about to destroy them with the earth." And, as we know, that's exactly what transpires, but not before Noah builds an ark for himself, entering it with his sons, his wife, his sons' wives, and two of all that lives. "Noah did," emphasizes the Bible, "just as God commanded him."[24] (Genesis 6)

That's why Noah was considered a "blameless [prophet *only*] in his generation," as opposed to Abraham, who is considered "blameless" and true throughout the ages.[25] When Noah learned of the future, teaches Rabbi Harvey Fields, "he said nothing on behalf of the people of his generation; he was indifferent to their inevitable suffering."[26] On the other hand, "when Abraham hears God's plan to destroy Sodom and Gomorrah, he argues on behalf of their citizens, though they were corrupt."[27] Therefore, we learn, it's not the Word of the Lord that makes one blameless, righteous, or true, but how that knowledge of the future is put to use.

Fine, but unlike doctors, movers, and mechanics, many of us are not on the lookout for a true prophet these days (attested by the fact that they're not on Angie's list… yet!). Nonetheless, we can't go far before hearing someone claiming to know the future: it's the politician's assertions; it's the stock broker's projections, it's the meteorologist's predictions. In fact, in a recent comic, one such forecast went like this: "Some areas can expect up to a foot of frogs, followed by lice, locust, and darkness 'till the end of days;" to which, a viewing couple responds, "Man, the Weather Channel's getting pretty creepy these days."[28]

---

[23] Deuteronomy 18:22
[24] Genesis 6
[25] Genesis 6:9, Noah is called "blameless in his generation, as he walked with God;" whereas, in Genesis 17:1, Abraham is called to "walk with God and be blameless."
[26] Harvey Fields. *A Torah Commentary for Our Times: Genesis.* UAHC Press: New York, 1990. p. 30
[27] Ibid.
[28] Walt Handelsman. "Forecast." Newsday: 2005

No doubt about it. Like the prophets of old, today's over-dramatized assertions, projections, and predictions are made with the hopes of influencing and redirecting the present, thereby changing the future. But, for whom? If, like old Biff Tannen from *Back to the Future – Part II*, it's done for their own personal gain, then he – along with the fortune-teller and inside-trader – become suspect.[29] For, while such individuals may initially be championed as true, righteous, or blameless in their generation, that status – like Noah's – will eventually be challenged by later ones, as their selfishness comes to light.

For, a true prophet makes no profit. They are the original non-profit agencies, directed by their CEO: God. It's no wonder then that so many initially refuse His call. Along with labor and lament, they know they'll likely have to persevere under great torment. "The prophet's present," writes Achad ha-Am, "is a wilderness, life far removed from the ideal. He therefore turns to the past and the future, from which he quarries."[30] But, what he pulls up cannot be weighed on any scale: it's not power or privilege, it's not prestige or private accounts. Rather a true prophet's success, like that of Abraham, Moses, and Jeremiah, is measured best by the progress of their populace.

This standard – by which to detect a true prophet from a false one – is much more reliable than the test administered by the Bible. For, by that qualification, a true prophet could be disqualified as such if the people heed his/her words, changing the future, thereby throwing off the forecast. But, one who uses their future knowledge to benefit others remains true, righteous, and blameless throughout the generations. May we – like that long line of true prophets – continue to use our visions in these productive ways. Thereby, we shall not only be a nation of priests, but a nation of prophets, directing our present to a more profitable and prosperous future for all.

Noach // Noah
Bite 2 – *"You Can't Win, If You Don't Play"*

Come on! Step right up! Take a chance," shouted a carnie at the 150th annual Mississippi State Fair. "You can't win, if you don't play!" "Sure," I responded. "But, I can't lose either." "Really?" retorted the carnie. "Uh… really," I replied, attempting to conceal my uncertainty. But, already, doubt had saturated my voice and suspicion grew like a fungus in my mind. Could my witty response (which I had happily congratulated myself for) be incorrect? Had I somehow not avoided a loss even though I avoided the game?

---

[29] In *Back to the Future – Part II*, an elderly Biff Tannen steals the time-traveling DeLorean, traveling from 2015 to his younger self in 1955. He presents himself with *Gray's Sports Almanac*, a book detailing the results of major sporting events for the second half of the 20th century. The younger Biff then uses this future information only for his own benefit, amassing a great fortune. Initially he is given the nickname, "luckiest man alive;" only later is he found to be a selfish fraud, as his hometown of Hill Valley comes to ruin.
[30] Ahad ha-Am. "Moses" *Selected Essays of Ahad ha-Am*, translated by L. Simon. 1912

An answer to this question may lie in this portion of *Noach*. As Noah steps out from the ark into the world, you could almost hear God saying to him, "Come on Noah! Step right up! Take a chance!" Believing that God would "never again destroy every living being" (Genesis 8:21), Noah takes a chance on life by becoming a farmer. According to Genesis 9, "Noah, the tiller of the soil, was the first to plant a vineyard." However, the result was not favorable. After tending his field, Noah "drinks the [fruit of his produce], wine, and [subsequently] becomes drunk, uncovering himself within his tent." (Genesis 9:20-21)

With one ill-fated step, the once revered "righteous man; blameless in his generation" is labeled a loser. Rabbi Ovadiah Sforno is particularly harsh on him. He writes: "Noah began with an unsuitable project; therefore, unsavory deeds resulted from it. For a small fault at the beginning will cause many more at the end."[31] But, how can we condemn him so? After all, considering the harsh ride of the flood, Noah may have deserved to let loose a little. Please understand. I am not condoning the copious drinking of an old man, nor anyone for that matter. Hopefully, we all have learned – some maybe the hard way – that drinking prolific amounts of alcohol is, in Sforno's words, "unsuitable." But, can we really say Noah had that lesson in hand? Being "the first to plant a vineyard," as our portion states, can we really assume that Noah knew what would transpire? Probably not. However, today, we are fully aware that all of life is really a series of firsts, each engrained with a degree of risk.

Whether it is in the relationships we attempt to sow or in the new initiatives we plow at work, whenever we break ground for the first time there is a chance that the tilled earth may prove to be either fallow or fertile. Often, this risk is known and even calculated into the equation of our deeds. We plug it, along with a potential reward, into a mental formula which determines whether or not the ensuing action is indeed "worth it." For example: when taking our first steps, when riding our first bike, when pursuing our first love (or every one thereafter), we are well aware that we may fall and feel pain.

Nevertheless, we continue the activity, even engaging in tactics that will hopefully assure protection from such projected risks: we hold hands with a parent or latch onto the nearest piece of furniture when taking our first steps; we wear pads, helmets and possibly even training wheels when riding our first bike; and when pursuing our first love….well, all the above apply. However, there are some risks in life that we cannot foresee and for which we cannot prepare. We are, after all, human, created in the Divine image, but not Divine ourselves. While God may – we can argue – know everything that has and will forever be, we cannot. Therefore, the potential exists that we, like Noah, may end up in a drunken stupor, completely exposed to the harsh outcome of the situation.

---

[31] See Sforno commentary to Genesis 9:21

At that moment, when we face our own failure, one of life's most pivotal questions will be presented: "Despite the best preparations and calculations, what are we to do when the ground upon which we were tilling has proven unfavorable?" Do we give up, abandoning our mission? Or should we continue, trying to find something else that may take root? As you consider what type of tiller you are, please allow me to share with you a story from Thomas Edison. As we all know, Edison invented the light bulb. But, what we may not know is that he tried 2,000 different experiments before it worked. When a reporter asked him how it felt to fail so many times. He said, "I did not fail, not even once. In fact, I invented the light bulb. It was just a 2,000 step process."

It's the same with Noah and the vineyard. Noah didn't fail. He just started a process; one that took many steps until it eventually led to the appropriate use of wine as the substance through which we sanctify our Holy days. This process is fitting, for just as wine gets better with age, so too do we. That is, as long as we are willing to take the risk – both the seen and the unforeseen – and step up to try our hand at life. Because, our failure in life will not be measured by how many times we tried and did not succeed. Rather, our failure will be evident in our inability to step up and try in the first place.

This is the lesson the carnie at the State Fair was presenting me. Had I tried my luck and lost, I would have still won. Maybe not the large prize that hung from the top of the carnie's booth. Instead, I would have received a valuable consolation prize: a small lesson, stuffed with what doesn't work. I know. It doesn't seem like much at the time. But, according to the rules, I can eventually trade these smaller prizes in for a grand-prize: a valuable lesson on what does work in the game of life. Because, by understanding what doesn't work, I will eventually come to understand what does. So, come on! Step right up! Take a chance! You can't win, if you don't play!

Noach // Noah
Bite 3 – *Standing Tall: A Framework for a Firmer Foundation*

There's an activity, nearly as old as time, which remains popular even among today's youth: stacking… one thing, on top of another, on top of another, on top of another, whether it's markers in grade-school, soda-cans in high-school, or pizza boxes in graduate-school. For, the only thing more exciting than building up is witnessing the much anticipated falling down. Yes! Eventually, we know that all those efforts will soon tumble to the ground. Why? Because, in buildings such as these, there is a fatal flaw found in the very foundation of their construction. Plainly put: the foundation is much too small, much too narrow, much too singular to support substantial and sustainable growth.

That's the lesson God provided the people near the beginning of Creation. According to this portion, humanity began on a very narrow foundation, as "everyone of earth had the same language and the same words." Upon this singularity, they said to one another, "Let's build a city and a tower with its top to the sky, so that we can make for us a name, lest we be scattered." Yet, ironically, that's what happens from their building. With the inherent dangers of this activity, God not only stopped the building but further "scattered the people from there over the face of the earth." (Genesis 11:1-8)

Why? What danger did God perceive that the people did not? Did they not take the proper safety precautions, like wearing hard yarmulkes? No, says Rabbi David Kimchi. By his account, the problem began with the people's reluctance to follow God's guidelines in constructing the world. According to the Divine building permit, God instructed: "Be fruitful and multiply. Fill the [whole] earth."[32] Yet, the people wished to dwell together. So, believes Rabbi Kimchi, God forced man's hand to fulfill the Divine command. For when we are pushed out of our homogeneous comfort zones to enter diversity, there resides a firmer foundation for more substantial and sustainable growth of our society.[33]

But, some argue, we have been pushed too far, grown too fast. Like dressing spread too thinly over salad, no longer is there enough cohesive contact to bring the parts together. As a result, over the last few decades, we have witnessed a surge of ethnocentrism, as more and more individuals embrace their roots to the exclusion of embracing one another. Even those not consciously on this path are moving that way, as our society grows increasingly more insular around one's particular region or religion, one's ethnicity or family. Take the decreased use in public transportation for example. Rather than hopping on a bus or train, many now rely upon private conveyances, that is, if we leave home at all.

For, at our fingertips, information has proliferated. Yet, our interactions have deteriorated. "This is the greatest challenge facing America today," summarized Bishop Ronnie Crudup. "Not overcoming our differences," Crudup clarified, "but merely coming in contact with them."[34] For, in the lack of the familial, we tend to see the "other" as inconsequential. And thus, as evident from far too many news reports, we are more prone to act towards the "other" in ways that hurt us all: whether passively by turning a blind eye or deaf ear to their suffering or actively by throwing sticks or stones, or something much worse.

To be clear, no one is immune from this. As long as we remain islands in the sea of the world, the tide could easily change on any of us. The only real way then to prevent erosion of our shore is to intertwine our roots with those of "others." The Sequoias in California do this. Standing as tall as skyscrapers, their roots go no deeper than just below the surface. A lone sequoia's roots, in fact, are so shallow that even the mildest of breezes could topple one over. So, how do they grow so tall? The answer is because a Sequoia tree never stands

---

[32] Genesis 1:28
[33] See RaDaK commentary to Genesis 11:1-8
[34] Spoken at the eighth annual Institute for Interfaith Dialog Dinner in Jackson, MS on 18 November 2011.

alone. They spring up in groves, and allow their independent roots to intertwine with "others," thus supporting one another against the angriest of winds.

This should be the case for us all, taught Thomas Jefferson. In a letter to the historic Mickve Israel congregation of Savannah, Jefferson said: "The great maxim of our civil government – United we Stand, Divided we Fall – should be reversed. Its true form is Divided we Stand, United we Fall."[35] For only a diverse base, one spread from sea to shining sea, can provide the firm foundation our society needs to not only have substantial growth, but sustainable growth from generation to generation. May we continue to follow this Divine instruction. May we leave our singularity to enter diversity, thereby providing a firmer foundation upon which our children may continue to build.

---

[35] For a copy of the letter, see: http://www.dividist.com/2008/03/maxim-of-civil-government-being.html

Portion 3:
Lech-l'cha // Go Forth
Torah Portion: Genesis 12:1-17:27

"GO FORTH FROM YOUR LAND, FROM THE PLACE OF YOUR BIRTH, FROM YOUR FATHER'S HOUSE, TO THE LAND THAT I WILL SHOW YOU." This opening command, along with the promise, "I will make of you a great nation, and I will bless you," (Genesis 12:2) becomes the basis of a long lasting relationship between God and Abram, along with his wife Sarai. It is the beginning of their physical journey to a new land, along with a transformational journey of becoming a new people.

In an act of great faith, Abram, Sarai, their nephew Lot, and a large entourage, allow God to guide them to Canaan, the land promised to Abram's descendants. But, due to a famine in that land, the family is forced to leave. They go down to Egypt, and then back to Canaan again, encountering adventure and adversity along the way. However, it was the hardship of not yet having children of their own that truly allowed discomfort and doubt to creep into their household. In such a state, Sarai grew bitter and resentful. Jealousy overcomes her, as Sarai deals harshly with Hagar, her maidservant, who had given birth to Abram's first son Ishmael.

Nonetheless, throughout the portion and those to come, God reassures Abram and Sarai that their descendants will be as numerous as the stars in Heaven. At first, this promise was one-sided, as God was the main player in the drama. However, as the story unfolds, a true Covenant will develop, with Abram stepping up to take a part. As he seals the sign of the Covenant on his flesh and on the flesh of all males in his house, Abram's name changes to Abraham: "the father of many nations." Finally, the barren wife Sarai receives Divine news that she will bear a son of her own: Isaac. With that promise, Sarai becomes Sarah, establishing her own sacred relationship with God.

Lech-l'cha // Go Forth
Bite 1 – *Just Like Your Parents*

Just so we're not confused, Harry Potter is a work of fiction (apologies, Potter enthusiasts). But if the fantastical sport of Quidditch, a whomping willow, and a talking spider named Aragog weren't enough to make this clear, then it should have been evident when, after being compared to his parents, Harry smiles. Because, what adolescent boy enjoys hearing the words: "You're just like your parents, when they were your age?"

Rest assured, we will not be embarrassed by a similar comparison, "You're just like your father Abraham, when he was your age." Because, only at the mature age of 75 does Abraham step-out from the shadows of history to take center stage in our people's drama. Until this moment little, if any, information is given about Abraham's formative years. By most accounts, his story simply begins with this portion of *Lech-l'cha,* when the Lord says to Abraham at the age of 75, "*Lech-l'cha*/Go forth from your land, from the place of your birth, from your father's house, to the land that I will show you." (Genesis 12:1)

From the perspective of the early rabbis, however, Abraham's departure from his father began much earlier. According to Rabbi Chiyya, Abraham separated from his father, Terach, "at age 50, [when] Abraham was put in charge of his father's idol shop. While attending the idols, a woman came with a plateful of flour and requested him to 'take this and offer it to them.' Instead of doing as the woman had asked, Abraham took a stick, broke the idols, and put the stick in the hand of the largest idol, [which he had left untouched].

Upon his return, Terach demanded to know what happened. Abraham replied, 'I cannot conceal it from you, father. While offering a meal to the idols, one demanded: *I must eat first.* Then, another screamed: *No, it's I who must eat first.* Thereupon, the largest idol rose and broke the others.' Terach cried, 'That's impossible! They're made of stone. There's no soul or spirit in any of them!' To which, Abraham questioned, 'Why then do you worship them?'"[36] In his own unique way, Abraham distances his course from that of his father. And in doing so, stated the rabbis, Abraham is able to stand on his own in front of God.

Many of us understand all too well the impetus of children to forge new paths in order to stand on their own. As Plato stated it, "A child who is led by what amuses his mind, will eventually discover himself." His claim is supported by our rabbis in the rare construction of *lech-l'cha* (which occurs only two times in the Bible – Genesis 12:1 and 22:2). Literally translated, *lech-l'cha* means "go/*lech* for yourself/*l'cha*." While this translation may ring of selfishness, the rabbis have long understood it to mean that "one cannot find one's authentic self

---

[36] Genesis Rabbah 38:13

without going forth. For when we go forth, we are free from the constraints of who we were, so that we may find who we are supposed to be."[37]

Understanding this, however, doesn't make it any easier to witness the growing space, whether emotionally or physically, which can occur between parent and child. So torn, we are, that we attempt to re-sew those closely knit relationships once experienced with our children in their more formative years. Suddenly, 'family game night' springs up, attendance around the dinner table is conscripted, and – when our children move out of the home – we continue to follow them through phone calls, e-mails, as well as visits (which hopefully have been scheduled with advance warning). These and other steps to shorten the growing distance between us and our children should always be taken.

However, there is a point in which a parent must stop following his/her children and allow them to continue on by themselves. Even Abraham's father, Terach, understood this. For it was neither Abraham who, nor God's command which, initiated the journey to Canaan (see Genesis 12:5). Rather, that journey began with Terach. As we read in Genesis 11:31, it was "Terach, [who] took his son Abram, his grandson Lot, and his daughter-in-law Sarai, and set out from Ur of the Chaldeans for the land of Canaan. But, when they had come as far as Haran, [Terach] settled there." In doing so, he left Abraham to continue the journey.

At some point, we too must settle and allow our children to *lech-l'cha*/go forth into the world to forge a new path for themselves. Undoubtedly, this moment will be wrought with uncertainty, concerned for what our children will have to experience on their own. But, as it has been taught, "It's not the job of a parent to raise children," whose steps must be continually supported; rather, "a parent's responsibility is to raise adults," who can stand and walk on their own. And, as our children continue to walk on their own, let us pray that they will come to realize that their new path – like Abraham's – is really a continuation of the old. Only then will they discover the great truth in the statement: "You are just like your parents, especially when they were your age."

Lech-l'cha // Go Forth
Bite 2 – *Go for Yourself*

I've always been an active person: rock climbing, camping, running, etc. My youngest brother, on the other hand, claims to be allergic to such activity. So, upon arriving in Israel to visit me, he wasn't thrilled to learn that we were going on a hike with some other rabbinic students in the desert. As expected, he complained the entire way. "It's hot; I'm tired; I can't go on; come on, guys! Let's take a rest!" That was until a group of young Israeli women, about his age, briskly walked by. Then it was, "Come on, guys! Can't you keep up!" as my brother quickly pulled ahead of us all.

---

[37] Mei HaShiloah

I suppose I should not have been surprised by his new found energy for this communal journey, as a similar thing happened with Abraham in *Lech-l'cha*. No, Abraham didn't see some lovely ladies, which motivated him to begin our Jewish journey. Rather, he happened upon God, who commanded him to "'*lech-l'cha*, go forth from your land, from the place of your birth, from your father's house to the land that I will show you. I will show you...' And Avram, just as the Lord [and the rock band U2] commanded, walked on." (Genesis 12:1-2) Though, what's interesting here isn't the last two words: "walk on." It's the first two: "*lech-l'cha*." Often understood simply as "go" or "go forth," a more exact translation would be "go/*lech* for yourself/*l'cha*;" specifically, states RaSHI, for "your own pleasure as well as for your own benefit."[38] For, God our Creator understood, what truly moves us isn't always a communal destination, but a personal motivation.[39]

Ideally, a communal command should be all that is needed to not only think about the greater good, but make strides towards those ends. Take the health initiative called "Let's Go Walking, Mississippi." Attempting to motivate Mississippians to move from their last place finish in our nation's health statistics, reporters have said: "This is not about one person's waistline, but America's bottom-line," as the news goes on to show how reducing our personal weight can reduce our state's rising healthcare cost.[40] For, it is hoped, if one can see the entire forest from behind the individual tree, we could then find our way into the clearing.

Such foresight, however, will not work for everyone, especially not in this nearsighted society. Think of WWII when this nation knew what was going on in Nazi Europe and did not mobilize until personally attacked at Pearl Harbor. Think of all those religious oriented people of MS, who sat silently on the white-picket fence of segregation, with its countless points of injustice, until the issue struck home with a KKK bombing of Rabbi Perry Nussbaum's home in an all-white neighborhood.[41] And, just think of all those people who continue to wait until they have a heart attack before engaging in a healthier lifestyle.

This reality of waiting until something moves us before we move for something is a far cry from the ideal. Yet, even in this less-than-perfect state, God still calls us to: "*Lech-l'cha*, go forth…" not for others, not for your nation,

---

[38] RaSHI (1040-1105 C.E.) commentary on Genesis 12:1

[39] Hence, why God told Abraham, "I will make your name great and you shall be a blessing."

[40] For an example, check out David Wright's piece, *America Lags Behind*, aired on ABC's World News on 05 October 2010.

[41] From the history page of the ISJL website (www.isjl.org): "On the night of 18 September 1967, a group of Ku Klux Klan members planted a bomb which destroyed much of Rabbi Perry Nussbaum's office and part of the library [at Temple Beth Israel in Jackson, MS]... Two months later, the same Klan members bombed Nussbaum's home, while the rabbi and his wife were there. Miraculously, no one was hurt. In response to the events, 42 clergymen and sympathetic citizens joined a 'walk of penance' to Temple Beth Israel, where they held a vigil, which attracted a large crowd... The attacks are [seen as] a turning point [in this issue of segregation and civil rights] as many white Jacksonians finally realized that the violence had gone too far, and it was time to change."

your people, or your family. But, God said, "go for yourself." Because, what truly moves us to reach a communal destination (whether it's the Promised Land or this land filled with Promise) isn't a glimpse of our collective future, but a perspective of personal progress. For without it, there is little reason to individually continue on when we feel as if – in our limited view – collectively we are going nowhere.

That shall not be our fate. No longer are we aimlessly hiking through the desert. Since the time of Abraham, we have been called to achieve a common goal, accomplish a collective mission, attain a corporate vision: making this world a healthier place. May we heed that call, finding the personal within the communal. For, in recognizing the individual benefit within a communal advancement, we can continue to make significant strides towards that Divine destination: a world filled with good health, great spirits and everlasting Peace.

Lech-l'cha // Go Forth
Bite 3 – Go! Leave No Man Behind!

Not long ago, Jews around the world rejoiced. Not simply in celebration for Simchat Torah, marking our return to "the beginning" of God's word. We rejoiced as well in the return of Israeli soldier Gilad Shalit, who had been held captive under immense duress by the terrorist group Hamas for five years. The cost of his release: 1,027 Palestinian prisoners, 315 of whom were serving life sentences for serious crimes against Israeli citizens. Though, with wishes that such unpleasant times were behind us, as well as with worry about what this exchange means for those times ahead, we nonetheless rejoiced in that moment, witnessing the fulfillment of God's command to "leave no man behind."

Traditionally this command is coined *pidyon hash'vuyim*, meaning "redeem the captives," whose origins come from this portion of *Lech-l'cha*. Sometime after Abram was instructed to "go forth," a war raged in the land that God instructed him to go. In this unpleasant time, "invaders seized Lot, the son of Abram's brother... And, upon hearing that his kinsman had been taken," continues the Bible, Abram engaged in an extraordinary measure, "mustering 318 men, born into his household, and went in pursuit." Eventually, Abram redeems Lot, bringing him with his entire household to safety. (Genesis 14:1-16)

Commenting on this, Rabbi Yochanan taught: "Redeeming captives is a great mitzvah, for captivity is harsher than all calamities: death from natural causes, death from sword, death from hunger, as captivity may include them all."[42] If so, adds RaMBaM, "there is no greater mitzvah than redeeming captives." So important is this duty, he continues, "that it takes priority over feeding and clothing the poor. For, the captive is regarded as suffering from both, plus he is

---

[42] *Babylonian Talmud*, Bava Batra, 8b

in mortal danger. If a society disregards this command," concludes RaMBaM, "they violate several Biblical prohibitions as well as several positive commands all at once."[43] In other words, redeeming captives takes priority in Judaism not solely because of the individual held captive but, as well, for what it would say about a society willing to keep one of their own in harm's way.

Knowing as much, Israel – time and again – engages in remarkable measures to redeem the captive. Sometimes, like those recently, it's done through clandestine conversations that broker prisoner exchanges. At others, it's covert military operations like Entebbe. Under the cover of a blackened sky, in 1976, Israeli commandos traveled to Entebbe Airport in Uganda to free 101 Israeli civilians and 1 French citizen held captive on an Air France plane by hijackers. Although the operation took a week of planning, it culminated in just 90 minutes, with 102 captives redeemed safely. However, it came at a cost. Five Israeli commandos were injured and one, their commander, Lt. Col. Yonatan Netanyahu (eldest brother of P.M. Benjamin Netanyahu) lost his life.

Though considered one of the most daring operations in history, even by those outside Israel, the cost of this effort and others to redeem individuals from captivity often raises concern. Not necessarily for those in the theater of operations, as service members often understand and accept the risks inherent in leaving no man behind. "That's how I would want to be treated," stated one soldier, "if, God forbid, something would happen to me."[44] Rather, the concern comes from those who live behind the civilian curtain in society. Do not such high costs only encourage future acts of terrorism?[45] Concluding as much, America has a stance of not openly engaging in such negotiations.

But, not Israel. Why? Because, in these unpleasant times, Israel is not concerned about encouraging future acts of terrorism. These terrorists are already highly motivated, states Israeli ambassador to the United States, Michael Oren, "attempting kidnappings on a weekly basis."[46] Therefore, in these instances, we must base such difficult decisions not on the values suspected to be held by others, but on those we know are held by us. And, make no mistake about it: we value the life of the individual. For, as the sages taught, "Saving one life is equivalent to saving the whole world."[47] And so, we honor that teaching, which "goes to the heart of Israeli society," by not leaving a single person behind.[48] A mandate, former Entebbe Operation pilot, Maj.

---

[43] Mishneh Torah, Hilchot Matanot Aniyim 8:10
[44] Stated in a counseling session with an airman, while in service as a USAF 2nd Lt, Chaplain Candidate.
[45] Such questions are raised in tractate *Gittin* in the *Mishnah* (4:6), as well as in the *Babylonian Talmud* (45a). Specifically, it was questioning whether this value needed to have a limit, as "not to encourage the capture of more people by the assailants, who could then bring them to ransom."
[46] Michael Oren. Stated at a breakfast in Washington D.C., hosted by The Christian Science Monitor on Tuesday, 25 October 2011. For more, please check out: www.csmonitor.com, keyword: Israeli Ambassador + Video
[47] *Mishnah* Sanhedrin 4:4
[48] *Ibid.*

General Doron Almog believes should extend beyond the military to enter everyday life. As he stated:[49]

> After our son was born, he was diagnosed with a severe physical and cognitive disability. In that instant, my world was turned upside down. At first, I had a very hard time coming to terms with the fact that my beloved son would always be dependent on others. But, my "no man left behind" philosophy – learned at Entebbe – prevailed, and I soon found the strength to be the father that Eran, my son, needed me to be. In fact, Eran allowed me to develop this philosophy even further, as I became committed to changing the way society views the disabled. I realized that it is not enough to make sure that these wonderful children don't get left behind. We must ensure that they are given every opportunity to excel and reach their greatest potentials. For, they too are captives. We don't need to launch any complex tactical mission to redeem them. But, make no mistake about it, our commitment to care for the disabled is immeasurably more difficult than any military campaign I have ever led. Nevertheless, we must stand up and fight to provide them with the care they deserve. Because, in the end, our society will be judged by how well we complete this mission.

Maj. General Almog is right. Our society will be judged on how well we accomplish this mission of *pidyon hash'vuyim*, of going forth to "redeem the captives." And, while some may insist that such an uncompromising value on the sanctity of each individual life threatens or weakens our society, we understand just the opposite. The confidence and cohesion this value creates among every member of society only infuses our society with additional strength. For then we know, no matter how bad it gets, there will always be others to reinforce our individual efforts, others who will "have our back," others who will not leave us behind. And, for that, we have just reason to rejoice now and forever more.

---

[49] Doron Almog. "Leave No Man Behind: Entebbe operation lessons relevant for Israeli attitude towards disabled members of society." Ynetnews.com: 04 July 2011. See: http://www.ynetnews.com/articles/0,7340,L-4090633,00.html

Portion 4:

Vayeira // He Appeared
Torah Portion: Genesis 18:1-22:24

"THE LORD APPEARED…" In the Eternal's presence, we are faced with that age-old question: "Is anything too wondrous for the Lord?" (Genesis 18:14) From numerous events in this portion, the answer is clearly "no." God can give life and take it away, protect and condemn, all for reasons only God understands. This awareness of our finite understanding in the face of the Infinite One only compounds the already complicated human relationships found throughout the portion.

It begins when Sarah overhears three Divine visitors inform Abraham that she will give birth to a son in her old age. Sarah laughs at this news, amazed at the abilities of the Eternal. Abraham is then forced to confront God's plan to destroy Sodom and Gomorrah in order to save his nephew Lot along with his family, as they reside there. With the cities destroyed, and Lot's wife dead, his daughters mistakenly believe they are the last surviving people on earth, and therefore decide to become pregnant by him.

Concern, spawned by limited knowledge, also causes Abraham to fret over the fate of his son Ishmael, as Sarah wishes to exile him and his mother Hagar from their household. God directs Abraham to heed the words of his wife, reassuring him that the Eternal's protection will be with Hagar and Ishmael in the wilderness. In fact, Hagar's and Ishmael's struggle – under God's protection – can be seen as the counterpart to the next episode of the *Akeidah*, "the binding of Isaac," as both son and mother likely struggle to understand God's command.

Thankfully, that test is halted before its deathly conclusion, as the portion then ends with the birth of Rebekah, Isaac's future wife, foreshadowing the next generation of God's people.

Vayeira // He Appeared
Bite 1 – *Time Out! A Challenge has been Issued on the Play!*

It's a bird! It's a plane! No, it's Supernanny! Faster than a speeding toddler, more powerful than their outbursts, able to leap tall Lego buildings in a single bound, Jo Frost (a.k.a. "the Supernanny") uses her amazing powers to put children in timeout![50] Seriously! Because, psychologists suggest, rather than forcing a child to address the undesirable action in the moment, "offending behavior is weakened best by removing the child from the reinforcing situation."[51] That is to say, rather than resuming the game of life immediately upon a penalty, sometimes it's best – for all involved – to call a "timeout."

As a tool in behavioral development, "timeout" was first coined and later advanced by psychologists Arthur Staats and Montrose Wolf in the early 1960s.[52] But, we understand, this form of discipline was at play much earlier. As we read in *Vayeira*, upon the child Isaac having been born and weaned, "Sarah saw the son whom Hagar the Egyptian had borne to Abraham playing [with him]. She thereupon said to Abraham, 'Remove that slave woman and her son, for the son of that slave shall not share in the inheritance with my son Isaac.'" Though, this demand distressed Abraham greatly, God said: "Do not be distressed…whatever Sarah says, you shall do." (Genesis 21:8-13)

"S'woorlll!" rolls the ball in the referee's whistle. "A challenge has been issued on the play." But surprisingly it is not in regards to Sarah's demand. Rather, the sages rush to her defense by calling into question the play of Ishmael, suggesting that it was somehow offensive or unsportsmanlike. Specifically, some charge that Ishmael's play included "illegal contact."[53] And, while this controversial call continues to arouse official reviews and debates, the Divine Referee's ruling stands: Hagar and Ishmael were to be ejected, removed from the reinforcing situation. Why? Because, as psychologists concluded, separation has the potential for long-term reconciliation between the opposing forces.

We see this time and again. Not just in sports arenas, but the Bible is loaded with examples of kinsmen finding separation as a first-stage solution to their

---

[50] *Supernanny* is a reality TV program. It features professional nanny Joanne "Jo" Frost, who helps families struggling with parenting. Through observation and instruction, Frost shows parents discipline alternatives. Of note is Frost's prominent use of the "naughty chair" (a.k.a. timeout).

[51] Psychologist Arthur Staats first printed the term "timeout" in his 1968 book *Learning, Language and Cognition*, published by Holt, Rinehart and Winston. In it, Staats describes the discipline of his 2-year old daughter in 1962: "I would put her in her crib and indicate that she had to stay there until she stopped crying. If we were in a public place, I would pick her up and go outside [until she stopped the offensive behavior]." In brief, he "intended timeout to constitute a very mild punishment."

[52] Montrose Madison Wolf, PhD, was born in Houston, TX and became a student and later colleague of psychologist Arthur Staats, PhD. After Staats first introduced the concept of "timeout" as a learning tool to shape childhood behavior, Wolf advanced the technique and its application.

[53] In Hebrew, the word for "play/*m'tzaheik*" can mean anything from innocent play to idolatry (see Ex. 32:6) to illicit sexual relations (see Gen. 39:17). For rabbinic speculations about how these connotations played out in this Biblical scenario see Genesis Rabbah 53:11. Additionally, suggests Robert Alter, "given that *m'tzaheik* is the verb form of Isaac's name (*Yitzhak*), we may construe that Ishmael was 'Isaac-ing;' that is to say, Ishmael was presuming the role of Isaac, playing the legitimate heir."

confrontations. For example, when quarrelling erupted between the herdsman of Abraham and those of his nephew Lot, Abraham said to Lot: "Let there be no strife between you and me, between my herdsmen and yours, for we are kinsmen… Let us separate: if you go north, I will go south; and if you go south, I will go north."[54] It's a precedent that continues here with Isaac and Ishmael, and one that will be with Jacob and Esau.[55] Each reaches the conclusion that it is far better to be apart and in harmony than to be together in disharmony.

Though we may have reservations in such separations, there seems to be a measure of truth in this approach, attested to most clearly in cases of siblings. As many of us have observed, during the awkward stages of development, siblings on occasion will foster an exaggerated sense of competition between one another, even to the point of being at each other's throats. Yet, when one sibling moves away from home, for college or a profession, magically years of tension, hostility, and aggression seemingly evaporate overnight. Why? Simple: the distance. It creates a space – in terms of both time and place – for proper ventilation, as we gain a better perspective which allows us to cool down.

But, we are advised in such moments to check the thermostat often. For while a temporary separation may lead to reconciliation, if prolonged the ventilated space between becomes a breeding ground for the spores of negativity: suspicion, distrust, even further acts of aggression as we no longer see the other as our brother, but as some inconsequential obstacle along our path easily squashed. One saw those dynamics at play in both the Civil and Cold Wars, and arguably they're still at play in the continued confrontation between we, the descendants of Isaac, and those descendants of Ishmael. What started as a means to cool down, has prolonged into a hard-freeze on the field of play, preventing the resumption of further good-will interactions.

So, how much time is an effective timeout? Psychologists recommend one minute for every year of the child. But, honestly, it varies upon the individual. I suppose, it could be said, that an appropriate time out is as long as one needs to move beyond the immediate emotional response to reach the rational one. It is, at this moment, when we will have a chance to become "supernannies" ourselves. For, while giving ourselves a timeout is a task worthy of the mightiest of men and women, what is truly awe-inspiring is having the courage, conviction, and faith to resume play, reengaging more appropriately with the other. May we all be so heroic this week and every week!

---

[54] Genesis 13:7-9
[55] Genesis 28

Vayeira // He Appeared
Bite 2 – *To Love is to be Vulnerable*

What is the toughest three-word sentiment to say in the English language? I would bet a quick survey of any community would actually elicit not one, but three such statements: 'I am sorry;' 'I forgive you;' 'I love you;' Coincidently, in our relationships, these three statements function symbiotically with one another, exponentially producing positive effects when all three are said and, consequently, multiplying the negative effects should even one go unstated.

Sadly, the latter is illustrated in the story of the *Akeidah*, "the binding of Isaac." According to the story, God tests Abraham by calling upon him to "take [his] son, [his] favored one, Isaac, whom" the Bible expresses, Abraham "loves and go to the land of Moriah and offer him there as a burnt offering." (Genesis 22:2) However, before the act can be consummated, an angel of the Lord calls out: "Abraham! Abraham! Do not raise your hand against the boy or do anything to him. For now I know that you revere God since you did not withhold from Me," and here the Bible reiterates, "your son, your favored one, Isaac." (Genesis 22:12) Yet missing in this reiteration are the words, "whom you love."

Its absence is not the Bible's way of relating to the reader that at this dramatic moment Abraham was somehow *verklempt* with emotion. Rather, according to modern commentator Nachum Sarna, the reason the Bible does not express the statement of love for a second time is because at that moment Abraham felt vulnerable, "realizing that Isaac, for the rest of his life, would remember that his father almost killed him."[56] In other words, what was sacrificed in those final moments of the ordeal was not a sheep. Instead, by failing to confront his vulnerability with the words 'I am sorry,' thus giving Isaac a chance to say 'I forgive you,' Abraham sacrificed the loving relationship they shared.

Now, one could argue that there are just some things 'I am sorry' cannot cover, like the attempted murder of a son for example. However, no matter how complicated or simple the case may be, 'I am sorry' is not intended to be a cure-all. These three little words are simply intended to initiate a process, one that will eventually include other similar statements and actions on the path towards restoration of the relationship. But, if we fail to articulate 'I am sorry' as well as 'I forgive you' in the moments that matter, we – like Abraham – ultimately sacrifice our ability to say within these relationships: 'I love you.'

It's not just Abraham. To some degree, we all feel a sense of vulnerability when initiating this process of reconciliation. Not in the fleeting way we experienced as children, when parents conducted a brief ceremony that compelled our lips to utter 'I am sorry' and 'I forgive you' in order to resume play. No. As adults, saying these words seems more complicated. As if, by saying 'I am sorry' we expose ourselves to an indefensible position, vulnerable to the offendee in the

---

[56] Nachum Sarna. *Etz Hayim: Torah and Commentary*. Rabbinical Assembly: New York, 2001. p.121

future. By the way, being the offendee can be equally unnerving. In fact, many of us are so ill at ease with the three words of 'I forgive you' that we attempt to replace them with three others: "that is okay;" "it is alright;" or even "forget about it." But, really, we fear forgetting. We feel that saying 'I forgive you' lowers this protective shield called memory, thereby making us once again vulnerable to the offender in the future.

Hopefully, then, it comes as a bit of comfort to know that both offender and offendee enter the process of reconciliation feeling vulnerable. I offer this perspective because all too often, in our relationships, we respond to these vulnerable moments in less than productive ways. We scramble to secure our boundaries, building up walls and scuttling off to conceal our positions through deployment of the silent treatment. Some of us, admittedly, even rush to arm ourselves with all sorts of words and deeds as a measure to reinforce our defenses. While these tactics can be effective on the battlefield, love (despite Pat Benatar's claim) is not one. Thus, to entrench ourselves in our positions is tantamount to a withdrawal from those we claim to care about.

Therefore, to ensure the integrity of our loving relationships we must actually remain vulnerable. I know it seems odd, but C.S. Lewis correctly pointed out: "To love is to be vulnerable."[57] However, he associated vulnerability to weakness, believing that our hearts are merely fragile vessels, constantly under threat of shattering. Thus, to protect the love the heart contains we must "wrap it carefully…avoiding all entanglements…locking it up safe."[58] But that cannot be the case. For our hearts are muscles and the love they contain grows, as all muscles do, from an open exchange of forces. Therefore, vulnerability may be better understood not in terms of weakness but openness, not in terms of fragility but permeability, as our hearts are perceptive and receptive to the constant give and take which occurs in healthy relationships. We just happen to feel the vulnerability more acutely when engaged in the give and take of beseeching and granting forgiveness.

Abraham too felt this vulnerability at the end of the story of the *Akeidah*. But, instead of facing and embracing this feeling as corollary to the loving relationship he shared with his son, Abraham remained silent. And, as we know, that silent treatment often becomes a vicious cycle difficult to break. A consequence Abraham and Isaac knew all too well, as the Bible never mentions that they speak to one another again. Let us not make the same mistake. May we continue to strengthen our current relationships and even create new ones by embracing our moments of vulnerability. For life is and will continue to be full of them. But, if we are able to express those vulnerabilities through the words 'I am sorry' and 'I forgive you,' what will be heard and understood is 'I love you.'

---

[57] C.S. Lewis. *The Four Loves*. Harvest Books, 1960.
[58] Ibid.

Vayeira // He Appeared
Bite 3 – *Fuel of Faith: What Drives our Judaism?*

To keep America moving forward, so that it can continue to be a leading presence in the world, we have always looked for more efficient forms of energy. We have gone from steam to coal to oil to nuclear fission. One can only guess what dominant form of energy will emerge next. Will it be wind? Perhaps. Water? Maybe. Solar? Still a possibility. How about... fear? After all, we do seem to have a lot of it these days. And, I do not know about you, but when I'm in the ocean and someone yells "shark," nothing gets me moving faster than the fear of being eaten.

I mention this because, throughout the year we experience small pit-stops, moments – like Shabbat – when we are encouraged to pull over and fill up our souls. Though, when we do, it often seems like the only thing on tap is fear: unleaded, of course. This is particularly evident in the *Akeidah*, "the binding of Isaac." At the end of this frightening tale, an angel of the Lord cried out to Abraham, saying: "Abraham! Abraham! Do not raise your hand against the boy or do anything to him, for now I know that you <u>fear</u> God." (Genesis 22:12)

But, it's not just here. A quick scan of Torah will reveal "the fear of God" numerous times, whether as a judicial qualification in Exodus,[59] a legal standard in the Holiness Code of Leviticus,[60] or even as a formal name of God. As we read later in the book of Genesis, Jacob states to Laban, "Had not the God of my fathers," whom Jacob qualifies as "the God of Abraham and the <u>Fear</u> [with a capital "F"] of Isaac, been with me, you would have left me empty handed."[61] In fact, according to the Bible, it's the lack of fear that precipitated both Pharaoh's and Amalek's transgressions against the people of Israel.[62]

So clearly, as we consider what energy will fuel our Judaism, the Bible stands like a gas-jockey, seemingly ready and more than willing to fill us with fear. And, why not? While fear can sometimes cause people to stall or break down, often times – as my phobia of sharks highlights – it can be a real boost to our engines, driving us to do something faster, and maybe better. In fact, I imagine that – for some of us – fear has even brought us closer to God. Such was the case with a Scottish fisherman, who once considered himself a devout atheist:

> While fishing one day on the ole Loch Ness, the Loch Ness monster billowed forth out of the water. With a strong flick of her tail, she sent the fisherman flying high into the air, while she – with mouth open wide – waited below, ready to swallow him whole. In that frightening moment, the fisherman screamed: "Oh, God! Please save me!" The whole scene froze. The Loch Ness monster was still below, mouth wide open, and the fisherman was stuck in mid-air just above her.

---

[59] Exodus 18:21
[60] Leviticus 19:14, 32; Leviticus 25:17,36,43
[61] Genesis 31:42, 53
[62] Exodus 9:30 and Deuteronomy 25:18

Then, a booming voice was heard from Heaven: "I thought you didn't believe in Me!" "Hey!" exclaimed the fisherman. "I didn't believe in the Loch Ness monster a moment ago either."[63]

While humorous, this scenario – as well as others – begs the serious question: what happens after that moment? What happens when the fear fades, when the terror is tamed, when the adrenaline wanes? Does our hyper-awareness fade as well? Absolutely. Just take, for example, the fear Jews had when they first came to this country: would our place here be secure? This fear provoked many to engage outside their Jewish communities, joining civic clubs, participating in politics, marching into the military. Yet, generations later, as our place here has become secure, that fear has waned and so too has our engagement outside Jewish walls, causing one prominent Jewish leader to say, even among many liberal congregations, "we are re-ghettoizing ourselves."[64]

Despite our propensity for repentance, there's no need for flagellations here. Because, as psychologists have pointed out, this is not a shortcoming of us; it's a shortcoming of fear. Whether it's physical or emotional, mental or spiritual, our bodies eventually acclimate to that heightened state of arousal, thus requiring an ever increasing amount of fear to provoke the same response. In other words, fear – by nature – is a non-renewable resource: abundant in the short run, but ill-equipped for a long trip. So, like America at large, we too find ourselves in need of a more efficient form of energy, a fuel for faith that can – as the Voice in the movie, *Field of Dreams,* stated – "go the distance."[65]

Thankfully, we don't have to go far to find it. As our prayer books teach, "*Ahavat olam Beit Yisrael amcha ahavta //* Eternal, unending, everlasting <u>love</u>, You [God] offered Your people, the House of Israel."[66] This isn't some hippy trip, but an interstate highway to holiness. For, unlike fear, love cannot be exhausted; its affection cannot be outgrown; its acceptance will not wane. And because it is so distinct from fear in those ways, the Bible actually expects us to pass love along. Not solely by "loving God with all of our hearts, with all of our souls, with all of our might,"[67] but more to the point by "loving [our] neighbors as we do [our]selves."[68] So, whereas fear is meant to go nowhere, love – as the Muppets once sang – is meant to keep us "movin' right along."[69]

Jackie Lantry, a mother of four, understands the powerful advantage love has over fear as well. In her own words, she says, "I believe in the

[63] Albert Tapper and Peter Press. *A Minister, a Priest, and a Rabbi.* Andrews McMeel Publishing: Kansas City: 2000. p.115
[64] Macy B. Hart, CEO of the Goldring/Woldenberg Institute of Southern Jewish Life, whose department of Community Engagement (directed by Malkie Schwartz) promotes community-wide engagement by Jewish communities throughout the South.
[65] Phil Alden Robinson. *Field of Dreams.* Universal Studios: 1989. Based on *Shoeless Joe* by W.P. Kinsella.
[66] These are the beginning words to *Ahavat Olam* prayer in the evening service.
[67] Deuteronomy 6:5
[68] Leviticus 19:18, 34. In fact, while love is meant to power us to do many positive things, the only thing the Bible has us do with fear is either have it (when it comes to God) or get rid of it (when it comes to other people and their ways of life).
[69] Paul Williams and Kenny Ascher. "Movin' Right Along." *The Muppet Movie: Soundtrack.* Atlantic Records: 1979.

ingredients of love, the elements from which it is made. I believe in love's humble, practical components and their combined power. I understand, because four years ago we – my husband and I – adopted our son Luke from China. The orphanage people simply dropped him off at our hotel room, without saying goodbye. He was six, weighed only 28 pounds, and his face was crisscrossed with scars. Clearly, he was terrified. 'What are his favorite things?' I yelled, as they hurried out the door. 'Noodles' was the reply, as the elevator closed tight.

Luke kicked and screamed. Not knowing exactly what to do, I stood between him and the door to keep him from bolting. His cries were anguished, animal-like. He'd never seen a mirror and tried to escape by running through one. I wound my arms around him, in love, hoping to prevent further harm. After an hour or so, he finally fell asleep, exhausted. I called room service. They delivered every noodle dish on the menu. Luke woke, looked at me and started sobbing again. I handed him chopsticks and pointed at the food. He stopped crying and started to eat. He ate until I was sure he would be sick. The screams of terror came again when I tried to give him a bath. I played with the water. And, by the end, the bathroom was soaked, but he was clean and giggling (for what seemed like the first time in his life).

The next day we met the orphanage officials to do paperwork. Luke was on my lap as they filed into the room. He looked at them and wrapped his arms tightly around my waist. For some time afterwards, Luke continued to be a skittish boy. He cried easily, withdrew often in fear. He hid food in his pillowcase and foraged in garbage cans. Though I wondered then if he would ever get over the wounds of fear the orphanage beat into him, today I only wonder how this abused, terrified little creature transformed into my smart, funny, well-adjusted son with tremendous charm. It was not therapy, counselors, or medications. It did not cost money, just time and energy. It was the power of love: simple, plain, easy to give."[70]

Like America, we too find ourselves in a moment of transition. But rather than going from steam to coal to oil to nuclear fission, in our faith we can go from fear to love. As any gas pump will remind us, during the pit-stops of our year, we have a choice as to which form of energy we wish to fuel our faith. We can go with fear, knowing that its boost goes out as quickly as it comes in. Or, we can choose to go with love. It may cost a little more in terms of time and energy but, as Jackie Lantry points out, it makes a world of difference in the long run. So, like a billboard advertisement along the highway of life, I am encouraging us all to select the more efficient form of energy to fuel our faith. Rather than fear, let us select the higher grade of love. For by it, we and our Jewish community are guaranteed to lead the way this day and every day!

---

[70] Jackie Lantry. "The Power of Love to Transform and Heal." *This I Believe*. NPR: 1 August 2005.

Portion 5:
Chayei Sarah // The Life of Sarah
Torah Portion: Genesis 23:1-25:18

"THE LIFE OF SARAH CAME TO 127 YEARS." No explanation other than her age is given for Sarah's death, which has led some commentators to draw a connection between "The Binding of Isaac" in the last chapter and her death at the opening of this one. Sarah's death prompts Abraham to purchase a burial plot for her: a cave in the field of Machpelah. This process is explained in detail, showing us how important it was for Abraham and his descendants, as Isaac and Rebekah, Jacob and Leah will be buried there as well. By purchasing this site, Abraham solidifies God's promise regarding the Land.

Additionally, Abraham ensures his Covenant with God by sending his servant to the land of his birth to find a wife for Isaac. Only there may a suitable partner be found, as opposed to taking a wife from the women of Canaan. Rebekah is seen at a well, a symbol of marriage in the Bible. Her generous character is confirmed when she offers to draw water for Abraham's servant and his camels. When she announces that she is the granddaughter of Abraham's brother, the reader understands that she is *beshert*, fated for Isaac.

But, it is not just God that holds them together; it is love. When Rebekah sees Isaac for the first time, she falls off her camel. Commentators have interpreted this to mean that she fell in love at first sight. Isaac loves Rebekah as well, indicating the first time we ever read about a man's love for a woman in the Torah. When Rebekah moves into Sarah's tent, she comforts Isaac after the loss of his mother and we see that Sarah's legacy lives on through the next matriarch.

At the end of the portion, Abraham dies and is buried in the same cave as Sarah. The Torah notes that both his sons, Isaac and Ishmael, were present at his burial; an honorable end to the portion as well as the progenitors of the Divine promise.

Chayei Sarah // The Life of Sarah
Bite 1 – *The Hallmark of Aging*

On a search for a birthday card for a mentor of mine, I came across many which captured the general human reaction to aging. For example, on the cover of one card, it stated in a comforting tone: "Happy 40th and cheer up! In time you'll learn to love being 40…," as the inside of the card read, "…like in ten years, when you turn 50!" But, at the age of 50, our reservations for getting older do not seem to diminish, as another card pointed out: "On your 50th birthday, studies show that wrinkles add depth and character." While on the inside the card read: "I do not know about you, but I would prefer to remain shallow and uninteresting. Happy 50th!" What once was a celebrated occasion of the anniversary of our birth has become, with each passing decade, a mile marker on the road of life approached with greater and greater reluctance.

Trepidation in the face of aging, however, is not the message that we are to glean from *Chayei Sarah*. On the contrary, we are to revel in our old age, as the Torah portion begins by trumpeting the years of Sarah's life. As it is stated, "Sarah lived to be 100 YEARS, and 20 YEARS, and 7 YEARS!" (Genesis 23:1) Now, most translations simply ignore the repetitious word *shanah* ("year") in the Hebrew, printing the English as "Sarah lived to be 127 years." This editorial decision undoubtedly saves ink, which in a time of economic recession and environmental consciousness is obviously advantageous. However, in doing so – the rabbis point out – we miss a wonderful lesson about the value of growing older in the Jewish culture.

According to the rabbis, the years of Sarah's life are broken up as they are to teach us that "at the age of 100 years she maintained the beauty of a 20 year-old. And at the age of 20 years she had the innocence of a 7 year-old."[71] I know what you're thinking: "What moisturizing cream did she use and where can I get some?" But, the intention of this beautiful rabbinic sentiment (which – by the way – could easily compete with Hallmark) is not that at the age of 127 Sarah actually looked 20. For Sarah had already stated a few chapters earlier that she was "withered."[72] Rather, this rabbinic statement encourages us to see within the process of aging that one's value, even to the likes of which we experienced in our youth, can be retained.

In the face of what we know, the retention of our worth in society – especially one that places such a high value on youthfulness – as we age seems almost impossible. Whether we are 7 years-old, 20 years-old, or even 100 years-old, most of us have or, at some point soon, will realize there's no way to pass through life without life passing and leaving its indelible mark upon us. Our eyes will eventually not see as far as they once could. Our ears will gradually not hear as clear as they once did. Our bones, bit-by-bit, will become brittle.

---

[71] Genesis Rabbah 58:1
[72] Genesis 18:12

Our hair will gray, whiten, and possibly fall out. But these flaws which amass on the human form by the torturous hands of time cannot reduce our value.

For the value in which the rabbis speak, the value which is inherent in the process of aging, is cultivated internally. From a verse found slightly later in this portion, Abraham is referred to as being "old (*zakein*) and advanced in years."[73] These seemingly repetitive accolades are not God's way of adding "worse to wear." No, by the standards of rabbinic tradition, "advanced in years" is simply an indication of chronological time, while "old/*zakein*" is an attribute of wisdom. For the rabbis believe <u>z</u>akein/old is the acronym from the Hebrew expression: <u>z</u>eh <u>ka</u><u>n</u>a, meaning "this one has acquired."[74] And, according to modern commentator Nachum Sarna, the specific inference is to Wisdom, a.k.a. the Torah.[75] For, the Torah is "a Tree of Life to all who hold it fast."

However, it is not enough for us to hold onto the Tree of Life and the wisdom we reap from its branches. In order to truly age with value, we must become *of* value to others, willing to pass our knowledge (gleaned from the written word and from our own life experiences) onto the next generation. As it is stated in *Pirkei Avot*: "One who learns Torah from the young, to what can this be likened? To one who eats unripe grapes and drinks from unfermented wine. But one who learns Torah from the old, to what can this be likened? To one who eats ripe grapes and drinks fine-aged wine."[76] In other words, the value we amass from the lessons learned through life are meaningless if they are forever contained in the vessel, the bottle of ourselves. Rather to age with value, we must become uncorked, allowing the contents of our minds to flow into the world so that others may drink and be replenished through our wisdom.

By these means, pursuing and imparting wisdom, we can retain our value in society even as we undergo the aging process and the changes it inevitably brings. As another card I came across recounts: "Now that you're 40, do you realize that 40 years ago call-waiting referred to a line outside of a phone booth, an airbag was someone who talked too much, spam was found only in kitchens, a cell-phone was what you used to make your one call from jail, and finally, a birthday was something you actually looked forward to!" Well, according to this portion, that last one is something that does not need to change as we get older. For, in Judaism, we are not supposed to sit in perpetual *shiva*, mourning the long lost days of our youth. Rather, we are encouraged to revel in our old age, understanding that as we rise in age, so too do we rise in value in society.

---

[73] Genesis 24:1
[74] Genesis Rabbah 59:6
[75] See Proverbs 8
[76] Pirkie Avot 4:26

Chayei Sarah // The Life of Sarah
Bite 2 – *Honor in Deed, Not in Dollar*

How shall our culture be valued? Is it by the towers we build, art we create, wars we wage and win, land we possess? According to Gandhi, it's none of the above. To know the true value of any culture, he taught, one needs only to observe the way they treat the least among them: the poor, the orphan, the elderly, even the deceased.[77] For, in these acts, there is no anticipated incentive for doing that which is just, no sense of entitled reward which motivates the deed, no expectation of payback. Such acts, between individuals, lay bare the culture's true values of what is right and what is righteous.

So, then, it could be said that the monotheistic culture – begun by Abraham – was to be amongst the most righteous cultures in the world. For, upon Sarah's death at the age of 127 years, Abraham spared no expense to secure her burial place. "Sell me a burial site among you," pleaded Abraham, as a resident alien to the Hittites, who then possessed the land. "No, my lord," replied Ephron the Hittite. "I will give it to you." Although generous, Abraham could not accept. "Allow me to pay the price of the land… to bury my dead," insisted Abraham. Thereupon, Ephron asked a steep price, 400 shekels of silver, which Abraham accepted without argument. (Genesis 23:1-16)

Why? Why did Abraham not attempt to negotiate such a steep price? After all, bargaining was an accepted practice of the region, and Abraham had already shown a disposition for being a great negotiator with God over the lives in Sodom and Gomorrah.[78] Some answer this question from the standpoint of Jewish Law. As it is written, "[Nothing] should eclipse the need to make arrangements for the prompt burial of the deceased," for in such speed we honor our loved ones.[79] Others suggest Abraham's lack of response connotes the general ill-ease we feel when forced to engage in fiscal matters in times of great grief. Among this latter group, there are even those who feel no need to negotiate, believing the amount paid is equivalent to the amount loved.

If correct, then such miscalculations in times of great significance are ubiquitous in every era. Far too often today, many of us still equate how much we spend with how much we love, whether it's with our partners or our spouses, our parents or our children, our friends or our extended families. Even those who consider themselves too smart to buy into advertisements – like "every kiss begins with Kay" – throw their equations off balance as special moments in the year approach: birthdays, anniversaries, holidays. Think about it. How crazy do we get trying to find that supposedly "perfect" gift that can precisely convey the true value of our loving relationships?

---

[77] Specifically, Gandhi is attributed as saying, "A nation's greatness is measured by how it treats its weakest members."
[78] Genesis 18:20-33
[79] Shulchan Aruch, YD 357:1

Seriously! We drive ourselves nuts on this fool's errand, as any gift – even the most costly – will pale in comparison to our feelings. They are, as the MasterCard commercial states, "priceless." Hence, this is the reason why our sages steer us away from the ostentatious and move us instead towards the modest. In the case of burial, writes Maurice Lamm in *The Jewish Way in Death and Mourning*, modesty goes beyond ensuring democracy in death, as no one is then embarrassed about what they can or cannot provide.[80] By requiring a simple shroud or wood casket, "the sages [generally] acknowledge expense as a poor barometer of honoring our relationships."[81]

This standard of modesty is not meant to discourage charitable giving in the name of loved ones. Nor is it meant to diminish the sincerity of public displays of private affection. Merely, when life calls upon us to recognize such moments of meaning, our sages wished to direct our attentions away from the dollar and onto the deed. For, in deed, we not only honor our loved ones, we keep our relationships with them – even in their absence – moving forward. What may start with personal participation in burial (i.e. placing dirt upon the grave), can and should continue with all the various actions of our lives, as we become mobile markers of meaning to a life well-lived.

It is through us and these meaningful and thoughtful acts that the true value of our culture shall be assessed. For, despite the outward appearance of modesty, which some may mistakenly equate as poverty, we know there is a deep and rich reservoir just below the surface. Rather than tapping it for ourselves, we divert it to the least advantaged members among us: the poor, the orphan, the elderly. And, in doing so, we honor all those who came before us and – we pray – all those who may come after us, giving them the greatest gift of all: not just a world that is right, but one that is more righteous.

Chayei Sarah // The Life of Sarah
Bite 3 – *One Foot In and the Other Out*

In 2005, a short documentary on Jewish history was released, called: *The Tribe*. Narrated by actor and fellow tribe member, Peter Coyote, the documentary states: "Throughout history, the Jewish tribe has been treated as outsiders," positing then that "the essential Jewish perspective must be one by which we are standing on the outside and looking in... This may explain," the film goes on to suggest, "why Jews invented a bread with only an outside:" the bagel.[82]

---

[80] A modest wood coffin is also required for burial by Jewish Law as to not hinder the natural process of decomposition as understood by the Bible: "from dust to dust." (Genesis 3:19)
[81] An example of this modest value in action may be understood from Jacqueline Kennedy's last minute decision to move her husband's remains from the bronze coffin provided by the Government to a casket made of mahogany wood. As Lamm notes, "John F. Kennedy's widow wisely decided that the President's spirit and life demanded a simple coffin, as he was removed from the bronze coffin and interred in a wooden casket." (p. 21)
[82] Tiffany Shlain and Ken Goldberg. *The Tribe*. 2005 www.tribethefilm.com

That delectable outside perspective pervades our Biblical texts, especially in *Chayei Sarah*. Immediately after the death of his wife, Abraham states to the Hittites, "I am a resident alien." In other words, "I am an outsider." Though now, desiring to take a step inward, Abraham appeals to the Hittites, saying: "Sell me a burial site among you." "No, my lord," answers the Hittite Ephron. "I will [not sell you this land. I will] *give* it to you: the field and the cave within it...to bury your dead." Though contrary to expectations and potentially even a few of our inclinations, Abraham rejects the idea, insisting: "Let me pay for the land," adding "at full price." (Genesis 23:4-13)

What?! Why would Abraham insist on paying for something, remarkably "at full price," when he could have gotten it for free? It may be that Abraham acknowledged, as so many politicians, economists, and local deli owners have, that "there's no such thing as a free lunch..." not even if it comes on a bagel.[83] Rather, to move securely from the outside to the inside of any society, as Abraham did, the beneficial *schmear* must cover both parties: those on the outside (as Abraham was) and those already on the inside (i.e. the Hittites).

Throughout much of history that perceived benefit, which allowed Jews to move from the periphery to the centrality of society, was – as it was primarily here with Abraham – fiscal. For example, in the year 1244 C.E., King Frederick of Austria issued an invitation to the Jews of the world to come into his kingdom for mutual economic benefit. As the charter states: "Inasmuch as we desire that men of all classes dwell in our land, and share our favor and good will, we do henceforth decree these [favorable] laws for all Jews."[84] According to renowned historian, Jacob Rader Marcus (*z"l*), these 'favorable' laws, which followed in the charter, "granted the Jews ample opportunity to sell their wares and [encouraged them], above all, to lend money."[85] For, as he and countless other historians have articulated, "Jews" and "merchants" were practically synonymous terms.[86] This was especially true in the Middle Ages, as the unfortunate Diaspora created the fortunate presence of multiple Jewish economic centers throughout the known world, allowing – at this early time – for international trade through extended family relations.[87] Besides, it must also be acknowledged that – at this point in history – one of the very few careers open to Jews outside their ghettos and inside the larger society was money-lending.

Though, as we now know, history would prove tragically ironic. Because, this role – through which we were welcomed in – is the same one that would be used unjustly to throw us out of France, Italy, Spain, England, and countless

---

[83] This popular adage conveys the idea that you cannot get something for nothing. Although the phrase's origin is unknown, it has appeared countless times in American culture. For example, the phrase was popularized by Robert Heinlein's 1966 novel, *The Moon is a Harsh Mistress*, and in economist Milton Friedman's 1975 book, *There's No Such Thing as a Free Lunch*.

[84] Jacob Rader Marcus. *The Jew in the Medieval World: A Source Book 315-1791*. Hebrew Union College Press: Cincinnati, OH. 1999. p. 31

[85] Ibid.

[86] See W. Roscher. "The Status of the Jews in the Middle Ages." *Historia Judaica*: April 1944, p.17 for an example.

[87] Max Dimont. *Jews, God, and History*, Second Edition. Penguin Books Ltd.: New York, 1990. p. 265

other places.[88] But rather than becoming more cautious and scaling back our investments upon arriving in a new place, as that would have been a rational response, subsequent Jewish history teaches us that we actually invested more. Such was the case in Lake Charles, LA.

> At the end of the 19th century, a member of the Meyer family, William, first came to Lake Charles from Alsace. According to an 1870 U.S. Census report, William was a druggist, and immediately set up shop, providing an indispensable pharmaceutical service to the community. By 1880, his younger brother – Adolph – became a business partner. But, helping his community economically was not enough for young Adolph. During the Civil War, he fought for the South in the Confederate Army, achieving the rank of Adjutant General. Then, from 1874 to 1888, he went on to serve Lake Charles as the city's mayor. And, from 1890 to 1908, he proved advantageous for the entire state of Louisiana, representing its populations' various interests successfully in the U.S. House of Representatives for nine consecutive terms.[89]

Wonderfully, his story is not unique. From Virginia Beach, VA (with Meyera Ellenson Oberndorf, who in 1996 was recognized by Newsweek as one of the best mayors in America) to Waco, TX (with Daniel Sternberg, who escaped Poland just before WWII to become dean of the Baylor School of Music and conductor of the Baylor Symphony Orchestra), examples of Jews investing more than their money for the benefit of their communities abound.[90] In fact, everyday across America, Jews engage themselves fully outside their homes: from the PTA to little league, from running for a cure to stopping in to support local food pantries. And, in return for offering this "full price," many believed – as Abraham did – that our place within our new homes would be secure.

Not necessarily. While we have fared far better in the center of American life as a result of investing our skills and talents along with our finances in our cities and towns, some will still caution, "we should not confuse insular with insulated." Because, something history has also shown us is that no matter how integrated we are within a society, there can be no guarantees of absolute security. One needs only to recall the horrors of the Holocaust – merely 65 years ago – for a painful reminder. But, let us not fear or fret. Because, while there is no such thing as absolute security there are certainly things we can do to bring us greater stability. In addition to investing in the New World, we cannot afford to divest completely out of the Old. If we do, we may ultimately

---

[88] For example: Welcomed in as money-lenders by King Louis X in 1315 C.E., the Jewish community was forcibly removed 80 years later by a decree of King Charles VI, who - among other reasons - grew uneasy with the economic expansion of the Jewish community.
[89] Thanks to ISJL Historian, Dr. Stuart Rockoff, for his help in combing the census archives for this information.
[90] Ibid. For further reading, please check out The Encyclopedia of Southern Jewish Communities at www.isjl.org

put ourselves at risk – falling, once more, through the proverbial hole in the bagel.

Therefore, let not history repeat itself. Let us, in our gradual move from the periphery of the world to its center, which began with Abraham and continues with us here today, learn that we must maintain a wider stance, keeping one "foot in," as the *Hokey Pokey* would say, and the other "foot out. [Because, truly,] that's what it is all about!" By maintaining a connection to that substance from which our lives have been nourished (i.e. the bread of our unique and noble heritage), we maintain our ability to share it and its benefits with the world. And thereby, we pray dear Lord, that our continued movement from outside in will grow ever more and more secure, as all Your creations – O' God – will be covered in a *schmear* of goodness.

Portion 6:
Toldot // Generations
Genesis 25:19-28:9

"THIS IS THE GENERATION OF ISAAC…" Specifically, these opening words of this portion are referring to Isaac's twin sons: Jacob and Esau. However, it is really their mother Rebekah who takes a lead role in the portion. During her pregnancy, Rebekah receives a prophecy from God that the younger son will rule over the older. As the twins grow and enter young-adulthood, their different characteristics become more discernible. Esau – "a man of the outdoors" – is favored by Isaac, while Jacob – "a homespun man" – is favored by Rebekah.

In the midst of the brothers' narrative, whereby Esau sold his birthright to Jacob, we learn of another famine in the land, driving Isaac and Rebekah to Gerar, in the land of the Philistines. Similar to an earlier story of Abraham and Sarah, Isaac lies and tells the people that Rebekah is his sister in order to protect himself. When Abimelech, king of the Philistines, realizes they are married, he warns his people not to touch Isaac or Rebekah. This risky venture pays off when Isaac is able to prosper in the Philistines' land.

The portion then shifts back to Rebekah and her understanding of the Divine plan. In order for this plan to come to fruition, she must ensure that Jacob receives his father's blessing. Although most of our rabbinic sages praise Rebekah for her actions, many modern commentators are more skeptical. Is Rebekah simply an implementer of a Divine plan or a manipulative schemer, placing her favored son in line for prosperity? No matter how one views her intentions, Rebekah's actions are clearly central to this narrative, leading Jacob to receive Isaac's blessing and causing Esau's scorn, so that Jacob is thereupon forced to flee to Haran and live with her brother Laban.

Toldot // Generations
Bite 1 – *Walking Upright*

In October of 2010, the U.S. publicly apologized for infecting Guatemalans with syphilis in order to test the effectiveness of penicillin on STDs. In a joint statement, the U.S. Secretary of State as well as the Health and Human Services Secretary expressed: "Although these events occurred more than 64 years ago, we are outraged that such reprehensible research could have occurred under the guise of public health. We deeply regret that it happened, and we apologize to all of the individuals who were affected by such abhorrent research practices."[91] Obviously, we are appalled and embarrassed that Americans would conduct such experiments. Yet, the researchers involved must have believed that the ends (a significant medical benefit) justified the means (harming others).

A similar ethical dilemma develops in this portion of *Toldot*. According to it, Esau – Jacob's twin brother – has just returned to the family tent, having spent the entire day hunting in the fields. Starving, he pleads to Jacob: "Give me some of that red stuff to gulp down, for I am famished…" But, rather than helping his brother, Jacob takes advantage of Esau's vulnerability, saying: "First sell me your birthright." Consenting, Esau responds, "I am at the point of death, so what use is my birthright to me?" (25:30-32) Okay, it's not experimenting on human beings (thank God!), nor is it outright stealing (even though Jacob *does* steal his father's blessing from Esau a few verses later). But, really, isn't forcing someone to pay for food when they're starving still morally wrong?

Strangely, though, some rabbis attempt to justify Jacob's actions. RaSHI, for example, states: "the Holy Blessed One affixed the Divine seal to the sale of the birthright which Jacob purchased from Esau."[92] Why? Rabbi Yossy Goldman writes, "[Because] generations later, when his children had gone through the 'smelting pit' of Egypt and still, with amazing faith and tenacity, kept their heritage – then they were deemed worthy of the honor of the birthright."[93] In other words, these rabbis believe that the ends (a future generation of Israel, devoted to God, in spite of incredible hardships) justified the unfavorable way Jacob acquired that birthright from Esau.

So, is that what we are to learn from this portion? That we can do anything – no matter how unjust – if the ends are favorable to us? Maybe… just consider the following:

> **Scenario 1:** Billionaires Warren Buffet and Bill Gates recently traveled to China to recruit donors to join the group of 40 millionaires that have pledged a least half of their net worth to charity. However, many

---

[91] Dr. Donald G. McNeal. "US Sorry for Guatemala Syphilis Experiment" *New York Times*, Research: 1 October 2010. http://www.nytimes.com/2010/10/02/health/research/02infect.html
[92] Quoted in Rabbi Yossy Goldman's "Beans and Birthrights." www.chabad.org
[93] Ibid.

have taken issue with how China's richest have acquired their wealth. So, is it okay to accept donations to charity, even if the money was acquired in an unethical way?[94]

Scenario 2: At the end of WWII, the U.S. decided to drop the atomic bomb on Nagasaki and Hiroshima. Although an estimated 120,000 lives were ended immediately and thousands more in the aftermath, some believe that dropping the bombs was the only way to end the war, which therefore saved thousands of lives. So, is it okay to end hundreds or thousands of lives in order to save thousands more?[95]

Scenario 3: Imagine that a dying loved one desperately needs medicine you cannot afford or they will die. You are aware of a location where you will be able to steal the medicine, but you know that there is a chance that you will be stealing it from somebody else, who may need it, and you'll likely end up in jail. So, is it okay to steal such a precious resource from others so that your loved one will survive?

No one is judging these difficult decisions, as there is only one true Judge in Heaven as on Earth. But, if we were to say 'yes' to any one of these, then we must also be willing to accept the consequences when our unjust actions catch up with us. For example, the American government eventually had to take responsibility and apologize for an atrocity that took place over 60 years ago. And Jacob, even though he attempted to avoid the responsibility by fleeing to Haran, eventually had to come face to face with the consequences of stealing the blessing from Esau. As we read later on, in Genesis 32, "A man wrestled with [Jacob] until the rise of dawn. When [the man] saw that he could not overcome him, he struck Jacob's hip-socket, so that Jacob's hip-socket was wrenched."[96] While some commentators say that Jacob was wrestling with his inner demons, others suggest that he was wrestling with Esau or his spirit, who confronted Jacob because of his unjust actions in the past.

Jacob survived the confrontation. But, he paid a heavy price for his actions, forced to spend the rest of his life walking with a limp. Yet, we know there is a way to avoid these costs in the first place and that's by ensuring that the means are as just as the ends. In each of the ethical scenarios we have explored, there is a fork in the road – a choice to take the righteous or unrighteous path to reach our desired ends. The unrighteous path is often shorter and easier, while the righteous path is often longer and loaded with challenges. Though, ultimately, it's the latter path we must walk down. God says as much to the Israelites, when they left Egypt: "[Do not go] by the way of the land of the

---

[94] Heng He. "Why Warren Buffet and Bill Gates returned Empty-Handed from China." The Epoch Times: 13 October 2010. www.theepochtimes.com
[95] "The Bombing of Hiroshima and Nagasaki," http://www.history.com/topics/bombing-of-hiroshima-and-nagasaki
[96] Genesis 32:25-26

Philistines, although it is shorter... [Instead,] go round about [the long way], by way of the wilderness at the Sea of Reeds."[97]

In other words, while taking the just route in life may take longer and more effort, it is ultimately not just the right thing to do, it's the Jewish thing to do. As Jews, we are taught to treat others with respect, to welcome the stranger, to not place stumbling blocks before the blind and to treat our family and community with compassion. If we take the time in our own lives to infuse these values into each and every one of our steps, then our means are as just as our ends, and will – with God's help – come out walking upright, instead of walking with a limp!

Toldot // Generations
Bite 2 – *Putting the "Give" into Thanksgiving*

With Thanksgiving just around the corner, let us take a moment to recap the story of the pilgrims: A group of people felt religiously oppressed and decide to flee from the oppressive environment, by crossing a body of water. They arrive on dry land and make a connection with a certain large rock: "Plymouth Rock." At first, the harshness of their new environment challenges them in many ways: physically as well as spiritually. Despite the adversities, they persevered in the Land of Promise, eventually making it the "Promised Land of Opportunity!" Oh... and let us not forget. There is also a special meal tied to this event, which offers thanks to God for a safe deliverance. This doesn't sound like anything to which the Jew could relate? Does it?

The fact is that this genesis story of America so closely resembles our own people's pilgrimage from Egypt to the Promised Land of Israel that Benjamin Franklin proposed, in the formative years of the United States, a seal other than the eagle with olive branches in one talon and arrows in the other. According to Franklin's own notes, "Moses [would be] standing on the shore, and extending his hand over the sea, [allowing the Israelites to pass freely, while] causing the sea to overwhelm Pharaoh who is sitting in an open chariot, a crown on his head and a sword in his hand."[98] Undoubtedly, in Franklin's mind, the King of England is Pharaoh and the Israelites were the pilgrims and later immigrants who longed to be free in America. Directly in this vein, there was even a proposal during these formative years of our country to have Hebrew become the national language of the U.S.

From these early reverberations of Thanksgiving to more modern occurrences like Charlie Brown's Thanksgiving, the theme of thanks and giving resonates throughout so many aspects of our lives. What is it about the Thanksgiving story that makes it so popular? Do we relish in the triumph of new beginnings? Or do we just have an affinity for eating and need any excuse to eat so much?

---

[97] Exodus 13:17-18
[98] Noam Zion and David Dishon. *A Different Night: The Family Participation Haggadah.* The Shalom Hartman Institute: Jerusalem, 2003. p. 121

Because, whether it is turkey and stuffing to signify the resilience of America's pioneers, or *al ha-esh* (the barbeque feast) celebrated in Israel to commemorate the culmination of the Zionist plan on our Jewish nation's Independence Day (*Yom HaAtzma-ut)*, or *matzah* and all the fixings during the feast of Passover, the 'thanks/giving' motif of triumph over a meal recurs time and time again, including in this portion of *Toldot*.

This time it is Isaac who flees from the hostile environment of the Philistine city of Gerar, only to experience adversity in his attempts to establish a new beginning elsewhere. As this portion relates these attempts, "When Isaac's servants, digging in the wadi found there a well of water, the Gerar's herdsmen quarreled with him, saying, 'The water is ours.' …When they dug another well, they disputed over that one also…He (Isaac) moved from there and *he* dug yet another well and [finally] they did not quarrel over it…saying, 'Now at last the Lord has granted us ample space to increase in the land.'" (Genesis 26:19-22) After the hostility came to a formal end with the King of Gerar, Scripture tells us that "then Isaac made…a feast and they ate and drank." (Genesis 26:30)

Our sages ask, "Why was there no dispute the third time?" To which the answer is given: "Only then did Isaac give of himself." In the first two diggings it was his servants who did the work. But, when the third time arose, Scripture states: "he (Isaac) dug" and only then did "the Lord appear to him." (Genesis 26:24) Through this explanation we are taught the reason why Thanksgiving has reserved a special spot in our lives, even as Jews. It is to remind us that this is not just a day of thanks, but more importantly, a day of giving; giving of ourselves for the betterment of the world.

> Once there was a little boy, who couldn't have been more than 9 years-old. He desired to find God. So one day he packed his little suitcase with the bare-essentials for such a journey: a six-pack of root beer and a box of 'Twinkies,' and headed out the door.
>
> Having traveled far (in childhood terms this was no more than three blocks), he felt tired and decided to take a break at the neighborhood park. There, he found a spot on a bench next to an old lady, feeding pigeons. He sat down, opened one of his root-beers, and gulped down the foaming liquid. As he did so, his eyes glanced over to the old woman, who was staring at him. He thought "maybe she's hungry." So, he reached into his suitcase and pulled out a 'Twinkie' for her.
>
> She smiled and he liked her smile. Somehow it made him feel warm inside, so he wanted to see it again. He dug down, once more, this time pulling out for her one of his root-beers. Once again, she gave him a smile. They went on like this for the rest of the afternoon: eating, drinking, smiling, but without exchanging a word.
>
> Before they knew it, the sun was setting and the boy closed his suitcase and made his way back home. But just before he did, he ran back to

the old woman and gave her a hug. And she gave him her biggest smile ever. As the little boy opened the door to his house, his mother, worriedly jumped up to ask, "Where have you been all day?"

The boy responded, "I was in the park... having lunch... with God." The mother thought, "Boy, does my son have an imagination!" But before his mother could say anything else, the boy added, "and she has the most beautiful smile ever!"

Well, just as the boy was telling his mother about his meeting with God, the old woman returned home to find her worried son asking, "So mom, where were you all day?" The old woman responded, "I was in the park... eating a snack... with God." The son was stunned. He thought, "Finally, Mom has lost it!" But, before he could say a word, the old woman continued, "...and you know what? He's a lot younger than I thought."[99]

What this story and our Torah portion come to teach us is that Thanksgiving deserves a rightful place within our year. Not because we are given an opportunity to thank God, for as Jews we have this opportunity daily, within our prayers and our deeds. But, Thanksgiving is integral to our lives, because it is a yearly reminder of the power of *giving*. For not only does the act of giving generate the opportunity to render thanks, but as the story demonstrates, the act of giving generates the Divine presence here on earth. When we give of ourselves we live Divinely.

Typically, on Thanksgiving we think about all those reasons we have to be thankful. But, I believe a more appropriate question for us as Jews – with Thanksgiving upon us – is, "Have we created opportunities of thanks by the selfless giving of ourselves to others?" Let us take a moment to think how we have given in this past year and how we will continue to give of ourselves in this year to come. With this thought in mind, let us pray that as Thanksgiving approaches we will not forget our Divine mandate to live ethical and moral lives by giving to others. May we continue to give of ourselves along our path of life, for in this way we walk in step with God wherever our path may take us. As one of America's leaders, Abraham Lincoln, said in his second inaugural address, "With malice toward none, with charity for all, with firmness in the right as God gives us to see the right, may we strive to finish the work we are in...to do all which may achieve and cherish a just and lasting peace among ourselves, and with all nations."

---

[99] Original story by Julie A. Manhan. "An Afternoon in the Park." *A 3rd Serving of Chicken Soup for the Soul.* Health Communications, Inc.: Deerfield Beach, Florida, 1996. pp. 65-66.

Toldot // Generations
Bite 3 – *The Play of Deception*

In the fall of 2010, the Driscoll Middle School football team in Corpus Christi, TX became a viral sensation on YouTube. Here's what happened: As the Driscoll team breaks out of a huddle, its quarterback lines up over the football. From the sideline, the Driscoll assistant coach calls out that his team deserves a five-yard gain because of a supposed infraction made by the other team. At this point, the Driscoll center casually hands the ball over his shoulder to the quarterback (a release perfectly acceptable, though often not done). The quarterback, with football in hand, begins walking straight forward through the defensive line, counting off the alleged five-yards unmolested. Once clear of the confused opposition, he takes off, dashing 67 yards for a touchdown.[100]

According to the rule book, this play was perfectly legal. Surprisingly, according to our Holy Book, it seems – on the surface – all good as well. For, when Isaac's eyes grew dimmed with age in this portion, he called for his eldest son Esau, in order to present him with the blessing of the first born. Though, as we know from the story, Rebekah sends Jacob in his brother's place. "But my brother is a hairy man and I am smooth-skinned," stated Jacob. "If my father touches me, I shall appear to him a trickster and bring upon myself a curse, not a blessing." But, his mother said to him, "Your curse be upon me, my son!" Be a good boy, and "do as I say." (Genesis 27:11-13) And, of course, Isaac did, acquiring – through an act of deception – his brother's blessing.

Like today's sports critics, Biblical commentators are quick to offer varying views on this problematic play. Some sound like spin-doctors, attempting to benign its true negativity by claiming the play was not a ruse but a stunt, "not deceit but cleverness, otherwise Isaac would have never blessed Jacob."[101] Others go a step further, stating that here a deceptive play was necessary to ensure the win, because "a prophet may at times speak falsehoods, as long as the prophetic message is not distorted."[102] Since the younger not the elder child was destined to be blessed, Jacob's deception was more than justified. Not so quick, argues Rabbi Harold Kushner. "It is not the way of Torah to moralize over questionable plays, but to show how such plays have consequences in people's lives."[103] For, though one may believe deception bears blessings, it creates plenty of curses as well.

Particularly, this becomes evident in the life of the individual who first instigates the deception. Why? Well, simply put, it's because trick plays are not unique to any one individual's playbook. This was true even in Jacob's case. In the second quarter of Jacob's life, he leaves home to work for his uncle Laban. "Just because you are a kinsman, should you serve me for nothing?" asked Laban to Jacob. "Tell me, what shall be your wage?" Now, Laban had two

---

[100] See: http://www.youtube.com/watch?v=0UIdI8khMkw
[101] RaSHI's commentary to Genesis 27:35
[102] Ibn Ezra commentary to Genesis 27:19
[103] Rabbi Harold Kushner. *Etz Hayim: Torah and Commentary.* Rabbinical Assembly: New York, 2001. p. 170

daughters: the elder Leah and the younger Rachel. "Jacob loved Rachel," states the Bible, so he answered: "I will serve seven years for your younger daughter Rachel." Laban agreed. But, when seven years came and went, Laban did an ol' switch-a-roo, putting the elder Leah in place of the younger Rachel (exactly reverse of the deception Jacob pulled on his father).[104]

Yet, not the instigator alone receives a cursed taste of his/her own deceptive medicine. There are those on the sidelines, who may get injured in the play as well: family, friends, etc. This part of the curse arrives in the third quarter of Jacob's life. "Come now," stated the sons of Jacob. "Let's kill our brother Joseph... Then, we shall [deceive our father], saying, 'A savage beast devoured him.'" Though they sold Joseph into slavery, the brothers still came to their father with his ornamented tunic stained in blood. "We found this," they said, playing innocent. "Isn't it your son's?" Recognizing it immediately, Jacob exclaimed in great grief, "My son's tunic! A savage beast has devoured him." Jacob mourned inconsolably. For he knew, in his heart, he was to blame.[105] His original deception now compounded to an agonizing 22-year separation which cursed him, his family, and all those innocently in his care.

Innocent bystanders are not the only ones in harm's way along the sidelines. Deception also threatens those in the stands, as it has a way of spilling over, spoiling the entire game for those who wish to watch and learn from the glorious play of others. This is most evident in the old World Wrestling Federation (WWF), for example. As children, we may have flocked to our TV screens to watch the outrageous plays of Brutus the Barber Beefcake, Ravish Rick Rude, and – who could forget – the amazing Hulk Hogan. "O yeah, brother!"[106] But, as we matured, our eyes were opened. We began to see missed kicks which still sent an opponent to the ropes, hits which appeared like a gentle slap, and figure four leg-locks which seemed little more than playing footsy. With such lies, there is little truth to live by.[107] Thus, we soon turned the game off, having been turned off by the game.

We cannot allow this to happen with our lives. For the sake of both our ancestors as well as our descendants, we – the adults – have the responsibility to call out deception whenever it occurs as well as to discourage it from occurring again.[108] For, though we may believe that – should any curse come – it will be upon us, the story of Jacob reminds us that the cursed ball has a way of getting away from us in a hurry, striking hard those along the sidelines as well as those in the stands. Therefore, may we set a better example for our children, showing them that through integrity and passion, through truth and

---

[104] Genesis 29:15-30

[105] Another interesting twist in this Game of Deception, for just as a son, Jacob deceived his father, so too did his sons come to deceive him.

[106] Often one of Hulk Hogan's catch phrases.

[107] This happens in other sports as well...

[108] Deception fits under the Jewish prohibition of g'neivat da'at, literally meaning "theft of knowledge." And this theft may include stealing one's mind, thoughts, wisdom, or knowledge, and/or fooling someone and thereby causing him or her to have a mistaken assumption, belief, and/or impression. (BT Chullin 94a and Sefer Yereim 224). While some connect this prohibition to the eighth commandment, "Thou shalt not steal," others believe it is not Biblical but rabbinic (see Semak, 262).

real competition, not only will they cross the goal line; they'll do so with their heads held high. For, as the sportswriter Grantland Rice, once wrote: "When the great Scorer comes to write about your name, God marks not that you won or lost but how you played the Game." May we continue to play it well!

Portion 7:
Vayeitzei // He Left
Genesis 28:10-32:3

"AND JACOB LEFT BEERSHEVA AND SET OUT FOR HARAN." The portion begins with Jacob's hurried departure from his home after tricking his father into giving him the blessing meant for his brother Esau. In truth, a more apt title for this portion could be "The Trail of Trickery," as deception and irony marks each of Jacob's steps... with one exception. On his journey to Haran, Jacob stops for the night at a "certain place" and dreams of a ladder that connects Heaven to earth. As angels go up and down it, God appears to Jacob in this dream, promising him this land upon which he lies.

Continuing his journey, Jacob comes upon a certain well, beholding the beauty of Rachel. So overcome by her that he is able to lift the stone that covers the well and gives drink to her flocks, a job that typically required a group of shepherds working together. Though desiring to be with Rachel, Laban – her father – deceives Jacob into marring his older daughter Leah, a similar deception Jacob had pulled with his own father. Though Jacob is eventually permitted to marry Rachel, the irony of the narrative continues. Rachel – the wife that is most loved – is initially barren, while Leah is fertile, giving birth to many.

Despite Laban's repeated attempts to swindle him, Jacob has prospered both in terms of family and in property while in Haran. After overhearing Laban's sons complaining that Jacob has taken the wealth of their father, God tells Jacob it is time for him to return home. Jacob convinces his wives to leave and, fearing that Laban would prevent him from leaving with his family and property, they depart in secrecy. Laban pursues Jacob and when they meet, Jacob stands up to his father-in-law. Laban and Jacob make a pact at Galeid, attested to by a pile of stones, and Jacob proceeds back home.

Vayeitzei // He Left
Bite 1 – *Prayer: the Soul's Food*

With Thanksgiving upon us and Chanukah not too far away, it's hard not to think about that infamous four-letter F-word: FOOD! Whether it's the smorgasbord of fine delectables that we gorge ourselves on during the feast of thanks or the oil-drenched latkes that we stuff ourselves with during the celebration of lights, it seems that all of us – at some point, during this season – will engage in a personal relationship with food. That relationship, according to nutritionists, must be purely functional, supplying the physical body with the basic nutrition needed to sustain life. Food-critics, however, disagree, maintaining that food must be first and foremost a source of enjoyment. As Anton Ego, the fictional food-critic from the movie *Ratatouille,* stated: "I don't LIKE food. I LOVE it. If I don't LOVE it, I don't SWALLOW!"

These diverse perspectives – when it comes to our relationship with food – are, in many ways, like the diverse positions we take when it comes to our relationship with prayer, which coincidently is instituted in this Torah portion of *Vayeitzei.* As we read from Genesis 28:11, "He (Jacob) encountered/*vayifga* the place/*hamakom* and stopped there for the night, for the sun was going down." Jacob thereupon slept and had a revelatory dream in which angels descended and ascended a ladder which connected Heaven and earth. And, when Jacob awoke, he stated in awe: "Surely the Lord is present in this place and I did not know it!" Fittingly, the Bible states that Jacob then "named the site *Beit-El,*" meaning "the House of God." (Genesis 28:16-19)

Within this 'House of God,' the rabbis maintain that Jacob introduced the practice of evening prayer. As RaSHI explained: "'*Vayifga*/encountered' [from the verses above] is an expression of prayer, for it is similarly stated in the book of Jeremiah (7:16), 'do not pray on their behalf, do not encounter/*tifga* with Me.' Thus, it is taught, that as the sun was going down Jacob instituted the ritual of evening prayer for he too *vayifga*/encountered (i.e. he prayed) with *haMakom,*" a Hebrew word which literally means 'the place' but has long functioned in our Jewish faith as one of the many names of God.

But, like the disagreement between the nutritionists and the food-critics, a debate has arisen in contemporary times over the purpose of these prayerful encounters. In the vein of the nutritionists, some understand prayer as simply a function of life. Not as MC Hammer once proposed: "We have to pray just to make it today. That's why we pray." Rather, this perspective sees prayer as a means to satisfy the needs of God, our Creator. As it is stated in Numbers 28:2, we must "be punctilious in presenting to God, at the stated times, offerings of food… offerings by fire with an odor that is pleasing, satisfying to God." Thus, just as the body is sustained by the nutrients in our food, God is sustained by the prayers on our lips – our modern sacrifice.

However, in the vein of the food-critics, that which crosses our lips must be enjoyable. In other words, prayer is not prayer unless it provides us – not God

– with satisfaction or meaning. Rabbi David Aaron once wrote: "Prayer is exclusively a vehicle of self-transformation. It is not offered with the hope of influencing God. True prayer is a sermon to our own selves, cultivating our power to change our own lives."[109] Echoing this critical perspective of prayer, the great poet George Meredith wrote: "He who rises from prayer a better man, has had his prayer answered."[110]

Yet, either answer – whether it's from the perspective of the nutritionists or the critics – seems to serve up only 50% of the recommended daily value of prayer. I mean, if prayer was only made to satisfy God, then it could be said that prayer would lack the essential ingredients of passion, fervor, zeal. And, if prayer was only true prayer when it was personally meaningful, then it could be said that prayer would lack the power to rise beyond the self to impact and influence the world. Each perspective, therefore, lacks the complete substance and sustenance needed to satiate the soul, because the soul is neither entirely Divine nor mortal. It is a combination thereof.

Thus, for the soul to receive the full nutritional benefit of prayer, we must provide it with a balanced diet. Fortunately, the recipe is illustrated in Jacob's dream. Like the ladder, when we connect the intention of our prayers to Heaven and earth, when we fortify our prayers with both the needs of God and those of man, we allow prayer to traverse the space in between, bringing what is needed to each part of our soul. This, writes Rabbi Herbert Goldstein in his famous *Letter on Prayer*, is "the double charm of prayer, bringing God down to man and lifting man upward to God." So, at this time of year, when we give so much thought about what goes into our mouths, let us be equally as conscious about what goes out of them. For when our prayers, like our food, contain both ingredients – a pinch of the Divine nutrition here and a dash of the mortal enjoyment there – then truly does our soul receive its ample fill.

Vayeitzei // He Left
Bite 2 – *Marriage: A Romantic Business*

"I came here tonight because when you realize that you want to spend the rest of your life with somebody, you want the rest of your life to start as soon as possible." – [When Harry Met Sally] "I'm just a girl, standing in front of a boy, asking him to love her." – [Notting Hill] "I may not be a smart man, Jenny. But I know what love is." – [Forrest Gump] "You should be kissed. And often. And by someone who knows how." – [Gone with the Wind] "You had me at 'Hello.'" – [Jerry McGuire]

While Hollywood may be known for such romantic sentiments, the same cannot be said of the Holy Word. Yet, in this portion of *Vayeitzei*, we come across one of the most romantic statements of all time. After waking up from

[109] David Aaron. *Endless Light: The Ancient Path of Kabbalah*. Berkley Publishing Group: New York, 1998
[110] George Meredith. *The Ordeal of Richard Feverel*. Chapman and Hall: United Kingdom, 1859

his wedding night and realizing he had been deceived by Laban into marrying his older daughter, Leah, Jacob was forced to labor for another seven years to marry Laban's younger daughter, Rachel, with whom he had fallen in love. (Genesis 29:18) And, while – to us – this situation may seem unbearable and even unbelievable, the Bible very tenderly and passionately reveals that these fourteen years in which Jacob worked "seemed to him but a few days because of his [great] love for her." (Genesis 29:20)

Romantic, isn't it? And, some may say, surprisingly so! Because, during Jacob's time, marriage was ordinarily a simple fiscal arrangement, business between a potential bride's father and a would-be suitor, void of emotional investment. But here, in this portion, we get a rare glimpse that marriage – even by Biblical standards – can and should be so much more. As our sages have taught, "An arranged marriage, based upon sound economic considerations, garners some guarantee of a future. Though, when the business of marriage is coupled with love, then – as it was with Jacob and Rachel – such a relationship can be far more successful." For, then the marriage possesses both components necessary to overcome the sometimes tragic forces that occur in life.

Yet despite being warned by Don Henley and Patty Smyth that "sometimes love just ain't enough," we – just as it is with Hollywood – tend to place a far greater emphasis on love, relying upon it and it alone to see us through the tough times.[111] As a result, we are often shocked – as Jacob was – when, long after the wedding is over, we wake up one day feeling as if the person we fell in love with is not the same person we married. Reflecting on this phenomenon, the American author and playwright – Jean Kerr – once stated: "Marrying someone is often like buying something you've only admired for a long time in a shop window. You may love it. But, when you get it home, you realize it doesn't always go so nicely with the furniture."

It is, at this point in a relationship, that some will argue it is far easier to find a new spouse than to find new furniture; a perspective pervasive in American culture as divorce rates have continued to climb in our nation year after year after year. Please don't misunderstand me. I am not saying that everyone makes this difficult decision to divorce haphazardly. Being a child of divorced parents, I know very intimately how truly agonizing this decision can oftentimes be. In fact, some will suggest, it is because of this potential and agonizing reality that Jacob worked as hard as he did. For he, like many of us, reasoned that if we just labor hard and long enough we can ensure our marriage's success.

For some marriages, there is a degree of truth in this statement. Nevertheless, at a certain point, we just stop trying. Typically this happens when we feel that our marriage has become more work than pleasure. But, not Jacob; year after year after year, challenge after challenge after challenge, he continued to labor. How did he do it? Because, as Nachum Sarna notes, Jacob never forgot that

---

[111] Patty Smyth. "Sometimes Love Just Ain't Enough." *Patty Smyth*: MCS Records, 1992

every loving relationship also needs to be a business partnership in a company named "family."[112] For by this vision of the future, which he lovingly shared with Rachel, he was able to see beyond the daily grind of life, thereby moving him and his family from a present challenge to a future success. As Sarna writes: "A person looking forward to attaining a goal welcomes everything that brings him or her a step closer to that goal," even if that step is a difficult step to take.[113]

"I came here tonight because when you realize that you want to start investing with somebody, you want that investment to start as soon as possible." "I'm just a girl, standing in front of a boy, asking him if he has a diversified stock portfolio." "I may not be a smart man, Jenny. But, I know what a savings account is." "You should be audited. And often. And by someone who knows how." "You had me at 0% financing." These lines may not be romantic. But, they are nonetheless important in our relationships. For, they remind us that if we wish to enjoy a successful loving relationship, we must also work at having a successful business partnership. So, let us – with God's help – continue to work towards this goal. Thereby, as it was with Jacob, we may enjoy a future filled with promise for us and our families.

Vayeitzei // He Left
Bite 3 – *The More We Know, the More We Appreciate*

Ask any teenager and they'll likely tell you that Youth Group is truly miraculous. Unfortunately, they are not always speaking about the engaging religious or educational programs, which encourage our youth to embrace their noble heritage. Typically, they're talking about the overtly social components of the program, which often result in them embracing one another. "It's amazing!" remarked one teenager. "Upon my arrival, there appeared to be no one of interest here. But, as we got to know one another over the weekend, there they were, all around! Surely," she concluded, "greatness is in this place and I did not know it!"

A similar sense of astonishment was felt by our forefather Jacob in *Vayeitzei*. Having left Beersheva for Haran, Jacob came upon a certain place that appeared – upon first glance – to be nothing extraordinary. Though, upon lying down for the night, Jacob dreamt of a stairway to Heaven with angels moving up and down, as the Lord stood beside him. "I am the Lord," stated God. "[As promised to your forefathers, Abraham and Isaac,] I will assign to you and your offspring the ground upon which you lay." Jacob awoke and remarked in astonishment: "Surely God is present in this place and I did not know it!"[114]

---

[112] Nachum Sarna. *Etz Hayim: Torah and Commentary.* Rabbinical Assembly: New York, 2001. p. 171
[113] Ibid.
[114] Genesis 28:10-16

But, how could that be? After all, according to RaSHI, the place Jacob encountered was none other than Mt. Moriah, the mountain upon which his grandfather Abraham attempted to sacrifice his father Isaac.[115] Such amazement, comments Nachum Sarna, suggests that while the place may have held great significance for his forefathers, "it was merely a convenient spot for Jacob to lodge for the night, possessing no intrinsic value to *him…*"[116] That is until he learned of its importance in the dream. Thereupon, he awoke to comprehend its true value, not as ordinary but extraordinary, not as bland but beautiful, not as standard but sacred.

This sudden reevaluation is not confined to Mt. Moriah alone. It can and often does occur quite frequently in our lives: from places to people, from food to art. It seems, the more we know, the more we appreciate. Take, for example, the experience of looking at a Jackson Pollock painting. Without knowing the artist, one may conclude that the work is nothing more than a toddler's scribble. However, upon learning that the piece was created by the famed hand of Pollock, then suddenly the scribbles transform into lines of unimaginable meaning, unimaginable genius, not to mention… unimaginable price!

"That's because," states psychologist Dr. Paul Bloom, "value is not solely based upon what we see, touch, hear, taste, or smell. It is also based upon what we think."[117] In essence, sensory data is inputted into the computer of our minds, which thereupon renders a conclusion in the form of a feeling: "I like or I don't like such-and-such." Yet, as the youth grouper demonstrated, all too often we make such calculations based on incomplete data: physical appearances, environmental surroundings, others' opinions. As a result, our conclusions are frequently off, as we tend to over value or under appreciate many of the people, places, and things in our lives.

> This misfortune transpired for many D.C. subway goers on January 12, 2007. A violinist, shabbily dressed, fiddled with precision for nearly an hour on a subway platform. Some dropped a few cents into his open case. Most, considering him just another hurdle on their way to work, ignored his presence all together. There was, however, one businesswoman who didn't. Though pressed for time, she remained there for the entire performance. "Wow!" she exclaimed with great joy upon its conclusion. "Can you believe it?!"
>
> "Believe what?" inquired a man, standing nearby. "That! Gosh, do you know who *that* was?" continued the woman in astonishment. "No," replied the man, growing more curious. "Who was he?" She answered, "That was Joshua Bell, one of the best violinists in the world. A few nights ago he played Boston Symphony Hall to a packed house. And, you can bet, it cost more than a few cents to see him.

---

[115] RaSHI commentary to Genesis 28:11
[116] Nachum Sarna. *JPS Torah Commentary: Genesis*. The Jewish Publication Society: Philadelphia, 1989. p. 199
[117] Ira Flado. "Why Do We Like, What We Like?" NPR: *Science Friday*. July 23, 2010.

Surely, greatness was in this place and I'm thankful to have known it."[118]

So, we may wonder, how can we be similarly blessed? How can we ensure a more objective valuation, as to not miss such moments of meaning in our own lives, particularly if all we have to base our opinions on is subjective data? Some say it's by refraining from making conclusions in the first place. Simply allow, as Jacob did, the natural essence of the individual person, place or thing to reveal itself. Sure, that's the ideal. But, the world rarely allows us time to see the ideal unfold. So, with the time we do have, researchers suggest gathering more data. That is to say, we must learn as much as possible. For, while there will always be a measurable degree of variance in our results, this larger pool of information makes any conclusions drawn more valid as well as more valued.

The former Chief Rabbi of Israel, Abraham Isaac Kook, summarized this secondary approach in the following: "Nothing is unholy. There is only the holy and the yet to be holy."[119] All education from *Talmud* study to chemistry helps us reveal the holiness around us. So, let us continue that holy process of revelation, which began with Abraham, Isaac, and Jacob. May we gather as much information about the people, places, and things around us, so that we may expose the bland as beautiful, the ordinary as extraordinary, the standard as truly sacred. Then, may all be blessed to comprehend, as Jacob did, that "greatness, godliness, is in this place and now we surely know it!"

---

[118] Based upon Gene Weingarten's report "Pearls Before Breakfast," which appeared in the Washington Post on 8 April 2007.
[119] Quoted in Abraham Weiss's *Principles of Spiritual Activism*. Ktav Publishing House, Inc: New Jersey. p. 69

Portion 8:
Vayishlach // He Sent
Torah Portion: Genesis 32:4-36:43

"JACOB SENT MESSENGERS…" As Jacob anxiously prepares for his reunion with his brother Esau, he is interrupted by a man that wrestles with him until the rise of dawn. At the end of this match, Jacob is blessed with a new name: "Israel," meaning "he who struggled with God," lending itself to countless interpretations. For the reader, this battle stands in place of the much anticipated one between Jacob and his brother Esau. Instead of a fight, Jacob and Esau have a heartfelt reconciliation, with hugging and tears, after twenty years of separation. Jacob offers gifts to his brother in an attempt to correct the wrongs he did. Though the brothers reconcile, Jacob and Esau nonetheless go their separate ways.

When Jacob and his family arrive in Shechem, the portion turns its focus on Leah's daughter Dinah, who goes out to meet the local women. The local prince there spots Dinah and engages her in some sexual manner. However this act is interpreted, her brothers are enraged at her defilement. They devise a plan to slaughter the people of Shechem, as they recover from circumcision. Though this episode centers on Dinah, her voice is never heard. Thereby, Dinah has come to stand as a silent symbol of the marginalized woman in Israel, a society largely focused on men.

From there, Jacob and his family continue on to Beth-El, the place where Jacob previously encountered God. There, he erects an altar and eliminates the foreign gods in the people's midst. As a result, God reestablishes the Eternal Covenant with Israel. En route to their next stop, Rachel goes into a difficult labor with her second son. She dies during childbirth but bears Benjamin. Jacob sets up a pillar to memorialize Rachel's burial site in Bethlehem. This is not the only death Jacob will experience. This portion's journey ends with the death of Jacob's father, Isaac, as both Jacob and his brother Esau come together to bury him.

Vayishlach // He Sent
Bite 1 – *Flexing the Muscle of the Mind*

"Don't go chasing waterfalls. Please stick to the rhythms and the beats that you're used to." As a young boy, I used to sing those words from the song *Waterfall* by the female R&B group TLC everywhere. Small problem, those weren't the words to the song. The real words are, "Don't go chasing waterfalls." And, continuing with the theme of water, "Please stick to the rivers (not rhythms) and the lakes (not beats) that you're used to." It was an honest mistake in the transmission from what the lips uttered to what the ears heard. Similar mistakes, between what is said and what is heard, happen all the time. This portion of *Vayishlach* is of no exception.

In this Torah portion, Jacob undergoes an important, if not – arguably – the *most* important, event of his life: the nighttime encounter with the mysterious stranger and the subsequent presentation of the new name, *Yisrael*. However, just before the encounter, Jacob prays to God, quoting within the prayer what he thought to be God's promise: "For You have said God, 'I will surely deal bountifully with you." (Genesis 32:13) Small problem, this was not what God promised. As it was recorded in Genesis 31:3, the actual words by which God assured Jacob were simply: "I (God) will be with you."

A mistake, right? Not so, comments Nachum Sarna, who believes that all such alterations are not so accidental. They are really, writes Sarna, whether consciously or not, interpretations of what we want to believe was said. Thus, "this phrase – 'I will surely deal bountifully with you' – is likely one of the first examples of the interpretation of God's word."[120] When God said 'I will be with you,' Jacob hoped that the ever-abiding Presence of God meant things would forever be 'bountiful' or from the literal Hebrew translation 'good with him,' providing Jacob with safe passage through the approaching confrontation.

Many of us share the same hope. When God says, "He will be with us," we want to hear that "everything will [therefore] be good with us." This interpretive license, from what was said to what was heard, is not only beneficial, some will go even as far to say it's necessary, as we steer into moments of great uncertainty and potential difficulty. For such interpretations provide us with the faith and fortitude to continue forward in a time of flooding fears and frustrations. In a sense, these interpretations – like that of Jacob's – function as prayers, speaking to the hopes born in the heart and soul of man when traversing tribulations; a prayer for triumphant results.

Yet, far too often, we have experienced moments in life when it felt as if our prayers went unanswered; moments in our history when the outcome of a confrontation did not immediately appear favorable: from our slavery to Pharaoh in Egypt to our slavery to the vices in our society, from the

---

[120] Nachum Sarna. *Etz Hayim: Torah and Commentary*. Rabbinical Assembly: New York, 2001. p. 199

destruction of our Temple in Jerusalem to the destruction of our places of worship wherever our foundations were laid, from the ovens of Auschwitz to the heated hands of hatred that have risen against us time and time again. Thank God, from each and every one of these confrontations, we have emerged! But, not without a limp, as if – within the confrontation – the hip of our people was wrenched from its socket, leaving a pain that the children of Israel feel to this very day.

To some, that pain born from the inconsistency between what is believed and what is experienced is not merely physical. It's also deeply spiritual. The scar of this spiritual pain and loss is often expressed in words: "Surely, God has left me," or worse "God no longer exists." Justifiably, we question, "How could these difficult circumstances happen, how could these confrontations occur, if God was still with me?" To resolve this tension, many turn to the easiest of answers: God's absence. When it was time for God to be counted and be counted upon, these individuals understand God's silence as an admission that the Eternal was no longer there. And, while this answer may resolve the tension, it leaves little in the way of addressing the pain we feel in our soul, the loss we may feel in our spirit. In fact, it only compounds it.

To really tend to that soulful bruise incurred in these unfavorable times, we cannot take the easy path by abrogating our beliefs or resigning our faith. On the contrary, by holding onto them, by wrestling – as Jacob did – with beings both Divine and mortal, we may be able to more adequately address the pain we bear. For example, some believe that whenever people suffer, so too does God, as it is stated in Psalm 91, "I (the Lord) am with them in their distress." Or, as it is stated in Isaiah 63, "In all their troubles, God is troubled." Others address the pain, as Jacob did, with an interpretation that maintains that no matter how the confrontation is resolved, with faith in God there can be found within it a measure of goodness.

There will always be inconsistencies in the course of life: inconsistencies between what was said and what was heard, between what was read and what was interpreted, between what was taught and what was experienced. But, to fulfill our namesake as being *b'nai Yisrael*, literally "children who wrestle with God," we must continue in the face of these inconsistencies, these confrontations to flex – not just our physical might – but more importantly the muscle of our mind. For when we continue to engage in these moments, attempting to comprehend the inconsistencies, truly then we merit God's presence in our lives as well as God's blessing.

Vayishlach // He Sent
Bite 2 – *Welcome to the Main Event*

Ladies and gentlemen, in this corner, hailing from the great city of Seir, we have the red mantle of Edom, the skillful hunter of the outdoors... Esau! And, in our other corner, hailing from here, there, and just about everywhere, we have the once mild man of many sons and now the great wrestler of man and God alike... Jacob! So, without further ado, let's get ready to... *hug, kiss, and cry?!*

Yes, as strange as that may sound, that's exactly what transpires in *Vayishlach*. After Jacob divides his people and possessions in anticipation for a brotherly battle, and after Esau makes a demonstration of force, showing up for the royal rumble with 400 men, the bell rings on this Biblical bout. Ding, ding, ding! But rather than coming out of their corners, arms swinging, both Jacob and Esau open them up wide. As the Bible tells us, Esau embraced his brother Jacob. "He kissed him/*vayishkeihu* and they both wept." (Genesis 33:4)

"What?! You cannot be serious!" says John McEnroe, who knows a thing or two about getting into a scuffle. And, surprisingly, some of the *midrashic* sages concur. Expecting something more, Rabbi Yannai transforms Esau into a modern-day Mike Tyson: "Esau did not *vayishkeihu*/kiss him. As the dots written above this word in the Torah indicate, Esau wished to *vayishcheihu*/bite him."[121] "Now we're talking," interjects McEnroe. For, it is uncomfortable to imagine that such strong Biblical characters would show such emotion.

And, it's not just our sages. Even today our comfort wanes when seemingly strong men hug, kiss, whimper, etc., particularly when it's done in public and especially when it's among other men. Yet, it has happened to presidents and preachers alike. It was also the case, for example, with the great grandfather of the grid-iron, the slippery silver fox of the pigskin pocket, Brett Favre. During a 2008 press-conference to announce his retirement, MS native Favre – fighting tears – stated to reporters: "I promised I wasn't going to...(sniffle) It's never easy... (sniffle) But, I hope that the Packers feel that every penny they spent on me (sniffle) was worth it... As hard as it is for me to say, (sniffle) it's over."[122]

"Man up, Favre!" responded one sports commentator in response to his emotional display. For, like the rabbis of old, we continue to teach – sometimes intentionally and at other times unintentionally – that it is not appropriate for men to express themselves in these ways. Rather, they should take their feelings out onto the field, use them in the gym, implement them on the courts; for such physical ways are the only real way emotions are of any use. But, if we continue to transmit such a message, we may cripple not just our men, but our society, leaving it to limp from one generation to the next. While more constructive than a battle, these physical contests rarely deal adequately with the emotions. In fact, they can even compound an internal pain with an external one, as was the case with Jacob when he wrestled with the unknown entity.

But, what Jacob learned the hard way, we are given the blessed chance – through this Torah portion – to learn the easy way. In addition to encouraging

---

[121] Genesis Rabbah 78:9
[122] March 2008

our boys as well as our men to engage in some type of physical release, we must also encourage them, and thus be comfortable with it ourselves, to have an emotional release as well. For as Mr. Jeffrey Lebowski reminds us in the movie, *The Big Lebowski*, "Strong men also cry...strong men also cry."[123] And when they do, when our men – in addition to hitting, kicking and tearing – can express themselves through hugging, kissing, and crying not only will our men be stronger and more loving, but – God willing – so too will be our society.

Vayishlach // He Sent
Bite 3 – *Setting the Pace to our Recovery*

There is little doubt that our society is fracturing. Its once fast pace has resulted in a few pulling forward, scattering many behind. In this split a fundamental debate has arisen: who shall lead the way back to a healthier, more cohesive society? Who shall restore the Promise of America, where everyone – regardless of origin – has a chance to succeed? Shall it be the financially strong, allowing them to pave the way, so the rest can follow? Or, shall our focus be on the financially weak, looking to them to set the pace to our recovery?

Based upon *Vayishlach*, Judaism seems to come down decidedly on one side of this debate. After a positive brotherly reunion, Esau suggests joining Jacob on his journey. But, Jacob hesitates, saying to him, "My lord knows that the children are frail and that the flocks and herds, nursing, are a care to me. If they are driven hard a single day, all the flocks will die." Therefore, Jacob advises the physically fit Esau to "go on ahead, while [he] travels slowly at the pace of the cattle before [him] and at the pace of the children." (Genesis 33:12-14)

Yet, we know there's another reason Jacob desired to progress slowly (not his injured hip).[124] Rather, Jacob knew that when passing through precarious moments (like those found in the wilderness), it's far better to stay as a group. But, if their pace was set by the strong, ultimately it would have been too fast for the weak to keep up, resulting in a few soaring ahead while many lag behind. This separation is a liability for the entire group. Thus, Jacob wisely sets their pace by the weakest among them. In doing so, *b'nai Yisrael* is able to stay together, fulfilling God's promise of returning to the Land safely.[125]

But, to many, setting the pace of return or recovery by the weak just doesn't make a lot of sense. They reason that allowing the weak to lead, leads to a weak society. Wouldn't you want the strong out front, braving the way for the rest of society to follow? Besides, they argue, allowing the financially strong to lead encourages the weak to catch up, as they have a standard by which to aspire. We see this phenomenon, after all, within the sports arena. When a higher

---

[123] Ethan and Joel Coen. *The Big Lebowski*. PolyGram Filmed Entertainment: 1996.
[124] Genesis 32:32
[125] Genesis 28:15

ranked athlete competes against a lower ranked one, sometimes this interaction heightens the game of the "weaker" athlete, even if he/she ultimately loses.

Sure that happens, but not for all. Many others, decimated by such a heightened pace, simply fall farther and farther behind, until they are lost all together. "Good riddance!" some may say, claiming this as a necessary loss along the path towards a stronger society. "It's natural selection at its best, weeding out the weak while ensuring the strong survive!" The famed Spartans embraced this perspective in their efforts to have the strongest society imaginable. Specifically, they sent frail children (some as young as seven) into the wilderness. Those who returned were honored in great ceremony. Those who didn't, didn't receive a thing, not even a funeral.

But I say, "Where are the Spartans now?" Gone. Yet b'nai Yisrael, the children of Israel remain. Why? Very simply, it's because of the pace Jacob set for our collective journey in this Torah portion, calibrating it to the weak not the strong. For "in raising the poor from the dust, [in bringing them forward] and setting them before the nobles," we are lifting everyone up.[126] As it is further written in the book of Samuel, the weak, the poor, the orphan, the widow, the stranger, "these are the pillars of the earth; God has set the world upon them."[127] If they are weak, then we too are weak. If they are strong, we all are strong.

Thus, in debating our recovery, let us consider this lesson. Because, through its countless trials and tribulations, through its countless returns and recoveries, Judaism has learned that the pace of return cannot be set by the strong. For that pace will merely lead to the continued fracturing of our fragile society, eventually to the ruin of the entire world. Rather, in order to l'takein et ha-olam, in order to repair our world and our society, the pace must be set by the weakest of our members, looking to them to lead the way. May we continue to lift them up, thereby lifting ourselves up as well, returning, restoring our society back to a state of shalem (wholeness) and shalom (peace).

---

[126] I Samuel 2:8
[127] Ibid.

Portion 9:
Vayeishev // He Dwelt
Torah Portion: Genesis 37:1-40:23

"NOW JACOB WAS SETTLED IN THE LAND…" Just as Israel becomes settled, Joseph and his narrative begin to stir. The overt favoritism of Joseph from Jacob causes animosity between the children of Israel. Joseph does nothing to help his own case, as he seemingly taunts them with tales of things to come: one day they will bow to him, as he rules over them. That future, however, seems so far away, as Joseph is sold to an Ishmaelite caravan headed to Egypt. To cover their misdeed, the brother's dip Joseph's coat in blood, deceiving their father with a story that a wild beast devoured him.

Leaving Jacob in a state of great grief, the Torah now turns from Joseph to Judah, who had married a Canaanite woman named Shua. With her did he have three sons: Er, Onan, and Shelah. Yet, just as Judah had deceived his father about Joseph, a woman named Tamar will come to deceive him. Left in a precarious position within Israelite society by some unfortunate circumstances, Tamar tricks her father-in-law Judah into impregnating her. When the deception is finally unveiled, Judah is forced to admit: "She is more in the right than I," or – to put it another way – "I was more wrong than she." Thereby, Tamar's position in Israel becomes secure, as she is blessed with twins by Judah.

Our narrative returns once more to Joseph, this time in Egypt, where he serves Potiphar, an officer of Pharaoh. There, the Eternal is with him, though sometimes in unexpected ways. While in the service of Potiphar, the lady of the house attempts to seduce Joseph. He flees, though leaving his garment behind. She – just like Joseph's brothers before – uses his clothes in an act of deception: this slave has tried to toy with her, but she escaped his advances. As such, Joseph is enchained once more. It is there, in the prison of Pharaoh, where he transforms from a mere dreamer to a dream interpreter.

Vayeishev // He Dwelt
Bite 1 – *Destiny: A Joint Venture*

In the unforgettable motion picture, *Forrest Gump*, there comes a scene at the end of the movie where Forrest is standing over the grave of his belated, and eternally beloved wife, Jenny. After seamlessly streaming through some of the most pivotal points in American history, and shaping the lives of countless individuals, Forrest – through a flood of emotions – questions: "I don't know if Momma was right or if, if it's Lieutenant Dan. I don't know if we each have a destiny, or if we're all just floating around accidental-like on a breeze. But I, I think maybe it's both. Maybe both is happening at the same time."[128]

Interestingly, the opening lines of this portion and the commentaries that follow lead us to this same question. After Jacob settles his clan in the land of Canaan, we read that "Israel loved Joseph best of all his sons, for he was the child of his old age... But, when his brothers saw that their father loved him more than any of his brothers, they hated him so that they could not speak a friendly word to him." (Genesis 37:3-4) Thereupon, we learn that Joseph experiences a most unbelievable path in life. Being sold into slavery by his brothers, Joseph eventually winds-up as a leader of Egypt, second only to Pharaoh.

And, similar to Forrest, our commentators are uncertain about the root cause of these unusual circumstances. Was Jacob's favoritism, Joseph's arrogance, or his brothers' hatred part of some Divine plan? Or, are they merely a series of random coincidences, happenstances which by chance ended favorably? The commentators, expectedly, do not respond in one voice to this question. Nevertheless, they do agree that life is not random. We are not just feathers floating on the breeze. According to our sages, there is some logic governing life's course... we just don't always know whose logic it is.

First, there is the argument for human agency. Some blame Jacob for the whole mess. He, who of all people should have known better, whose relationship with his own brother was poisoned by parental favoritism, inadvertently prompted his older sons' cruelty with his inequitable treatment.[129] Others focus on Joseph's impertinence and arrogance (i.e. his tattling on his brothers as well as his insufferable dreams) and argue that Joseph brought his woes on himself.[130] Elie Wiesel, finely attuned to the plight of the persecuted, faults the brothers, writing: "They should have felt sorry for their small orphaned brother, whose mother died tragically; instead they

---

[128] Winston Groom and Eric Roth. *Forrest Gump*. Paramount Pictures: 1994.

[129] Beresheit Rabbah 84:8 - "Resh Lakish, in the name of Rabbi Eleazar ben Azariah, said: 'A man must not favor one child over another, for on account of Jacob showing Joseph favor through the coat of many colors, they (i.e. Joseph's brothers) hated him.'" Another example comes from Julian Morgenstern, who wrote: "Jacob was at fault for manifesting greater love for Joseph than for his other sons and for spoiling him as he did. Partiality is always a form of injustice, and injustice is always wrong and causes evil." (Morgenstern. *The Book of Genesis*. Schocken Books: New York, 1965. pp. 264-265).

[130] See RaSHI commentary on Genesis 37:2

pounded on him, harassed him. They should have tried to console him; instead they made him feel unwanted, an outsider."[131]

Any of these perspectives, however, would suggest that we have a great deal of control over how our lives and the lives of our children turn out. That is to say, the assumption underlying these commentaries is 'how we treat others has a direct impact on how they treat us;' a reassuring thought, indeed! But, the problem is – of course – that the world does not always work this way. Accidents happen, both good and bad; events transpire that cannot be traced to a rational cause. I mean, is it reasonable to presume that Jacob's favoritism, Joseph's arrogance, or his brothers' hatred directly caused either the salvation of an entire region from starvation or the Israelites' 400-year sojourn in slavery?

Of course not! None of the actors in this family drama had these ends in mind, as they played out their chosen roles. Maybe that's why Joseph, at the end of the story, says to his brothers: "Do not be distressed... it was to save life that God sent me ahead of you. God has sent me ahead of you to ensure your survival on earth, and to save your lives in an extraordinary deliverance. So, it was not you who sent me here. It was God." (Genesis 45:5-8) The thought that God has a plan for each of us is comforting and beautiful for those who can believe it. But what if our faith does not measure up to Joseph's? Granting the severe limitations of human control over the course of history, if we don't believe in Divine control, must we give ourselves over to the forces of chaos?

No. For notwithstanding scientific advances that have identified meaningful patterns in chaos, I believe there's still another possibility. Like Forrest, "I think maybe it's both. Maybe both is happening at the same time." That is to say, God and the beings the Eternal created in the Divine image are constantly engaged with one another in each and every moment. As the 20th century Jewish philosopher, Henry Slonimsky, once wrote: "The creation of Man with such power of freedom means that God has made room for a co-determining power alongside Himself. Man," he continues, "is at the crossroads of the world" and together – God and Man – shape the course of destiny.[132] For as Rabbi Abraham Joshua Heschel notes: "Not only does man need God, God is also in need of man."[133] May we continue to be instrumental in and thankful for this joint venture, we call Destiny.

Vayeishev // He Dwelt
Bite 2 – *Service to our Siblings*

Rabbi Joshua ben Levi once had the great fortune to meet Elijah, who – it was foretold – would herald the coming of the Messiah. Rabbi Joshua asked Elijah, "When exactly will the Messiah come?" Elijah

---

[131] Elie Wiesel. *Messengers of God: Biblical Portraits and Legends*. Simon and Schuster: 1985. p. 153
[132] Henry Slonimsky. *Slonimsky Papers (1920-1965)*. American Jewish Archives. Manuscript Collection, no. 637
[133] Abraham Joshua Heschel. *Man is Not Alone: A Philosophy of Religion*. Farrar, Straus, and Giroux: 1976.

answered, "Go and ask him, yourself?" "You mean," began Rabbi Joshua in amazement, "I can find him here?" "Yes," replied Elijah. "at the gates of Rome." "But," asked Rabbi Joshua, "how will I recognize him?" Elijah told him, "There he sits among the lepers, a lowly soul, unwrapping and rewrapping bandages, theirs as well as his own."

Keeping in mind Elijah's advice on how to identify the Messiah, in the most unlikely of places, among the most unlikely of people, he quickly spotted a poor sufferer who was unwrapping and rewrapping one painful sore at a time. Rabbi Joshua approached him and said, "Peace be upon you, my master and teacher." The leper looked at him knowingly and replied, "Upon you, may there be Peace, son of Levi." Then, Rabbi Joshua asked, "Speaking of Peace, say when – may I ask – will you deliver it to our world?" The leper said, "Today."

Rabbi Joshua returned to Elijah in the blink of an eye. Elijah said to him, "What did the Messiah say to you?" Rabbi Joshua replied, "He said, 'Upon you, may there be Peace, son of Levi.' But then, strangely, he lied to me, saying that "today" he would come and deliver Peace. But he has not come!" Elijah said calmly, "No, he has not; for his 'today' was not this day, but the day spoken of in Psalms. Written there, it says, "O' today, if you would but heed his voice!"[134]

Darn these cell-phones! Because, even when listening intently, God's voice message – as it was in this story – still gets distorted. According to its garbled recording in *Vayeishev*, God apparently tells us to play favorites with our children, placing the younger before the older. For though Jacob had twelve distinguished sons, it's clear – states the Bible – that he "loved [the younger] Joseph best of all; because Joseph was a child of his old age." Highlighting his preference, Jacob "made Joseph an ornamented tunic." Though, "when his [older] brothers saw that their father loved [him] more than them, they hated Joseph so much so that they could not speak a friendly word." (Genesis 37:3-4)

This inability to articulate friendly words, we know, would result in the most foul of human deeds, as Joseph's brothers would throw him into a pit and sell him into slavery. Given this and other disastrous consequences, born from playing favorites with our children, surely we – like Rabbi Joshua ben Levi – have heard God incorrectly. Surely, God would not want us to prefer one child over any other. No, he wouldn't, comments Rabbi Harold Kushner. Yet, in God's command to reverse the natural order, placing the younger before the older, God is leaving us a not-so-subtle reminder that "eminence is not a function of birth, but of individual character," a character that must be willing and able to take care of others, even the least among us.[135]

Like Post-it Notes placed around an office, reminders of this essential character building technique are found scattered throughout the Torah: from

---

[134] BT Sanhedrin 98a. The Psalm being referenced here is Ps. 95:7
[135] Harold KUShner, ed. *Etz Hayim: Torah and Commentary*. Rabbinical Assembly: New York, 2001. p. 296.

God selecting the sacrifice of the younger Abel over that of his older brother Cain, to Abraham passing the *Brit Olam* (the Eternal Covenant) to the younger Isaac rather than the older Ishmael, and Isaac similarly passing it on to the younger Jacob rather than the older Esau.[136] And, it's not just younger sons who come to surpass their elder siblings. This seems to be the case among some of the female character pairs of the Bible as well, for its text tells us that the younger "Rachel was more loved by Jacob than [her older sister] Leah."[137]

This reoccurring phenomenon of the Biblical texts led a friend and colleague of mine, Rabbi Noah Fabricant, to remark that "the most overrated role in the entire Bible has got to be that of the firstborn. In spite of having it made with the birthright, a special blessing, and the major portion of any inheritance, the Bible nonetheless shows us time and time again that it is not the older but the younger child who is truly preferred."[138] Unfortunately, that preference has profound consequences: from Cain's mistrust which led to Abel's murder, from Isaac's apathy which led to Ishmael's abandonment, from Jacob's betrayal which led to his battle with Esau, to the brothers' jealousy – in this portion – which led to Joseph's captivity and their own misery.

Clearly, this is far from the Peace for which we pray. Why? Well, writes Dr. Richard Friedman, it's because God's message has been misunderstood for generations.[139] When we hear, for example, that "the older the younger shall serve" earlier in Genesis, it can mean that "the older shall serve the younger." However, it can also mean "the older, the younger shall serve." It's intentionally and brilliantly ambiguous! For Peace will never be a product born of placement, setting one of God's children up as servant and, the other, master. That dynamic leads only to ruin not renewal, devastation not restoration. Though, by reading it both ways, then we are shown that through mutual service to our siblings in humanity we can achieve Peace.

So, Elijah the Prophet is right! The Messiah is very likely right here, right now, among us. For, in Judaism, we believe any one of us could be the Messiah. How? Well, it is not by playing favorites among God's children, saying one is more blessed than another. Rather, we bring about the Divine potential within us by allowing ourselves to serve as well as to be served by others. For, in the human family of God, each and every one of our siblings has something to give, something of value to contribute to the betterment of this world. May we create that world, where all are blessed, where all receive a mighty portion of our Divine inheritance known as Peace.

---

[136] Added to this list could be the younger Ephraim over the older Menasseh as well as the younger Moses over his older brother Aaron.
[137] Genesis 29:30
[138] Noah Fabricant. "Fourth Year Sermon." Delivered at K.K. B'nei Israel/Rockdale Temple on Erev Shabbat Vayeishev 5768.
[139] Richard Elliott Friedman. *Commentary on the Torah.* HarperOne: New York, 2001. p. 88. This point is in reference to Genesis 25:23.

Vayeishev // He Dwelt
Bite 3 – *The Value of a Second Look*

At first glance, in a sky saturated with stars,
I saw – by chance – a spot that seemed scarred.
This part of the night, framed by light, appeared in contrast dark and dim;
Not even the slightest light, at first sight, shown within.
But, upon a second look, gazing not glancing this time,
I saw – within the scar – a small star that shined.[140]

In this portion of *Vayeishev*, Joseph's brothers are the stars, at least as much as they are depicted as such in one of Joseph's dreams. (Genesis 37:9) And, similar to the patch of sky I observed that night, they too do not immediately shimmer or shine so bright. In fact, according to Joseph's first report in Genesis 37:2, they are rather dark and dim. It, therefore, begs the question: Why would Jacob send his beloved Joseph – just a few verses later – to once again "see how [his] brothers are... and bring back word." (Genesis 37:14) Was not the tension, created by the first report, enough for the family?

Indeed it was, some contest, leading them to understand Jacob's second dispatch as inherently different from the first. A literal translation of the Hebrew makes the difference clearer, as Jacob requests Joseph not simply to report, but to "go and see the *shalom* of [his] brothers." (Genesis 37:14) According to Rav Simcha Bunim, Joseph was in essence charged with "discovering the admirable qualities of his brothers," which could not occur from just one observation. Rather, to see and truly discover the *shalom*, the wholeness or the integrity of any individual we must be willing to take at least a second look.

Some would say that a second look in today's society is not nearly enough. For, today, we have become so comfortable with and accustomed to drawing immediate conclusions about individuals that sometimes we do so even before a first encounter. Whether it is from across a room or from a photo posted on the web, our minds – without delay – begin to process and report on a situation, doling-out a list of labels upon the participants: 'he's hot,' 'she's not,' etc. And, to these labels, we actually affix value, determining whether or not it's worth getting to know them.

Surely, some will argue that this response – which seems so natural – is in our best interest. For, the ability to appraise and evaluate a situation helps us to navigate the endless new encounters that arise along our path in life. Their logic – regrettably – is sound, for this natural reflex may be understood as part of our evolutionary development to ensure that we emerge from unprecedented moments unscathed, untouched, but ultimately unaware. Unaware that, by our own self-interest, we may have actually overlooked the real worth of an individual and the value they may have contributed to our

---

[140] Written by the author, Rabbi Marshal Klaven.

lives. Such was the mistake made by Col. James Moschgot of the USAF when he attended the Academy. In his words:

William Crawford certainly was an unimpressive figure, one you could easily overlook during a hectic day at the Academy. While we – cadets – busied ourselves, preparing for academic exams, athletic events, Saturday morning parades and room inspections, Mr. Crawford – our janitor – quietly moved about the squadron mopping and buffing floors, emptying trash cans, cleaning toilets, or just tidying up the mess 100 college-age kids can leave in a dormitory.

Sadly, few of us gave him much notice. Why? Well, perhaps it was his physical appearance that made him disappear into the background, or his job cleaning toilets, in which none of us wanted to be a part of. Or, maybe still, it was Mr. Crawford's personality that rendered him almost invisible to the young people around him. He was – after all – shy, almost painfully so. He seldom spoke to a cadet unless they addressed him first, and that didn't happen very often. Face it, Mr. Crawford was just an old man – a janitor – working in a young person's world. What did he have to offer us on a personal level?

One fall Saturday afternoon, I found out. I was reading a book about World War II and the tough Allied campaign in Italy, when I stumbled across an incredible story. On 13 September 1943, a private assigned to the 36th Infantry Division had been involved in some bloody fighting near Altavilla, Italy. Alone, the private took out three enemy machine guns before darkness fell, halting the advance of an enemy platoon. Yet, it was the next words in the story which leapt out at me from the pages of the book:

"In the face of intense and overwhelming hostile fire... with no regard for personal safety on his own initiative, Private **William Crawford** single-handedly attacked multiple fortified enemy positions." It continued, "For conspicuous gallantry and courageousness at risk of life above and beyond the call of duty, the President of the United States......"

"Holy cow," I thought, "our janitor is a Medal of Honor winner!" With much anticipation and a ton of doubt painted on my face, I met with Mr. Crawford the next morning and showed him the page in question from the book. Mr. Crawford stared at it for a few silent moments and then quietly uttered, "Yep, that's me." Mouth agape, I looked at our janitor, then back at the book, and then quickly back at our janitor...our hero. I then stuttered, "Why didn't you ever tell us about it?" He slowly replied after some thought, "That was just one day in my life and it happened so long ago."

I guess we were both at a loss for words. However, after that brief exchange, things were never again the same. Almost overnight, Mr. Crawford went from being a simple fixture in our squadron to one of our teammates.[141]

This is a powerful example of the lesson contained within this Torah portion. By asking one of *b'nai Yisrael* – Joseph – to go again and take a second look to discover the admirable qualities of his brothers, all of *b'nai Yisrael* (every child of Israel) is charged with taking a second look to discover the admirable qualities of each and every one of our brothers and sisters in the world. This lesson is particularly important for us during this holiday season of Chanukah. In our quest to bring light into the world, we cannot afford to overlook the light which already exists within it; the light contained within the vessel of the heart and soul of our neighbors. Let us, therefore, take a second look and see the star within, instead of assuming there's only a spot, scarred dark and dim.

---

[141] You can read his citation at http://www.history.army.mil/html/moh/wwII-a-f.html

CHANUKAH:

Rachel Jarman Myers' Hush Puppy Latkes

Ingredients:
2 medium Russet potatoes (peel, then shred coarsely, like hash browns)
½ yellow onion (peel and shred coarsely)
¾ cup of course yellow corn meal (not the mix)
1 cup of whole kernel sweet corn (fresh off the cob or canned)
3 scallions (chopped)   1 jalapeno (seeded and chopped) *optional*
1 teaspoon of kosher salt   1 tablespoon of Cajun seasoning of choice
½ teaspoon of black pepper $^1/_8$ cup of buttermilk (or whole milk)
2 eggs

Pour the potato onion mixture into a cheese cloth, wrap it up, and squeeze out as much juice as possible over the sink. In a large bowl, whisk the remaining ingredients together. Stir in the potato onion mixture until all pieces are evenly coated. In a medium skillet, heat 2 tablespoons of vegetable oil until shimmering. Drop packed teaspoons of the potato mixture into the skillet and flatten them with the back of a spoon. Cook the latkes over moderately high heat until the edges are golden, about 1½ minutes; flip and cook until golden on the bottom, about 1 minute. Drain on paper towels. Repeat with the remaining potato mixture, adding more oil to the skillet as needed.

Ann Zivitz Kientz's Sufgoniot and Strawberries (a.k.a. Beignets and Berries)

Ingredients:
1 can of biscuits (any kind, but not "flaky")
1 can of strawberry-pie filling
Flour (to prepare working surface)
Vegetable oil for the fryer - 2 bottles in a fry baby or a heavy pot on the stove
Powdered sugar (to heavily dust the beignets before serving)

Set the temperature on your fryer to 360 degrees. Open the can of biscuits and separate them out. Roll one at a time very thin (about $^1/_8$"). Put a teaspoon of filling in the middle, fold over and pinch together to seal. Place four at a time into the basket and lower into the oil. If you are using a pot, lower in and remove with a strainer or slotted spoon. When they float and brown (it happens quickly) turn over to brown the other side. Remove the basket and allow them to drain while you are preparing the next batch. If you are using a pot, they will need to be put on paper towels to finish draining. Put them on a serving tray and dust heavily with powdered sugar and enjoy hot and fresh!

Portion 10:
Mikeitz // At the End
Torah Portion: Genesis 41:1-44:17

"Now, at the end of two years' time, Pharaoh had a dream." Though, this dream was more of a nightmare. For Pharaoh first saw seven skinny cows consuming seven fat cows, followed by another dream of seven stalks, thin and scorched by the wind, overtaking seven healthy stalks. Disturbed, Pharaoh calls Joseph out of prison, demanding him to interpret his dreams. Whereupon, Joseph delivers the news of an impending doom: for the land, there will be seven years of plenty followed by seven years of drought.

Pharaoh's nightmare, however, would prove to be Joseph's dream come true. Pardoned from prison, Pharaoh sets him up as vizier of Egypt. Additionally, Joseph lives up to his name sake, as he *yuseph* (collects/adds) the abundant grain in the healthy years to Egypt's store houses, in order that they shall be available for the people of the land in the hard years to come. It is, in that time, that Jacob sends his sons down to Egypt to procure food. Standing before their brother Joseph, who they do not recognize, the sons of Israel bow down (fulfilling Joseph's dream from the prior portion).

This would not be the only trip the brothers would make to Egypt. Having successfully scored some food on the first go-around, they were hard pressed to return to Egypt as those rations ran out. Yet, by the command of Joseph, they could not return without their youngest brother Benjamin. He had not left his father's side. But the severity of the famine changed that, as Jacob eventually consented to his leave, placing him specifically in the care of Judah.

Even so, it would not be a smooth visit. Upon their return to Egypt, Joseph uses his position to toy with his brothers, possibly as payback. By the end of the portion, Benjamin's life is supposedly at stake for the alleged crime of stealing from this great representative of Egypt.

Mikeitz // At the End
Bite 1 – *Fashioning a Future from a Dreamer's Design*

"I want to be a princess... a Ghostbuster... an official representative of Earth to some foreign planet." Childhood dreams, such as these, have entertained parents for generations. Yet, in all that time, the same words – if uttered by an adult – have been met by skepticism and ridicule. For, our culture maintains a standard: its members, at a certain age, must abandon dreams and embrace reality. As best-selling business author Chin-Ning Chu wrote, "A successful life is one lived through understanding [and reason]... not chasing after dreams."[142]

Even Pharaoh, who believed in dreams and the power they may contain, showed some reluctance to rely upon them completely. We are told, at the beginning of this portion, that "Pharaoh dreamed that he was standing [literally] *al haY'or* (on the Nile)." (Genesis 41:1) Yet, when he recounts the dream to Joseph, Pharaoh states: "In my dream I was standing *al s'fat haY'or*," meaning, "on the <u>banks</u> of the Nile." (Genesis 41:17) To the best of my knowledge and research, the sages have not commented on this disparity, except to say that "such variations between an initial version and its repeat are common in the Bible."[143]

That's not surprising. We may find within our own lives that recalling dreams with exactitude often proves quite difficult, as if even the shortest hands of time can steal the greatest visions from our mind's eye. So who, then, can say for certain that Pharaoh's alteration was not made by design, as if to suggest Pharaoh consciously changed the irrational dream of walking "on water" to fit the rational rules of reality, the ability to walk "on the water's banks." For when confronted with reality, Pharaoh – like many of us – abandoned a dream for reason, or at least for what was believed to be reasonable.

And, why not? Has it not been said by one of the great founders of our nation, Thomas Jefferson, that "reason and free inquiry are the only effectual agents against error?"[144] Thus, to correctly see the world and navigate it successfully, not even Judaism espouses a complete reliance upon faith. Rather, we are taught to wed our faith to reason. In light of this holy bond, the preeminent Jewish scholar RaMBaM, wrote: "Never should man throw his reason behind him, for his eyes are not in the back [of his head], but in the front."[145]

But, it takes more than reason to see what lies in front of us. To envision a future where the impossible becomes possible, we must dream. For, within our dreams, we are not restrained by the restrictive rules of reason. In our dreams, we are free; free to see the world not merely for what it is, but – more

---

[142]Chin-Ning Chu. *Thick Face, Black Heart: The Warrior Philosophy for Conquering the Challenges of Business and Life.* Warner Books, Inc.: New York, 1994.
[143] Nachum Sarna. *The JPS Torah Commentary.* Jewish Publication Society: Philadelphia, 1989. p. 283
[144] Thomas Jefferson. *Notes on the State of Virginia*, 1787.
[145] RaMBaM. *Epistle to the Jews of Marseilles.*

importantly – for what it could be. Dreams are, if you will, a mental blue-print, guiding us, inspiring us to achieve that which was once thought to be inconceivable. From space exploration to racial integration, from cross-continental transportation to global communication... all started with a dream.

Started, but not completed. Because, unfortunately, the mental blue-print we call a dream is only roughly sketched. Marked with its beginning as well as its glorious end, the instructions on how to connect Part A (our dreams) with Part B (our reality) are missing. That's why we need people. Not like Pharaoh, who deemed it reasonable to alter his dreams when confronted with the unknown reality. Rather, we need people like Joseph – people of both conviction and action – who will confront the bumpy road of reality, with its unexpected twists and turns, and still hold onto their dreams. For Joseph understood, as another great pioneer – Theodor Herzl – once did, that "if you will it, it is no dream."

We too are pioneers, each attempting to fashion a future for ourselves where the impossible becomes possible. In this construction, our Torah portion wants us to be aware that alongside reason there hangs another great instrument on the tool-belt of our lives: the power to dream. For reason may assist us in laying a foundation of what is, but only a dream – at whatever age – can help us build an extension of what could and hopefully will be; whether it's to be a princess... a Ghostbuster... or an official representative of Earth to some foreign planet. So, as John Lennon poignantly sang: "You may say I'm a dreamer. But, I'm not the only one. I hope someday you'll join us. And the world will live as one."[146]

Mikeitz // At the End
Bite 2 – *An Inspirational Gift to Keep or Not Keep in Mind*

As we are in the midst of Chanukah, it is appropriate to ask you to imagine, for a moment, that you were given an extraordinary gift, an idea – perhaps – that was guaranteed to change the world for the better. What would you do with this gifted idea? Would you give it away immediately, sharing it freely with others? Or, would you hold onto it, waiting until you felt it was most opportune to release it? This was the dilemma, the sages speculate, that faced Joseph in this Torah portion of *Mikeitz.*

After two disheartening dreams, which aggravated his spirit, "Pharaoh called for all the magicians of Egypt and all its wise men. Pharaoh told them his dreams," hoping that one among them may present a solution to his problem. "Yet, none could interpret them for Pharaoh;" none, that is, except for Joseph. On temporary release from prison, Joseph was brought forward to offer an interpretation, an idea, which the Bible states, "was pleasing to Pharaoh." For,

---

[146] John Lennon. "Imagine" *Imagine.* Apple: 1971.

in this gift of interpretation, the Egyptian world would change, saving countless lives. (Genesis 41:8-37)

Yet, the sages question: "With such a valued gift, why didn't Joseph hold onto his interpretation until there was some guarantee of permanent release? After all, his earlier attempt to secure his freedom by way of the Cup Bearer proved fruitless.[147] Some suggest Joseph was in no position to negotiate with Pharaoh, who held ultimate control over his life or potential death. Conceding, others say it wasn't because Joseph was inferior to Pharaoh. Rather Joseph was in no position to negotiate because those ideas were not his to sell. They were God's and thereby belonged to all.

Let me explain. In our highly creative and competitive culture we work hard and long to come up with innovative ideas that we believe can and will change the world. And, whether it's fiscal compensation or name recognition, these acknowledgements seem just given the amount of time and energy expended on such beneficial efforts. In fact, according to Jewish Law, "failure to recognize our sources of inspiration is tantamount to *g'neivah* (thievery), for it not only presents a false impression of wisdom on the one who has not, it also robs the one who has of gratitude."[148]

But, what if there were no guarantees of gratitude, no reassurances of recognition, as was the case with Joseph? Do we have the right to refuse the idea's release, keeping it locked safely in the security box of our minds? Sure we do. We always have the right. But – let's be clear – if we exercise that right, then the vaults of our minds become nothing more than prisons for our ideas. And we, in turn, become their hostage-takers, waiting for the world to pony-up the cash to secure the idea's release. In the meantime, the world suffers.[149]

Having recently been incarcerated, it's likely that Joseph understood those dynamics. In his mind, there was no choice but to release the idea without condition. For, being inspired literally means being "in the spirit" of God. And, upon acting in accordance with that spirit, giving freely for the benefit of others, not only do we have a chance to be recognized, more importantly, we have a chance to bring recognition to the One who really deserves it: God. As Pharaoh excitedly exclaims, upon receiving Joseph's gift, "Could there be another like him, in whom there is the spirit of God!"[150]

The answer is, of course, "Yes! Yes! Yes!" In each and every one of us there is the spirit of God. Occasionally, that spirit will present us with a gift, an idea, a spark of inspiration. While we may desire to hold onto it until we are promised

---

[147] See Genesis 40:23 – "The chief cupbearer did not think of Joseph; he forgot him."

[148] Rabbi Moshe Feinstein, *Iggeros Moshe, Choshen Mishpat* vol. 2 no. 30

[149] This, some will argue, transpired with the automakers in America. In a dramatic shift, this past summer, car manufacturers reversed their long standing opposition to use the technology they had on hand to raise fuel economy standards. According to the reports, fuel consumption will rise from the current standard of 27 miles per gallon to 54.5 miles per gallon by the year 2025. This technology's release, states economists, can largely be attributed to the multi-billion dollar auto-bailout which taxpayers paid a few years back. [See Bill Vlasic's piece in *The New York Times*, "Carmakers Back Strict New Rules for Gas Mileage." 28 July 2011

[150] See Genesis 41:38-43

some form of compensation or recognition, our Torah portion is guiding us to give it away without reservation. Why? Because it is all too human to seek gain; it is all together Divine to give. And, if we wish to be a light unto the nations on this Chanukah, may we embrace our Divine potential to give – even of our minds – freely and without reservation. Thereby, like it was with Joseph in Egypt, we pray our world will be changed for the better.

Mikeitz // At the End
Bite 3 – *Express Yourself*

"*Tis the season to be shopping, fa lalalala lala la la.*" And, since this is the busiest shopping season in our year, many of us may recall that common complicated moment on many parent-child shopping expeditions, specifically those that had the goal of securing a new outfit. After many hours in a crowded shop, after shop, after shop, the parent excitedly holds up what she believes to be the perfect clothing choice. "See, honey! It's perfect." But the child's face, showing the sourest of cringes, says otherwise. "What?" asks the parent confused. "Isn't this, as you say, 'the bomb?' Doesn't it say that I am cool and hip, but responsible and smart?" "No, mother," responds the child, through tightened lips. "It says I want to be shoved inside a locker. Oh, but please take my lunch money first, I insist!"

Today's teens are not the only ones that have a complicated relationship when it comes to clothing. This was the case even in the Bible. Already presented and then stripped of his clothing twice as a young man (once when his brothers took his coat of many colors, throwing him into the pit, and a second time when Potiphar's wife tore his clothing from him, before he was thrown into prison), we read in *Mikeitz* that Joseph receives two new outfits for his wardrobe, though thankfully with better results. First, upon emerging from the pit of prison, we read that Joseph "had his hair cut and his clothes changed, in order to appear before Pharaoh," who thereupon elevates Joseph to the position of vizier of Egypt. (Genesis 41:14) And, as such, Pharaoh "has him dressed in robes of fine linen," accentuating them with some major bling, "a signet ring" and "a gold chain around his neck." (Genesis 41:42)

Some commentators, like Robert Alter, see these wardrobe changes as merely a practical necessity, writing: "The putting on of fresh garments is realistically motivated, for it is obvious that an imprisoned slave would have to make himself presentable before appearing in [the royal] court [of Egypt]."[151] Though not dissenting, others believe these strategically placed clothing changes also have symbolic significance. More than practical necessity, Dr. Tamara Cohn Eskenazi writes, "Joseph's clothes have served as a symbol of his fate. In each case he received clothing, it was a sign of a positive shift in his

---

[151] Robert Alter. *The Five Books of Moses: A Translation and Commentary.* W.W. Norton & Company: New York and London, 2004. p.232

identity."[152] And, conversely, in each case his clothing was removed, it signaled a negative shift in his identity. "Thus," continues Eskenazi, "garments function [not just practically for warmth or modesty, but clothing can oftentimes serve] as a symbol of its wearer," a medium – says Madonna – to "express yourself."[153]

From our own history, we have witnessed the absolute truth of her words, as each and every generation has donned clothing as a medium for its unique and personal message. For example, in the 1950's, the iconic tight jeans and white t-shirt with rolled sleeves came to represent the tough American resolve after WWII. That toughness, though, would later give way to the free flowing and flowery vestments of the 1960's and its message of unbridled liberation; a message which seemed to only fade and wither under the reflected lights of the 1970's Disco Fever and its message of glitz and glam. The 1980's bore the message of sleek success on the padded shoulders of power suits for both men and women; a style which dramatically clashed with the 1990's counter-culture message, as teens purposefully tore holes in jeans, which sometimes barely hung onto the human frame. Remembrance characterized the early 2000's, as previous styles from earlier generations were retrofitted for the new millennium; a contrast to the current movement, which projects – through tight jeans, flannel shirts, and wild hair – that the future cannot be defined. So from hippies to hipsters, from grunge to ghetto, every generation has tailored their clothing – whether consciously or unconsciously – to express the individual self.

And, while those within any particular generation as well as Billy Crystal may say, "You look marvelous," those outside that generation rarely give it such praise.[154] For example, the 1950's tough-guy was, to the Greatest Generation of the 1940's, a rebel without a cause. The 1960's hippie was, to the 1950's, a "wasted" generation. The 1970's soul man was considered soulless to those who experienced the revolutions of the 1960's. Even Joseph, who believed his technicolored dream coat was a symbol of righteousness and Divine grace, learned the hard way that others – specifically his older brothers – perceived the ornamented tunic with suspicion, understanding its message to be self-aggrandizing, arrogant, and boastful. But misunderstandings such as these are bound to occur. Because clothing, like any symbol, is open to a variety of interpretations. Take head coverings for example. Some wear them as a sign of humility. Others take them, especially if worn indoors, as a sign of disrespect. Thus, we see that what the wearer intends and what the viewer interprets can often be two dramatically and conflicting messages.

Therefore, in order to ensure the best presentation of oneself, it is vital to consider not simply our own intended message, but also how our message may be interpreted by others. This could be said with regards to anything, from our

---

[152] Tamara Cohn Eskenazi and Andrea L. Weiss. *The Torah: A Women's Commentary*. URJ Press: New York, 2008. p. 236
[153] Eskenazi, p.211 and Madonna. "Express Yourself." *Like a Prayer*. Warner Brothers: 1989
[154] The catch phrase is from Billy Crystal's famous character on Saturday Night Live, Fernando Lamas. 1985

choice in wardrobes to our choice in words. "But why?" cries the youth of each generation. "Why should I allow another's perception to stifle my presentation of self?" Because, as the 16th century English poet John Donne reminds us, "No man is an island, entire of him[/her]self; every person is a piece of the continent, a part of the main. If a clod be washed away by the sea, is not the [entire] land the lesser."[155] In other words, rarely – if ever – are our actions contained within a vacuum of self, separated and sterilized from the remainder of the world. Like a pebble dropped into a pond, an individual's act can ripple out to the rest of humanity, as is evident in the story of Joseph. His dramatic tale is really a culmination of individual choices: from Jacob's to Joseph's, from his brothers' to Pharaoh's.

Therefore, in expressing ourselves we have the responsibility to – as the knight from *Indiana Jones and the Last Crusade* advised – "choose wisely."[156] We hopefully do as much when it comes to our faith, realizing that every Jew is by default a de facto representative of the whole of Judaism. But, through this portion, we are reminded to do as much with our secular decisions as well. For when we consider other voices not just in our wardrobe or our words, but in all the actions of our lives, we have the potential to express the very best of ourselves to the world, and thus represent the world at its best.

---

[155] John Donne. "Meditation XVII." *Devotions upon Emergent Occasions*. London: 1624
[156] George Lucas. *Indiana Jones and the Last Crusade*. Paramount Pictures: 1989

Portion 11:
Vayigash // He Approached
Torah Portion: Genesis 44:18-47:27

"THEN JUDAH APPROACHED HIM…" While this portion approaches the end of Jacob's life, it picks up where the last one left off: the climax of the Joseph saga. Benjamin is caught with Joseph's goblet in his sack and Joseph announces his plan to make Benjamin his slave. However, Judah approaches Joseph and pleads for his brother's release. He uses the petition, "If he leaves his father, our father shall surely die!" Playing on Joseph's heartstrings works, but in a way the brothers could not have imagined. This strange Egyptian is neither a stranger nor an Egyptian at all. It is their brother Joseph, who thereupon reveals himself.

In this moving narrative of families reuniting, Joseph reminds his brothers that his time spent in Egypt was the will of God. Rather than holding a grudge, Joseph releases his brothers from their guilt. Pharaoh even helps Joseph's family, providing them with provisions for their journey home and inviting them all back to Egypt, where Joseph had prospered. When the brothers arrive home they tell their father Jacob that Joseph is still alive. Although readers of the Bible are rarely privy to the feelings of our Biblical characters, in this passage we learn that Jacob's frozen heart revives with spirit.

Within renewed energy and the Divine's promise that "I Myself will go down with you to Egypt, and will most assuredly bring you back as well," Jacob journeys down to Egypt to meet his son. This is the climax of the Joseph story. In this tearful reunion, Jacob announces, "Now that I've seen your face – for you are still alive – I can die at last." It is the approaching death of the patriarch Jacob that will take readers into the next portion. The man once bent with grief, is now standing tall, ready to greet the world beyond.

Vayigash // He Approached
Bite 1 – *The Precious Present*

When asked, "what's your favorite Jewish holiday," invariably the most popular answer given by children is... Chanukah! But, not because of Chanukah's meaningful message about the human capacity to create miracles; nor, unfortunately, is Chanukah so appealing because it is a time for joyous family celebrations, fully equipped with delicious *latkes* (potato pancakes) and *sufganiot* (jelly-filled donuts). No, the real reason Chanukah is so often reserved a special place in the hearts of our children is – as we know – *presents*! More than the menorah itself, it's the present which has come to symbolize this Festival of Lights. Through the process of wishing and waiting, children and even some adults build up an expectation that when the time comes to present the present there will be – contained within a beautifully wrapped box – happiness (batteries not included). In fact, this assumption led a lonely stone-cutter, many years ago, on one of the most exceptional journeys of all time.

Every morning, before the sun rose, this stone-cutter would leave his meager hut to venture many miles to a mammoth mountain, upon which – by the king's order – he worked. After a relentless day under the sun, the stone-cutter would return home, exhausted. He was greatly unhappy with having to work so hard to survive. But, what choice did he have? So, he continued to do so, until one day when the stone-cutter – by chance or Providence – came across something miraculous.

Lifting his pick high into the air, the stone-cutter soundly struck a round boulder, which split open like a nut. Contained, therein, was a lamp. He had heard the stories of these lamps, but considered them a mere matter of myth. But, here it was! So, without delay, he began rubbing the lamp. And, just as it was in those legends, a genie bellowed forth, offering the stone-cutter an endless supply of wishes.

"Master, I am the Genie of the Lamp. How can I be of service?" "Genie," said the stone-cutter, with hesitation. "I wish to be the king, for then I will be happy." With a poof, the stone-cutter was transformed into the king. No longer did he have to work from early morning to late night. As he slept in, others worked for him. Indeed, being waited on brought him a measure of happiness. Though, it was only fleeting. For, one day, he basked too long in the sun and got a severe burn.

In that unhappy moment, the former stone-cutter rubbed the lamp and said, "Genie, I have another wish. I wish to be the sun, for then I will be truly happy." With a poof, the former stone-cutter turned king was transformed into the brilliant sun; and, boy, was he happy! Besides the splendid view, the stone-cutter enjoyed his power to shine upon the whole world. That was, until one day, when a large cloud came and blocked his rays. And, once again, the stone-cutter was unhappy.

So, he made another wish. "Genie," said the stone-cutter. "I no longer want to be the sun. I wish to be a cloud, for then I will be truly happy." With a poof, the former stone-cutter turned king, turned sun was transformed into a cloud. Indeed, he felt happy. Besides blocking the sun, he was delighted to bring shade and rain to the earth. That was, until the day, when a stiff breeze came and blew him off course. Utterly upset, the stone-cutter made another wish. "Genie!" he bellowed.

"Yes," responded the Genie calmly. "I have another wish. I'm no longer happy being the cloud. I wish to be the wind, for then I will be truly happy." With a poof, the former stone-cutter turned king, turned sun, turned cloud was transformed into the wind. For a while, he was happy. Besides directing the clouds, he found amazing enjoyment in swooping down low amongst the trees and flying high with the birds. Until the day he smacked-up against a mountain. Unlike so many things, the mountain would not be moved.

Unhappy once more, the stone-cutter hollowed: "Genie! I'm no longer satisfied with being the wind. I wish to be the mountain, for then I will be truly happy." With a poof, the former stone-cutter turned king, turned sun, turned cloud, turned wind transformed into the mountain and, boy, was he pleased! He reveled in the fact that he was an immoveable force, able to withstand the angriest of winds and repel the most torrential of rains. That was, until one day, when a lonely stone-cutter came and began to chip away at him.

"Genie," stated the stone-cutter with resounding assurance. "I wish to make one final wish." "Yes master," humbly responded the Genie. "I wish to be a stone-cutter, for then I will be truly happy."

The end of this amazing journey is similar to the conclusion reached by *b'nai Yisrael*, the shepherding children of our forefather Jacob. After enduring hardship, after hardship, after hardship and making their way down to Egypt, Jacob's children are advised in *Vayigash* to tell Pharaoh that they are "breeders of livestock from time immemorial, [because] shepherding is abhorrent to the Egyptians." But, rather than wishing to be something else, they tell Pharaoh: "We are shepherds," adding "as were our fathers." (Genesis 46:34, 47:3)

But, why? Why defiantly resist this advice meant only to bring about a happier ending for *b'nai Yisrael*? Because, like this story, we learn that the only present that can truly deliver happiness is... the present (i.e. the present moment). Sure, life can often be tough. In those moments, it's understandable to want to find happiness somewhere or through something or someone else. But that is a fool's errand. For, as long as we are displeased with ourselves, disappointment is bound to follow us, wherever we go. Thus, if we truly wish to find happiness, then we must begin by unwrapping ourselves, dealing with those various layers of disappointment, regret, and heartache which have surrounded our lives. For contained beneath them is a precious truth: "each of us are" – as taught by Rabbenu Yonah – "a precious and treasured gem in the crown of God."[157] And, as God appreciates us, so may we come to appreciate ourselves.

Vayigash // He Approached
Bite 2 – "When in Rome..."

As parents, many of us have received or eventually will receive _the_ briefing; the infamous one our growing children deem necessary to deliver just before we visit them in their new environment away from home. Generally, it begins with a short list of the things we _can_ do, followed by a much longer list of the things we absolutely _cannot_ do. Finally, the briefing concludes with: "And, whatever you do, please, don't embarrass me!"

In _Vayigash_, the father of the Israelites receives a similar briefing from one of his sons, Joseph. Poised to enter Joseph's new home in Egypt, Jacob is told exactly what to say when Pharaoh summons him and asks, "What is your occupation?" Joseph states, "[Father], you shall answer, 'Your servants have been breeders of livestock from time immemorial...' For [although you are really shepherds], shepherding is abhorrent to the Egyptians. [So, please, don't embarrass me!]" (Genesis 46:33-34) Foreseeing the potential for a cross-cultural wrinkle between Israel's high value for shepherding and its low status among the Egyptians, Joseph's words can be heard as an attempt to iron-out a smooth parental visit. I suppose, though, Joseph should have used a little starch, because his briefing did not exactly hold. When – just a few verses later – Pharaoh asks, "what is your occupation," the answer given is: "We, your servants, are shepherds." D'oh! And to make matters worse, Jacob adds, "...as were also our fathers." (Genesis 47:3)

According to our sages, Jacob's disregard for Joseph's words was not an act of disrespect towards his son. For, even in his absence from the ancestral home, Joseph remained his father's beloved. Rather, comments Nachum Sarna, Jacob's response "reflects a healthy self-esteem of a [person and his] people raised in their own land" and steeped in their own traditions.[158] Traditions Joseph – as with many of our own children – recommend changing when entering their new environment. After all, "when in Rome, do as the Romans."

This adage is actually regenerative; that is to say, it renews itself with each successive generation. In Joseph's time, it may well have been 'when in Egypt, do as the Egyptians' and today it may be 'when in America, do as the

---

[157] 13th century sage. See his commentary to Pirkei Avot 2:5 recorded in _Pirkei Avot: The Sages Guide to Living_. Mesorah Publications, ltd., 1995. p.74

[158] Nachum Sarna. _Etz Hayim: Torah and Commentary_. Rabbinical Assembly: New York, 2001. p. 284

Americans.' For children in any era – as we may recall ourselves – typically measure success in life by the degree to which one acclimates, and dare I say assimilates, into a new environment. As a first generation American, Louis Brandeis once declared: "However great his outward conformity, the immigrant is not Americanized unless he is brought into complete harmony with our ideals and aspirations, and cooperates with us for their attainment. Only then will America truly embrace his consciousness as that of an American."[159] Brandeis captures a sentiment held by many children, who believe that the extent to which they accept society is correlated to the extent society will accept them.

But, that acceptance comes with a feeling of rejection on behalf of even the most progressive parents. As each generation makes a name for itself, certain aspects of the previous generation are adapted or altogether abandoned. It is only natural that parents are upset by these changes and interpret them as a sign of embarrassment. However, we must remember that our children adapted to their new environment not because they do not appreciate our heritage, but because they desire to be successful in their new life. And, isn't that what we want for our children?

We want them to be successful. We just maintain a different perspective, gleaned from our life experiences, on how to get there. Not by forsaking the past for a chance at a future, instead we believe the best chances for success in life are often found when we allow the past to work for our future. A perfect example of this lesson comes from the aforementioned Biblical episode. After Jacob confidently embraces his past role as a shepherd, Pharaoh does not reject him as Joseph had feared. In fact, Pharaoh – in turn – embraces him, stating to Joseph: "Let your father and your brothers stay in the land of Goshen… [and, furthermore,] put them in charge of my livestock." (Genesis 47:6) For Pharaoh understood that one's past experiences, one's traditions, are not a barrier to success in a new environment. Actually, they can be the seed of that success.

Yet, there's no guarantee how the past and its traditions will bloom in the new homes of our children. As we see from this portion, Jacob's tradition of shepherding in the ancestral homeland was transformed into a new career as a breeder of livestock in Egypt. There are, in fact, many other examples of our traditions changing over the centuries, as we have entered new lands. So, I suppose, the next time our children sit us down for _the_ briefing and explain to us what may need to change, we can brief them on one of the greatest traditions of our people: change. Our ability to adapt to a new environment has allowed us to be the only people on the face of the earth to survive not one, but two expulsions from our ancestral homeland to still be around today. And, God willing, let us pray that we will still be around for centuries to come, by embracing both tradition and our tradition to change. Then, no one, neither parent nor child will have reason to feel embarrassed.

---

[159] Louis Brandeis. _Address at Faneuil Hall_, Boston – 4 July 1915

Vayigash // He Approached
Bite 3 – *The Echo of Our Deeds*

As a child, I was pretty clumsy: stubbing my toes, bumping my head, smashing my fingers. I always understood these painful moments as the natural (though undesired) side-effects of growth, the missteps – if you will – in these often turbulent and transformative years, as I attempted to gain a more stable foothold towards the future. My mother, on the other hand, had a wholly or holy different theory. After each unfortunate bump, bruise or bang, she would articulate her masterful theory in the words: "That's God getting back at you!" "For what?!" I would question, argumentatively. "Oh," she would say, "you know."

It's too bad Joseph didn't know my mother or her theory. Had he, maybe he would have avoided a most unfortunate misstep in Jewish history: Egyptian slavery. For, in the third year of their famine, "the Egyptians came to Joseph and said: 'Give us bread, lest we die before your very eyes; for our money is already gone.' Joseph replied, 'Then bring your livestock, and I will sell it to you...' So they brought their livestock." But, by the next year, that ration was consumed as well and the people once again came to Joseph, saying: "Let us not perish before your eyes... Take us and our land in exchange for bread." And, by their word, it was so. (Genesis 47:13-27)

Commenting on this exchange, scholar Nachum Sarna writes: "The severity of the remaining years of the famine was such that the people became wholly dependent upon the state for their survival. In effect," Joseph's policies, adds Sarna, "nationalized the land and livestock and turned the populace into [what the Bible calls] *avadim l'Pharaoh*," meaning "servants," "serfs," or even "slaves to *Pharaoh*."[160] Many of us are likely familiar with this phrase. After all, it appears in the Passover *Haggadah* as "*avadim hayinu l'Pharaoh*." That is to say, sometime after Joseph, "we were slaves to Pharaoh." Why? Well, my mother would say, "that's God getting back at us."

In other words, because one of *b'nai Yisrael* helped enslave the Egyptians, it is fitting – by this theory – that *b'nai Yisrael* eventually became enslaved themselves. While certainly callous, many of us would, in theory, like to believe that this is the way the world works. It is, after all, so simple and yet so profound. Like an echo being released into the world, our actions can and will reverberate back to us. If we put out good, then good will come back. And if we, let's say, treat our brothers unkindly, well then – for the sake of this argument – one can surmise that unkind action will ensue, like stubbing one's toes, bumping one's head, or smashing one's fingers.

But, in truth, that's not always the way the world works. Likely, we have observed good individuals treated poorly and bad people treated kindly. Why? What can explain these irregularities? Well, some say, there's no need for

---

[160] Nachum Sarna. *The JPS Torah Commentary: Genesis*. JPS: Philadelphia, 1989. pp. 320-323

explanation, as they only appear irregular to us. From God's point of view, even these problems have a purpose that we cannot entirely perceive. Okay. Maybe. But, what we *can* perceive is the nature of our world, which is far from being a hollow, cavernous pit, able to reverberate the echo of our actions in perfect pitch. Rather, it's filled with people, whose own actions and resulting echo can affect the echo of our actions, distorting it or sometimes stopping it all together.

So, does that mean we should give up on this theory? To my mother's relief, no; for, in believing that our actions will one day come back to us, we often become more thoughtful about when first sending them out. This was the likely intent behind such teachings as "what is hateful to you, do not do to another,"[161] or "love your neighbor as yourself, for you were once strangers in the land of Egypt."[162] Yet, even these teachings can be distorted. So, how can we maintain their integrity? Simple, we need to amplify our message by working in concert with others. Only then can we produce a sound wave strong enough to counter the current of negativity that sometimes interferes with our good deeds.

As the new secular year *vayigash*, "approaches," this teaching couldn't have come at a better time. For all too often, in this past year, the good deeds of many – but ultimately unconnected individuals – were distorted or silenced by the negative broadcasts of a very few. But, as *Vayigash* reminds us, we have the power to change that by approaching one another. May we do so and, in doing so, connect our Power Source for positive change with others. Thereby, we may produce a signal so strong that it will echo and reverberate from sea to shining sea and all the spaces in between, without interruptions. Then may we see the validity of our parent's theory: "in doing good, we create good… for others as well as ourselves." That, my friends, is "God [truly] getting back at us!"

---

[161] Stated by the sage Hillel and recorded in the *Babylonian Talmud*, tractate Shabbat 31a.
[162] Leviticus 19:34

Portion 12:
Vay'chi // He Lived
Torah Portion: Genesis 47:28-50:26

"JACOB LIVED IN THE LAND OF EGYPT FOR SEVENTEEN YEARS." And, there Jacob would die. The majority of the portion is therefore devoted to how the father of Israel, Jacob, confronts this moment. Appropriately, as his 147 years of life draw to a close, he draws close to his children, delivering unto each one a unique blessing. "Blessing" may be putting it too broadly, as the words uttered here are not all optimistic, but speak to the individual human strengths and weakness contained within his sons, reflections – if you will – of his own imperfections.

Additionally, his words point to both the past and future. Featured therein are the Divine promises of abundant offspring and security in the land, which God had sworn to Abraham, Isaac, and Jacob. In highlighting these, it could be said that Jacob was sowing the seeds for their eventual Exodus from Egypt back to the Promised Land. For, Jacob made his children and children's children swear to return his bones to the Land upon his passing, placing them alongside the bones of his fathers in the cave of Machpelah.

Jacob will not be the only prominent character in the course of this last portion of Genesis to die, nor will he be the only one who commands that his bones not rest in Egypt. Joseph, who passes at the very end of this portion, also makes a similar request before his death: "I am about to die. God will surely take note of you and bring you up from this land to the land that the Eternal promised an oath to Abraham, Isaac, and Jacob." So, Joseph made the children of Israel swear, "When God has taken notice of you, you shall carry up my bones from here."

Though the family of Israel eventually dies, from here the nation of Israel is born. They are brought together, forged into a single identity, by the smelting pit of Egypt.

Vay'chi // He Lived
Bite 1 – *It's the Beginning of the End!*

"It's the beginning of the end!" a statement perfectly fitting for a doomsayer, but for a rabbi? However, before we conclude to the contrary, let us consider for a moment that both tend to stand upon a soapbox at times to speak to a community who may not be so enthusiastically inclined to listen. Furthermore, what is said is eerily similar as well, as both encourage us not only to adjust our outlooks on life, but – more importantly – adjust our actions. And, now, the similarities abound as this rabbi joins the doomsayer in saying: "Let us make this adjustment now, because *it's the beginning of the end*!"

I sound this alarm not simply because we stand poised to end one decade to begin another, nor because we are presently concluding one Biblical book – Genesis – in order to begin another – Exodus. Rather, I present this precarious prediction because of the prophetic forecaster, Jacob, who foresees the beginning of his own end in this portion of *Vay'chi*. Here, we read, "When the time approached for Israel to die, he summoned his son Joseph and said to him, '…Don't bury me in Egypt. When I lie down with my fathers, take me up from Egypt and bury me in their burial place.'" (Genesis 47:29-30)

That's not all Jacob did. In addition to making this final request to Joseph, Jacob also assembles all of his children and even two of his grandchildren – Menasseh and Ephraim – and blesses them individually. According to our sages, Jacob knew he had time to do this because "he prayed for a sign (i.e. 'sickness' in Genesis 48:1) that his death was approaching, in order that he would be able to number his days."[163] In other words, Jacob knew exactly when he was going to die. It makes us wonder, doesn't it? Would we pray the same? Would we want to know when it was going to be the beginning of our end?

"No way, dude!" exclaims the extreme-sport enthusiast, who believes that knowing the exact time of death will somehow 'chill the thrill' of those near-death experiences like bungee-jumping, sky-diving, and synchronized-swimming. Alright, maybe not synchronized-swimming; but, the adverse effects of this knowledge of the future on the present are why many of us would object to offering the same prayer that Jacob so willingly extended to God. Knowing our death, it is believed, can only result in filling every moment of life with fear and anxiety for that very future. In essence, seeing the future obscures our perspective of the present.

But, one person's obstruction is another's clarification, a lens helping us to focus on what is really important in the present. For example, elsewhere in the *Talmud* there's a story told of Alexander the Great and his quest to find *Gan Eden*.[164] In his insatiable hunger for wealth and power, Alexander believed that

---

[163] BT Bava Metzia 87a
[164] Gan Eden is Hebrew for the Garden of Eden. BT Tamid 32b

the fabled treasure which grew on the trees of the Garden would be the crown jewel of his expansive kingdom. According to the story:

> As Alexander the Great approached the gates of Eden, a voice from inside the Garden bellowed: *"This is the gateway of the Lord. Only the righteous shall enter through it."*[165] Although Alexander had always considered himself righteous, the gate would not open. Hanging his head low, Alexander pleaded with 'the Power that is and will forever be' to be given something from the Garden to prove that he was there, something that would help him become righteous. He was given a human eye with the instruction: "Ponder its meaning."

> Upon his return, Alexander sought to discover the eye's value. He began by weighing it against a few bars of gold from his treasury. What he observed was the eye, when placed on a scale, easily outweighed the few bars of gold. So, Alexander added more. Yet again, the eye was heavier. Not deterred, Alexander kept adding more and more gold, each time the scale tilted down towards the direction of the eye. Confused at what this meant, Alexander sought out the wisest sage of his kingdom.

> When found, Alexander asked the Sage, "Tell me rabbi, what does this mean? I was given this eye from the Garden of Eden. It's supposed to teach me righteousness. Yet, each time I place it upon the scale to determine its worth, it outweighs all the gold I've amassed in my conquests. What then is the value of the eye?" To answer that, the great Sage said, "You must return the eye to the scale, Alexander. But, this time, instead of gold, place on the other side a small handful of dirt."

> Alexander did as the Sage instructed. Lo and behold, the scale tipped downwards, towards the direction of the dirt as the eye lifted upward. "What could this mean?!" questioned Alexander. To which, the Sage answered, "It's clear. As long as we hunger for wealth or power the eye will never be satisfied. But, as soon as a little dirt from the grave comes into view, only then are we given a righteous perspective on life, becoming satisfied with what is really important."

The Sage's words are echoed in the Psalms, which prayerfully states: "Teach us to number our days, O' Lord, so we may obtain a heart of wisdom."[166] But how, exactly? How does this perspective of the future help us to see the value of the present? To answer this question we must – for a moment – imagine that there'll be no tomorrow, no chance to make up for what should have been done today. How then would we spend these last remaining moments of life? Would we squander them so cheaply on things which are fleeting: the pursuit of wealth, possessions, and power? Or, would we choose to invest these last

---

[165] Psalm 118:20
[166] Psalm 90:12

moments – as Jacob did – with things that are lasting: *actions* which demonstrate our love for our family and friends and *time* spent honoring our relationship with God?

Surely, for those who aspire to live lives of righteousness, the answer cannot be in doubt. But, surprisingly, the question may be. Because to truly live lives of righteousness our faith desires us not to question whether we would or would not like to know the future details of our death. Rather, to effectively live lives of righteousness, our faith inspires us to live as if each moment was the beginning of our end. As Rabbi Joshua Liebman once wrote: "Death is not the enemy of life, but its friend. For it is the constant and continual knowledge that our days are limited which makes them so precious."[167] This knowledge is not meant to "chill the thrill" of life nor invoke fear, paralyzing our ability to live. Rather the ability to number our days is meant to be a catalyst, spurring us to invest the fleeting moments of our years, months, days, hours and even seconds with ever-abiding worth.

"It's the beginning of the end!" So, as we count down the remaining moments of our secular year, cramming them with joy, love, peace, and harmony, let us also do this for all the days of our lives, counting them one by one so that we understand that we have a limited time to manifest our limitless potential.

Vay'chi // He Lived
Bite 2 – *God: A Community of People*

In October of 2009, Pope Benedict XVI issued an invitation that rocked the Christian world. It was not a friend request, inviting everyone to join his Facebook page. Rather, Pope Benedict XVI issued a papal invitation to Anglican priests, permitting them entrance into the Catholic priesthood without forgoing their previously established marital status. Yes, you heard me right... married priests! And, "with as many as 200 Catholic priests who are married right now in America...this invitation is expected to increase that number dramatically," reported Brian Taff of ABC News.[168] Responding to that potential reality, some Catholic leaders questioned its practicality. "If you look at it from a practical point of view, in terms of all the demands that are made time wise and otherwise on priests in this culture," stated Monsignor Michael Carroll, "there isn't time for family."[169]

Although we will never experience this struggle, at least not to the same degree as our Catholic brothers and sisters, we still are susceptible to the tension that sometimes exists between loving God and loving our fellow man or woman. This struggle, in fact, was pronounced in this portion of *Vay'chi*. Reflecting on his life, in his final moments, Jacob reveals to Joseph that "El Shaddai appeared

---

[167] Joshua Liebman. *Peace of Mind*, 1948
[168] Brian Taff. "Door Opening for Married Catholic Priests." ABC News: WPVI-TV Philadelphia, 21 November 2009. http://abclocal.go.com/wpvi/story?section=news/special_reports&id=7130952
[169] ibid.

to [him] at Luz, in the land of Canaan, and He blessed [him] and said to [him], 'I will make you fertile and numerous, making of you a community of peoples.'" Yet, in the process of fulfilling this Divine vision, "Rachel died, to [Jacob's] sorrow," states the Bible, "while [he] was sojourning [at God's command] in the land of Canaan. [And so,] when still some distance from Ephrat (now Bethlehem), [Jacob] buried her on the road." (Genesis 48:3-7)

Commentators have a "conclave" of sorts over these two revelations so close to the setting of Jacob's life. Sforno, for example, imagines Jacob pleading with Joseph to understand the reason his mother did not receive a proper burial. "So intense was my grief," says Jacob, according to Sforno, "that I had not the strength even to carry her to the cemetery."[170] RaMBaN, however, provided another explanation. Considering the interesting juxtaposition of the two revelations, RaMBaN suggested that "Jacob spoke to Joseph in an apologetic tone... stating, '[Although I loved her dearly], I buried her there by the word of God.'"[171] In other words, Jacob hoped that Joseph, while he may not be happy with what transpired, would – at the very least – come to understand the great consternation he experienced at that difficult moment, choosing to love God versus loving his wife.

It's not that he or we, for that matter, can't understand. Many of us know all too well the tension that sometimes can arise over what appears to be dueling responsibilities: the obligation to fulfill God's commands and the desire to fulfill that which was requested of us by those we love. For example, do we serve our beloved team in a vital sports competition or do we fulfill our religious service in love of God? Do we attend our child's PTA meeting or our congregation's Sisterhood or Brotherhood meeting? Do we engage in work for the Lord or do we engage in work for our families? These real life struggles, which flood our consciousness on a weekly – if not daily – basis, allow us to intimately understand the great consternation Jacob must have experienced in this difficult moment on his Divine path.

But, what may still elude our mind's grasp is neither the experience, nor the conflicting feelings therein; it's the choice. Are we – like Jacob – always supposed to choose the love of God, known as *Kiddush HaShem* (sanctification of God's name), over our love for our families, our friends, even the stranger in our midst? According to many, the answer would be most definitely "yes," and not just by Catholic clergy. Even in the Jewish world we have come up with many explanations on why we should turn our backs on our fellow in order to turn and face God. These reasons include but are not limited to understanding this personal sacrifice as the necessary repayment for the Divine gift of life; a payment many proudly profess Sandy Koufax deposited on Yom Kippur 5726 (1965). In her biography on the Hall-of-Famer, author Jane Leavy wrote: "By

---

[170] Sforno commentary to Genesis 48:7. For a good translation see *Sforno: Commentary on the Torah* by Raphael Pelcovitz (Artscroll Mesorah Publications, Ltd.: Brooklyn, NY. 2004), p. 258

[171] RaMBaN commentary to Genesis 48:7. Some of his statements are attributed to RaSHI. For a good translation see *RaMBaN: Nachmanides Commentary on the Torah*, Genesis, by Rabbi C. Chavel (Shilo Publishing House, Inc.: Brooklyn, NY. 1999), pp. 573-575

refusing to pitch that [Yom Kippur] day, Koufax defined himself as a man of principle, who placed faith above craft. He became inextricably linked to the American Jewish experience... He is the New Patriarch," boast Leavy. "There was Abraham. There was Isaac. There was Jacob. And, now there's Sandy."[172]

Sandy?! But, where's Joseph? That place in the patriarchal chain was reserved for his link, not Sandy's. But, unlike Sandy, Joseph likely didn't agree with his father or his great grandfather, Abraham, who consistently put God before family; hence the reason Jacob, according to the sages, needed to plead with his son. For Joseph's life experience taught him something different. After serving the people of Egypt as vizier, Joseph not once said it was because of his love of them. Rather, he tells his brothers: "I saved life because it was God who sent me... God had sent me [on this errand] to ensure your survival on earth."[173] In other words, Joseph understood what many of us miss in this struggle. Namely, one does not have to choose one's commitment to God over our commitments to people. Because, by loving and serving our fellow man or woman, we are – in fact – loving and serving God.

Allow me to be clear. This does not mean that we are free from coming together in communal prayer and service directly to God in our houses of worship. As they, and these times, are the well from which we draw our strength to serve others. But, what it means is that we cannot forego our relationships with one another, hoping that we can still have one with God. Because the fact is that if we wish to walk hand-in-hand with God, we must also walk hand-in-hand with our neighbors. This is indeed a struggle as the Monsignor mentioned. Yet, in making time for our family, our friends and our neighbors, we are making time for God. In honoring our commitments with those we profess to love, we honor our commitment to God who constantly loves us. May we continue to honor God in these ways, ensuring that His vision – spoken to Jacob – will indeed come true, that we will indeed grow to become "a community of people."

Vay'chi // He Lived
Bite 3 – *A Painful Lesson*

"If you could change one thing about the world, what would it be?" That was the question asked of a long-legged contestant in a national beauty pageant. With a huge smile that stretched from ear to ear, she responded confidently: "Well, to be honest, I would do away with pain." Her response, as one can imagine, garnered much applause. After all, who in this world has not felt hampered or hindered by the aches and pains of life? However, it's unclear whether or not the Bible would join in the ovation.

---

[172] Jane Leavy. *Sandy Koufax: A Lefty's Legacy*. HarperCollins: p. 171
[173] Genesis 45:5 & 7

Because, according to this portion of *Vay'chi*, Jacob actually expends a great amount of his remaining energy wishing some of his children… pain. Yes, you heard me right: pain. In a blessing that sounds unmistakably like a curse, we hear Jacob state to his first born son, Reuben: "You are my might and first fruit of my vigor, exceeding in rank and exceeding in honor. Yet, you are as unstable as water; you shall excel no more." (Genesis 49:3-4) And, it's not just with him. Simon, Levi, Issachar, even the beloved Joseph become slighted in one way or another by the last words of their father.

Is this because, in his old age, Jacob has become an impaired blessor? Believing so, Rabbi Jack Bloom writes: "This was a task he was not up to… There was not one word of blessing for them – cold, accurate, pungent descriptions, yes, but no blessings."[174] Yet, others say, precisely because Jacob knew the character of his children so accurately, his words should be taken – as the Bible portrays them – as blessings.[175] For, in Jacob's life of great ups and downs, he has come to understand pain as the unwanted, but sometimes welcomed teacher, who can transmit valuable wisdom about the future, setting his children up for success.

To be clear, this is not an endorsement of abuse. That type of intentional pain teaches only pain and nothing more. Yet, we are also well aware of another type of pain that comes from the unexpected bumps along life's path: the touch and subsequent burn from a hot pan, for example, which teaches us to be more aware of our surroundings, or the fall into love and subsequent heartbreak, which teaches us to approach matters of affection with great care. These pains, as Jacob imparted, are blessings too, for they not only teach us how to avoid such hurt, they can also teach us how to better deal with pain should it occur again in the future.[176]

Even so, many of us – like the beauty contestant – may wish to avoid such unpleasant lessons. Not simply because we do not want to feel pain, but because of how pain affects and interferes with other parts of our lives. For example, TIME Magazine reports that nearly $60 billion is lost annually from American production due to employees who suffer from chronic pain.[177] That report doesn't even calculate the priceless time lost from family and friends. So, it's not hard – even for the casual pain sufferer – to understand how pain-killers often seem like the answers to our prayers. "Halleluyah! Thank God!"

---

[174] Rabbi Jack Bloom. "Being Blessed is not Enough" *CCAR Journal: A Reform Jewish Quarterly*. CCAR Press: New York, Winter 2003. pp. 29-30. RaSHI also alludes to Jacob's diminished abilities, writing: "Jacob wished to reveal the end [of Days] to his sons, but the immanent Presence of God departed from him, so that he began to say other things to them." [See RaSHI commentary to Genesis 49:1]

[175] Dr. Rabbi J. H. Hertz characterizes Jacob's words as blessings, because "the counsel and benediction which Israel imparts to them (i.e. his children) are such that their descendants have remained 'children of Israel' for all time." [See Hertz commentary to Genesis 49:1]

[176] Thomas Wayne, the father of Batman, once explained this concept to his son in the rhetorical question: "Why do we fall, Bruce? So," continued Thomas Wayne, "we can learn [how] to pick ourselves up." [David S. Goyer and Christopher Nolan. *Batman Begins*. Warner Brothers Pictures: 15 June 2005]

[177] Kathleen Kingsbury. "Millions of Americans in Chronic Pain." TIME Magazine: 2 May 2008. Read more: http://www.time.com/time/health/article/0,8599,1737255,00.html#ixzz1iQoviWiH

we exclaim, in great joy, as we open a bottle of aspirin to swallow down our pain.

Yet, when we do this not for pain-management but for pain-avoidance, we are turning a budding blessing into a certain curse. For, in our pain, the mind, the heart, the soul are all receiving valuable information that something, as we say down here in the South, "just ain't right!" The pain is warning us, it's advising us to alter our current status: whether it's merely our diets, having experienced the pain of eating too much or too little, or whether – as was the case with Reuben – it's a pain delivered from a deficit in our moral character. In other words, if we fail to heed the pain, there is little doubt that we will also fail to heed its lesson, resulting in even greater aches in the future.

That was the painful lesson implicit in Jacob's blessing. With the story of our patriarchs' ending and the story of our enslavement and subsequent Exodus from Egypt just beginning, Jacob wanted *b'nai Yisrael* (the children of Israel) to understand that pain is not the end of life's course; it is merely a pit-stop, encouraging us to make the necessary realignments to ourselves so that we may continue more smoothly along our future path. For even with the bumps and bangs that we will likely experience along the way, we pray that we may not only go from strength to strength, but – with the wisdom gained from those bumps and bangs – we pray that we may also go from pain to strength.

Chazak, chazak, v'nitchazeik!
From strength to strength, we are strengthened!

EXODUS

Sh'mot

Portion 1:
Sh'mot // Names
Torah Portion: Exodus 1:1-6:1

"THESE ARE THE NAMES OF THE SONS OF ISRAEL WHO CAME TO EGYPT WITH JACOB." The book of Exodus, known simply as *Sh'mot* in Hebrew, opens with a recounting of the members of Joseph's family who had migrated to Egypt. However, a new king arose over Egypt, who did not know Joseph, or – more to the point – knew nothing of his deeds in saving the whole of Egypt during the famine.

Thus, any prior goodwill afforded the Israelites on behalf of Joseph's actions is replaced by fear, as Pharaoh grows concerned that the Israelites could one day use the power inherent in their large number to his disadvantage. Therefore, he sets out, not to harm them per se, but to restrain their power. When slavery fails, Pharaoh decrees all male babies to be killed. This plan also fails, because of the midwives – Shiphrah and Puah – who allow the males to live.

At this time, Moses' mother hides him in a basket, which is sent down the Nile; Pharaoh's own daughter saves Moses and raises him as her own. When grown, Moses attacks an Egyptian taskmaster and flees to Midian. There, he aids a group of sisters. In gratitude, their father – a Midianite priest – allows Moses to marry one of his daughters, Zipporah. Later, while serving as a shepherd in Midian, Moses happens upon the Burning Bush. From it, God first speaks to Moses, revealing the Divine Name as "*Eh'yeh-Asher-Eh'yeh* / I Am What I Will Be." (Exodus 3:14)

After several refusals, Moses agrees to be the leader of the Israelites, with the help of Aaron, his brother. The brothers appeal to Pharaoh to let the Israelites leave to worship their God, but Pharaoh responds by increasing the Israelites' workload. The portion closes with the Israelites complaining and God foreshadowing the plagues as a demonstration of God's power, which is greater than Pharaoh's power.

Sh'mot // Names
Bite 1 – *Facing Our Fears*

Wherever you are right now, whatever you're doing… stop! Right now, it's imperative that you sing the following aloud: "When Israel was in Egypt land… *let my people go*! Oppressed so hard they could not stand… *let my people go*! Go down, Moses, way down in Egypt land. Tell ol' Pharaoh… *let my people go*!" Thank you. And, I'd especially like to thank any Decantophobics who may have sung along. Decantophobia, of course, is the fear of singing. Even for those who aren't full-blown Decantophobes, I'd venture to guess that had you been among a group willing to sing along as well, it would have made offering your individual voice a little less intimidating.

That's because Decantophobia – like many fears – is incredibly hard, if not impossible, to face and overcome alone. So, thanks to all who sang along. I'm appreciative not because this song is so relevant to our festival of freedom, which should be honored year round, but because the very act of stepping out of our comfort zones to face our fears is at the very core of our people's triumphant story. What?! You don't think the Exodus is about facing our fears?! Well, obviously you didn't try eating g'filta fish at the Passover seder as a child. Though, if this is not enough to prove my point, fear not. With the help of author Beth Kander, I present some of the phobias in this triumphant and transformative story, which has come to define us as a people: past, present, and future.[1]

For example, take Xenophobia (the fear of strangers). Most explicitly, the dangers of xenophobia are present at the very beginning of the book of Exodus. There we read that "a new king arose over Egypt, who did not know Joseph. He said to his people: 'Behold, the children of Israel! Look how they're flourishing and getting strong. Come! Let us deal shrewdly with them, lest they become more powerful and – in the event of war – join our enemies. For, if they fight against us, they would surely gain control over the region.'" (Exodus 1:8-10) Make no mistake about it. It was xenophobia, the fear of the mass he did not know, that hardened Pharaoh's heart and resulted in our enslavement.

And from this negative example, we gain a positive lesson: DO NOT BE LIKE PHARAOH. In fact, more frequent than "loving God" or "keeping the Sabbath," or refraining from or adhering to any other commandment in the Torah is God's instruction to regard the stranger as the native, "for we were once strangers in the land of Egypt."[2] The great sage Hillel articulated this cumulative lesson of Torah in the following words: "What is hateful to you, do not do to any other. That is the whole Torah; all the rest is commentary. Go and learn it." We learn, because through accumulating knowledge we can

---

[1] Beth Kander is an ISJL colleague, who shared this teaching to the staff in 2012. She has also written a children's book called *Glubbery Gray, the Knight-Eating Beast.*
[2] Exodus 20:22 for example.

confront and combat our fears, telling them what's true and what is merely a manifestation of our minds.

That is, unless that confrontation takes place in public. For the fear of public speaking, Glossophobia, is the number one phobia among all peoples. "What's number two?" you may ask. Death. So, as the great sage Jerry Seinfield pointed out, "that means at any given funeral, most people would rather be in the casket than giving the eulogy." This fear is so prevalent that even Moses, our great leader, experienced it. Having been singled out by God to lead our people to freedom, Moses said: "Oh, Lord, I am not a man of words, neither heretofore nor since You have spoken to Your servant; for I am slow of speech and slow of tongue… Please, O Lord, make someone else your agent." (Exodus 4:10)

How familiar Moses' words must sound to so many of us who have felt the anxiety of being asked to speak in public. "No. Not me. Surely, you can ask someone else." Yet, as we know from the story, there was no one else, as Moses goes on to become one of the greatest leaders the world has ever known. But, how? What caused this transition? Once again, one can say, "knowledge," as Moses' path only begins after he went out to witness the harsh labor of his kinfolk. After all, as was alluded to a moment ago, from knowledge comes familiarity, from familiarity comes comfort, from comfort comes confidence, and from confidence comes a poise and a passion that can truly touch people's souls, transforming a nation.

But, even with his awareness, his understanding, his knowledge, Moses experienced moments of great doubt, moments in which fear crept back in, threatening to drive our redemption off course. So, what happens then? What happens when, in spite of our pursuits of knowledge, fear drives a wedge in our tracks, threatening to derail our train to freedom? Well, then and there we find God or God finds us. Either way, God reminds us, as the Eternal reminded Moses, that we are not alone. We exist in community. And, from that communal existence, comes a Divine strength to help us not only face our fears but rise above them, whether it's Decantophobia (fear of singing), Ranidaphobia (fear of frogs), Nacrophobia (fear of death) or, perhaps the most challenging of all, Eleutherophobia.

Eleutherophobia is the fear of freedom. For our ancestors this fear seemed so real, expressed in their cries to return to Egypt/*Mitzrayim* ("narrow places"). For us, with Egypt long behind us, it is seen in our distress to leave the narrow places that still exist in our lives, places where fear continues to confine us. Therefore, as we recall the betterment which occurred to our people in the past, may we also work at making better our collective present. Let us continue to grow both in knowledge and in community with one another, for in this dual growth comes both the confidence and the strength to face our fears and, with God's help, rise above them. Then, we shall not only celebrate our Exodus from Egypt, but our exodus from fear!

Though once confined by despair...*Let my people go!*
Together we can conquer fear... *Let me people go!*
Go down, Moses, way down in Egypt land. Tell ol', FEAR-O,
'Let my people go!

Sh'mot // Names
Bite 2 – *The Light of our Children*

Once, a bubbie took her two grandchildren to the park, when another bubbie asked the ages of the children. The first bubbie replied, "Well, dear, the lawyer's one and the doctor's three." As grandparents and parents, we have a special gift: the power to see something in our children that no one else can. For example, if our child builds a beautiful Lego house, we can see immediately that he/she will become a great architect. If, however, our child chooses to play with bugs, we are neither discouraged nor disgusted, because we can see that he/she is destined to become a famous biologist. And, if our child just happens to part the water every time he/she enters the bathtub, well then, clearly we can see that our child is going to be a little prophet.

Moses, however, gives no such indication in his formative years... at least not by Biblical accounts. Nevertheless, his mother saw something in him that no one else could see. As we read in this portion, "A certain man from the house of Levi went and married a Levite woman. The woman conceived and bore a son; and when she saw that he was good, she hid him for three months." (Exodus 2:1-2) The rabbis question, "What need is there to say that 'she saw that he was good?'" A mother, after all, would likely hide her child – whether good or not – if threatened. Therefore, RaMBaN teaches, "This statement must mean that she saw in him some unique quality which, in her opinion, foreshadowed the miracles that would later surround him."[3]

The 'unique quality' she saw, as further expounded in the *Talmud*, was "a light, which filled the room the minute Moses was born."[4] No, the midwives – Shiphrah and Puah – didn't accidently shine the exam-light into Moses' mother's eyes. Nor is this light simply the glorious light of joy which illuminates the hearts of all parents the minute their child is born. Rather, it can be explained that this is the light of the child's internal potential, which the parents can readily see, while the rest of the world remains in the dark, unaware until much later.

For that luminous potential to be realized, many parents feel – like Moses' mother – that they must hide their children away, securing them safely from the harsh realities of this world. Assisting us, in what has been dubbed the 'helicopter method of parenting' (since we hover over our children every minute of every day), are such things like Baby Kneepads, Baby Helmets, and

---

[3] RaMBaN's comment to Exodus 2:2
[4] BT Sotah 12a

Kinderkords (a.k.a. "child-leashes," allowing three full feet of freedom before snapping the child back towards the parent). Sure, while some may balk at these measures, it does protect our children from harm. After all, in the context of the rabbinic explanation, our children are like light bulbs, fragile, and therefore must be treated with extreme care.

But, as we can already intuit, if a light bulb remains hidden, surrounded by Styrofoam, stored in a box, and secured safely in a closet, then there's little chance for it to shine at all. By this reasoning, a countermovement of parenting has developed called 'slow-parenting' or 'free-range parenting.' True to its namesake, this mode of parenting is expressed by parents stepping back and being a little slower to respond to their children's needs. As one member of this movement stated, "If you really want your children to succeed, sometimes you have to let them fail."[5] For, only in stepping back, do we give them a chance to step up; from outside our shadow, they can learn, grow, and shine on their own.

> Even Moses' mother seems to have found some merit in this method of parenting, as she eventually abandons her "hovering" – or, dare I say, "hiding" – method of parenting, placing her child in a basket and sending him down river alone. As it is written: Moses' mother let him go "when she realized he [or, in the Hebrew, 'it,' implying 'his potential/light'] could no longer be hidden" from the world. For, it was taught, "There is a time for all things under Heaven... a time to be close and a time to be far away."[6]

But, understanding and embracing that time when our kids must navigate the waters of life on their own, in order to realize their full potential, is not easy. In fact, it's one of – if not – the hardest things we have to do as parents. And, while there's no definitive answer to how we must go about this, a source of comfort can be found from one word in this portion: teivah.[7] It's the name for the basket in which Moses was placed. It also happens to be the name of the ark Noah built.[8] Thus, just as that vessel was steered by God, so too do we – as parents – pray that the Lord will help steer our children through all the waters of life. Thereby, their light, their potential, which we saw all along, illuminating our homes, will be seen by all, illuminating the dark places which still exist in this world. And, should the waters of life turn rough, please remind them dear Lord, as our Divine co-Parent, that we may still be a light to them through our unending love, helping them to see themselves once again to safe shores.

---

[5] Nancy Gribbs. "The Growing Backlash Against Over-parenting." *Time Magazine*: 20 November 2009.
[6] Exodus 2:3; Ecclesiastes 3:5
[7] Ibid.
[8] Genesis 6:4. These two places are the only occurrences of *teivah* in the entire Torah.

Sh'mot // Names
Bite 3 – *Herstory*

"Standing behind every great man, there's an even greater woman." This statement, some will say, is not only old, but outdated, antiquated, clearly ill-equipped for an egalitarian modernity which understands women not simply as equal to men, but sometimes even superior. Take the news reports, for example, which testify that "in 147 out of 150 of the biggest cities in the U.S., the median full-time salaries of young women are 8% higher than those of the guys in their peer group. In two cities, Atlanta and Memphis, those women are making about 20% more!"[9] Yet, despite this and other advances towards genuine equality, this statement – "standing behind every great man, there's an even greater woman" – can still be heard, echoing down the halls of our world. A world, some will say, that may be run by men, but – as we will learn from this portion – is built upon the pivotal role women have consistently played in the course of history (or should we say, "herstory").

Because, at the beginning of our people's story, it's not the men who receive acknowledgment; it is the women, as we read in chapter two of the book of Exodus. A certain Levite "woman conceived and bore a son... She put the child into [a wicker basket] and placed it among the reeds by the bank of the Nile, with his sister stationing herself at a distance to learn what would befall of him." (Exodus 2:2-4) And what was that? Well, according to the story, it is a path only God could have fashioned, as "the daughter of Pharaoh, spying the basket among the reeds, sent her slave girl to fetch it... Taking pity on him...she named [the child] Moses, explaining 'for I drew him out of the water,'" and will raise him to be a prince of Egypt. (Exodus 2:5-10)

From here, we know, Moses goes on to have great success redeeming our people from Egypt. Yet, some will say that success (i.e. our freedom), is not solely his. According to the *Mekhilta*, "the Israelites were worthy of being redeemed precisely because they did not assimilate. Through all the years of slavery, they did not change their names, their language, or their mode of dress."[10] Others, however, say that it was not by the efforts of the entire people that we merited redemption from slavery. Rather, according to the sages, it was only "because of those righteous women," who were mentioned above, "that we – the people of Israel – were redeemed from Egypt."[11]

"Girrrl Power!" roars some members of the feminist movement, who see within these women a stirring example of the great influence women can have in the world, even one so dominated by males. By the way, it's not just these women. From the prophetess Miriam to the former Israeli Prime Minister Golda Meir, from the brave post-exilic Esther to the pioneer of journalism Jane Eisner, from the Israelite Judge Deborah to the modern Israeli Supreme Court

---

[9] Belinda Luscombe. "Workplace Salaries: At Last, Women on Top." *Time Magazine*: 01 September 2010. For more information: http://www.time.com/time/business/article/0,8599,2015274,00.html#ixzz18m5pE0vi
[10] Mekhilta Bo 5
[11] BT Sotah 11b

President Dorit Beinisch, from the Biblical warrior Yael to the Nobel Prize winner for Chemistry Ada Yonath, Judaism has a long and proud history of strong and influential women, whose impact on the world – it can be argued – is on par with their male counterparts.

But, before we get too excited, we are reminded by scholar Dr. Tikva Frymer-Kensky that these Biblical women were powerful not because they broke from their traditional roles, but because they utilized them. Hence why none of their names are mentioned in this Biblical excerpt, but their family roles as mother, sister, and daughter were. Because – as Dr. Frymer-Kensky explains – while slavery turned the realm of men, outside the home, upside down, "the external oppression did not change the lives [of women] in fundamental ways. Certainly, oppression intensified their suffering...but, because women [at this time] were used to ignoring outside events to follow personal imperatives like helping their husbands, protecting their children, and being loyal to their God, these women were able to be proactive and assertive even while the men were passive, reactive, or absent."[12]

Reinforcing the distinction of gender roles may make some uncomfortable; a fair response to be sure, for in our secular culture gender roles have often been used to subjugate women. But, not in Judaism. Even as Judaism has preserved the uniqueness of our different gender roles, it has never confused gender equality with gender homogeneity. A beneficial approach, to be sure, that can be felt in the rise of female rabbis, including the recent Orthodox ordination of Rabbah (the female equivalent to Rabbi) Sarah Hurwitz. Commenting on this new reality, author Anita Diamant, stated: "Many of the ceremonies that have come to bless the women as well as the men of our people, particular those of the *mikvah*, owe a great deal to the insights and efforts of female rabbis who were ordained in the last 30 years."[13] For they have preserved and highlighted a wonderful thread that has always been woven into the fabric of our people; namely, "her" story is integral to "his" story.

Though, let us be clear. "We should not focus on setting and sitting at separate tables," states Rabbi Sandy Eisenberg Sasso.[14] "Ultimately, what we want to do is to bring women's voices and stories to the traditional [male] table of Jewish life." In other words, no longer is it enough to recognize the pivotal role women have had in history with the passive acknowledgement of "behind every great man, there's an even greater woman." Rather, Judaism – while it maintains a gender distinction – envisions women and men standing side-by-side as equal and compatible forces, advancing towards the full liberation of our people in mind, body, and soul. So that together we may, as Moses did standing beside his sister Miriam, sing in one accord: "*Mi chamocha*...who is like you, O' God, who blessed us to be different but valued the same."

---

[12] Tikva Frymer-Kensky (1943-2006). *Reading the Women of the Bible: A New Interpretation of their Stories*. Schocken Books: New York, 2002. p. 32
[13] Penny Schwartz. "Barriers Broken: Female Rabbis Look to Broader Influence." *Jewish Telegraphic Agency* (JTA): 13 December 2010.
[14] First female rabbi ordained from the Reconstructionist Movement of Judaism

Portion 2:
Va-era // I Appeared
Torah Portion: Exodus 6:2-9:35

"GOD SPOKE TO MOSES AND SAID TO HIM, 'I AM THE LORD (YUD-HEY-VAV-HEY).'" The portion begins with the revelation of God's proper Name (i.e. the Tetragrammaton) and a quick recap of the redemption story thus far: the failures of Pharaoh, God's call to Moses, his reluctance to fulfill the mission, and God's marvels to come.

But, before that can happen, a strange confrontation occurs in the night, in which God sought to kill Moses or his son Gershom. Like the night encounter of Jacob, who emerges with renewed purpose as Israel, ready to confront his past (Esau), Moses too will emerge from this nightly confrontation confirmed in his role as Israel's true prophet who will confront his past (Pharaoh).

Thus, the first seven plagues are brought about through Moses and Aaron, each failing to affect Pharaoh's ever hardening heart.

1. God turns the Nile into blood, but Pharaoh's magicians do so as well.
2. God brings frogs upon the land, but the magicians do the same. Pharaoh agrees to free the Israelites if the plague ceases; but, once the frogs die, he refuses.
3. God turns the dust into lice; the magicians cannot.
4. God brings swarms of insects that infest only the Egyptians' homes. Pharaoh agrees to let the Israelites go into the wilderness to sacrifice, but – once the insects were removed – again he refuses.
5. God brings pestilence upon only the Egyptian livestock.
6. God brings boils upon the Egyptians and their beasts.
7. God brings fiery hail upon the Egyptian. Though knowing that Pharaoh still did not fear God, God stopped the hail at Pharaoh's plea through Moses. But again Pharaoh reverted, as God had foretold to Moses.

Va-era // I Appeared
Bite 1 – *To Fear, To Revere, To Relate*

A dear friend, from one of our Southern congregations, recently received an advertisement about a new book. It was called, *Yud-Hey-Vav-Hey: His Hallowed Name Revealed... Again!* According to the advertisement, the book's author – Pastor Keith Johnson (a former chaplain of the NFL's Minnesota Vikings) – challenges a long standing tradition in both Judaism and Christianity regarding the use of the Divine name. The press continued, "Johnson just didn't accept the idea that the Bible would both command believers to hallow the Father's Name [in reverence], but prohibit it from being spoken [out of fear]."[15] A perspective that provoked my friend to ask: "So, really, how do we – Jews – approach God's Name? Are we supposed to fear it or revere it?"

I suppose I could have responded with Hermione's line from *Harry Potter*: "Fear of a name, increases fear of the thing itself."[16] But, that response would have been grossly insufficient for such a great and difficult question. One made even more challenging, to be sure, in light of the accounts of *Va-era*. In this portion, we read about the first seven plagues to be inflicted upon Egypt: *dam*/blood, *tz'fardeia*/frogs, *kinnim*/vermin, *arov*/wild beasts, *dever*/pestilence, *sh'chin*/boils, and *barad*/hail. And, just to be clear, this great devastation – which ravaged Egypt – was brought on by none other than "God, who spoke to Moses, saying unto him, 'I am the Lord (*Yud-Hey-Vav-Hey*). I appeared to Abraham, to Isaac, and to Jacob as *El Shaddai*. But, I did not make Myself known to them by My Name: *Yud-Hey-Vav-Hey*.'" (Exodus 6:2)

Why? Well, suggests commentator Nachum Sarna, it's because "in the ancient Near East names in general, and the name of a god in particular, possessed a dynamic quality and served to express character as well as power. Thus, to say, 'I did not make Myself know to them by My Name: *Yud-Hey-Vav-Hey*,' is to state that the patriarchs – Abraham, Isaac, and Jacob – did not experience the specific power associated with the name *Yud-Hey-Vav-Hey*."[17] They, adds 19th century Rabbi Benno Jacob, "experienced God as *El Shaddai*, a nurturing mothering God, as *Shaddai* may be related to the Hebrew word *shadayim*, meaning 'breasts.'"[18] A fitting attribute indeed for the infancy stage of our faith, but one ill-equipped – many would argue – to deal with the might of Pharaoh. To confront him as well as any modern day Pharaoh, we need to relate to God through God's other attributes, in this particular case: power.

---

[15] "Hundreds of Years of Jewish/Christian Tradition Wrong: Author Challenges Orthodoxy of Not Speaking/Writing the Name of God." *World Net Daily: A Free Press for Free People*: Washington, D.C. 16 December 2010

[16] J.K. Rowling. *Harry Potter and the Philosopher's Stone* (British Ed.). Bloomsbury Publishing: London, 1997. p.216

[17] Nachum Sarna. *The JPS Torah Commentary: Exodus*. The Jewish Publication Society: Philadelphia, 1991. p.31

[18] Benno Jacob (1862-1945), translated by Walter Jacob. *The Second Book of the Bible, Exodus*. United States of America: 1992. pp.143-156

It's a power described all too well in the Torah, as well as in that other great traditional source: *The Ten Commandments*, with Charlton Heston. Depicted in these sources is a power so great that we would have good reason to fear the Name of God. By simply evoking it, one could be put in harm's way, as Moses exclaims: "Ever since I came to Pharaoh to speak Your Name, it has become worse for Your people."[19] But, this fear is not of God. Mostly it's of ourselves, fearing our potential inability to handle the Divine power we call forth. For example, when the Temple stood in Jerusalem, the High Priest of Israel would go into the Holy of Holies on Yom Kippur to pronounce God's Name. But, before doing so, he would tie a rope around his ankle. Because, should he become overwhelmed – even to the point of death – his lifeless carcass could then be retrieved without putting another in harm's way.

Clearly, a lot has changed since then, as you don't commonly see rabbis today stepping out onto the pulpit to lead services with a rope tied around their ankles. Still, there are many Jewish professionals and others who restrain themselves from stating God's Name outright. Instead of saying, "thanks be to God," we say in Hebrew, "*baruch HaShem*" (meaning, 'blessed is the Name'). Instead of saying, "may it be God's will," we say, "*b'ezrat HaShem*," (meaning, 'may it be with the Name's help'). And, in case we may think this is just part of some religious superstition, let me remind you that in our common parlance we resist pronouncing God's Name as well. For example, while it is often considered improper to say "God darn," many people will not hesitate to say "Gosh darn." Instead of saying, "God bless you," when someone sneezes, it has become appropriate just to say: "bless you."

Why? Why do we so often take God's name out of the picture? Typically, today, it's not out of any misplaced sense of fear. Nor is it entirely out of reverence, reserving the utterance of God's Name for only the most sacred of occasions, as was the likely motive for many of the examples above. Rather, from a Jewish perspective, it's because of a fundamental idea that God's entirety cannot be contained in a name. God, as Sarna's commentary alluded to, is manifest through an expansive and varied list of dynamic qualities. In this way, we hold faith with a God who is able to extend far beyond a Divine Oneness to pervade the many places of our world and the many stages of our lives. In other words, by relating to God through an unending list of attributes, we never exhaust the Divine's usefulness. We can turn to God when we need a nurturing Presence. As well, we can turn to that same Oneness when we need a powerful Presence, able to help us oppose the oppressive forces in our lives.

So, really, how do we approach God's name? This is indeed a great and challenging question, one whose answer is as varied as God's qualities are varied. For some it may be with fear. For others, it is to revere. But, at all times, we are challenged – according to our Jewish faith – to relate to God in our own way. For, in God's varied Oneness, there is always a part of God that is open and available to us: a God who can meet us in the varied places and stages of

---

[19] Exodus 5:23

our lives. As such, a more appropriate title for Pastor Keith Johnson's new book may be, *Yud-Hey-Vav-Hey: His Hallowed Name Revealed....Again, and Again, and Again*, as we continue to pronounce this and God's other names, evoking God's power and Presence in our lives, this day and every day!

Va-era // I Appeared
Bite 2 – *Your Quan: The Measure of Your Soul*

Metrics are all the rage these days, as we attempt to quantify the internal quality of everything and anything in this rapidly expanding world. Some believe these quantifiable numbers help us determine what is truly valuable and what is not, thereby saving us limited time and precious energy. But, it's not just things we measure, is it? In an effort to capitalize on our full human potential, we apply these measures to individuals. We use feet to measure one's height, pounds to measure one's weight, units of time to measure one's age, I.Q. points to measure one's intelligence. But, what about measuring the value of one's soul? How do we account for that?

That question likely faced Aaron, elder brother of Moses, in this portion of *Va-era*. Despite being among the leadership of Israel, as they labored in the trenches of Egypt year after year, it was not he who was selected for a battle-field promotion as the Savior of Israel. It was Moses. Aaron, as this portion makes clear, was the enlisted man, responsible for merely following orders. As it is written: "The Lord said to Moses, 'Say to Aaron: take your rod, Aaron;' 'hold out your hand, Aaron;' 'speak Aaron;'" do this and do that, Aaron![20] As such, one can understand if Aaron felt a little undervalued and greatly overworked.

But, lo and behold, the Bible states: "This is the same Aaron and Moses of whom the Lord said, '[They will] bring forth the Israelites from the land of Egypt, troop by troop.'" (Exodus 6:26) What is so unusual about this wording is that the name of Aaron precedes the name of Moses. In most other instances, within the Bible, it's the reverse. Rabbi Moshe Feinstein suggests that occasionally Aaron's name will be mentioned prior to Moses' as a reminder that both were equally valuable in our redemption. For "on God's scale," he writes, "value, the worth of one's soul, is measured only by how well one fulfills one's own personal mission."[21]

Yet, somewhere along life's trek, we lose sight of our mission. As if it were some form of *gematria*, we begin to think of meaning in terms of the numbers on our paychecks, success in terms of the titles before our names, happiness in terms of cushy corner offices with windows.[22] This disorientation may start as early as childhood. The nurse, the fire-fighter, the teacher, the artist we

---

[20] Exodus 7:9, 19; 8:1, 12; 16:9
[21] Rabbi Moshe Feinstein. *Stone Chumash, 11th Edition*. Mesorah Publications, Ltd.: New York, 2000. p. 323
[22] *Gematria* is the exegetical rabbinical process of assigning meaning to numbers.

yearned to be as children is redirected to other aspirations that grown-ups tell us are more valuable. "But honey," caringly stated one parent, "if you work harder, you can become a doctor, a lawyer, a corporate leader, and have anything you wanted. Wouldn't you like that?"

Sure! Who wouldn't? But – even in such blessed positions – if we only gauge our value by these external factors, eventually an unsettling truth creeps into our lives: we have become slaves ourselves. Not to some human taskmaster, as was the case in Egypt. Rather, we set upon ourselves the almighty dollar, which pokes and prods us forward incessantly in spite of our displeasure. And, should we be so fortunate to weather these torrential economic winds that can rip such false measures away in an instant, ultimately we'll become resentful of this self-imposed servitude, screaming – as did Rod Tidwell in *Jerry McGuire* – "Show me the money!"[23]

In fact, we see from Tidwell's story that it wasn't until he rediscovered his *quan* (his greater sense of purpose) did his life dramatically improve. Why? How can the discovery of one's personal mission make such a positive impact? Simple. In finding our purpose – that internal gauge of value – we become empowered to cast off such external taskmasters like money or titles. We become liberated, free to pursue that which truly makes us happy, that which makes us feel truly fulfilled, that which we hold as truly meaningful. That worth weighed on God's eternal scale, taught Rabbi Feinstein, is worth more in the long run than any amount of money.

Surely, Aaron came to recognize this, as he tapped into his Divine gift of speech and leadership, guiding the people spiritually, internally as the High Priest of Israel until the end of his days. So, what is your measure? What special gift did God give you to set you apart, that makes you unique, that makes you of value to your world, your community, your congregation, your family, and – most importantly – yourself? For once you find that measure and mission, that purpose and potential, there's no telling how far your value will stretch. May it and you stretch far and wide, inspiring us all to reach our own potentials and fulfill our own Promise!

Va-era // I Appeared
Bite 3 – *To Break a Heart*

Heartbreak – it's the only heart-condition of which most children are aware. Only later, as we mature, are we alerted to a wide range of other ailments which can afflict the human heart, having disastrous effects on our overall well-being. One, however, will never appear on any medical list though it's equally – if not more – of a threat to our overall health, a condition known as 'hard heart.' First diagnosed by our Divine Doctor (not to be confused with Dr. McDreamy from *Grey's Anatomy*), 'hard heart' is a reoccurring ailment

---

[23] Cameron Crow. *Jerry McGuire*. TriStar Pictures: 1996

which plagues Pharaoh numerous times in this portion. As we may recall from our years spent around the Passover table, the Lord instructs Moses to "Go down…way down in Egypt land. Tell ol' Pharaoh, 'Let My people go!'"[24] But, shortly thereafter, God cautions Moses that Pharaoh may not heed his call for "Pharaoh has a [heart condition, known as] *kaved lev,*" a heavy or hard heart. (Exodus 7:14)

Rarely is this condition, as one scholastic practitioner stated, a good thing, as if it could be mistaken for a "firm resolve." Rather, hardheartedness most often exhibits itself as "stubbornness, insensitivity, arrogance, and inflexibility."[25] If the Divine Doctor's repeated warnings go ignored, counsels RaMBaN: "God may lock the door [of his practice], leaving one to suffer from this sin[ful ailment] forever, without [the needed treatment of] forgiveness."[26] Therefore, Judaism clearly recommends maintaining a soft heart, one that's pliable to the many stimuli of this world. For, through these stimuli, the God who exists out there has a chance to interact with the Divine potential inside each of us; a potential, which Moses taught, is engrained into our very hearts. In the medical journal of Deuteronomy, we read, "The Lord [recommends that you] open," literally "that you circumcise (i.e. remove any barrier between) your heart and the Lord in order that you may live."[27]

Understandably, some of us believe that a soft heart may actually put our lives in greater jeopardy, for then we are vulnerable to hurt. Sentiments to this effect have been captured for generations in the classic Psalms like "Stop! In the name of love, before you break my heart,"[28] as well as the infamous, "Don't tell my heart, my achy breaky heart."[29] And, it is not just from unrequited love. We justifiably worry that a soft heart would make us susceptible to a full range of hurt from those who would pervert God's teachings and take advantage of our open nature. So, whether proactively by being stubborn, insensitive, arrogant, or inflexible, or reactively by relying upon vices like alcohol, drugs, or impulsive eating to numb the pain, we choose to harden our hearts as an act of protection, a sort of self-administered vaccination.

It's a measure of self-preservation we believe will always be within our control, willfully stopped at any time in order to return to the Divine Doctor's recommendation of a soft heart. However, as Rabbi Hillel Silverman once wrote, this belief is a fallacy. "Each time we choose to disobey the Voice of conscience, it becomes fainter and feebler. And, consequently, the human heart becomes harder and harder to reach," until, one day, when we attempt to flex our free will, only to find it unresponsive.[30] This point is well highlighted by Pharaoh, who initially had the will to "harden his own heart," as stated in

---

[24] Spiritual by the Jubilee Singers 1872, based upon Exodus 7:2
[25] Robert Alter. *The Five Books of Moses.* W.W. Norton & Company: New York, 2004. p. 345
[26] RaMBaN comment to Exodus 7:3
[27] Deuteronomy 30:6. Though the Hebrew says "circumcise," most translations read "open."
[28] The Supremes, 1965
[29] Billy Ray Cyrus, 1992
[30] Hillel Silverman. *From Week to Week.* Hartmore House: New York, 1975. p. 57

Exodus 8:2. Though, a chapter later, we simply read "his heart was hardened,' as if to indicate it transpired without Pharaoh's control. (Exodus 9:35)

Uncontrolled and potentially contagious, it is then that RaMBaN envisions God closing the door of His practice to the one afflicted with hardheartedness. At first, this may appear insensitive. But, it is important to note that God did not lock the door. He merely shut it. Why? Because while "one unhealthy act can certainly bring on another," as it is written in *Pirkei Avot*, God is also aware that "one healthy decision can bring on another," leading the way to a *r'fuah shleimah*: a complete healing of mind, body, and heart.[31] All it takes to start the process is one conscious, healthy decision to open the door of our hearts to God. Then the Divine Doctor, who fashioned the human from the clay of the earth (Genesis 2:7), can also practice the skills of sculptor, transforming – with our assistance – the hard granite of our hearts into a smooth work of art.

---

[31] Pirkei Avot (Ethics of our Ancestors) 4:2

Portion 3:

Bo // Go
Torah Portion: Exodus 10:1-13:16

"THEN THE LORD SAID TO MOSES, 'GO TO PHARAOH. FOR I HAVE HARDENED HIS HEART… IN ORDER THAT I MAY DISPLAY THESE – MY SIGNS – AMONG THEM.'" Thus, the bulk of this portion continues where the last one ended, deep into the heart-wrenching plagues (numbers 8-10), which God was forced to deliver upon the Egyptians in order for the Israelites to be set free by Pharaoh.

8. God sends Moses and Aaron to warn Pharaoh of another plague. After Pharaoh agrees to let only the men (as opposed to the entire congregation of Israel) go to worship, God brings locusts. When God removed the locusts, Pharaoh still would not let the Israelites go.

9. God then brings darkness over Egypt, but not the Israelites. In response, Pharaoh agrees to let all the people go, but the livestock should remain. Without proper sacrifices, God hardened Pharaoh's heart once more.

Prior to the final plague, Moses forewarns Pharaoh that all the firstborn males in Egypt will be killed. God then dictates this month as the beginning of the year as well as the laws for the Pesach (Passover) offering on the 14th of the month: it shall be eaten on that night with unleavened bread and bitter herbs. The blood of the offering placed on the doorposts will serve as protection from the Divine plague.

10. During the night, God kills the firstborn Egyptians. In the morning, when Pharaoh hears the cry of Egypt, he immediately releases the Israelites, hurrying them out, with their unleavened dough and valuables from their neighbors. Thus, the Israelites and a mixed multitude left Egypt with their animals. God then dictates the rules for redeeming the firstborn, which are consecrated to God because they were spared.

Bo // Go
Bite 1 – *Letting Go of Control*

You know you're a control freak when, instead of a leash, you walk your dog with marionette strings attached to a puppeteer's control. You know you're a control freak when you point the television remote at your family, press mute, and expect their chatter to stop. You know you are a control freak when you wear a T-shirt that says, "I'm not a control freak. I'm just kindly expecting you to obey me." Finally, you know you're a control freak when – and I'm not naming names here, but – you enslave an entire people for more than 400 years, forcing them to build such garrison cities as Pithom and Rameses.

Okay. You got me. I'm talking about Pharaoh; fitting because – in this portion of *Bo* – Moses continues to help Pharaoh with his control issues by pleading: "Pharaoh, Pharaoh, whoa baby, let my people go! Whoo!"[32] For, God wonders "how long will you refuse to humble yourself? Let My people go," states the Lord, "so that they may worship Me." Even Pharaoh's courtiers begin to grasp the inescapable truth: the time had come for Pharaoh to let go of his control, saying unto him: "How long shall this one be a snare to us? Let the men go to worship their God. Are you not yet aware that Egypt is lost?" (Exodus 10:1-7)

That, identify psychologists, is the real sign of a true control freak. You know you're a control freak when you ignore and dismiss the helpful and insightful words from those you supposedly trust, choosing instead to rely upon yourself and yourself alone. For all that "I-know-best" attitude, taught the sages, what often results is calamities for yourself and others, as was heard in the courtiers' protest: "Are you not yet aware that Egypt is lost?"[33] No. A control freak isn't, not until it's too late. Yet, it's not too late for us. Through this portion, we can learn how to avoid becoming the Pharaoh in our own lives.

This does not mean that we should, as the movie *Eat, Pray, Love* promoted, "let ourselves go."[34] Because, seeking control over our environments is a natural survival instinct, as Maslow pointed out in his 1943 hierarchy of needs. In persistently seeking and obtaining a better understanding – a better grasp – of our world, there is a feeling that we can actually begin to predict the path of its endless variables, thereby directing our lives more soundly and securely therein. Many religious traditions share this perspective as the impetus for our on-going education.[35] Yet, there is only so much of the infinite world that we,

---

[32] These are not the exact Biblical remarks of Moses, but stylized ones from the song "Pharaoh, Pharaoh," written by Steve Brodsky, Ken Chasen and Josh Zweiback.

[33] Dr. J.H. Hertz, the late chief Rabbi of Great Britain, commented on this verse, stating: "Because they were willing to stand up to Pharaoh, their hearts were not as hard as their master," who continued to maintain complete control. [See his commentary on p. 249]

[34] Ryan Murphy and Jennifer Salt. *Eat. Pray. Love.* Columbia Pictures: 2010.

[35] By giving up total control of one's life, that individual is – in essence – giving up their free will, which was a highly stigmatized act in the Biblical world. As we can see in Leviticus 21: 5-6, "If a slave declares, 'I do not wish to go free (i.e. I wish to not be in control of my own life),' his master shall take him before God. He shall be brought to the door or the doorpost, and his master shall pierce his ear with an awl; and he shall then remain a slave for life."

finite beings, can comprehend. Thus, even Judaism appreciates such searches for control as really searches for a _sense_ of control.

That distinction, however, doesn't mean we should stop our attempts. Because, even in obtaining a mere sense of control over our lives, we often acquire confidence, courage, and faith (a little mixture, we call in Judaism, _chutzpah_), helpful in overcoming those countless trying moments of life. Yet, there are some – like Pharaoh – who go about obtaining this measure of control through power and force. These individuals, whether at home or the workplace, reinforce their sense of control through stifling imaginations, restricting choices, ultimately subjugating the free will of others. And, in spite of their efforts, they – like Pharaoh – are often surprised when the still unaccounted and uncontrolled variables of the world begin to plague their lives, building upon one another until all is left in ruin.

That is why, through Moses, God guides us onto a better path. Rather than using power, we can reach a real sense of control in our lives by actually sharing control with others, trusting them, allowing them to accompany us on this journey. As Moses insisted to Pharaoh, "We must all go: young and old, sons and daughters, flocks and herds."[36] As Moses understood it, the variables of this world are too numerous for one person to know and, thus, control. Even those we are aware of often seem too numerous to track. But, when we allow others into – what Jack Byrnes from the movie _Meet the Parents_ called – our "circle of trust," we can actually increase our sphere of influence, not decrease it.[37] In other words, in letting go of control, we actually receive a larger and truer sense of control over our lives.

So may we, attempt to control the control-freak that resides within each one of us. Let us control our inner-Pharaoh, as Zechariah encouraged, "not by might, nor by power, but [may we do so] by spirit alone."[38] For in sharing this spirit, in sharing this sense of control with others, we pray that a sphere of positive influence – born of trust – may increase one day to cover all the earth. And, on that day, dear Lord, our sense of control may yet be realized as Your true control over us all, allowing everyone to live safe, sound, and successful lives.

Bo // Go
Bite 2 – _Coming out of the Darkness of Depression_

Depression, it's a serious medical condition afflicting no less than one in five Americans.[39] According to the National Institute for Mental Health (NIMH), a depressive episode may be triggered by any number of factors, including – but not limited to – a natural disaster, financial distress, loss of a loved one,

---

[36] Exodus 10:9
[37] Jim Herzfeld and John Hamburg. _Meet the Parents._ Universal Studios: 2000.
[38] Zechariah 4:6
[39] CDC. _Treatment Works: Get Help for Depression._ www.cdc.gov/Features/Depression

personal trauma, and, of course, stress.[40] Is there any wonder, then, as images of these triggers are incessantly plastered on the news that experts predict by the year 2020 that depression will be the second most common health problem, not just in America, but around the world?[41]

It's a world that the ancient Egyptians saw firsthand ravaged by a series of events that were out of their control: (1) water turning into blood, (2) swarms of frogs, (3) an infestation of vermin and (4) insects, (5) pestilence, (6) an outbreak of boils, (7) hail which decimated the land, as well as (8) a throng of locusts which devoured anything which the hail had left behind. Only then, as we read in *Bo*, did "darkness descend upon *all* the land of Egypt." Well, that is, with one exception: the area of Goshen, where the Israelites continued – states the Bible – "to enjoy light in their dwellings." (Exodus 10:22-23)

But, how was it that the Israelites enjoyed light while the average Egyptian did not? Unlike the other eight plagues, could not the average Egyptian respond to this one? For example, by lighting a simple candle to dispel the darkness? "Since they did not," answers my former professor, Nachum Sarna, "then perhaps this plague was not a physical darkness caused by God, a sandstorm, or a solar eclipse."[42] Perhaps, instead, it is "a spiritual or psychological darkness…triggered by the realization that their [Egyptian] comfort was dependent upon [the discomfort], the enslavement of the Israelites."[43]

Artfully, Sarna's interpretation transforms an episode of darkness incurred by the ancient Egyptians into an episode of depression suffered by all who witness their world ravaged. It is a metaphor that is particularly poignant, not just for our contemporary circumstances, but for the Exodus events as well. For the text further indicates, immediately after darkness descends, that "the people could not see one another… and no one could rise from where he was." (Exodus 10:23) In its own way, the Torah highlights the real progression of this illness. First, it affects the way we see the world. Then, if left untreated, depression can actually affect us physically, depleting our energy to move.

As if these symptoms weren't enough, a worsening depression can make merely the act of living each day a significant challenge. As one survivor of depression wrote, "At first, it felt like the sun was rising, but little of its light reached me. However, shortly thereafter, I started to sag under a weight that was much stronger than I. Uncontrollably, my ankles twisted, my knees buckled. My waist began to break under a strain I was helpless to withstand. And, in the end, I was compacted… This thing had crushed my world to a circumference of me."[44] Eventually, many who suffer from a worsening depression (often called, "chronic depression"), feel that the only way out is death – the tenth plague.

---

[40] NIMH. *What Causes Depression?* www.nimh.nih.gov/health/publications/depression
[41] PBS. *Depression: Out of the Shadows*. www.pbs.org/wgbh/takeonestep/depression
[42] Lieber, ed. *Etz Hayim: Torah and Commentary*. The Rabbinical Assembly: New York, 2001. p. 377
[43] *Ibid*
[44] Andrew Solomon. *The Noonday Demon: An Atlas of Depression*. Simon & Schuster, 2002. p. 5

Yet there is another way. As many experts purport, a key to unlocking the mental and physical constraints of depression is found within our relationships. I know; the very notion of reaching out beyond our narrowing world even to a close family member or friend – not to mention a therapist or support group – can seem overwhelming. Yet, at these challenging moments, the extension of ourselves is exactly what is needed to halt the progression of the illness. For, when we share our situation with another, we invite him/her into our world, gently expanding its circumference to allow a little light to shine in. Certainly, this must have been what the sages meant when they stated: "only when we are able to recognize the face of our fellow has the light of dawn arrived."[45]

Likely this was how the Israelites continued "to enjoy light in their dwellings," despite the darkness that drenched Egypt. Instead of retreating, each one to his or her own dwelling to ponder such an awe-filled as well as an awful moment alone, the Israelites huddled together. We hear this call for communal support from Moses, who pronounced: "Let us all go, young and old. Let us all go with our sons and daughters, with our flocks and herds; for we [together] must observe this moment of the Lord." (Exodus 10:9) May this call be heard today. When darkness threatens our world, let us not shrink back alone. Instead, let us go out together to face it. Only then will we truly be able to halt depression's progress, seeing our way out of darkness by the light of mutual support.

Bo // Go
Bite 3 – *Reparations: A Resource for the Future*

In 2009's comedy blockbuster, *The Hangover*, one of the main characters somehow misplaces his grandmother's wedding band (which she managed to carry with her throughout the Holocaust). To be clear, this character misplaced it on the hand of an exotic dancer. Ouch! And, when realizing his predicament, he exclaims in horror, "She's wearing my grandmother's Holocaust ring!" To which his dimwitted friend states, "I didn't know they gave out rings in the Holocaust."[46] They didn't, of course. But many of us may still be surprised to learn that, after the Holocaust, the German government gave Israel $1.5 billion, as requested by the then Israeli Prime Minister, David Ben Gurion.[47]

This 1951 request resurrected a long standing debate in Judaism, one originally aired in response to *Bo*. In this portion, Moses and Aaron continue to engage Pharaoh, pleading with him to "let our people go!" As well, we read of the eventual consequences of the remaining three plagues (numbers 8-10), when Pharaoh continues to say: "No. No. No!" This part of the Exodus story is

---

[45] *Babylonian Talmud*, Berachot 9b
[46] Jon Lucas and Scott Moore. *The Hangover*. Warner Bros.: June 2009
[47] David Ben Gurion. *Israel: A Personal History*. Funk and Wagnalls, Inc. and Sabra Books: New York, 1971. pp.399-400

familiar to us. And yet, there is an element of the story that can be and often times is overlooked. Before the final plague, death of the first-born son, God instructs Moses to take gold and silver from the Egyptians. Moses follows God's instructions and "the Egyptians," according to the Bible, "*yishalu*/give objects of silver and gold and clothing" to the Israelites. (Exodus 12:35)

Yet, due to that unusual usage of *yishalu*, Biblical commentators have much to say about these "gifts." Some, like Rabbi Yose, regard them as gracious rewards, "for while the Israelites could have taken advantage of the Egyptians in their days of darkness, they did not."[48] Others, however, disagree. "The silver and gold," comments Rabbi Fields, "were not neighborly gifts, but the spoils of a justified Jewish victory over the Egyptians."[49] And, still others, interpret these gifts as the modern day equivalent to reparations. As the Talmudic sages tell it, "Do the Egyptians not owe the Israelites payment for all their years of slavery?"[50] A reasonable question, indeed; one that may – in fact – give rise to another: "How should we, today, approach the notion of reparations?"

For some, it will be to embrace them. Not out of selfishness or simply for the relief that comes from financial assistance. Instead, the impulse to accept these monies may come out of a sense of, as Tevye from *Fiddler on the Roof* reminds us, "tradition!" After all, citing precedent, these individuals will point out the various times our people accepted monetary compensation for injustices; a system introduced by the rabbis when they read "an eye for an eye and a tooth for a tooth."[51] By their understanding, when someone causes the loss of another's eye, justice does not demand that you take their eye. Rather, justice demands that the guilty party pay the equivalent for a loss of an eye.[52] Speaking to this approach, the 20th century Italian sage, Umberto Cassuto wrote: "The Hebrew slaves had worked for their masters...they were entitled to their freedom and, justice demanded, a farewell payment," as a way to reconcile the past.[53]

But specifically, because of the past, others have voiced hesitancy at best, an outright rejection at worse, in accepting reparations. "It's not just to accept these monies," they will say. "It's an injustice," as those reparations will stand as a constant reminder of the horrific event, tormenting the survivors over, and over, and over again. This position, for example, was voiced by the leader of the Israeli opposition in 1951, Menachem Begin. According to him, the acceptance of these German monies would amount to "the ultimate abomination!"[54] An argument not simply rooted in the past, as many will

---

[48] Mekhilta Bo, Exodus 12:36
[49] Harvey J. Fields. *A Torah Commentary for Our Times: Exodus.* UAHC Press: New York, 1991. p.28
[50] BT Sanhedrin 91a
[51] Exodus 21:24
[52] See RaSHI commentary to Exodus 21:24. According to him, "If he blinded his fellow's eye, he gives him the value of his eye, which is assessed in terms of how much his value was decreased by his blinding... And so, too, all of them [i.e. the limbs and organs mentioned in this verse]. It does not mean the literal taking of a limb of the offender."
[53] Cassuto commentary on Deuteronomy 23:8
[54] David Ben Gurion. *Israel: A Personal History.* pp.399-400

point out that no amount of money can ever truly compensate for the hurt one human being causes another. All the more so, any reparation would pale in light of the immeasurable pain and loss felt by we who survived the murder of six million of our brethren.

Indeed, that's true. No amount of money could ever be enough to make up for the great losses our people have endured throughout history, whether it's the smelting pit of Egypt or the furnaces of Auschwitz. But, maybe we can take a cue from Israel, both past and present. Because, according to the full story, when Ben Gurion asked for $1.5 billion from Germany, he made this request with a calculation that this amount would be "the minimal sum required for the absorption and rehabilitation of half a million immigrants from the countries subjected to the Nazi regime."[55] In other words, what Ben Gurion was acknowledging was a limitation with money. Money cannot heal nor can money change history. But money, he intimately understood as chief entrepreneur of a start-up nation, was a resource that can change the direction of the future.

This debate over the Jewish approach to reparations will likely rage on. For some, their approach will be made with great trepidation, choosing to keep a distance from the event by keeping a distance from the money. Others will embrace the reparations, understanding them as the regrettable but needed steps towards coming to terms with the past. Yet, it seems from the perspective of our history, that in either case reparations are not meant to help us forget about the past, but a way to deal with our future. So, God forbid, should we ever be in the position, may we – like Moses and David (Ben Gurion) – find a way to turn the destructive into the productive, the hurt into healing, the fettered into the free!

---

[55] Ibid.

Portion 4:
B'shallach // He Let Go
Torah Portion: Exodus 13:17-17:16

"Now when He (Pharaoh) let go of the people, God did not lead them by way of the land of the Philistines, although it was nearer…" The portion opens with the first movement of the people in their exodus from Egypt to the Promised Land. As a bit of foreshadowing, God makes clear, that this journey was not going to be a short trip but a long trek, as God leads them roundabout, by way of the wilderness at the Sea of Reeds.

Specifically, God's guidance appears as a pillar of clouds by day and a pillar of fire by night. Between Migdol and the sea, the Israelites encamp by the command of God. Seizing this moment of rest, Pharaoh sets out to overtake them. In fear, the Israelites cry out to Moses. Turning to God for help, God turns back to Moses: "Why do you cry out to Me? Tell the Israelites to move forward as you lift up your staff…" (Exodus 14:15-16)

With Moses' staff raised, the sea splits and the Israelites cross on dry ground. But, when the Egyptians follow, its walls collapse on top of them. The next passage contains the Song of the Sea (Miriam's Song), recounting God's deeds in this harrowing moment. This poem is believed to be, by scholastic reasoning, one of the oldest pieces of Jewish text, showing up artistically within the written Torah.

After travelling for three days with no water, they arrived at Marah, which only had bitter waters, which God turns sweet. As for food, God "rains" *manna* upon the Earth in the morning and quail in the evening. On the sixth day of the week they collect a double portion for Shabbat. At Rephidim, we find the first instance of receiving water from a rock as well as the initial attack of the Amalekites. In this battle the Israelites are successful as long as Moses' staff is raised; God commands that this battle not be forgotten.

B'shallach // He Let Go
Bite 1 – *Wherever You Go, I Will Go*

Many, probably, have never heard of Dr. Mathilde Krim. But, she's part of an esteemed list of individuals that includes but is not limited to Sammy Davis Jr., Jim Croce, Elizabeth Taylor, Connie Chung, and former NFL linebacker Andre Tippett. No, not all of them have earned the Presidential Medal of Freedom for their tireless efforts in AIDS research, as she did. Nor did they all become active members of Irgun (a Jewish resistance movement in Palestine during the 1940's), as she did. However, what they all have in common is equally important and worthy of admiration. They all chose, like our Biblical Ruth, to say: "Do not urge me to leave you or turn back and not follow you. For wherever you go, I will go; wherever you lodge, I will lodge, your people shall be my people, and your God my God.[56]

Ruth's decision to enter Judaism, like so many other Jews-by-Choice, has undeniably influenced the historical path of the Jewish people. Some would say it's an influence felt very early in our collective journey, as far back as "when Pharaoh [finally] let the people go [from Egypt]." (Exodus 13:17) As we read in this Torah portion of *B'shallach*, when the time came for the people to set out from slavery to freedom and eventual redemption in the Promised Land, "God did not lead them by way of the land of the Philistines, although [the Bible explicitly states] it was nearer." Rather, it is written, "God led the people round about, by way of the wilderness at the Sea of Reeds." (Exodus 13:18)

"Why?" we may ask. Why does God insist that the people take the long way around, instead of giving Moses the green light to fast-track the people's redemption to the Promised Land? Well, there are many answers. But, according to Rabbi Shimon bar Yochai, the fabled author of the Jewish book of Mysticism (the Zohar), God instructs Moses to take the long way around, because "the mass of people fleeing Egypt was a mixed multitude. It consisted of Israelites as well as converts;" individuals not born into the Israelite culture, but whom nonetheless chose to follow them in the Exodus from Egypt.[57] Thus, all the people were led the long way in order to allow the newcomers, these Israelites-by-Choice, time to acclimate into Israelite society.

And, no sooner had the people departed did the moaning begin: "Are we there yet?!... I'm hungry. Where's the food? When are we going to stop? I have to use the restroom!" Okay. These weren't their actual words. Nevertheless, those who felt entitled to the short route wasted no time expressing their urgency and anxiety. In a way, one can almost understand their impatience. Especially in our "get 'er done" era, with a "time-is-money" mentality, we can imagine that some within the mixed multitude were just ready to go through the remaining motions of redemption. After hundreds of years of slavery, any detour was likely considered a colossal waste of time, a waste of energy, and a

---

[56] Book of Ruth 1:16
[57] Book of Zohar, 2, p. 45

waste of resources! Not to mention, the longer trek was – according to Maimonides – considerably harder, both physically and psychologically.[58]

It's not like the Israelite-by-Choice would have been ignorant of these hardships that lie along the long path to the Jewish homeland as well as reaching a state of feeling at home within Judaism. Along with witnessing and learning the difficulties facing the Israelite nation, our tradition demands that we warn a potential convert with the words, "Do you not know that at present Israel is sorely afflicted, oppressed, despised, confounded, and beset by suffering?"[59] It's a unique rendition of Jewish history that would likely lead the prospective convert down the first off-ramp on this highway before entering the city limits of conversion. However, Adina Yaffe (a recent Jew-by-Choice) writes, "On the contrary, the more I learned about the long and sometimes difficult path of Judaism, the greater my desire was to join that path and become a Jew."[60]

Given the awareness of the costs, many would consider the choice to continue down the long and more difficult road absurd. But, to those – like our ancestors of old – who chose to join the nation of Israel nothing could be more rational. Not simply because of the old adage that "life is a journey and not a destination."[61] Although, it's interesting to point out that the Torah is more of a journey story than anything else, as it actually ends before the people reach their destination of the Promised Land. But, more to the point, those who make the choice to take the long route to Judaism understand that the rewards of life are directly correlated to the labor exerted in life. As Rabbi Harold Kushner wrote, "Maybe in plane geometry the shortest distance between two points is a straight line. But, in life, the shortest distance between us and our goals can be an indirect, roundabout route."[62] For by this roundabout path we are given the time as well as the opportunity to discover who we really are.

And the results of that discovery have blessed our community time and time again. Each year thousands discover who they really are, entering Judaism by choice and becoming some of the most knowledgeable and active members of the Jewish community. But, as this portion teaches, that should be the goal of every Jewish soul. For God did not separate the Israelites-by-Birth from the Israelites-by-Choice. No. God directs them down one path together in order that we may all learn that Judaism can never be a short stroll down some Philistine beach. Judaism, rather, is an extraordinary exodus through the wilderness of life. So, let us all be – on some level – a Jew-by-Choice. Let us all choose to approach our Judaism every day and with every step. Only then will we be able to rightfully say to one another: "wherever you go, I will go; wherever you lodge, I will lodge, your people are my people, and your God is my God."

---

[58] See *Etz Hayim: Torah and Commentary*. The Rabbinical Assembly: New York, 2001. p. 399

[59] RaMBaM. *Mishneh Torah*. "Laws of Forbidden Intercourse," 14:1; BT Yevamot 47a-b

[60] Allan Berkowitz and Patti Moskovitz. *Embracing the Covenant*. Jewish Lights Publishing: Woodstock, 1996. p. 51

[61] Ralph Waldo Emerson

[62] Harold Kushner. *The Lord is My Shepherd*. Random House, Inc.: New York, 2003. p.73

B'shallach // He Let Go
Bite 2 – *Prayer and Action: A Path between the Currents*

I don't hide it, nor – to be fair – do I broadcast it either. So, when people first learn that I'm a rabbi, their immediate response is to transform me into some sort of priest, confessing: "Forgive me Rabbi, for I have sinned. Because of work, it's been nearly 6 months since my last attendance at synagogue." Momentarily, I contemplate responding with: "Well, my son/daughter, that'll be three hail-Miriams." But, I don't. Because, honestly, I'm wondering: "Why are you asking *me* for forgiveness? Am I the one preventing you from praying?"

Though not from lack of prayer, a similar question was presented by God to Moses in this portion of *B'shallach*. Facing the Sea of Reeds, with the Egyptian army at their backs, our ancestors cried out. "Have no fear!" stated Moses. "Stand by and witness the deliverance which the Lord will work for you today… It will be the Lord who will battle for you, as you hold your peace." "Who? Me?" responded the Lord, surprised. "Why do you cry out to Me? [Am I the one preventing] the Israelites from moving forward?" (Exodus 14:10-15)

Much has been made of this response. Rabbi Yehudah taught that "Nachshon ben Aminadav heeded these words of God by leaping into the sea before it was split."[63] Seeing his faith in action, "God thereupon splits the sea and grants Nachshon's tribe of Judah ruling authority over Israel."[64] To modern Biblical scholar, Nachum Sarna, this was the first ecclesiastical moment of the Bible. Just as there is a time to be born and a time to die, a time to lay roots and a time to uproot, so too is there "a time to pray and a time to act."[65]

Yet, today's trend is to split these two conjoined currents of life into separate sides. On the one side, we have those who become overly dependent upon prayer. When someone is ill and in need of professional medical care, they pray. When someone is acting unkind and in need of reprimand, they pray. When disasters strike and there is a call for help, again they pray and pray and pray. This is not to say that prayer cannot be responsive to both internal and external concerns. I believe it can. But, even some prayer books acknowledge: "While prayer can water an arid soul, mend a broken heart, and rebuild a weakened will, it cannot bring water to parched fields, nor mend a broken bridge, nor rebuild a ruined city."[66]

That is why others feel justified in abandoning prayer for action… the other side of this divided sea. Whether it's for their families or communities, such actions are often equated to the work of God, as if to say – in the words of Rabbi Abraham Joshua Heschel – "[their] feet are praying." Yet, even in the

---

[63] BT Sota 36b-37a

[64] *Ibid*. And his proof text comes from Psalm 114:2-3, "Judah became His holy one and Israel His dominion, the sea saw them and fled."

[65] Ecclesiastes 3; Nachum Sarna. *Etz Hayim: Torah and Commentary*. Rabbinical Assembly: New York, 2001. p. 403

[66] Elyse D. Frishman, ed. *MishkanT'filah: A Reform Siddur*. Central Conference of American Rabbis: New York, 2007. p. 75

noblest of deeds, there comes a point of exhaustion; a point when we are not just physically tired but mentally and spiritually drained. At such points, we may wonder, "how can we be refilled in order to feel fulfilled to move forward?" One answer is, of course, prayer. As WWII Army Chaplain, Rabbi Robert I. Kahn, once taught his soldiers: "Prayer isn't words shouted into an empty void, answered only by its own echo. Prayer is a means to reach that spirit within us, so we may respond to the world."[67]

Life will always require us to move forward. Yet, as we see from this portion, there is little hope of advancement if we rely upon prayer or upon action alone. To do so is really equivalent to getting caught up in a single current of life and dragged down stream, helplessly watching the world pass by. Thus, as it was for our ancestors, so may it be for us. May we strike a balanced approach between the waters: the current of prayer and the current of action. Thereby, through this middle path, we may all reach the dry land of our redemption in peace.

B'shallach // He Let Go
Bite 3 – *A Personal Plea*

In the midst of Haiti's devastating cholera epidemic, a group of American volunteers traveled to the remote and isolated mountain village of Medor on a 12-day mission to save lives. With no easy way in and, as of yet, no way out, this group of brave volunteers parachuted into Medor to treat more than a thousand people suffering and dying from cholera. Also on their agenda was an airstrip. The American team hoped that by building a runway, on this tough terrain, the village would be connected to outside help for more long term support and sustainable care. But, with only days left in their mission and still meters and meters of land left to clear, an obstacle arose.

It was not a boulder or tree that stood in their way; it was a mentality. Demoralized by their situation, the local villagers – assisting in the project – made the fateful decision to give up rather than pursuing a future that seemed uncertain at best. It's a thought many of us may have had at some difficult moment in our lives, and one that would have likely continued in Medor had it not been for a solution – engineered by the team leader – which motivated the workers to continue their efforts. "What was it?" you may ask. Very simply, it was arranging for the workers to have three square-meals a day, something these Americans took, and many of us tend to take, for granted.[68]

Not these Haitians and clearly not our Israelite ancestors either. Similarly calling for a halt in their forward progress, the Israelites shouted: "Was it for want of graves in Egypt that you brought us to die in the wilderness. You should have let us be... for it is better to serve and live than to be free and die!"

---

[67] *Ibid.*
[68] Ann Curry. "Rescue in the Mountains." *NBC, Dateline*: 9 January 2011.

(Exodus 14:11-12) In response, God does not offer immediate salvation in the Promised Land. Instead, their protests – as it was in Haiti – were answered with a deliverance of another kind... food. Yes, as it is written in *B'shallach*, "By the evening you, [*b'nai Yisrael*], shall eat meat and in the morning bread; by this you shall know that I, the Lord, am your God." (Exodus 16:12)

Indeed this food, as well as the knowledge of God as food-for-thought, allowed the Israelites to continue. Yet, some will ask, "How is that possible? How can a mere morsel make such a momentous difference?" These doubtful souls have obviously never gone hungry nor tasted my bubbie's matzah ball soup! Had they, they would have known well the lengths one would go to eat. But this response is more than shaking the proverbial carrot in front of a work horse. "According to the later sages," notes Rabbi Harold Kushner, "the Israelites' lack of food was a metaphor for their lack of Torah, the substance which will come to nourish their lives."[69] In other words, by receiving food (i.e. having a basic need met), the individual is free to focus their efforts on the larger issues at hand.

Yet, too often we misinterpret the protest of the poor, the whimpers of the weak, and the hankerings of the hungry. We take their muted calls for help as some personal attack on those who happen to have their fill in life. This misinterpretation, sadly, even occurred with Moses. After enduring the people's repeated complaints, Moses becomes unhinged: "Why do you quarrel with me!"[70] This, notes RaMBaN, happened because "previously the people only criticized their situation, not Moses. But here [Moses felt as if] they were quarrelling with him, stating: 'If we die, our blood will be on your hands!'"[71]

And, certainly, nobody wants that. But rather than prevent the hurt by helping, so often we shift the responsibility. We take it off ourselves and place it upon the one who is suffering. Yeah, you heard me right. We actually blame the individual for his/her dilapidated state with sentiments like: "you only have yourself to blame" and "help comes to only those who help themselves." It is not that there isn't a grain of truth in these words. In some degree, we all must take responsibility for our own lives. The Haitian villagers did so, for example, when they participated in their own recovery. And, the Israelites were instructed as such, in this portion, when God said: "By doing what is right, then your wellbeing will be secured."[72]

But, to leave the recovery process up to these individuals alone would be tantamount to putting a stumbling block before the blind.[73] And when they fall, which they likely will, they will bring us down with them. Thus, there is no other option than to take their calls for help personally. Not as a personal attack, as Moses misunderstood it. But, as a personal plea, one that expresses

---

[69] Harold Kushner, ed.. *Etz Hayim: Torah and Commentary.* The Rabbinical Assembly: New York, 2001. p. 413
[70] Exodus 17:2
[71] RaMBaN commentary to Exodus 17:2
[72] Paraphrase of Exodus 15:26
[73] Leviticus 19:14

our needs as much as it expresses their own. Responding to a question about why she would go to such lengths to help a stranger, one volunteer said, "I was not helping them. I was helping myself. As an immigrant to America from a torn nation, I heard in their cries my own cry for help."[74]

Therefore, let us be reminded from these volunteers as well as our Divine guide in the wilderness that, as members in a communal society, we have a responsibility to help remove the barriers that stand between the poor and the rest of society. This isn't as selfless as it sounds. For as the sages acknowledged in response to this portion, helping someone take care of their basic needs frees them to focus on the larger matters of society. For when they don't have to worry about from where their next meal will come, where they are going to lay their head at night, or how they are going to take care of those they love, then they are free to engage themselves fully in society. And, in that engagement, we all stand to be delivered to a better state of existence, a promised state where "truth and kindness shall meet, and justice and mercy embrace."[75]

[74] Curry, "Rescue."
[75] Psalm 85:11

Portion 5:

Yitro // Jethro
Torah Portion: Exodus 18:1-20:23

"JETHRO, PRIEST OF MIDIAN, MOSES' FATHER-IN-LAW, HEARD ALL THAT GOD HAD DONE..." This portion opens with Jethro's visit to Moses upon hearing that the Israelites were safe. Moses welcomes Jethro, Zipporah, and their sons Gershom and Eliezer, retelling all that God had done. Jethro responds by acknowledging God's power and sacrificing to God.

The next day, Jethro sees how the community functions and questions Moses' leadership. After all, "Moses would sit as magistrate among the people, while the people stood about Moses from morning until evening." (Exodus 18:13) In observing this, Jethro encourages Moses to delegate his responsibilities as judge, so as not to become too weary. Moses heeds Jethro's advice, sharing the burden of leadership by setting judges over groups within the community to judge smaller matters, while keeping for himself the task of judging larger cases and teaching the Law to the Israelites.

The Israelites then arrive at Sinai, where God reminds them of all that God has done and brings them into the Covenant once again, a recommitment ceremony. The Israelites thereupon receive the instruction to prepare and purify for this ceremony, where God will reveal the marriage contract (i.e. the Eternal Covenant/*B'rit Olam*) begun with the first Ten Commandments (i.e. the Decalogue).

This moment has all the glamour one would expect from such a high-profile wedding. There's thunder, lightning, fire, smoke and the sound of the *shofar*. God appears at the *chuppah* (the wedding canopy) of Mt Sinai, waiting for the bride, Israel represented by Moses, to ascend. The Israelites, in awe of God's power, prefer to hear the words through Moses than directly from God. The people agree to the Covenant and, in the final verses of the portion, Moses receives the laws for building appropriate altars to God.

Yitro // Jethro
Bite 1 – *Display the Decalogue*

"Hear me! Hear me, O Israel!" heralds Mel Brooks, playing Moses in the classic comedy *History of the World – Part 1*. Stepping down from Mount Sinai, with three tablets in hand, Brooks continues: "The Lord has given unto you these fifteen… oy!" exclaims Brooks, as one of the three tablets slips from his grip to shatter at his feet. With two tablets remaining, Brooks attempts to cover his blunder: "…these ten, ten commandments for all to obey."[76] Whether it's in the movies, or in our houses of law and worship, or even outside a mattress store in Ridgeland, MS, the two tablets of the Ten Commandments are arguably among the most recognizable symbols in all the world.

To be fair, this public recognition did not happen by chance. Rather, according to this portion of *Yitro*, a public display of the Divine Law was a deliberate part of God's marketing strategy. Sparing no expense on theatrics like smoke machines, pyrotechnics and noise makers, "the Lord descends upon Mount Sinai, calling for Moses to ascend to the very top of the mountain. [Of course,] Moses went up." (Exodus 19:18-20) Because, from this very public place, the Lord would speak the words that would form the basis of our beliefs, the foundation of our faith, the roots of our religion, the core of our culture, the substance of our society: the Ten Commandments, inscribed publically on two tablets of stone.

But "why," question the sages, "was the Torah given publically in the wilderness and not more privately in the Land of Israel?" How exactly does Mount Sinai help facilitate the fulfillment of God's vision of a world at peace? "Mount Sinai is a place owned by no one," taught 2nd century sage Rabbi Ishmael. "Had Torah been given in the Land of Israel, then it would have been possible for the Israelites to say to the nations of the world: 'You have no portion in it.' But, as it was given in the wilderness, publically and openly, anyone desiring to accept it was free to do so."[77] Thereby, we come to understand today that a public presentation of the Ten Commandments is pivotal to the Divine plan of peace.

However, even those who agree with this teaching are uncertain as to where a public display of the Decalogue should take place. On the one side, there are those who argue that since the first three of the Ten Commandments refer explicitly to an individual's relationship with God, then – in accordance to our nation's policy of separating religion from state – the only fitting place for such a display would be within our community houses of worship.[78] In fact, beyond affixing replica tablets to our Arks and sanctuary walls, many congregations once crafted their windows with arches to resemble the tablets of the Ten

---

[76] Mel Brooks. *History of the World – Part 1*. 20th Century Fox: 1981.
[77] Mekhilta de-Rabbi Ishmael. Tractate BaChodesh, parasha 5. (Lauterbach. JPS Classic: p.318).
[78] For more information on this, see
http://www.adl.org/religious_freedom/resource_kit/ten_commandments.asp

Commandments, reminding the worshipper that their words – uttered in here – must also extend out there.

Indeed, on that basis, the other side of this debate argues that the Ten Commandments have a rightful place outside our congregations, whether it's in our schoolhouses or our courthouses. This isn't simply a nod to history, as if to show some deference to the Biblical roots of our modern legal system. Rather, as a majority of the Ten Commandments speak to universal mores (i.e. not murdering, not stealing, not slandering, etc.), there are those who believe more public displays of the Decalogue could only help our society act – not more religiously, but – more humanely. Observing our predicament, French Nobel Laureate Anatole France once humorously quipped: "America, where 40 million laws reinforce just Ten Commandments!"

And, in all likelihood, there will continue to be more and more laws crafted for just that purpose. Why? Why aren't the current laws enough? Well, it's not from a lack of displaying the Decalogue in public places; the real problem is the lack of displaying the Decalogue in public _people_. Not just in our politicians or our celebrities, but all of us are in some way public people and, thus, it becomes incumbent upon us to display the Ten Commandments in each and every one of our actions. As God declared to our ancestors, "In obeying Me, in keeping My Covenant, you shall be a treasured possession…a kingdom of priests."[79] And, what more is a priest than a physical reminder, a physical representation of the holy, the sacred, the most humane in action.

> In early 1943, Armin L. Robinson – an Austrian publisher – conceived an idea from a visit with Hermann Raushning (an early denouncer of the Nazi Party). The idea was to get ten internationally recognized authors to write ten short novels, each illustrating one of the Ten Commandments. Fittingly titled *The Ten Commandments*, the book was meant to indict Hitler's career of breaching time and time again the moral sanctions of a humane society.[80]
>
> Thomas Mann, another Nobel Prize Laureate, who fled Germany after the rise of Hitler, contributed the story for the first of the Ten Commandments. In his usual ethereal, mystical prose, Mann describes how Moses must have helped God formulate the Decalogue atop Mount Sinai. Moses, Mann relates, after jabbing and chiseling, after scraping and smoothing the two tablets, then hacking and engraving the letters, paints them with the blood coming from his own hands.
>
> "Here me! Hear me, O Israel! This is the blood of our ancestors," he said. "Take them! Hold them sacred…by your actions! For here is briefed what shall bind you; here is the Divine condensation; here is

---

[79] Exodus 19:5-6
[80] Armin L. Robinson, ed. *The Ten Commandments: Ten Short Novels of Hitler's War Against the Moral Code.* Simon and Schuster: New York, 1943.

the rock of decency... Into the stone of the mountain did I engrave the ABCs of human behavior, but it must be engraved also into your flesh and blood, O Israel."[81]

To be sure, there is no better way to display the Decalogue, no better presentation of God's Ten Commandments than to see those Divine words pulsing like blood through our veins, moving our flesh to action. So, may we continue to heed that lesson. May we focus a little less on inscribing God's words on the doorpost of our houses and on our gates (i.e. public buildings). Rather, may we focus a little more on binding them as a sign upon our hands (i.e. upon our very person), allowing them to be a symbol before our eyes and before the eyes of all who meet us.[82] For then, we pray, not only will the two tablets of the Ten Commandments be among the most recognizable symbols in all the world, but – with God's help – they may be among the most adhered to symbols as well.

Yitro // Jethro
Bite 2 – *WikiLeaks: Sinai Edition*

A revelation has come to ROCK our world... and, surprisingly, it's not Sinai! No, the revelation of which I speak is WikiLeaks. With literally hundreds of thousands of pages of information once deemed secret now revealed, reports project that the consequences of this revelation can and has already put hundreds of lives in danger and will deeply impact foreign relations around the globe.[83] Yet, despite this warning, Julian Assange – the founder of WikiLeaks – and his supporters continue to espouse their right, nay, their obligation to publish the truth.[84] "I don't understand the problem," charged one of his supporters. "How can revealing the truth be bad?"

It's an honest question, to be sure, and one which may be answered by looking at the prime example of revealed truth – the Revelation at Sinai – in this Torah portion of *Yitro*. After Moses, with the help of his father-in-law Jethro, set up a system of governance for the wandering Israelite nation, we read that the Lord came down upon Mount Sinai, where He spoke to Moses, saying: "I am the Lord, your God, who brought you out of the land of Egypt, the house of bondage. And, you shall have no other gods beside Me, nor shall you make for yourself sculpted images... nor [even] swear falsely by My name... And, you shall remember the Sabbath day and keep it holy." (Exodus 20:1-11)

---

[81] This excerpt comes from the Wartime Sermons of Rabbi Richard C. Hertz, maintained at the Jacob Rader Marcus Center of the American Jewish Archives in Cincinnati, OH. Collection #67, folder 5. Rabbi Hertz originally delivered the sermon at Ft. Ord in California on 2 June 1944.
[82] Deuteronomy 6:8-9
[83] Scott Shane and Andrew Lehren. "Leaked Cables Offer Raw Look at U.S. Diplomacy." *New York Times*: 28 November 2010.
[84] Howard Chua-Eoan. "WikiLeaks Founder Julian Assange Tells TIME: Hillary Clinton 'Should Resign.'" *TIME* Magazine: 30 November 2010.

Thereupon, it is not just the remainder of the Ten Commandments that God goes on to reveal to Moses. (Exodus 20:12-14) According to some views of Jewish tradition, at that very moment on Mount Sinai, God reveals to Moses the whole of the Written Torah (i.e. the Five Books of Moses, the Prophets, and the later Writings) as well as the complete Oral Torah (i.e. the *Mishnah*, the *Talmud*, the codes of Jewish Law, etc.) And, similar to WikiLeaks, this enormous cable of information – as it was recorded in *Pirkei Avot* – was quickly transmitted from "Moses to Joshua, from Joshua to the Elders, from the Elders to the Prophets, from the Prophets to the sages of the Great Assembly" and eventually to the entire world.[85]

"And, what's wrong with that?" you may ask. Well, honestly, nothing. As a people who have based our very survival on the pursuit of hidden truths, we know intimately well the importance of disseminating knowledge. And, it's not just us. Every culture which has or will make an impact on this world knows – through our example – that success as a nation depends upon the education of the individual. Plato understood this principle of knowledge as the key to free the fettered.[86] According to him, most people live their lives chained in a cave, with their conception of reality mounting to little more than faint and passing shadows reflected upon the wall. And, if they ever hope to make a difference in society, they must move towards the light of truth.

"But," writes Plato, "what if one should be forcibly dragged out to the light?" as one may argue was the case with WikiLeaks. "Wouldn't he be distressed," Plato continues, "and unable to see?"[87] With the help of Plato's rhetorical question we move beyond the all too common debate between "rights and responsibility," between "I *could* do this, but *should* I do this" dilemma. For when it comes to knowledge, there can be no question. It must be shared. But, the question that remains is... *how*? How can we transmit that knowledge responsibly? For, if done too quickly, or all at once, we – as the character in Plato's analogy – may end up blind. And what should have helped us rise to greatness, could result in our fall down the mountain.

So, to ensure that the revelation of truth is a blessing rather than a curse, it should behoove us to move more gradually towards the light. This concept is not foreign to Judaism. Fortunately, for us, many Jewish thinkers have formulated the concept of revelation as a gradual process. For example, take the writings of Hermann Cohen, who taught that God revealed His truth by instilling His Divine genius in man and, through this faculty, we can gradually come to comprehend a measure of Divine logic and ethics through nature and history.[88] And though "these truths will always be culturally conditioned,"

---

[85] *Mishnah*, Pirkei Avot 1:1
[86] See Plato's Allegory of the Cave in his work, *The Republic*. It is written as a fictional dialogue between Plato's teacher Socrates and Plato's brother Glaucon, at the beginning of Book VII (chapter IX in Robin Waterfield's translation: 514a–520a).
[87] Ibid. 516a
[88] Hermann Cohen. *Die Religion der Vernunft aus den Quellen des Judentums*. Gustav Fock: Leipzig, 1919. pp. 82-92. See also the interesting analysis in *Encyclopedia Judaica*, vol. 14. "Revelation." Keter Publishing House: Jerusalem. 1972. pp. 117-126

notes Dr. Robert Gordis, "they are nevertheless parts of God's ultimate truth."[89]

Thus, we have arrived at an answer to that question which was proposed by the supporter of Julian Assange: "How can revealing the truth be bad?" An answer: when the revelation of truth is presented as a one-time event. For such a large amount of information will likely result in sensory overload, putting people's lives in real danger. However, when we approach our right, nay, our obligation to transmit the truth through a gradual revelation of knowledge, well then, we give people the time necessary to adequately adjust to their new concept of reality. And thus, we pray, that information will transform our world, being a blessing not a curse, used for life and not for death. May we continue this progressive approach to revelation, which started with Moses and continues with us today.

Yitro // Jethro
Bite 3 – *The Greatest Generation*

Undoubtedly, many of our thoughts over these past few weeks have been occupied with one thing and with one thing only… No, not the New Orleans Saints and their bid to be Super Bowl champs (although our prayers are certainly with them). Rather, our thoughts and prayers have been directed towards Haiti and the earthquake which shattered that nation, leaving many of its citizens in shambles. However, just this week we received news of a miracle! A full half month, fifteen days, after the initial earthquake a teenage girl was pulled out of the rubble alive! And, thank God she was, for as ABC reporter David Wright poignantly stated: "In addition to medical supplies, food, and water, Haiti is badly in need of miracles!"[90]

But, who isn't? I mean, with all due deference to the Haitian people and their plight, how long has it been since any of us have seen a real miracle like the pillar of smoke that protected the Israelites in the desert by day or the pillar of fire whose light guided them at night? You know, grand miracles, like the splitting of the sea or the one we read about in this Torah portion of *Yitro*? As it is written there: "All the people witnessed [something miraculous]: thunder, lightning, a blare of a horn, [all on top of] a mountain which was ablaze." (Exodus 20:15)

According to tradition, it wasn't just the ancient Israelites who witnessed this miracle on Mount Sinai. "Even those not there that day," as Moses recounts later in the Torah, beheld God's miraculous powers displayed atop the mountain.[91] And let us not think that 'those not there' simply implies some straggling group of young Israelites who were fashionably late to the party. For,

---

[89] Robert Gordis, chairperson. *Emet Ve-emunah: Statement of Principles of Conservative Judaism*. JTS, RA, and The United Synagogues of America: New York, 1988. pp. 19-20
[90] ABC *World News Tonight*. "Miracle Rescue." 28 January 2010
[91] Deuteronomy 29:14

RaSHI comments that "these words – 'those not there' – refer to future generations yet to be born;" individuals like you and I, who should feel as if we too stood at Sinai.[92]

But, what RaSHI doesn't tell us is that there are varying opinions regarding the significance of where we stand (i.e. our distance) in relation to Sinai. By Orthodox standards, the greatest generation is the one who stood closest; in this case, the ancient Israelites. Since then, each successive generation "has been falling back, standing at a [growing] distance [from God]." (Exodus 20:15) As a result, God's word has needed to be pushed back through the generational lines until it finally reaches us, way back in the last row. This may seem inconsequential. But, to an Orthodox perspective, each time the message is transmitted – like a childhood game of telephone – God's word becomes susceptible to distortion.

Which is why, in the Jewish practice of mysticism (called *kabbalah*), every generation since Sinai is inspired to regain the distance created between Israel and God. Only by shortening that distance can we hope to receive the most pure form of God without the additives from other generations. "This principle task, [coined *devekut* in Hebrew], comes from the Biblical commandment – 'Thou shall cleave/*davok* to God.'[93] It is," writes the 12th century Kabbalistic rebbe, Yitzhak Nehor, "a central principle of Torah and of prayer, bringing one's thoughts close to God, conjoining our world with His."[94]

Yet, before we rush out to buy the superglue needed to complete that endeavor, I have come to believe that this is not our true task. For, we are not the ones who have backed away from God. God, likely, is the one who has gradually backed off of us. This Divine move is consciously enacted, as evident in God's steady transition from the grand miracles of the desert to the small miracles we experience in our daily lives: having clothing to protect our bodies, shelter to cover our heads, and food to satiate our hunger. While we may be inclined to interpret this move as a punishment, the *Talmud* reminds us that "the small act of providing food is as great of a miracle as splitting the sea."[95]

The difference between those earlier ostentatious miracles and God's later modesty is that small acts of God allow for greater acts by people. In other words, by moving backwards, God is granting us room to move forward, realizing our full potential to be miracle makers of our own. This isn't simply what Paula Abdul sang about in the 80's: "[We] take two steps forward while [God] takes two steps back."[96] More to the point, it's what Dr. Phil preaches: "If you need a miracle, be a miracle!"[97] And a miracle we were. For what was

---

[92] RaSHI (Rabbi Shlomo Yitzaki, 1040-1105) comment to Deuteronomy 29:14
[93] Deuteronomy 13:5
[94] Yitzhak Saggi Nehor - Quoted by Gershom Scholem "Kabbalah: The Mystic Way." *Encyclopedia Judaica*, vol. 10. Keter Publishing House: Jerusalem, 1972. p. 623
[95] BT Pesachim 118a
[96] Paula Abdul. "Opposites Attract." Forever Your Girl. 1988
[97] This line can be heard in the opening sequence to the Dr. Phil show.

miraculous in Haiti was not solely that God sustained a young girl in the rubble for 15 days. What was equally as miraculous was that God did not need to do it for a sixteenth day, as it was people – like you and I – who became miracle workers, bringing a little girl alive out of the rubble.

Such miracles can and should be the case every day, all over the world. We cannot wait around for God to save humanity. Rather we must realize our own strength to pull humanity out of the rubble, to capitalize on our potential to deliver our people to a better state of existence. When this occurs, when we act in accordance with the Divine image in which we were first cast, when each of us creates miracles in our own lives as well as in the lives of others – whether friend or foe, whether familiar or unknown – then no longer will the greatest generation be the one that stood that day, long ago, at Sinai. Instead, the greatest generation will be the one who is standing here today.

Portion 6:
Mishpatim // Rules
Torah Portion: Exodus 21:1-24:18

"THESE ARE THE RULES THAT YOU SHALL SET BEFORE THEM."
This portion details (as its name suggests) laws for the
Israelite community, which roughly can be categorized
topically.

The first group of laws (21:2-11) concern slavery and the
release of slaves. The next set of laws (21:12-36) regards the
punishment for various injuries imposed by an individual or
their animal against another individual or their animal. The
third section of laws (21:37-22:14) deals with property law.
The portion moves from civic law into laws governing moral
behavior (22:15-23:9). The fifth section (23:10-19) pertains
to ritual observance and "cultic law," including the
command to celebrate the three festivals: Passover, Shavuot
and Sukkot.

As the chapter concludes, God provides a synopsis of what
will happen as the people enter the Promised Land: an angel,
a plague and God's terror will go before the people and the
inhabitants of the land will be overtaken and driven from the
land. Moses repeats to the people all that God has said, and
the people affirm the Covenant and offer sacrifices to God.

In the final verses of the portion, Moses, Aaron, Nadav and
Avihu (two of Aaron's sons) "behold God" and Moses
ascends the mountain to receive the tablets with the
teachings and commandments that God will inscribe. The
portion concludes with Moses' ascension into the fiery cloud
and remaining on the mountain forty days and nights,
leaving Aaron and Hur in charge of the people in his absence.

Mishpatim // Rules
Bite 1 – *The Domino Defense*

In this era of high tech toys, some of us may have forgotten many of those low tech favorites: jacks, tiddlywinks, marbles, pick-up sticks, and my personal favorite...dominos. Okay, I was no Robin Weijers (a.k.a. "Mr. Domino"), who set a world record in 2009 by toppling 4,491,863 dominos in one giant course.[98] But – in my childhood mind – I was equally as crafty, spending hours upon hours engineering elaborate and ordered courses around my room. And, on one particular occasion, just as I was nearing the completion of an exceptionally complicated set-up, one of my brothers barged into the room. Knocking into just a few dominos sent the entire design into motion prematurely. Angered, I released a fury of emotions. But rather than accepting blame, he absolved himself by saying: "Geez, Marshal! It's not like I meant to do it."

"Uhhgg!" I exclaimed, in my best Charlie Brown impression. For, in that heated moment, my brother's argument of "no-intent" rather than "ill-intent" seemed like a weak defense. Even today, when we hear people insist on their innocence because they had no intent behind the resulting action may make us similarly cringe. Yet, this defense is not without potency or precedent. On the heels of the Ten Commandments, we read in *Mishpatim* a series of laws, commonly referred to among Biblical scholars as *Seifer HaBrit* ("Book of the Covenant"). Included among these Divine judgments is the following legislation: "He who fatally strikes a human soul shall be put to death. But, if he did not do it by design [i.e. he had no intent], as it came about by an act of God," so stated the Lord, then "I will assign you a place to which he can flee." (Exodus 21:12-13)

And, the sages of our people further clarify this defense. For example, according to Biblical scholar Nachum Sarna, "The reference in these verses is to homicide. Where malice aforethought has been established beyond question, the act is considered murder and capital punishment must be carried out. However, unintentional homicide should be treated differently from murder. Because, in a civil society, crime is punished by the state, not by means of private vengeance. And thus these measures," surmised Sarna, "were designed into the Covenant to protect the innocent manslayer and allow the established legal procedure to take its course."[99] In other words, if we wish to have a civil society, the one who committed a crime without intent cannot and should not be held to the same standard of responsibility as the one who criminalizes intentionally.

---

[98] For more information on Robin Paul Weijers and his previously held records, check out www.dominodomain.com

[99] Nachum Sarna. *The JPS Torah Commentary: Exodus.* The Jewish Publication Society: Philadelphia, New York, Jerusalem, 1991. pp.121-122

Yet, in that leniency, some will hear complete absolution, as they transform themselves into the reggae star Shaggy, singing: "It wasn't me!"[100] And, not only do they sing of their own innocence, they will also chant of another's guilt. It was the crazy lone gunman, the hyperbolic speech of the media, the music, the drugs. That's at fault; not themselves. Some will even attempt to pass off responsibility onto God. And though it may be hard to say, sometimes there is a grain of truth in that perspective. Even the great sage RaSHI would agree. Reading the selected text above literally, he understood that "God's hand was involved in the death, relinquishing the individual of guilt," as he was nothing more than the unwitting accomplice in God's elaborate design.[101]

Well, with all due respect to this intellectual heavyweight in our tradition, that is not the only way we may understand the dynamics at play. Rather than seeing God's hand as intimately involved in every aspect of our lives (though that may legitimately bring some of us comfort), one can also understand that the "God element" indicated in the text is indicative of those unknown repercussions that are inherent in every action of human life. For an allegory of this teaching, one need only to look back at that childhood game of dominos. Like dominos, God – at the beginning of creation – set out an elaborate and ordered design to preserve life. Though, when that order is disrupted, when we act outside those Divine guidelines (whether intentionally or not), we may set into motion a series of events that could eventually lead to another's fall.

In light of this Divine involvement, we may reasonably question then: "Does that mean that I am absolved of responsibility?" Or, to say it another way, just because I was not the one to hold the gun, does that then mean that I hold none of the guilt? Well, according to the 15th century sage Sforno, the answer would be definitely "no." As members in a communal society, we always carry the weight of others with us. Their involvement in the course of our individual actions (the "God element"), may help take some of the burden of responsibility off our shoulders. But, let us be clear, a measure of it will always remain with us. For "even the unintentional killer," continues Sforno upon reflection of this portion, "is exiled to a place in order to atone for his iniquity."[102]

So, then, we are left to ask: "How do we atone for the unknown?" Well, it is not, as my brother did, to simply say that "I did not intend, thus I did not offend," and continue to stand back and watch the dominos of life fall. Rather, in that moment, we must realize that there is still a role to play. Not just as the unintentional instigators of evil, we can also be the intentional instigators of good. As the sage, Ben Azzai, stated in Pirkei Avot: "*Mitzvah goreret mitzvah, aveirah goreret aveirah.*"[103] That is to say, just as one evil can lead to another, which can lead to another, which can lead to another (even if committed unintentionally), so too can one solitary good deed lead to another, which can

---

[100] Shaggy. "It wasn't me." *Hot Shot*. MCA Records: 2000.
[101] RaSHI commentary to Exodus 21:13
[102] Sforno commentary to Exodus 21:13
[103] Pirkei Avot 4:2

lead to another, which can lead to another (especially when it's intentional). And so, may we continue to focus our efforts to be the instigators of this positive counter movement, which may – we pray – help us to properly atone for the unknown as well as halt the progress of evil in our world.

Mishpatim // Rules
Bite 2 – *Pardon Me: Navigating the Intersection of Justice and Mercy*

What must a society have to function well? That enduring question has plagued human beings ever since we first realized that our survival was contingent upon the survival of others. Because, even in establishing a communal existence, challenges remain, particularly when individual paths cross and intersect. In those moments of intersection, life holds great potential for either a painful collision or a pleasurable cohesion. So, how do we achieve the latter and not the former? What must we have to achieve a good, strong and stable society?

For some, the answer to this question rests in obtaining a strong communication system and a stable transportation system. For others, it's in establishing a strong education system and a stable health system. And still, for others, it's in achieving a strong military and a stable economy. Well, not according to the Bible. For the Bible, a strong and stable society simply comes from "justice" and "mercy," as all other societal factors can be contained therein. As the prophet Micah famously instructed: "God has told you, O man, what is good and what the Lord requires: 'Simply do justice and love mercy. [Then one may] walk humbly with your God.'"[104]

Yet, all too often we do not really understand how these two fundamental factors of a well-functioning society work. Frequently, the prevailing perspective is that justice and mercy are parallel paths headed towards the Divine dream of Peace. Thus, there's a tendency to race down these paths at neck-breaking speeds. For, who really wants to keep God waiting?! However, like a sign of caution on the highway to Heaven, this portion of *Mishpatim* comes to advise us travelers of an approaching reality: justice and mercy are not parallel paths. Rather, justice and mercy are crossing currents, an intersection, which must be navigated with great care.

From Hammurabi's Code to the Torah to the US Constitution, we know that a stable society rests upon a strong foundation of Law and Order (not the TV show). In fact, our Constitution begins with "We the people of the United States, in order to form a more perfect Union, [must] establish justice [to] ensure domestic tranquility." Why? How does that strong sense of justice work? Because, as our sages taught, "when one comprehends that in hurting another, I'm hurting myself," there is a chance to stop crime before it ever

---

[104] Micah 6:8

begins.[105] And, arguably, there is no stronger deterrent than this teaching of "life for life, eye for eye, tooth for tooth, etc." (Exodus 21:23-24)

Yet, for many, this goes way too far. In this measure-for-measure justice, there appears to be no measure of mercy. That, some say, is the reason why the sages of blessed memory tempered justice's harsh decree by altering the punishment from a physical retaliation to a fiscal compensation. As RaSHI noted, "'Life for life, etc.' does not have to be taken literally. There are those who understand it to mean 'the value of a life for a life.'"[106] But, for many others, this too seems wrong. "No one can precisely determine the value of a life," stated Sforno.[107] Thus, when a murderer has his/her sentenced reduced or pardoned on account of mercy, justice – and thereby our society – seems to be deeply disturbed.

And this disturbance, this feeling of instability, is absolutely appropriate. Because, as we see from this portion, the closer we get to mercy, the farther we are from justice. And, the closer we get to justice, the farther we are from mercy. Therefore, if we wish to have a stronger and more stable society, we are instructed to find that sweet spot in the middle, that moment where justice and mercy intersect. Because, in finding and navigating that place "where mercy and truth embrace, where justice and well-being kiss," states the 85th Psalm, "the Lord will favor our land and restore our fortune."[108] For there, in that pleasurable cohesion, Divine peace truly has a place to dwell.

As travelers along this Highway to Heaven, let us heed these words of warning. May we slow down, being more cautious and careful, as we approach all matters of justice and mercy. For in navigating the intersection of these fundamental factors for a well-functioning society successfully, we pray that our society may continue to grow ever more strong and ever more stable, allowing everyone therein to continue to walk humbly with God.

Mishpatim // Rules
Bite 3 – *Out of Revenge*

Just what is revenge? Many people would think first of its Biblical definition: ". . . the penalty shall be life for life, eye for eye, tooth for tooth, hand for hand, foot for foot, burn for burn, wound for wound, bruise for bruise." (Exodus 21:23-25) This verse, from the portion of *Mishpatim*, would lead to the erroneous conclusion that the proper response to being hurt is to demand an equal hurt from the person who wronged us; even though, as Mahatma Gandhi notes, "If we truly practiced 'an eye for an eye and a tooth for a tooth,' soon the whole world would be blind and toothless."

---

[105] For example, the sage Hillel once taught: "What is hateful to you, do not do to another." BT, Shabbat 31a.
[106] See RaSHI commentary to Exodus 21:23
[107] See Sforno commentary to Exodus 21:24
[108] Psalm 85:11

It is hard not to think of revenge as parallel hurts. The English novelist, George Orwell, understands this desire for equilibrium stemming from a state of disequilibrium. In his essay, *Revenge is Sour*, Orwell writes: "Revenge is an act which you want to commit when you are powerless and because you are powerless. . . ." Laura Blumenfeld, whose father – Rabbi David Blumenfeld – was shot by a Palestinian on his way back from praying at the Western Wall, adds to Orwell's understanding: Revenge comes from a state of shame, as many cultures believe it restores honor.[109]

Oh, but how destructive shame and revenge can really be (as Gandhi so told)! This awareness is not unique to Ghandi's native India. We, the Jewish people, also know well the retributive hurt that comes from the hurt of others, a reverberation of pain that leaves all lame, deaf, dumb and blind. For example, according to the *Talmud*, the destruction of our sacred city of Jerusalem and its holy Temple by the Romans happened because – as told by the sages – a man was publicly shamed. The story goes:

> A certain man had a friend Kamtza and an enemy Bar Kamtza. He once made a party and said to his servant, "Go and bring Kamtza." The man went and brought Bar Kamtza. When the man [who gave the party] found him there he said, "Behold, you – who tells tales about me – what are you doing here! Get out!"

> Said the other, "Since I am here, let me stay; I will pay you for whatever I eat and drink." He said, "I won't". Said Bar Kamtza, "Then let me give you half the cost of the party." The other said, "No." Replied Bar Kamtza, "Then let me pay for the whole party." He still said, "No," and he took him by the hand and put him out.[110]

From this public embarrassment – and the fact that no one stood up for him – Bar Kamza takes his revenge, an act which initiates a series of events which eventually caused the Jews to revolt against Rome and for Rome to wage war against the Jews. In the end, not only did many of those who shamed Bar Kamtza fall; so did Bar Kamtza and all he loved. It's amazing how something so small can result in something as devastating as the destruction of Jerusalem and the Temple. But, that's part of understanding the true effects of revenge.

But, let's be clear. Revenge cannot only destroy a temple or city; it can also destroy the sacred temple of our lives. When we focus on revenge, the negative energy required to keep the grudge going can suck the strength from the rest of our being. We see this in our language when we speak of "nursing a grudge." We define ourselves as victims and never get to move forward and heal. In this stagnate state, the temple of our lives begins to deteriorate. So too does it suffer when filled with such hate, there leaves no room within for any positive thing or person to participate.

---

[109] Laura Blumenfeld. *Revenge: A Story of Hope*. Washington Square Press: New York, 2002.
[110] BT Gittin 55b

In the end, revenge isn't worth it. Not simply for the hurt it causes others as well as ourselves, but because it is truly impossible to achieve. As Blumenfeld questions in her own self-discovery of revenge, "How much revenge is enough? The most honest reply I ever heard," she says, "came from Leah Rabin, the widow of assassinated Israeli prime minister, Yitzhak Rabin." Mrs. Rabin told me, with her green eyes, hard as marbles: "None… there's not enough revenge in the entire world" to bring back a loved one, to restore the life that was, to make one feel whole again.

Thus, there are other choices to be made in the face of hurt. Blumenfeld calls this "constructive revenge." This type of revenge is seen in people who have suffered some challenge and use the challenge as the impetus for positive change not only in their lives, but in the lives of others: the parents who lost a child because of drugs/alcohol who educate other children about such consequences, the child who witnesses the challenge of his/her senior parents and enters politics to make life better for them and others, the disease-ridden soul who becomes a spokesperson for the cause.

So, when we read "life for life, eye for eye, tooth for tooth, etc." in this portion of *Mishpatim*, may we understand this revenge as constructive revenge: saving life when our life is threatened, protecting that vision of a better tomorrow even as our sights may be obscured, giving reason to smile though we may not feel like doing it ourselves. In these ways and more, may we come to see the reverse of Ghandi's warning. Rather than a world that is blind and toothless, may we see it wide-eyed and smiling, as we hold hands and march together towards that Promised Land!

Portion 7:
T'rumah // Gifts
Torah Portion: Exodus 25:1-27:19

"THE LORD SPOKE TO MOSES, SAYING, 'TELL THE ISRAELITE PEOPLE TO BRING ME GIFTS.'" These gifts, in which the portion begins, initiate the building of the Tabernacle (the *Mishkan*), the sanctuary of the Divine, so that God may dwell among the Israelites. Though, there is a caveat; God, through Moses, shall only accept gifts from those individuals whose hearts are so moved – not obligated – to give.

Then God gives the instructions for building the Ark, in which the tablets of the Covenant will be placed. The entire piece – inside and out – will be overlaid with pure gold. At the two ends of its cover, there will be two *cherubim* from which God will speak to Moses, issuing forth commands to the Israelites.

In addition to the Ark, which will take a central place in the developing Israelite culture, God delivers unto Moses instructions for the Table and its vessels, the lampstand (*menorah*), the Tabernacle structure, and a tent for over the Tabernacle with its elements: a screen, an altar, and an enclosure.

For each element of the Tabernacle, God declares the exact measurements (in cubits), the materials to be used, the materials to cover it with, their colors and designs, as well as their locations in the Tabernacle. Nothing is left to the human imagination. Nearly every detail for the Tabernacle is given and every piece should be made according to God's instructions to Moses.

The prescribed materials used are progressively more precious the more sacred that part is to the Tabernacle. For the holiest part – the Ark of the Covenant – there is gold, then silver, and finally copper for the least sacred. Thus, the major instructions for the Tabernacle are concluded.

T'rumah // Gifts
Bite 1 – *Bringing Balance to our Accounts of Love*

In the famous comic strip, *Calvin & Hobbes*, the young Calvin awakens in the middle of the night and yells: "Mom! Wake up! Come quick!" Frantic, Calvin's mother runs over to her son's room and asks with great concern: "What's wrong? What's the matter?" Calvin very cerebrally and calmly responds: "Mom, do you think love is nothing more than a biochemical reaction designed to make sure genes get passed on?" Attempting to restrain her anger for this gross interruption in sleep, his mother answers, "Well Calvin, whatever it is, it's all that's keeping me from strangling you right now."

Surely, with the aroma of roses still blowing in the breeze and the sweetness of sugar still pulsing vigorously through our veins, it is likely that our senses remain stimulated to that same question: "What is love?" From a cultural cue, one may be inclined to conclude that love is nothing more than an act of giving: from cards to carnations, from jumbo teddy-bears to jewelry. A message, coincidently, that is echoed in this Torah portion of *T'rumah*. Because, according to Exodus 25:2, our commandment to love God requires us to "give Me (i.e. God) gifts…from every person whose heart is so moved."[111]

Defining love in this way – as an act of giving – is also the conclusion made by some of the great sages of our people. As RaSHI understands the verse above, nothing says I love you more than "the gift of money, which should be set aside for God" and used at the Divine's discretion to build the Tabernacle.[112] And, it's not just with the gift of money. According to the rabbis of the *midrash*, one 'whose heart is moved' can also demonstrate his/her love with the gift of time.[113] For, it is stated, "A loving favor is better than silver or gold."[114] Thus, at first glance, it appears that Jewish tradition defines love too as an act of giving.

And, why not? Love has long been expressed by the giving of gifts, whether it's with the gift of our time or with the gift of our money, whether it's with the gift of our words or with the gift of our gestures. Even our sanity, on occasion, has been given with the gift of our hearts. As the great American writer, Elbert Hubbard, so poignantly stated: "Love grows by giving. The love we give away is the only love we keep. The only way to retain love is to give it away."[115] For, in this act of giving we say, 'I care more about you, than I care about myself.' It is through these selfless gestures that the heart can truly be moved.

Which explains, I suppose, why so many people today measure the love in their lives by how much they give or how much they receive. But, sadly, this

---

[111] Deuteronomy 6:5
[112] RaSHI comment to Exodus 25:2
[113] Exodus Rabbah 33:5
[114] Proverbs 22:1
[115] Fra Elbert Hubbard. *Philistia: Elbert Hubbard's Selected Writings, part 9*. The Roycrofters: 1922. p. 41

counting leads to a perverse account of love, which produces statements from the giver like, 'Of course I love you, just look what I bought you!' or, as Janet Jackson sang from the perspective of the recipient, 'What have you done for me lately?'[116] These statements clearly indicate a problem in our accounts. Sure, gifts appear to reinvigorate our investment in love. But no sooner are these gifts made, does their impact begin to depreciate, leaving us in need of another deposit to bring our accounts of love back to good standing.

That is why RaMBaN suggests that we should not read the Biblical verse in question as "give Me [i.e. God] a gift," as it is so often rendered in English translations. Rather, we should read it as "take Me as a gift," which is closer to the original Hebrew. Because, according to RaMBaN, this verse alludes to the mutual communion that exists between God and the people, as if to say "God shall be my gift and God's gift shall be me."[117] It is a linguistic formula which has a parallel in the great Biblical love story between Israel and God. As we read there, in the Song of Songs, "I am for my Beloved and my Beloved is for me."[118] Such formulas bring balance to our accounts.

How? Because when we ask, "What is love?" these words from our portion remind us that love is not an act of giving or receiving. True love is an act of sharing. As Elie Weisel once stated: "Love risks degenerating into an obsession [of things], if it weren't for a relationship born of sharing." Because, when we share, we stop defining love and its participants in terms of *objects* of affection, which are tallied on a ledger and recorded as profit or loss. Instead, defining love as an act of sharing allows us to understand love's participants as *partners* of affection, who mutually invest not in things but in moments, not in gifts but in each other.

Let us, therefore, truly love. Not merely for one day, nor simply for one week or one year. Let us love – with the time God grants us to love – with all our heart, with all our soul, and with all our might each day, seeing each moment in life as an opportunity to share in the joy of each other.

T'rumah // Gifts
Bite 2 – A Mishkan Meeting

Recently, I had the pleasure of visiting with the Jewish community of Mishkan Israel in Selma, AL, where we celebrated our Jewish faith together. For those who may be unfamiliar with this particular Jewish community, its story is similar to the history of many of our Southern congregations. First established by a strong body of Jewish merchants in 1899, Mishkan Israel became a cornerstone of the Selma community, as every individual member of its congregation fully engaged themselves in the betterment of the city. Though,

---

[116] Janet Jackson. "What have you done for me lately?" *Control*. A&M: 1986
[117] RaMBaN comment to Exodus 25:2
[118] Song of Songs 6:3

due to a dwindling Jewish population over recent years, their temple – the sacred symbol of this Jewish impact in Selma – has fallen into some disrepair.

Still, this modern Mishkan maintains the fullness of God's Presence, as experienced in the Mishkan of our Israelite ancestors in this portion of T'rumah. As it is written: "May it be the will of the Israelite people to bring [God] gifts...from every person whose heart is so moved: gold, silver, and copper; blue, purple, and crimson yarns, fine linen, goat hair, tanned ram skins, and dolphin skins... so that they may make [God] a sanctuary, (in Hebrew, a 'mishkan') to dwell among them."[119] Alright, there was no tanned ram skins, no dolphin skins, not even a single goat hair to speak of in the magnificent synagogue in Selma. Nevertheless, it was still evident that the individual gifts of the Jewish community there had – as described in the Bible – contributed in "making a [extraordinary] sanctuary in which [God] may dwell."

But, that Biblical statement may perplex many of us, for why would the omnipresent God require a building in which to dwell? Some commentators answer that question with an analogy, stating: "Just as great mortal kings of men have palaces, so too does the King of Kings deserve to dwell in luxury."[120] Most commentators, however, say that the building responded less to the needs of God and more to the needs of man. For example, the early 20th century sage Umberto Cassuto suggested that a Mishkan was needed by man because after the intimate Divine experience at Sinai "it seemed to the Israelites [in the vast void of the desert] that the link between them and God had been broken."[121]

Well, with all due respect to Cassuto's suggestion, this point seems to belittle our tradition. For just as Abraham met God on a mountain, Jacob on a lonely place along his path, Moses through an ordinary bush, there has not been a time or place that we did not know that we can encounter God anywhere and everywhere. Thus, it may be suggested that some other mortal need necessitated God's mandate to build Him a sacred space in which "to dwell among us," a need famously spelled out in the fabled story, Stone Soup. As we may recall:

> Once upon a time, a great famine fell upon the land. In that dearth, people jealously hoarded whatever food they could find, hiding it from friends and strangers alike. Therefore, it should come as no surprise that, one day, when a stranger came wandering into town, he was told: "Move along, for there is not a bite to eat in the whole province." "Oh, that's okay," said the stranger. "I have everything I need. In fact, I was just thinking of making some stone soup to share with y'all." And, with that, he pulled an iron cauldron from his wagon, filled it with water, and built a fire under it. Then, with great

---

[119] Exodus 25:1-8
[120] Rabbi Harvey Fields. *A Torah Commentary for Our Times: Exodus*. UAHC Press: New York, 1991. p. 64
[121] Cassuto commentary on Exodus 25:8

ceremony, he drew an ordinary-looking stone from a velvet bag and dropped it into the water.

Hearing the rumor of food, the villagers began to stare and gawk at the stranger from their homes, as he – with great care – stirred and sniffed the "broth," licking his lips in anticipation. And though they kept their distance for a time, hunger began to overcome their skepticism. As they approached, one of the town-folk questioned: "What are you making there?" "Stone soup," replied the stranger. "Stone soup?!" echoed back the man in bewilderment. Oh, yes. It's very famous where I come from. Though," admitted the stranger, "it would taste a lot better if it had a little seasoning. Say, a dab of salt or pepper perhaps?" With that, the man darted off to his home and returned with some spice, which he gladly sprinkled into the boiling water.

"That's great!" continued the stranger. "Of course, with a little cabbage, this stone soup would be hard to beat, even by my own peop..." Before he could even finish his statement, a young woman appeared at his side with a head of cabbage. With a gracious "thanks," he added it into the pot. "Though," added the stranger. "I once had stone soup with a little roasted chicken in it, and – I tell you God's honest truth – it was a meal fit for a king!" Upon hearing those words, the village butcher emerged from his boarded-up shop with a full chicken in hand. And so it went, with each member of the community coming out to add a little something of their own into the pot. By day's end, there was a hearty soup prepared, large enough to feed the entire community.

"Please," pleaded the town's mayor, as the stranger began to pack up his things. "Tell us the secret of this stone soup." "There's nothing to tell," responded the stranger. "All you need is a group of people willing to stop thinking of themselves and participate in making something together. Then," added the stranger, "you will find an abundance of blessings to nourish the soul."

"All you need is a group of people willing to stop thinking about themselves and participate in making something together... [to] find an abundance of blessings to nourish the soul." That's the human need God intended to fulfill in mandating the construction of a Mishkan, a sacred place to dwell among us. For, in tough times, it's natural for people to stop thinking of others and to start thinking only of themselves; a self-destructive thought that ultimately puts all lives in jeopardy. To counter that mortal inclination and set us up for success, God initiated a building project. Not to have a place to meet Him, but a place for us to meet each other. In those human connections we can establish a firm foundation for our Divine future. For, as the sages have taught, "Where two or more people meet and share of themselves, there God can be found."

And God was surely found in Selma, AL, as I was warmly welcomed into the Mishkan of that Jewish community. Yes, even in the face of a deteriorating building, the full Presence of God showed no wear. For, in their present challenge, they have recognized – as many of our Southern communities have – that it's not the place that makes for holiness. It is the people that do, people who – with relentless spirits – continue to give more and more of themselves to others, filling the places of their lives with the eternal values of our people. So that, should the time sadly come when a building no longer stands, at the very least these values will, testifying to all that God indeed has a place "to dwell among us" now and forever more.

T'rumah // Gifts
Bite 3 – *A Tabernacle in Our Hearts*

Mark Bennett is an artist who is known for his detailed blueprints of sitcom homes. Want a detailed rendering of the Manhattan apartment where Ricky and Lucy Ricardo lived on the sitcom *I Love Lucy*? He drew it. Interested in seeing a layout of Fred and Wilma Flintstone's home in Bedrock? He drew that one too. Bennett was able to do this because rather than focusing on their stories, while watching T.V. he focused on the details of their environments. For Bennett and those like him, this portion of *T'rumah* is ideal, because no longer is the text focused on our ancestors' story, but the setting.

Specifically, this portion focuses on the construction of the wilderness Tabernacle (the *Mishkan*): its many materials and its countless colors, its finishing and its furnishings. Yet, for others, those dry details make the skin diseases of Leviticus look appealing. Their problem is not necessarily reading details of something that they can't quite visualize, as Bennett could; rather, what's challenging is the theology behind the construction. Why would God need such a place and who are we to make – as God said – "a sanctuary (a *mikdash*)" for the Eternal "to dwell among [us]?" (Exodus 25:8)

There – did you hear – is an important distinction, helping us to answer our own question? In calling the *Mishkan* a *mikdash*, comments Nachum Sarna, the Eternal is acknowledging "that this holy place is not meant to be understood literally as God's abode, as were other such institutions in the pagan world. Rather, its function was to make perceptible and tangible the conception of God's immanence, that is, of the indwelling of the Divine Presence in the camp of Israel, to which the people may orient their hearts and minds.[122] Thus, this construction is not for God, but for us, reminding us of God's Presence.

Yet, there is something even more important here than the choice between *Mishkan* and *mikdash*; it's the phrase that follows: "to dwell among them." Rabbi Andrea Weiss suggests that "such language helps negotiate the tension between the freedom of God to be everywhere and the need of humans to have

---

[122] Nachum Sarna. *The JPS Torah Commentary: Genesis*. The Jewish Publication Society: Philadelphia, 2003.

tangible evidence of God's immanence and accessibility."[123] Possibly in realization of this, the Italian commentator Sforno explains that "I will dwell among them" to mean "I will dwell among them in order to receive their prayers and their worship (i.e. sacrifices)." [124] Because, more than a theological symbol of the nature of God, the wilderness Tabernacle speaks about the nature of our people, who – from time to time – needed reassurances of God's Presence.

We are millennia past the building of the *Mishkan* in the wilderness and our relationships with God are in some ways different from that of our ancestors. Perhaps, still, we can use the idea of building a *Mishkan* to speak to that part within us that yearns to dwell with the Eternal. To do this, Rabbi Menachem Mendel of Kotzk suggested reading the verse not as "build Me a sanctuary so that I may dwell in it," but "build Me a sanctuary so that I may dwell within them." [125] In this view, each of us then is obligated to build a tabernacle within our hearts, for the Holy One of Blessing to dwell within us.

Our ancestors built a tent in the wilderness, our sages a Temple in Jerusalem, and we a sanctuary in our hearts, not to contain God, but to have a space to turn to the Eternal and honor that Divine relationship. As this portion turns its attention there, may we turn ours. Thereby, we may ensure that our story has a sound and sustainable setting.

---

[123] Andrea Weiss. Commentary on Exodus 25:8. *The Torah: A Women's Commentary*. Editors: Tamara Cohn Eskenazi and Andrea Weiss. URJ Press: New York, 2007.
[124] Sforno on Exodus 25:8.
[125] Menachem Mendel of Kotzk on Exodus 25:8.

PURIM:
Rachel Jarman-Myers' Pecan Pie Hamantaschen

Ingredients (Crust):
3¾ cups of flour
1⅓ cups of powdered sugar
1½ teaspoons of baking powder
¼ teaspoon of salt
2 large eggs
1¼ cups of cold butter

Ingredients (Filling):
½ cup of pecans (finely chopped)
1 egg
½ cup of brown sugar
2 tablespoons butter (room temp.)
2 tablespoons of corn syrup
Flour

Combine flour, powdered sugar, baking powder, and salt in a large food processor. Process briefly to blend. Beat eggs in a small bowl. Scatter butter pieces over the flour mixture in the processor. Mix using on/off pulsing motion until mixture resembles coarse meal. Pour the beaten eggs evenly over the mixture. Process with an on/off motion, stopping to scrape the mixture down occasionally, until the dough begins to come together in a ball. If the crumbs are dry, sprinkle with 1 tablespoon of orange juice and process briefly; repeat if the crumbs are still dry. (Note: the top of the dough may seem dry, but bottom may be moist and will moisten the rest when you knead it.)

Transfer dough to a work surface. Knead it lightly to blend the ingredients. With a rubber spatula, transfer the dough to a sheet of plastic wrap. Wrap it and push it together, shaping it into a flat disk. Refrigerate the dough for three hours before using it.

Mix together the ingredients for the filling. If it is too wet, add flour. Roll out your dough and cut with a 3-inch cookie cutter. Brush their edges lightly with water. Put 1 teaspoon of filling in the center of each one. Pull up the edges of each round in three arcs that meet above the filling, covering it. Pinch the dough above the filling to close the hamantaschen firmly. Put them on a greased baking sheet and refrigerate uncovered for at least 30 minutes, before baking firm the dough. (If one is preparing to bake a lot of hamantaschen, it is suggested to place them in a refrigerator as you go, rather than waiting until all are shaped.)

At 350 degrees, bake for 14 minutes or until light golden at the edges. Cool them on a rack. Make sure that you bake the hamantaschen only until they are pale golden at the edges. If the hamantaschen are baked too long, the sugar in the dough may cause them to burn.

Portion 8:
T'tzaveh // You Shall Command
Torah Portion: Exodus 27:20-30:10

"YOU SHALL FURTHER COMMAND THE ISRAELITES TO BRING YOU CLEAR OIL OF BEATEN OLIVES FOR LIGHTING, FOR KINDLING THE LAMPS REGULARLY." This portion begins with a continuation on the rules for the Tabernacle, specifically with regards to instructing the priests in their responsibilities towards it.

God commands the Israelites to bring oil for the Eternal light (*Neir Tamid*) and the appointment of Aaron and his sons as priests. Those skilled enough in the community shall make the priestly vestments, the details of which are then prescribed: the ephod, the breastplate, cords, pomegranates, frontlet, fringed tunic, headdress, sash and breeches. And, for Aaron's sons, they should make a tunic, sash, turban, breeches. Again, the exact specifications as to how to construct each element are detailed.

The portion then moves on to the directions for consecrating the priests. Upon ordination, Aaron and his sons are told – in detail – the sacrifices they are to make as the priests of Israel, as well as the rules for taking their priestly share of such offerings. The entire process of ordination shall last seven days, as it will in the future when a new priest (one of Aaron's sons) will be ordained in Aaron's stead.

Following the details for ordination of priests, God commands the various daily sacrifices – a yearling lamb in the morning and evening with libations (the *Tamid* offerings). Through all of this, the Tent of Meeting will become sanctified and God will speak to the Israelite people.

The portion concludes with the command to make an altar for burning incense, with its specifications and instructions for offerings.

T'tzaveh // You Shall Command
Bite 1 – *Neir Tamid: God's Light Burns Eternally*

One item, above all, has helped children make it through the night – in their own beds – the longest. "What is it?" you may ask. Well, it's not Pampers or pull-ups. It's not Superman pajamas or My Little Ponies. It's not Teddy Bears or even special blankets. No; the one item that has long accompanied children throughout the night, helping to dispel the dread of darkness, is none other than the soft flicker of a small night-light.

In Biblical terms, the night-light is called a *Neir Tamid* (an Eternal Light). First described in this Torah portion of *T'tzaveh*, God commands Moses to "instruct the children of Israel to bring [him] clear oil of beaten olives for lighting, for kindling the *Neir Tamid*. Aaron and his sons shall set them up at the Tent of Meeting, outside the curtain, over the Pact, [to burn] from evening until morning before the Lord. It shall be a due from the Israelites for all time." (Exodus 27:20-21)

"But, why?" question many. "What necessity is there to maintain this light forever?" Surely, once the scary nights in the wilderness are over, as people are safe and sound at home in Israel, the light can go out. Not so, teach the sages. For, this light does not merely dispel darkness; it also draws us into the Divine.[126] In other words, God is symbolically light, a light which must continually be maintained if we are to ever have a chance at illuminating our world.

How does that work exactly? How can God's essence be articulated through the symbol of light? Well for one, like God, light is not an object in and of itself. Rather, light is a product born from a process of liberating dormant energy, whether hidden in a piece of wood or a lump of coal. In much the same way, taught Rabbi Harold Kushner, "When we liberate our contained energies for justice and mercy, for truth and love, God and God's vision for our world is seen by all."[127]

Though, in truth, God is not really seen, as God has no form. Rather, we only become aware of God by how God helps us to see other things: comfort during turmoil, hope in the midst of despair, and victory after suffering defeat after defeat after defeat. Much like light, God helps us see more of others than God, Himself, is seen. After all, only "Moses saw God face to face," states the Bible.[128] All others were simply overwhelmed by staring directly into the light of God.

---

[126] BT Shabbat 22b: In reference to this verse of the *Neir Tamid*, Rav Sheishet rhetorically questioned, "Does God need this light?" As the *Neir Tamid* was set-up outside the curtain, Rav Sheishet concludes that the light was not for God but for the people. "It (i.e. the light) is a testimony for all mankind that the Divine Presence dwells with Israel."

[127] Harold Kushner, ed. *Etz Hayim: Torah and Commentary*. Rabbinical Assembly: New York, 2001. p. 503

[128] Exodus 33:11; Deuteronomy 34:10

All the more reason why light is a fitting symbol for God. Because, like the light born from fire, the light of God is a co-dependent force. Sure, "people need God's light to show them the way," wrote Rabbi Harvey Fields. "But, God needs people to bring His light of justice and peace into the world."[129] If either party were to back away from their Covenantal responsibilities, then this Divine light would go out, leaving the world in the dark.

For the sake of every child (and, thus, every parent) wishing for a good night's rest, we cannot allow this to happen. We cannot allow this symbol of God's Presence, which has long brought comfort and strength in dark times, to go out. Therefore, like our priestly forefather Aaron, may we step up to fulfill our priestly duty by maintaining the *Neir Tamid*. Let us illuminate God in our daily actions: being more courteous and kind, being more comforting and compassionate.

For in being so courageous, spoke the prophet Isaiah, we become – as God designed – His "light to the nations, opening the eyes of those deprived of light, rescuing – from the dungeon – those who sit in darkness." May we continue to be this vessel of light. Through us, may God's eternal night-light of the *Neir Tamid* shine on. May we dispel the darkness, while drawing people into the Peace of the Divine.

T'tzaveh // You Shall Command
Bite 2 – *Power Point*

Over these past couple of weeks, it is likely that our attentions have been captivated and aroused by the images of a contentious match-up, one that has been a long time in the making. And, I am not referring to the showdown on the playing-field Sunday between the Green Bay Packers and the Pittsburgh Steelers. Rather, I am referring to the showdown on the political landscape of Egypt, where a young generation of Egyptians have squared-off with their long-time autocratic president, Hosni Mubarak. As one of the young demonstrators stated to ABC News: "Mubarak is a tragic figure. He started off fine, but – in later years – his concentration of power has become a real problem."[130] And now these young people, who have found the power of their own voice, are chanting: "Mubarak must go!"

Coincidentally, in this portion of *T'tzaveh*, it's the transition of power that occupies the entirety of the Biblical texts. As it is written, "You shall bring forward your brother Aaron, with his sons, from among the Israelites to serve Me as priests." (Exodus 28:1) Implying, "Not you;" that is to say, not Moses nor his sons shall continue to lead the people.[131] Rather, it shall be Aaron and his sons, as the text fittingly goes on to describe in great detail the priestly

---

[129] Harvey Fields. *A Torah Commentary for Our Times*: Volume 2. UAHC Press: New York, 1991. P. 73
[130] Christiane Amanpour. "This Week: Crisis in Egypt." *ABC News*: 6 February 2011.
[131] This point is also made in the *midrash* of *Leviticus Rabbah* 11:6. As it is written: "God said to him (Moses), 'It belongs not to you, but to your brother Aaron.'"

investiture and vestments in their service to God and our people. But, Moses' name (while implied) goes unmentioned. In fact, not only do we not read of Moses in *T'tzaveh*, this is the only Torah portion in the remaining four that we also do not hear from Moses, as no direct speech from him is made.

This literary uniqueness, captures the curiosity of many a commentator. For example, some commentators point out that the traditional understanding of Moses' death, the 7th of Adar, always falls during the week in which *T'tzaveh* is read.[132] Thus, they interpret Moses' absence from the Torah portion as symbolic of his departure from this world. Others, conceding his absence from the text is symbolic, interpret it not as emblematic of his departure from life but, as Nachum Sarna suggests, acknowledgement of Moses' soon-to-be-departure from political life. "For here," writes Sarna, "Moses is stepping aside to let the spotlight of leadership fall on Aaron and his priestly functions."[133]

In other words, particularly those words of the famed country singer Kenny Rogers, "knowing when to hold 'em and knowing when to fold 'em," is not only the mark of a good leader, the orderly transfer of power is also the mark of a healthy and stable society.[134] This, as we have seen recently, becomes painfully evident not only in places like Egypt and Tunisia. One can also observe the precarious position of a people when power is possessed by only a precious few here in America. Yes, take for example the multibillion dollar company of Apple. Simply on the news that its founder, brainchild, CEO, and its all-around guru – Steve Jobs – was ill, credible doubt was expressed about the future of the entire company.[135]

That's because, in these examples, power is structured like an inverted pyramid, as the majority of people are attempting to balance upon a single, solitary, individual point of power. And, should that individual be taken out of the picture, by force or by fate, then those being held up would undoubtedly fall. Not such a good recipe for stability. Thus, to have a more stable society, "a more perfect union" as noted in the preamble to our Constitution, it seems only reasonable to return the pyramid back to its natural resting position. In this picture, stability is created through shared power, spreading it over a larger base of people, as they – in turn – rely upon a fewer and fewer number of selected or elected individuals to guide them forward.

"Yeah," some will say, "but that doesn't necessarily solve the problem. For as long as power is contained in human hands there is always the chance that it

---

[132] *Tosefta Sotah* 11:5 (Lieberman ed., pp. 218-220). The date was determined by computing backwards from the 10th of Nisan, the date the Israelites crossed the Jordan River (Joshua 4:19).
[133] Nachum Sarna. *Etz Hayim: Torah and Commentary*. The Rabbinical Assembly: New York, 2001. p.503
[134] Originally written by Don Schlitz, these lyrics were rerecorded by Kenny Rogers. "The Gambler." *The Gambler*. United Artists Group: 1978.
[135] Jessica Guynn. "Apple's Steve Jobs to Take Medical Leave [Update]." *Los Angeles Times*: 17 January 2011. http://latimesblogs.latimes.com/technology/2011/01/apples-steve-jobs-to-take-medical-leave.html. Or, check out Shara Tibken. "Proxy Firm: Apple Should Disclose Succession Plan." *The Wall Street Journal*: 7 February 2011.

will corrupt and thus create instability for a society once more."[136]And, according to our Jewish faith, these concerned voices have a point. Hence the reason why countless sages understood Moses' absence in this portion not simply as emblematic of his departure from life nor from politics, but – like his absence in the Haggadah – as indicative of a conscious move to step aside in respect and recognition for the ultimate source of our power, God and God's law: Torah.[137] For, it is by the rule of law, and not of man, that a society has a real chance at knowing true safety and stability.

That, we can say, is the true Point of Power, which is thereupon invested into human hands... not to benefit ourselves, but to deliver blessings unto others! This lesson Moses knew most intimately, as he graciously began the process of stepping aside to allow for the future success of our people through the leadership of Aaron and the priesthood; a lesson, paradoxically, that Mubarak has forgotten. For as the one who demonstrated stated, what started out fine, ended with a problem with his concentration of power. Thus, may we learn from the success of Moses' humility as well as from the failure of Mubarak's pride: a society's stability cannot be based upon the point of one person's power. Rather, let our success and stability as a nation – dear Lord – be based upon the power of the people, who – we pray – will continue to be guided by the sound rule of law.

T'tzaveh // You Shall Command
Bite 3 – *Living is Moving*

Life is like a box of chocolates, you never know what you're gonna get.[138] Life is like a rollercoaster baby, I wanna ride.[139] Life is like a ten-speed bicycle, most of us have gears we've never used.[140] Life is like a foreign language, all people mispronounce it.[141] Nevertheless, that has not deterred us from trying, as another attempt to find the right pronunciation to define life was made recently in the film, *Up in the Air*. In this film, Ryan Bingham (played by George Clooney) lives an unencumbered life. Unattached to things or people, he travels 322 days a year in his career, packing everything he has or needs into one small carry-on suitcase. According to him, "living is moving."

If this is indeed the essence of life, then it could be said that the Israelites are and will continue to be "livin' large" as they move farther away from Egypt and move closer to the Promised Land. Because, in these movements, they not only progress in terms of space and time, but also in terms of soul and mind, establishing the foundations of our people's culture that would endure for

---

[136] One could say that the English Catholic historian, Lord Acton (1834-1902), would be among these individuals, as he famously stated: "All power tends to corrupt and absolute power corrupts absolutely."
[137] As it is written in the Haggadah: "The Lord brought us out of Egypt, not by an angel, not by a *seraph*, not by a messenger (i.e. Moses), but by the Holy One Blessed be God, by Himself."
[138] Eric Roth. *Forrest Gump*. 1994
[139] Adapted from Red Hot Chili Peppers' *Love Rollercoaster*. 1996
[140] Charles M. Schulz. *Life is Like a Ten-Speed Bicycle*. Harpercollins Pub.: 1998.
[141] Christopher Morley. *Thunder on the Left*. Garden City Doubleday Page & Co.: 1926.

generations. Fittingly, then, the Israelites are commanded in the portion of *Tetzaveh* – to "take two lapis lazuli stones, engrave on them the names of the sons of Israel, and…attach the two stones to the shoulder-pieces of the ephod, as stones of remembrance of the Israelite people." (Exodus 28:9-12)

According to Biblical commentator, Nachum Sarna, "the names of all the tribes engraved on the gems and affixed to the High Priest's vestments are to serve as a perpetual and humbling reminder that each of us, [as a priestly people,] are representatives of the entire community of Israel."[142] Thus, according to this Torah portion, life is not about standing on the shoulders of giants, who – it could be said – are our people (both past and present). Rather, it is like having those giants stand upon us, as wherever we go, wherever we move in this life, we are required to take our relationships, and our responsibilities to them, along for the ride.

Some may consider this Biblical requirement as an unnecessary burden beset upon us by a by-gone era, an antiquated nuisance for the nuances of a modern life that is continuously on the move. Seeing it as such, the character Ryan Bingham, in the movie, states: "Make no mistake. Your relationships are the heaviest components in your life: your brothers, your sisters, your children, your parents, and finally your husband or your wife, your boyfriend or your girlfriend. All those negotiations and arguments and secrets…the compromises! They weigh us down until we can no longer move. And the slower we move, the faster we die!"

That is why, to truly live, some people espouse that we drop the excess baggage and the weight it adds to our lives. This abandonment is not just limited to things, but – as many a Jedi Knight can attest to – it also means refraining from personal relationships. It's a move Ghandi referred to as "reducing oneself to zero," as he gave up many modern conveniences (modern clothing, city living, a meat diet) as well as sexual relations with his wife in order to focus his energy, his Jedi force if you will, on achieving independence for India through non-violent civil disobedience. As such, one can understand asceticism not necessarily as the selfish withdrawal from the weight of the world, but a particular flight-plan which may reserve one's fuel (i.e. one's energy) for the achievement of life's loftier heights.

Judaism, obviously, does not dissent from this perspective, calling upon us time and time again to ascend to great heights, for it is there where we have found God as well as the framework for our collective futures. Yet, we are taught to ground these flights towards the future with the weight of the past (i.e. the stones engraved with the names of our ancestors, indicating our responsibility to our people). Why? Because 'grounding,' in this case, does not mean to forgo flying. On the contrary, to be 'grounded' expresses the need to have a solid reference point to keep us on track as we continue to fly the friendly and sometimes not-so-friendly skies of life, if – God forbid – our own

---

[142] Nachum Sarna. *Etz Hayim: Torah and Commentary.* Rabbinical Assembly: New York, 2001. p.506

internal navigation equipment should somehow go awry. As many a philosopher has recognized: "There is no way to tell where you are going, unless you know where you have been."

So, maybe Ryan Bingham was right. Life is moving. And, more precisely, it could be said that life is like moving in an airplane. It matters less about how high, or for that matter, how fast we fly. All that really matters is that we arrive at our destination safe and sound. But, contrary to Bingham's testimony, this portion of *Tetzaveh* teaches that the best way to ensure that happens is by never flying solo. We all need a co-pilot, whether it be our brothers or our sisters, our children or our parents, our partners or our spouses, or even our ancestors or our God. For these extra pair of eyes from the past as well as additional ones from the present will serve us as a backup in our flights towards the future. With their help, may will all arrive together in safety and peace.

Portion 9:
Ki Tissa // When You Take
Torah Portion: Exodus 30:11-34:35

"THE LORD SPOKE TO MOSES, SAYING, 'WHEN YOU TAKE A CENSUS OF THE ISRAELITE PEOPLE...'" This portion completes the rules given to Moses atop Mount Sinai concerning the Tabernacle and priestly service.

God then instructs Moses on the first census of military-age Israelites by donating a half-shekel, the rules for the vessels for washing prior to making offerings, the "recipe" for the sacred fragrant oil and incense, and that Betzalel and Oholiab have been given the talents to make the Tabernacle and its array as God has commanded.

Just before Moses returns to the camp, with the first set of tablets, God reiterates the commandment to rest on Shabbat: "The Israelite people shall keep the Sabbath throughout the ages as a covenant for all time. It shall be a sign for all time between Me and the people of Israel, etc." (Exodus 31:16-17) These verses constitute the *V'shamru* prayer sung in many Jewish congregations to this day.

However, the people had become restless at Moses' delay and ask Aaron to make for them a "new" god. The scene of the Golden Calf ensues, including Moses shattering the first set of tablets. Moses pleads on behalf of the people twice, recalling the promise to Abraham and the Exodus as reasons to pardon the people. The people are punished by both Moses and God, but are not destroyed.

Following this incident, Moses asks if he has earned God's favor that God might let him see God's Presence, but God only lets Moses see God's back, lest Moses see God's face and die. The portion concludes with the creation of the second set of tablets, followed by the ritual Decalogue. When Moses returns to the camp, his face is radiant, as it remained anytime he spoke with God.

Ki Tissa // When You Take
Bite 1 – *As One Gives, One Receives: The Half Shekel Offering*

Many of us are aware that, on Purim, it is customary to read the scroll of Esther, retelling the story of our ancestors' salvation in Persia. Many of us are aware that, on Purim, it is customary to mask and unmask ourselves, symbolizing our task to unmask God in the world. And, many of us are aware that, on Purim, adults may be intoxicated to the point where they cannot hear the difference between "blessed be Mordechai" and "cursed be Haman," reminding us that the line between good and evil is never so easy to distinguish. Yet, despite this knowledge, many of us remain unaware that, on Purim, it is also customary to collect a half-shekel equivalent of the common currency as a gift to the poor.

The source of this custom comes from this Torah portion of *Ki Tissa*. After reading of the priestly costumes in the last portion, we begin this one with God's instruction to Moses concerning the counting of the Israelite *purim*, the Israelite "lots." The Lord spoke unto Moses: "When you take a census of the Israelite people according to their enrollment, each shall pay the Lord a ransom for himself on being enrolled, that no plague may come upon them through their being enrolled. This is what everyone who is entered into the records shall pay: a half-shekel by the sanctuary weight – twenty *gerahs* to the shekel – a half shekel as an offering to the Lord." (Exodus 30:11-13)

In its contexts, note the sages, the half-shekel offering seems to have functioned as a talisman of sorts, warding off evil. After all, those counted were soldiers, comments former Chief Rabbi of Great Britain Joseph H. Hertz. "As they will soon be in a position to take life – but not in circumstances that constitute murder – a ransom for life is required;" it stays the evil eye.[143] Indeed, adds RaSHI, "the evil eye rules over all census-taking," affecting civil life as well.[144] A census may spawn pride over the size of one's family or jealousy for the size of another's. If left unchecked, these feelings could plague the people. Thus, we are commanded to give to others in order to save ourselves.

The Proverb states, "*Tzedakah* saves from death."[145] Though, surely, that has to be a mistake! Although giving helps to fulfill many of the values passed down from generation to generation, in the transmission of our noble Jewish heritage, we know that giving – in and of itself – is not an act of love or mercy or even justice. In other words, in Judaism, giving is not an act of charity; it is a command, void of any personal motivation besides pleasing the Lord, as was the case with the half-shekel offering. In fact, it has been said that "giving should involve no more thought than breathing." In essence, Judaism

---

[143] Dr. Rabbi J. H. Hertz. *Pentateuch and Haftorahs.* Soncino Press: London, 1971. p. 352. See his commentary to Exodus 30:12.
[144] RaSHI commentary to Exodus 30:12
[145] Proverbs 10:2

considers giving just an involuntary reflex of life, simply enabling us (i.e. our society) to move onward and upward.

Yet, even in that teaching, there is the slight recognition – even if unintended or unwanted – that giving spawns benefits not just for the receiver, but also for the giver. For, just as one cannot live without breathing, one cannot live without giving. This does not mean necessarily, as the Vilna Gaon once taught, that "one gives today because they may have to receive tomorrow."[146] Rather, the mutual benefit giving spawns is more immediate, as alluded to in our Hebrew text. *V'natnu*, translated as "each shall give," is a palindrome, spelled the same way from right to left as it is left to right in Hebrew. This signifies, wrote Rabbi Harold Kushner, that "even as one gives, one receives."[147]

> That was certainly the case for a circuit riding preacher some years ago. Living off the small honoraria he received from his visits with each community, the preacher did not make a lot of money. Though, he wasn't complaining. In fact, having his family's basic needs met while doing this meaningful work of the Lord, made him feel abundantly blessed.
>
> On one particular visit, the preacher brought his son along to share with him this blessed experience. As they made their way down the back rural roads of the community, the son observed all around the challenging life circumstances created by these tough economic times: boarded up shops, many homes for sale, even the tone of the people seemed audibly depressed.
>
> "These people are really down, aren't they dad." stated the young boy. "Yes, my son" acknowledged the preacher. "That is why we are here… to lift their spirits!" And, boy did he! The preacher, utilizing the liturgy of the prayer book, the songs from the hymnal, and the teachings of their faith, provided a moving service and stirring sermon, which seemed to visibly lift the people up.
>
> Though, when it came time to pass around the collection plate for the weekly offering, the plate remained empty. The boy observed his father discreetly putting a crisp $20 bill into the plate. Shocked at his father's gift, the boy asked, "Dad, why do you give? Don't your words fulfill your offering?" To which the preacher responded: "Prayers without works, my son, are just empty vows and promises."
>
> At the end of the service, the preacher thanked everyone for their hospitality. The president of the congregation, in turn, thanked the preacher. "We really appreciate your visit and feel truly grateful for the great service you provided. We wish we could provide you a proper thanks. But, honestly, there is nothing to give."

---

[146] Quoted in *Etz Hayim: Torah and Commentary*. The Rabbinical Assembly: New York, 2001. p. 523.
[147] *Ibid.*

Though this would mean certain hardships for him and his family, the preacher sincerely stated to the President, "That's okay. You have already given me and my son so much: a time to celebrate our faith together, as a community, in a meaningful moment of prayer. That will suffice. Thank you."

As the preacher and his son loaded the car for their ride home, the president came running out of the building, waving a small white envelope. "We couldn't bear you leaving without a little something from us," stated the president in between deep breaths. "Bear in mind, it is small."

More thanks were offered, as they said their good-byes and headed home. When they hit a large bump at the end of the Church's driveway, out of the envelope popped a crisp $20 dollar bill, awkwardly similar to the one the preacher had placed in the collection plate a few moments before. Seeing the stunned face of his son, the preacher asked him: "So, my child, what did you learn from this?" The son responded with: "You should've put a little more in the collection plate."[148]

And, the boy is right. We should give more, because – as this portion tells us – consequently we receive more to sustain our lives. Not necessarily in terms of money or even public recognition. Rather, in the act of giving more, we receive something far more valuable (but less tangible): the pleasure in bringing joy to others, the satisfaction that our unique gifts are valued, the fulfillment in being the working tools of the Lord, etc., etc. And, this is nothing to be scoffed at or ashamed of, as if it somehow violates some sacred aspect of our faith's command to give. For, in these reciprocal gifts, we find great meaning and purpose for our lives, providing us not only the fuel to move forward, but also the direction on how to get there.

That, some say, is the reason why the Lord, our God, commanded our ancestors to give only half a shekel. It was a constant reminder to them then, as it should be for all of us today, that giving is only half the picture. The other half is receiving. And, by grasping that we all play both parts in this process, then we come to see everyone as having worth, everyone has something to give: whether tangible or intangible, whether small or big. May we continue to grasp both parts of this giving process, so that we may – we pray – go on to live and help others to live full, complete, and whole lives. Let us give the half-shekel. Let us be the whole shekel!

---

[148] I would like to thank my friend, Richard Klein – the Network Associate Director and Southeast Regional Director of the Jewish Federations of North America – for sharing this story with me.

Ki Tissa // When You Take
Bite 2 – *Being Gifted*

Like many youngsters, I once dreamt of being an Olympian, proudly representing my country on the world stage. I dreamt of harnessing every bit of energy that was me and deploying it just at the right moment, so that I could soar atop the leaders' board and gently come to rest on the medal podium to the grand applause of my countrymen as well as to the glorious sound of our national anthem: "Oh, say can you see by the dawn's early light. What so proudly we hailed at the twilight's last gleaming…" Ah, this was my dream; that is, before I learned that there are just some people blessed with athletic prowess and others who are not. And, unfortunately for me, I fell – literally sometimes – into the latter category.

I suppose I should have read the Bible first. Because, there, I would have learned a similar lesson (this time, without the bruises). According to *Ki Tissa*, God "singles out" certain people and "endows [them] with the Divine spirit of skill, ability, and knowledge." (Exodus 31:2-3) In its context, this Biblical verse refers to Betzalel son of Uri as well as others whom God "granted the gift of skill [in the wilderness]…so that they could make everything that God had commanded Moses: the Tent of Meeting, the Ark of the Covenant, the cover upon it, all the furnishings for the Tent, etc." (Exodus 31:6-11)

So, why does God get involved in this way? Couldn't God, who had already written the Ten Commandments once and will do so again in this portion, include a small instruction manual to be given to the selected workmen? After all, it works for IKEA! But, according to commentator, Nachum Sarna, it would not have worked well for the Israelites. "Because," he writes, "to construct most things, one needs only a set of specific instructions. But, to fashion something holy – something that will move others – being able to follow instructions is not enough. A measure of Divine inspiration is required."[149]

Indeed, there are some people we all recognize as inspired or gifted; individuals bestowed – one might say, from God – with an extra measure of skill, knowledge, or ability. We think of people like Picasso, Einstein, even snowboarder Shaun White, who performed a dramatic trick during the 2006 Olympic Winter Games that many considered impossible. It was called the *Double McTwist 1260*. And, it consisted of two back-flips while rotating the body three and a half times as one screams down a half-pipe at extreme altitudes. A trick, I am happy to report, White executed perfectly, earning him and our country a gold medal as well as redefining the statement – as Eli Saslow from the Washington Post pointed out – "to air is Divine."[150]

---

[149] Nachum Sarna. "Exodus." *Etz Hayim Torah and Commentary*. The Rabbinical Assembly: New York, 2001. p. 527

[150] Eli Saslow. "Snowboarder and skater Shaun White: To Air is Divine." *Washington Post*: 26 June 2006

Some, however, will argue that these dramatic efforts are not tricks, that there is nothing supernatural or Divine about these results. What allows the rest of us to marvel at the moments when the impossible becomes possible is nothing more than hard work and determination. It is argued that anybody who is driven to push the envelope of human potential farther would be able to achieve similar results. Rabbi Isaac testified to this fact in the *Talmud*, stating, "If a man says to you, 'I have worked hard and not succeeded,' he is not to be believed. Same goes if a man says, 'I have not worked hard and succeeded.' Rather, a man should only be believed if he says, 'I have worked hard and succeeded.'"[151]

Because, Rabbi Isaac understood – what many of us have embraced for generations as Americans – that 'hard work produces results.' But, to what extent? Because, I can honestly say that no matter how hard I may practice art, I'll never be a Picasso. No matter how hard I may study, I'll never be an Einstein. No matter how hard I may try to do a *Double McTwist 1260,* I'm more likely to be seriously injured than to be a Shaun White. This does not mean I or any of us who cannot pull-off a *Double McTwist* are losers, destined to watch the medal platform than to be on it. It just means that we are not snow-boarders, artists, or mathematicians. Instead, it shows that we are likely gifted by God in some other way. For, as the rabbis of the *midrash* remind us, "At the very first moment of creation, God prepared every person for one task under Heaven."[152]

For what purpose did God prepare you? What Divine gift was bestowed uniquely unto you? Are you great with words or with colors? Are you great with children or with numbers? Once each of us discovers what it is that makes us unique, our tradition encourages us to pursue this gift with all our mind, with all our heart, and with all our being. For it is then, and only then, that we will truly be recognized as gifted, radiating – as Moses did (Exodus: 34:30) – having reached the summit of our Divine potential. May we recommit ourselves to this sacred task. For when we open our Divine gift, we present the essence of holiness to our world, moving others to do the same.

Ki Tissa // When You Take
Bite 3 – *At One with our Imperfections*

Some months ago, I got an unexpected delivery in the mail. It was a new *smicha* (certifying that, indeed, I am *still* a rabbi...whew!). It was sent by the Hebrew Union College-Jewish Institute of Religion to replace the one I was handed on ordination day. The letter, which accompanied the new *smicha*, stated: "Due to the unfortunate discovery of typos in the Ordination *Smichot* of last year, we have reprinted them with the mistakes removed," adding "we think!"[153] While

---

[151] BT Megillah 6b
[152] Exodus Rabbah 40:2; RaMBaN commentary to Exodus 31:2
[153] Letter sent from my dear friend and mentor, Rabbi Ken Kanter - Director of the Rabbinical School, on 19 July 2010.

apparently some uncertainty remains with even the new *smicha*, one thing is for sure… I am now faced with a small dilemma. Do I hang this one up in place of the other, as one – without mistakes – would be most reflective of the prestige of the College-Institute as well as my sacred profession? Or, do I leave the one with the imperfections where it is, as a testimony to our imperfect natures?

Amazingly, Moses was faced with a similar scenario. No, he didn't receive a *smicha* from HUC-JIR full of imperfections. (His came out just fine!) Rather, Moses' similar dilemma was experienced after he witnessed the Israelites worshiping the Golden Calf in this portion of *Ki Tissa*. As we may recall from this story, Moses – on his way down from Mt. Sinai – saw his people engaged in some elicit behavior. Upset, "he hurled the tablets from his hands and shattered them at the foot of the mountain." (Exodus 32:19) Then, after the people repented, God invited Moses back to the summit of Sinai, commanding him to "carve two [new] tablets of stone like the first and," says the Lord, "I will inscribe upon the tablets the words that were on the first, [this time without the typos]." (Exodus 34:1)

Alright, as far as we know, there weren't really any typos. Nevertheless, having two sets of tablets – one "perfect" and the other unmistakably imperfect, as it was in pieces – Moses was faced with a dilemma: what to do with the imperfect tablets? Should they be left at the foot of the mountain or should they be dealt with in some special way? After all, the Bible does tell us that the hand of God was upon them.[154] According to a *midrash*, preserved within the writings of the *Talmud*, the rabbis tell us that "the broken tablets were placed into the Holy Ark, alongside the whole tablets."[155] Why? In order to teach us that only when the imperfect parts of ourselves are held together with those parts which are considered perfect, can we hope to obtain a true sense of wholeness.

> It is a lesson presented to a great king many, many years ago. According to the story, this great king had amassed an even greater treasure; a treasure whose crown jewel was a large, flawless diamond. Its color was pristine; its cut, exquisite. In truth, it was perfect. And, after each and every long, hard day governing his kingdom: witnessing injustices, making difficult decisions, and settling conflicts, the king would retire to his private chamber to meditate on the perfection of this diamond. It brought him great comfort to know that, with all the imperfections of this world, at least one thing could be perfect. But, one night a tragedy occurred. While the king was caressing the diamond, it fell from his imperfect hands and careened through the air, smashing onto the stone floor. With trembling fingers, the king picked it up and peered very intently at his precious jewel. To his horror, the king perceived a deep scratch running along

---

[154] Exodus 31:18, 32:16
[155] BT Bava Batra 14b

its side. The king was distraught. Grieving over the scarred jewel, he bewailed: "Aaaahhhh, the last perfect thing in all of Creation... gone."

Seeking to comfort their leader, the king's ministers and servants brought all sorts of experts to the royal court in the hope that they may be able to repair the diamond. Jewelers, gemologists, scientists, technicians, and even wizards were engaged in this task. But, all failed to repair the deep scratch. The diamond was undeniably flawed. Its perfection ruined forever... Or, was it? Just as all hope appeared lost, there came an old, wise craftsman into the royal court. Looking over the diamond carefully, the craftsman's gaze shifted upward, into the solemn face of the king. "A week," he said. "Give me a week, and I'll repair the diamond." "You can repair it?!" responded the king, astonished. "But, so many others have tried and failed!" "Yes. Give me a week and I'll bring it back to you more perfect than before." answered the craftsman. "*More* perfect than before?!" echoed the king. "Yes, even more perfect." With that, the king handed the precious gem to the craftsman and the craftsman got to work.

After a week, the king anxiously called for the craftsman. "Well, have you fixed it?" asked the king. "I have," replied the craftsman. "It's perfect once more. In fact, as promised, it's more than perfect." Upon having the diamond in his hands, the king immediately lifted it to the light. And there – just as before – the scratch remained: long, deep, marring the perfection of the gem. "Do you mock me, craftsman?" bellowed the king. "It's still flawed!" "Look again," assuredly advised the craftsman. And the king looked again. This time bringing the diamond closer, he saw that the scratch was really no longer a scratch. With great art and precision the craftsman had engraved a delicate rosebud around the tip of the imperfection, transforming the deep scratch into a beautiful stem.

When the king and his courtiers saw what he had done with such thought and ingenuity, they were amazed! "Indeed!" said the king, "It is truly more unique, more remarkable, more perfect than ever before." And then modeling for his kingdom an act of sincere appreciation, the king honored him with all sorts of extravagance, thanking the craftsman for making him feel whole and complete once more.[156]

Now, isn't that the feeling we so earnestly search for in light of our imperfections? Do we not desire to feel whole and complete once more? Sure, we do. Why wouldn't we? But, even with all our attempts to go back to some earlier state of being, which through the distorted lens of memory appears wholly perfect, we soon come to realize – as Frodo Baggins did in *The Lord of*

---

[156] Story was adapted from a Rabbi Edward M. Feinstein version found in *Capturing the Moon: Classic and Modern Jewish Tales*. Behrman House, Inc.: New Jersey, 2008.

the Rings – "there [really] is no going back. There are some things that time cannot mend. Some hurts that go too deep, that have taken hold."[157] In other words, sometimes when that imperfection is made, it can be there forever, scarring the present and – we believe – marring its limitless potential. So, what do we do in this moment? Do we bewail our loss; inconsolably mourn and grieve over "the last perfect thing in all of Creation," as the king did? Or do we, as Moses did with the tablets, as the craftsman did with the scratch, find a way to place our imperfections side-by-side with that which we perceive as perfect?

From our tradition's perspective, there can be no doubt. We must keep our perfections in view of our imperfections. For then we can see the fullness, the wholeness of ourselves. And, from this precious perspective, we have a chance to achieve true at-one-ment, true atonement. Not with ourselves alone do we become at one. By connecting our imperfections with our perfections we also come closer with God. As it was taught by our Chasidic sages: "Each human being is tied to God by a rope. If the rope breaks, and is later fixed with a knot, that individual is closer to God than ever before." Thus errors, mistakes, failures (i.e. our imperfections), when they are brought together with our perfections, have the potential of drawing us even closer to God and ourselves.

I suppose, then, there is only one thing left for me to do... Go to the store to frame my new *smicha*, so that it can hang side-by-side with the one that's already there. And there it can remain, as a sign of our complete human potential, which certainly makes mistakes, after mistakes, after mistakes. But, also contained within us is the Divine potential to create something perfect. And thus, in maintaining both, we maintain the wholeness of our lives as well as our connection to the holiness of our lives, the Holy One, blessed be God.

---

[157] Philippa Boyens, Peter Jackson, Fran Walsh. *The Lord of the Rings: Return of the King*, based on J.R.R. Tolkien's novel. New Line Cinema: 2003.

Double Portion 10 & 11:
Vayakheil-P'kudei // He Assembled-The Records
Torah Portion: Exodus 35:1-40:38

"Moses then assembled the entire congregation of Israel." This double portion opens with Moses conferring to the entire Israelite community all that God has commanded: to keep Shabbat and those regulations concerning the Tabernacle.

The Israelites work under Betzalel and Oholiab's guidance (as God commanded) with the freewill gifts they had given to build the Tabernacle. With an outpouring of support, the Israelites flood these master craftsmen with more gifts than what was needed for the building of the Tabernacle. And, so, Moses instructs them to stop.

With all the material necessary assembled, and with those skilled in labor enlisted and ready for the task, the building of the Tabernacle finally commences at the end of the first of these two portions. They are to follow in God's instructions laid out in detail in the previous portions.

"These are the records of the Tabernacle, the Tabernacle of the Pact, which were drawn up at Moses' bidding." In the continuation of the double portion, some of the construction work of the Israelites is recorded. Upon the Tabernacle's completion, they bring their work before Moses. Seeing that the Tabernacle was completed according to God's instructions, Moses blesses the people. God then speaks to Moses concerning setting up the Tabernacle and ordaining Aaron and his sons, which will take place on the first day of the first Biblical month, Nissan.

Thus, one year after the Exodus, the Tabernacle was erected and a cloud covered it and the Presence of the Eternal filled the Tabernacle. The pillar of cloud by day and fire by night directs the Israelites when to remain encamped and when to begin journeying.

Vayakheil-P'kudei // He Assembled-The Records
Bite 1 – *Extreme Makeover: Mishkan Edition*

"Move that bus!" Words which have moved countless individuals to joyful tears in the hit ABC television series, *Extreme Makeover: Home Edition*, as one family after another is presented with the truly transformative gift of a new home and a new lease on life. And while it has taken a show to organize this dramatic change, it is important to note, that the change is created not by the show but by countless ordinary citizens who come together for that most sacred of purposes: helping others. Some, as those of you who watch the show will know, are just good-hearted people, moved to give of their time and energy to remove debris from the old homes and/or to move furniture into the new homes. Others, however, are a wonderful cadre of skilled volunteers: carpenters and craftsmen, designers and decorators, bulldozer operators and builders.

In fact, if unaware of the contexts, one may actually confuse an account from the double Torah portion of *Vayakheil-P'kudei* as just another exciting episode of *Extreme Makeover... Mishkan Edition*! Oh yes, for after the budding Israelite family was left in the dark of the desert following the luminous moment of Sinai, Moses initiates a building project, the *Mishkan*, a home in which the Divine light of God will reside. "Take," says Moses, "from among you gifts to the Lord from everyone whose heart is so moved: gold, silver, copper, etc." (Exodus 35:5) Furthermore, "let all among you who are skilled come and make all that the Lord has commanded: the *Mishkan* with its tent, its covering, its clasps, etc." (Exodus 35:10-11) Finally, states Moses, "The Lord has singled out Betzalel, son of Uri son of Hur, of the tribe of Judah by name. He has endowed him with a Divine spirit of skill...to give directions." (Exodus 35:30-34)

What?! Why would God single out an individual (other than Moses) in this communal project? For surely that appears counter to its purpose, which was to create a space to bring people together, not to single them out from one another. Well, according to the *midrash*, Betzalel was singled out from amongst the people because of a tradition which states that "when the Israelites were about to serve an idol (i.e. the Golden Calf), Hur (the grandfather to Betzalel) risked his life on God's behalf to stop them from doing so, with the result that he was killed. Whereupon the Holy One, blessed be God, said: 'I assure you that I will repay you for this. By My life, I swear, I shall give all My children that descend from you a great name in this world.'"[158]

Yet, I suspect that Moses' selection of Betzalel was made with less consideration about the past and, certainly, with more and more concern regarding the future. For when it comes to nation building, often times the first step to laying a firm foundation for the future comes simply from good-hearted people willing to step-up and make a difference. We see this not only from this Torah portion, as the first group Moses calls for are people "whose

---

[158] Exodus Rabbah 48:3

hearts are so moved," but the transformative power of good-hearted people is also evident in latter parts of history with the pilgrims and other early settlers of America, the *chalutzim* (pioneers) of the early *yishuv* in Israel, and even the protesters of the Middle East who are helping to initiate an extreme national makeover of their own.

But, it is not enough to have good-hearted people to fuel national change. To really engage in nation building one must have some sort of proficient engine to make use of the energy of the people. Otherwise, "it is all sound and fury, signifying nothing," as no movement is made.[159] This reality was demonstrated most clearly in Egypt. As we now know, a feeling of national unrest long brewed underneath what appeared to be a calm and stable political surface; a calm that would have likely endured had it not been for the advent of a young generation skilled in the use of computer engines like Google, Facebook, Twitter, and YouTube. Through the use of such tools, this skilled group – like that of Moses' second group of skilled individuals – translated a national feeling into tangible words and pictures, inspiring a nation and the world.

But still, that movement could have gone – as Joni Mitchell sang – "round and round and round, in the circle game" forever had it not been for the selection of a driver, an individual who could steer the movement of the people, both good-hearted and skilled alike, forward.[160] In Egypt, it would not be Mohammed ElBaradei as many had projected.[161] For even while his credentials as a Nobel Prize winner seemed appealing, his self-exile made him an outsider. But that's not the case for Wael Ghonim, a young Google executive.[162] Born in Egypt and imprisoned for 12 days by the former regime for his protest efforts, Ghonim was singled-out – as was Betzalel – because he could provide a more impassioned and authentic voice for the next generation, helping his people to move beyond seeing and articulating a vision to actually building that vision (i.e. that new lease of life after oppression).

That is why it is important to note that it was not the show, *Extreme Makeover: Home Edition* which creates a similar amazing change in the lives of others every week. The power to make this transformative, lasting, and positive change came from ordinary citizens like you and me. For, as this Torah portion reminds us through the character of Betzalel, we can each be that change. We can each be "filled with the Divine spirit of skill" to stand up and give direction to a national feeling, moving us beyond words and pictures to concrete actions. And thus we pray to You, dear Lord, that You will help us to use this spirit for good, so that we may be the Betzalel, the Wael Ghonim, the Ty Pennington of our generation, as we say "move that bus," revealing a new lease on life for ourselves, our neighbors, and all the world.

[159] William Shakespeare. *MacBeth*, Act V, Scene V.
[160] Joni Mitchell. "Circle Game." *Ladies of the Canyon*. Reprise Records: 1970.
[161] Dean Praetorius. "Mohammed ElBaradei: Egypt's Potential Future Leader." *The Huffington Post*: 28 January 2011.
[162] "Profile: Egypt's Wael Ghonim." *BBC News*: 8 February 2011. http://www.bbc.co.uk/news/world-middle-east-12400529

Vayakheil-P'kudei // He Assembled-The Records
Bite 2 – *Mobile Mishkans*

Think about this for a moment… What do most synagogues around the world have in common? An answer: a modest design, especially in comparison to the houses of worship of our co-religionists, as many synagogues, temples, and shuls rarely stand above two-stories in height. Why? Well, it's not because we, as a people, are acrophobic (afraid of heights). Nor are we afraid of becoming repeat offenders of the Tower of Babel fiasco, thus safely keeping our buildings low to the ground. No. What keeps us approaching the buildings of our Jewish institutions with modesty is a teaching contained in this double portion of *Vayakheil-P'kudei*.

After reading for weeks about the minutia regarding the building of the *Mishkan* (God's dwelling place in the desert) and the unending list of what the Israelites must bring for its construction (i.e. their gifts of gold, silver, and copper; their fine linens, yarns, and goat-hairs; their valuable skins and spices, along with their precious stones and aromatic scents), we finally read in this portion that these efforts are to stop. Beseeching the people at the end of the book of Exodus, Moses exclaims: "Let no man or woman make further effort toward making gifts to the sanctuary!" And, as a result, the people stopped bringing gifts, for the Bible makes explicit that "their efforts had been more than enough to get the job done." (Exodus 36:6-7)

But, why stop? I mean, had the father of fundraising – Moses – been too persuasive in his building campaign, realizing only now that similar to rain, wine, and – dare I say – beignets from Café du Monde, it's possible to have too much of a good thing? Thank God (especially from the stand-point of the beignets) this is not the case… at least not here. For here, Rabbi Harvey Fields writes, "One must make a distinction between support for Israelite institutions and *tzedakah*/charity for Israelites."[163] In other words, Moses' plea is not meant to stop our giving completely. It is merely meant to direct our efforts more productively, giving to people not places, giving to individuals not institutions.

Yet, as it has been the case, buildings have long garnered a significant portion of our attention as well as our resources. For example, the new World Trade Center (a.k.a. the Freedom Tower) is designed to stand at a whopping 1,776 feet tall (an echo of that famous year – 1776 – when America declared its independence). In addition to its towering height, this building is also projected to have a towering cost, estimated at three billion dollars and taking at least six years to complete.[164] Though, when completed, there are those who say that it will be worth it, because this building will stand as a sign of our resilience, a symbolic statement of our unwavering dedication to the Divine values of freedom and justice for all.

---

[163] Harvey J. Fields. *A Torah Commentary for Our Times. Volume Two: Exodus and Leviticus.* UAHC Press: New York, NY, 1991. p. 90.
[164] Charles V. Bagli. "Unions to Rally to Build Towers at Ground Zero." *New York Times*: NY/Region, 08 March 2010.

It could be said that a similar message is made by our synagogues. As attested to in the new Reform *siddur* (prayer book), *Mishkan T'filah*: "Our ancestors built the synagogue as a visible sign of God's Presence in their midst. Throughout our long history and our endless wanderings, it has endured [as] a beacon of truth, love, and justice for all humanity."[165] So, in addition to providing a sacred space for those inside its walls, the synagogue also speaks to those outside, "combating" what the 15th century sage Abravanel called "the notion that God has forsaken the earth, choosing to reside exclusively in Heaven, remote from humanity."[166]

Maybe, then, we can understand why Judaism considers giving to the building funds of our Jewish institutions such a great *mitzvah*/command. For the building, itself, can remind us that God does not dwell on some lofty height, but among us. Even so, we are taught that this is not enough. It is not enough to erect buildings, no matter how grand, to prove God lives *among* us. We must also show God lives *within* us by feeding the hungry, by clothing the naked, by caring for the sick, by funding educational opportunities for the poor, etc. The value of these random acts of kindness to neighbor and stranger alike cannot be understated. For, as Rabbi Assi fittingly taught, "No other commandment stands taller than the *mitzvah* of *tzedakah*."[167]

> This message is highlighted in the story of a 10 year-old boy, Joshua, who came from a small southern town. Many years ago, when an ice-cream sundae cost much less, little Joshua entered a hotel coffee shop during the afternoon rush and sat at one of the empty tables. A waitress, who was barely able to make ends meet, was busy with what she believed were more substantial and important orders that would certainly garner more tips. Quickly throwing down a glass of water in front of the little boy, she asked: "So, what do ya' want?"

> "How much is an ice-cream sundae?" inquired Joshua. "50 cents," replied the waitress, as she nervously tapped away at a pad of paper with her pen. Little Joshua reached his hand into his pocket and pulled out a small handful of coins. He studied them slowly for a minute. With the waitress growing ever more impatient, Joshua asked, "Well, then how much is just a dish of plain ol' ice-cream?"

> "35 cents," she answered brusquely, as many people – who would undoubtedly have more to order than this boy – were now waiting to be seated and served. But, little Joshua was oblivious. He only counted his coins. "Okay," he finally spoke up, "I guess I'll just have the plain ice-cream, please."

---

[165] *Mishkan T'filah: A Reform Siddur*. CCAR Press: New York, NY, 2007. p. 124
[166] *Etz Hayim: Torah and Commentary*. The Rabbinical Assembly: New York, NY, 2001. p. 485
[167] BT Baba Bara 9a

A few seconds later, the waitress brought the ice-cream, putting it on the table with the bill and immediately walked away. She didn't say a word. And the boy didn't mind. He was just happy to have his ice-cream. And, when he finished, he went over to the cashier to pay the 35 cents and departed.

By the time the waitress finally came back, the boy was long gone. But there, on the table, she saw – neatly placed beside the empty ice-cream dish – two nickels and five pennies: 15 cents, her tip. She swallowed hard, realizing that the little boy stopped giving to himself so that he could give to her. From then on, she never over-looked anybody or any order no matter how small they may appear.

That is why Moses stopped our giving to the *Mishkan*, redirecting our giving hearts from places to people, from institutions to individuals. Because, there is more than one way to create space for the Divine to dwell. In addition to a physical place, when we give of ourselves to another person, we ultimately open up a space for the Divine to reside within us and others. In fact, earlier in the book of Exodus, God made a statement to this effect. God said: "Make Me a Temple, so that I may dwell in them." (Exodus 25:8) "Why 'in them' and not 'in it?'" we may ask, as surely 'in it' would be more grammatically consistent with the singular subject: Temple.

Because, states the Hasidic Rabbi Menachem Mendel Morgenstern, better known as the Kotzker Rebbe (1787-1859), "This is because 'in them' refers to each and every individual. God is asking us to become [mobile] *mishkanot*, [mobile] dwellings for the Divine Presence on earth."[168] In other words, by giving to others, by dealing with a little less so that someone else may have a little more, by focusing our efforts on people rather than places, no one will ever doubt where God is. For we will prove it with every breath we take and with every move we make.[169]

Vayakheil-P'kudei // He Assembled-The Records
Bite 3 – *"And, I'd Like to Thank God."*

If an alien to this planet were to spend any time here, how would it come to understand God? Possibly, I imagine that it may come to understand the Holy One, Blessed be God, as a very busy sports coach with no particular allegiance to any one team, or an over-worked cinema director with an eclectic taste in movies, or potentially even a very inspired composer of an array of musical genres. For how many times have we seen the victor on the field of play or the prize-recipient at some awards show attribute their mortal accomplishment to the Divine with the words: "And, I'd like to thank God for this achievement?"

---

[168] Quoted by Aharon Yaakov Greenberg in *Torah Gems*. Yavneh Publishing House LTD.: Tel Aviv, Israel, 1998. p. 172.
[169] Adapted from Police. "Every Breath You Take." *Synchronicity*, 1983.

It's not such a bad understanding, to be clear, as one may actually glean a similar association between human deeds and Divine accomplishments from *Vayakheil-P'kudei*. Because after engaging a considerable amount of human effort in the preparation, assembly, and building of the Tabernacle and all its furnishings (which was detailed to exhaustion in the last four Torah portions of the book of Exodus), the Israelites – under the artistic leadership of Betzalel – finally present the finished product to Moses, who thereupon – states the Bible – shows his thanks by "blessing them." (Exodus 39:43)

Or, did he? While on the surface it appears as if Moses' words acknowledge both his acceptance and appreciation of the Israelites' mortal deeds, rabbinic tradition may lend itself to a different conclusion. For preserved in the discourse of our sages are the fabled words of that blessing. As they are recorded in the *Tanchuma*: "Moses blessed the people, saying, 'May the Divine Presence continue to rest upon the works of your hands.'"[170] In other words, Moses said to them: "And, I'd like to thank God for *your* achievements."

God?! I mean, was it God who collected every bit of yarn and metal from the 600,000 plus Israelites, who then weaved as well as molded these items into a usable form when constructing the illustrious Tabernacle? Or, for that matter we can ask, is it God who throws the successful Hail Mary touchdown-pass to win the game, or who hits the grand-slam with a tie-game in the bottom of the ninth with two outs? If it is, well then, I'm picking God to be on my next fantasy sports team! In truth, we know that it is not God who does these things; we do. And, to thank God entirely for these human accomplishments, some say, belittles the important role we can play in the betterment of our world.

Though others don't waste a minute to "*baruch haShem*" (bless and thank God) for their human feats both big and small. Sure, among this group there are those who articulate such sentiments sincerely and humbly. They understand that in these moments of praise-worthy deeds, there is the chance of misplacing that praise upon the person (rather than the deed). So, to make it clear that is not what is or should be happening, the victor rightly and righteously acknowledges God, shifting the focus off him or herself. Yet others, as it has been asserted, make such noble statements only from the standpoint of political correctness, bowing less to God and more to cultural expectations.

But, for us in the Jewish world, we understand the words – *baruch haShem* – to mean so much more than humility and political correctness. These words can also help others to know and understand God and God's connection to our human endeavors. Such was the case with Abraham and Sarah, as captured in the *midrash* of our sages. As it is told:

---

[170] The *Tanchuma* is a collection of *midrashim* ascribed to Rabbi Tanchuma of the second half of the fourth century C.E. Noted in the *Etz Hayim: Torah and Commentary*. p. 568

It was the custom of Abraham to go forth and make rounds everywhere while he and his wife, Sarah, were stationed at the Terebinths of Mamre. And, where and when he found a traveler, he would bring him into their tent, which was – according to Abraham and Sarah's open and welcoming nature – open on all four sides.

To him who was unaccustomed to eating the luxury of wheat bread, Abraham and Sarah served wheat bread. To him who was unaccustomed to eating the luxury of meat, Abraham and Sarah served meat. And, to him who was unaccustomed to the luxury of drinking wine, Abraham and Sarah gave them wine to drink.

Abraham even went so far as to wash the feet of his guests; a grand gesture of genuine friendship among desert people. Then, as it would seem appropriate, the travelers would thank Abraham and Sarah for their generosity and hospitality. But, they would stop the travelers in mid-sentence:

"Thank us not," stated Abraham. "Rather, we ask that you offer thanks and blessings to the Holy One, Blessed be God. For, it is God who made everything in Heaven and on earth. We are merely the humble and thankful servants, who bring God's bounty before you."

And, as the *midrash* goes on to state, in this manner Abraham and Sarah made God's Name known throughout the world; an act, to which God responded by stating: "Until now My Name had not been known. Thus, I shall regard you as though you had worked with Me in the creation of the world."[171] In other words, by acknowledging God through our words of thanks, we do not diminish our role in the world. As a point of fact, from our tradition, we increase it. For as we make God a partner in the deeds of our hands, God also makes room for us to be partners to His deeds as well.

And that, my dear friends, is the understanding that any of us should glean about God in our world, whether we are an alien just stopping through on a fact-finding mission or a longtime resident searching for life's meaning. We exist in partnership with God whether as a football or baseball player and God is the coach, or as an actor, a musician, or a craftsman and God is the director, the composer, or the master architect. Let us continue to honor this partnership by making room in our speech as well as within our deeds for the Holy One, Blessed be God. For then, we pray – as Moses did – that the Divine Presence may continue to rest upon the works of our hands as we make this world a fitting place for us and God to reside.

Chazak, chazak, v'nitchazeik!
From strength to strength, we are strengthened!

---

[171] Genesis Rabbah 48:7 and Avot d'Rabbi Natan, chapter 7

LEVITICUS

Vayikra

Portion 1:
Vayikra // He Called
Torah Portion: Leviticus 1:1-5:26

"AND THE LORD CALLED TO MOSES AND SPOKE TO HIM FROM THE TENT OF MEETING." After all, the Tent of Meeting was completed just as the book of Exodus came to an end. It's fitting then to start Leviticus with God commanding Moses from the Tent of Meeting, informing him of that which was to take place in and around this sacred space.

Namely, it was the sacrifices: the burnt-offerings, the meal-offerings, and the peace-offerings. These sacrifices were designed to offer thanks to God as well as to atone for sins committed. The Israelite bringing the offering was legislated to come to the Tent of Meeting and lay his hand on the head of the animal that would be slaughtered. Aaron's sons, the priests, shall scatter the blood, light the fire on the altar, and burn the animal in a way pleasing to God. The meal-offering (unleavened cakes of flour or wafers with oil baked in) is described as an alternative to the animal sacrifice.

God also outlines the process of forgiveness for one who sins through error, whether it was an individual or the entire congregation of Israel. Many other categories of sins of omission and commission are given, in which God allows the Israelites to atone for these sins through the process of ritual sacrifice. One who fails to testify in court, one who touches an unclean thing, animal, or person, and one who utters an oath are all given a prescribed sacrifice to atone for their sin.

The portion concludes with a reassuring thought for this fledgling society of Israel, which shall be guided by justice and not by vengeance. Even one who deals deceitfully with his neighbor, robs or defrauds them, can be forgiven upon reparation of what he stole plus one-fifth. By making these offerings before man and God, "he shall be forgiven for whatever he may have done to draw blame thereby." (Leviticus 5:26)

Vayikra // He Called
Bite 1 – *A Student's First Steps*

With Passover approaching, we are once again reminded of our obligation to transmit Torah to the next generation. As we read in the Haggadah of Crosby, Stills, Nash, and Young: "Teach your children well, their father's hell, did slowly go by."[1] But where do we begin? Maybe it's fitting, as Passover approaches, to begin with the captivating story of the Exodus. After all, two great movies have been born from its pages: *The Ten Commandments* (1956) and more recently *The Prince of Egypt* (1998). Speaking of movies, maybe we should begin instead with the unusual text that inspired Shrek: Balaam and his talking donkey. (Numbers 22)

Or, I suppose, we could always go more traditionally and begin "in the beginning, [when] God created Heaven and the earth."[2] But, surprisingly, this first verse in the book of Genesis is not the traditional embarkation point for a child's Jewish journey through Torah. Traditionally, a child's educational exploration into our holy texts will begin in the book of Leviticus with the words: "The Lord *vayikra*/called to Moses and spoke to him from the Tent of Meeting, saying: 'Speak to the Israelites and say to them…'" (Leviticus 1:1-2) And what follows in this portion of *Vayikra,* as well as throughout the book of Leviticus, is verse after verse, chapter after chapter of ritual law.

"Woo, hoo!" exclaims one confused child, who thinks that a burnt-offering has something to do with barbequing. The rest of the children, though, remain silent; for they – like many of us – believe that the book of Leviticus is rarely that intellectually delectable. So, why then do some insist that our children begin their engagement with Judaism here, rather than in the dramatic narratives of Genesis? Addressing this question in the late 3rd century C.E., Rav Assi taught, "Children are pure. Therefore, it is fitting that they should begin their engagement with the study of ritual purity," which happens to be found in just about every chapter and verse of Leviticus."[3]

Yet, it's also possible that this astute pedagogic choice of Leviticus over Genesis was made, not because of any chapter or verse, but because of a single word: *vayikra,* meaning 'called,' as its final letter – *aleph* – is intentionally written smaller than the other letters in the Torah. This small and ever-so silent *aleph,* beginning the book of Leviticus, draws our attention ironically to a resounding lesson on learning. Namely, informed speech – which calls the world to change – cannot be achieved without a preparatory moment of silence. Or, to put it another way, holy speech is contingent upon first achieving a moment that is wholly silent.

---

[1] "Teach Your Children." *Déjà Vu.* Atlantic Records: 1970.
[2] Genesis 1:1
[3] Leviticus Rabbah 7:3

This task, however, is easier said than done. Even at the beginning of our lives we are rarely silent. For example, generations of parents have attempted to lull babies into a quiet rest with nursery rhymes, like "Hush, little baby, don't say a word…" And, it is not like we have gotten any quieter with age. In fact, now-a-days, the once customary greeting of any public address – "Ladies and Gentleman, welcome" – has been replaced with "Ladies and Gentlemen, please silence your cell-phones." At least in theaters we are provided with a reason, as many a movie screen will remind us: "Silence is Golden."

But gold is not what Judaism values. It's wisdom. Therefore, Judaism addresses the value of silence another way. Written in Proverbs, we read that "even a fool, if he keeps silent, is considered wise; intelligent, if he seals his lips."[4] Now, I suppose, one could argue that a fool blathering incessantly benefits no one. And, thus, his silence is only regarded as 'wise' by others, who wish him not to speak. Perhaps. Yet, it is also possible that the fool, realizing his limited knowledge, chooses the medium of silence as a teacher. Understanding the value of silence as a powerful educational medium is highlighted in a famous story from our tradition.[5] The story goes something like this:

> Several Jews were once having an argument. The first claimed that God had given the whole Torah, word by word. A second one said that God gave only the Ten Commandments. A third person, however, remembered the old legend from the *Talmud* which states that God didn't even give ten, but only directly gave the first two sayings: *I am the Lord your God and you shall not have any other gods besides Me.*[6] "After all," that person contested, "the first two sayings are the basis for all of Judaism. One who remembers that there is but one God and no other will probably go on to live a healthy Jewish life."
>
> "No. God didn't even say that much!" insisted a fourth person, who walked in on the conversation. "All God said was the first word of the first saying, *I* (or in the Hebrew, *Anochi*). And, all four agreed. If God had only said one word, it would have been *Anochi*, because it affirms the unity of the Divine soul that rests in every individual. However, just then, Rabbi Mendel who had overheard the entire argument came forward and said, "Not even the first word. All God said was the first letter of the first word of the first saying of the Ten Commandments, which in Hebrew is also the first letter of the aleph-bet: *aleph*."[7]
>
> "But we thought that the *aleph* was a silent letter," replied the others. "Almost, but not perfectly silent," answered Rabbi Mendel. "You see,

---

[4] Proverbs 17:28
[5] Adapted from Lawrence Kushner's "The Silent Sound of Aleph." *The Book of Miracles: A Young Person's Guide to Jewish Spiritual Awareness*. Jewish Lights Publishing: Woodstock, VT. 1997. p. 41-42
[6] BT Makkot 23a
[7] Rabbi Mendl Torum of Rimanov (1745-1815) was a German Hasidic Rebbe and author.

aleph makes a tiny, little sound that is the beginning of every other sound. Open your mouth. Go ahead. Open your mouth and begin to make a sound. Now, stop! That's an *aleph*. See," Rabbi Mendel continued, "God made the voice of the *aleph* so quiet that if you made any other noise you wouldn't be able to hear it. So, at Sinai, all the people of Israel needed to hear was the silent sound of the *aleph*. It meant that God and the Jewish people were ready to begin a conversation."

In other words, within the glittering gold of silence we not only are given a chance to perceive the beauty of the world, we are also presented with an opportunity to receive the knowledge it projects, understanding more completely what really makes us rich. Yet, silence is not always golden. According to a quote I recently came across, "Sometimes silence is just plain yellow!" When? It's when – after perceiving the world and reaping its knowledge through silence – we remain silent…cowardly…yellow. For silence should not be the end of our spiritual path. Silence is merely the beginning which should spur us onward to find our own prophetic voice, articulating the needs and dreams of those voices which have been muted by our society. As Moshe ben Ezra, the 11th century Spanish Jewish poet and religious philosopher stated, "The path to wisdom begins with silence, followed by hearing, then memory, and finished with action."

That is why we begin our Jewish journeys here, with Leviticus, rather than Genesis. For contained in this one word, *vayikra,* is the entire mission of Israel; a mission which calls upon us to first tap into our spiritual oil, before becoming a light unto the nations; a mission which calls upon us to first hear the ever-so silent voice of the *aleph* that is authentically speaking to us, before we can authentically speak to the world. As we approach this holiday of Passover, in which we are reminded to teach our children well, let us therefore begin at the beginning…with the first word of the Hebrew alphabet: *aleph*. Because, from this first and most basic building block of our vocabulary, we will be able to construct the words and sentences, which can serve as the firm foundation of complex thoughts, which may allow us to dwell in lives of meaning and action.

Vayikra // He Called
Bite 2 – *Taking a Ritual Stand*

In an attempt to combat the pressures of a world incessantly on the move, a young Jewish mother sets out to make a grand Shabbos meal for her family. Besides giving her family a chance to sit and enjoy time with one another, in this moment she knows that her daughter will have a chance to learn – as she did from her mother – the meaningful work it takes to bring family together. So, as the daughter observed her mother slicing the ends off a perfectly good brisket before placing it into a pan, she was perplexed. "Why, mother, do you cut off the ends?" she asked.

The mother paused for a moment and then said to her daughter: "You know... I am not really sure. That's just the way I observed my mother preparing a brisket. Let's call Grandma and ask." So, the young mother calls her mother and asks: "Mom, when I was young I always saw you cut off the ends of the brisket before roasting it. I now do the same and was wondering why it must be done." The grandmother pauses for a moment and then says to her daughter, "You know, darlin'... I'm not sure either. That's just the way I always saw *my* mother make it."

With all three women now curious, they decided to pay a visit to the great-grandmother of this family, who – thanks be to God – was still alive and being cared for at the nearby nursing home. "Bubbie," stated the young mother, "we have a question for you. We know that when we make a brisket, we must cut off the ends before roasting it. But," added the young mother, "we were wondering why we did this." The very elderly woman paused for a moment and then stated: "Well, I don't know why *you* do it. But, I can tell you why *I* did. *I* did it because that was the only way I could fit the brisket into my small pan!"

To some, the rituals of Leviticus (which begins with this portion of *Vayikra*) make as much sense as cutting the ends off a brisket. That is to say, there are some things that our ancestors did generations ago because they fit into their religious framework. But, within a more contemporary context, these rituals seem to make little, if any, real sense. Rituals like: "when a bull is slaughtered before the Lord, Aaron's sons shall offer up its blood, dashing it against all the sides of the altar." (Leviticus 1:5) I mean, yuk! What a mess! Or, "every grain offering shall be seasoned with salt." (Leviticus 2:13) Hey, that's not good for anyone's cholesterol! Or even, "you must not eat any of the fat, for all fat is the Lord's." (Leviticus 3:16-17). But, that's where all the flavor is stored!

And it's not just people today who are making the charge that these ancestral affairs seem remote from contemporary concerns. Standing in the ruins of the Temple in 70 C.E., Rabbi Yochanan ben Zakkai told his students, "Do not grieve [over the loss of the sacrifices]. For, we have a means of atonement that is far more effective. It is performing acts of loving-kindness. For God taught," from the prophet Hosea, "I desire mercy, not sacrifices."[8] Then why did God institute sacrifices to begin with? Because, according to *Leviticus Rabbah*, God thought: "Better that they bring their offerings to My table than they are brought before idols."[9] For within the religious framework at the time, the Israelites could not conceive of a religious culture without ritual sacrifice.

---

[8] Pirkei Avot d'Rabbi Natan 4; Hosea 6:6
[9] Leviticus Rabbah 22:8

But we can, as evident in the fact that we have maintained our faith over thousands of years without a Temple and the sacrifices that were performed therein. Yet despite our enlightened minds, which seem to prefer spontaneous spiritual expressions over religious ceremonies, some part of our soul still seems to yearn for proscribed practices, as we have merely replaced the ritual of sacrifice with the ritual of prayer. To be fair, these rituals represent – to some – only the start of a process. Like the journey our people took from sacrifices to prayer, prayer too could be understood as merely another step towards discovering our own words to spontaneously express the soul.

Yet, even then, others will insist that the human soul will still desire some semblance of a ritual. This latent desire has been documented well in the lives of children. According to research, children who embrace a daily routine, a daily ritual, at home have shown to perform far better in all other areas of their lives.[10] The reason, suggests the research, is that when a child knows what to expect from the environment, he/she can invest more energy learning about him/herself. In fact, it's a valuable lesson that grows exponentially with each and every ritual, which somehow our soul comes to appreciate as a handrail on the course of life, providing some confidence and security in an incessantly changing and moving world.

Though this confidence, to be clear, is more than a sense that we are simply "doing things right," because we can see from the ritual of the brisket that not all rituals are about doing things in the most efficient of ways. Rather, the confidence born from rituals comes from the knowledge that we are doing something that was done by our parents, and their parents, and their parents before them... possibly all the way back to Sinai! As it is stated in this portion, "It shall be a law for all time, throughout the ages." (Leviticus 3:17) So, how is that knowledge empowering? Because in knowing that this one act connects us to others, we are provided a tangible sense of communal support, strong enough to help us to stand confidently and securely in any moment.

This is not to say that rituals can't sometimes let us down. Whether, for example, it's driving to work unconsciously morning after morning after morning only to find ourselves there on our day-off, or embracing the environmentally-friendly habit of turning off the lights when we leave a room only to mindlessly leave someone in the dark in a public restroom, or even cutting off the ends of a brisket needlessly, rituals can get us and others into an occasional pickle. But, when done in a conscious way, with an awareness that these acts connect us with generations past, they can (as we continue to read of them) fill our days with an endless amount of strength and meaning.

---

[10] For more information as well as links to other resources about the value of routines in the lives of children, please check out PBS online at http://www.pbs.org/wholechild/providers/little.html

Vayikra // He Called
Bite 3 – *Pursue or Be Pursued*

After numerous rounds of respectful but tempered applause, typical of most conferences, I heard a speaker articulate convincingly the reasons for a preemptive strike against Iran. At that point, in the general session, the applause reached a feverish pitch. An overwhelming majority of attendees stood in a rousing ovation. I could not. My body was hunched over in pain, as my heart broke. It's not that I don't understand war or its occasional necessity. As a Jew and as a former USAF Chaplain, I understand all too well that – at times – we must physically confront evil to ensure good survives.[11] But, what caused so much pain for me at that moment was the pure, unadulterated, joy expressed by others, who hoped and even prayed for war.

I can tell you, at moments like those, a standing ovation is far from the typical response one would hear even from the most ardent military members.[12] With an intimate knowledge about the steep costs of war for themselves, for their families, for the communities in which these battles are waged, most service members – upon receiving their orders – sit in silence, becoming resigned to getting the job done, becoming resolved to getting back home as quickly as possible. In fact, it's that harmony of the home, which some believe motivated God in this portion of *Vayikra* to proscribe only domesticated animals to be used as sacrifices on the Holy altar: the bull and the cow, the sheep and the goat, the pigeon and the dove.

"Why?" asked the sages. "Why does God desire these animals and not others?" Because, answered Rabbi Eliezer, God seeks only those who live in harmony with nature (i.e. herbivores, who are pursued as prey). "The cow is pursued by the lion, the goat is pursued by the leopard, the sheep by the wolf, the pigeon by the fox. Therefore, God said, 'Do not offer Me those who pursue; offer me those who are pursued.'"[13] Rabbi Abahu, in the *Talmud*, applied this Divine desire to man. He taught, so too "should man always be among the pursued (i.e. those who live in harmony with nature) and not the pursuers. For, they are the only ones God happily accepts."[14] In other words, to ensure the Divine's acceptance, it seems ill-advised to encourage and pursue war.

Though given our unique Jewish history, which has had more than its fair-share of violent confrontations, this Biblical teaching seems odd, if not outright hypocritical. Because, that history has plainly taught us the benefits of standing up for our beliefs, even by physical force: whether it was the Maccabees and their war against the Hellenized Assyrians, the early rabbis and their revolts against the Romans, or our brethren in the modern State of Israel

---

[11] Edmund Burke is commonly attributed as saying: "All that is necessary for evil to triumph is for good men to do nothing."

[12] This is apparent, every year, in the US President's State of the Union address. The military officials, in attendance, take an attentive pose, without offering an emotional response.

[13] Vayikra Rabba 27:5

[14] BT Bava Kamma 93a

and their ceaseless battles to ensure their existence. Even in our losses, we have come to understand that doing something is far better than doing nothing. For not fighting back, when necessary, leads only to greater devastation, as we tragically experienced in the Holocaust.

So, then, how are we to make sense of this seemingly impractical teaching? For, surely, God would not want us to be prey, awaiting some pursuing beast to bring about our demise. "Definitely not," responds Ray from the movie *Rain Man*.[15] God desires our survival. Thus, it is best to understand this teaching as one of temperance rather than non-violence. For, when it comes to our "enemies," Moses advised that we will "not be able to put an end to them all at once, lest wild beasts multiply to [our] hurt."[16] Interpreting this enigmatic warning, Rabbi Israel taught, "This means that if we become too adept at war, too prone to violence, some of our people will come to enjoy it. Then, we will become like wild beasts, unfit for God's service."[17]

In fact, when lives are unfortunately taken to ensure God's values of freedom and justice for all, people are not the only ones affected (as we see much too often with our fighting men and women experiencing PTSD). The taking of life, even when justified, aggravates God as well. We see this in our Exodus from Egypt. Upon arriving on freedom's shore, God closes the Sea of Reeds around Pharaoh and his army. In our joy, our ancestors erupted in song: "*Mi chamocha ba-eilim Adonai...* / Who is like You, Adonai..."[18] Yet, God did not sing along. Instead, directing our attentions back to the sea, God silenced us, saying: "Why do you sing? Can you not see that they are my children too?"[19]

These, my friends, are some of the high costs of war. And, as such, it is painfully inappropriate to God and to our fellow men and women in uniform (to whom we owe so much) to approach the notion of going to battle so cavalierly: pursuing the fight, applauding the potential taking of human life. May we be more tempered than that. May we be both more humane and more Divine-like than that. May we, in contemplating future physical confrontations, weigh these costs thoughtfully. For, in doing so, we pray that our sacrifices, carried most heavily on the backs of our fighting men and women, will continue to be counted as a blessing in God's holy service.

---

[15] Barry Morrow. *Rain Main*. United Artists: 1988.
[16] Deuteronomy 7:22
[17] Harold Kushner, ed. *Etz Hayim: Torah and Commentary*. The Rabbinical Association: New York, 2001. p. 1038.
[18] Exodus 15:11
[19] *Midrash Avkir*; BT Sanhedrin 39b

Portion 2:
Tzav // Command
Torah Portion: Leviticus 6:1-8:36

"THE LORD SPOKE TO MOSES, SAYING: 'COMMAND AARON AND HIS SONS…'" After elaborating on the laws of the sacrificial rituals that were to take place in and around the Tent of Meeting in the previous portion, God proceeds to impart to Moses the role of Aaron and his sons, as the priests, who collectively will administer and minister the sacrificial cult of the congregation of Israel.

In carrying out the congregation's sacrifices, the priests must wear a special outfit of a linen garment and linen breeches. After lighting the fire and burning the sacrifices, the priests would eat what was left of the sacrifice "without leaven in a holy place… as a due forever throughout your generations." (Leviticus 6:11)

Moses then takes Aaron and his sons and anoints them as priests to the people of Israel. Moses assembles the people at the Tent of Meeting, washes Aaron and his sons with water, and clothes Aaron with the priestly tunic, sash, robe, ephod, headdress, diadem, and the holy breastplate as well as the *urim v'tumim* (sacred objects carried within the breastplate, used for communing with God). He similarly dresses Aaron's sons with tunics, sashes and turbans.

Aaron and his sons lay their hands on a bull, which is offered as a purification offering to God, a ram which is given for a burnt-offering, and a second ram, offered as an ordination offering. Moses takes anointing oil and blood from the sacrifices, sprinkles it on Aaron and his sons, and commands them to boil the flesh of the offerings and eat it, as well as the bread from the basket of ordination.

Their ordination at the entrance of the Tent of Meeting would take seven days, paralleling the seven days of Creation, for it indicated a new beginning for the people of Israel.

Tzav // Command
Bite 1 – *Sacrifice: A Vaccination from Greed*

Our country, and for that matter the world, is sick. The global economic system has been infected with a disease which started a few years ago with the collapse of the housing market and spread so quickly that – to many of us – nothing appeared immune. The viral contagion responsible for this societal sickness, this impurity of the American Dream, is 'Greed;' a condition spawned from a perversion of our human nature, which rightfully fights for survival. But, where this justifiable human response has gone awry is not in the desire to fight, but in the manner this battle is being waged. Instead of fighting for the survival of a people, each individual – infected with Greed – is battling for the preservation of self at the expense of the people. And, the cost is painfully felt by us all at this critical moment in our nation's history.

Yet, like an infomercial, our Torah text comes to advertise a simple and fast-acting solution to this serious problem. The remedy, as it is stated in this portion of *Tzav*, is… *Sacrifice*. Yes! Now you can rid yourself of 'Greed' in three easy steps. First, take a handful of choice flour. Second, pour oil and lay frankincense upon the flour. And, finally, hand it all to a priest so that it can be laid upon an altar and turned into smoke as a pleasing odor to the Lord. It is, according to Leviticus 6:11, guaranteed to work as "anything or anyone that touches these [holy sacrifices] shall become holy [themselves]."

Now, before we rush to our phones to call 1-800-GOD-IS-1 and hand over our credit cards, let us pause to understand what we are buying into. Is the Torah really stating that all we have to do to correct the problems of this world is to touch something holy? It's not out of the question, as this concept is common among many faiths. Every day, around the world, people cling to tangible items, especially those believed to be invested with holiness: iconography of deities, statues of leaders, symbols of faith. We touch these items hoping, thinking, praying that somehow – through these things – we will be inoculated from the disease of 'Greed' and the other countless evils that infect our world.

But, do such things really work? To answer this question I sought a second opinion from modern commentator Baruch Levine, who is well versed in the fine-print of Torah. He writes, "[In the Biblical world] the condition of holiness, unlike that of impurity, was not regarded as contagious." Thus, he suggests, the verse from Leviticus "would be better translated as: 'Anyone who is to touch these [holy sacrifices] must be already in a state of holiness."[20] In other words, we cannot go from a state of impurity to a state of purity simply by coming in contact with something or someone that is holy. Similar to the Biblical world, today the transformative change we desire and the type of change our world so desperately needs can only be generated when we engage in holy deeds (not in holy items).

---

[20] Baruch Levine. "Leviticus." *Etz Hayim: Torah and Commentary*. The Rabbinical Assembly: New York, 2001. p. 615.

Therefore, the pertinent question we must ask to counter Greed is not *should* we act; it's *how* should we act. As a society, we often are mistaken in this endeavor. We frequent the mall as <u>consumers</u> to feel as if we are worth something. We repeatedly <u>consume</u> food so that we feel fulfilled in some way. And, we <u>consummate</u> relationships that shouldn't be consummated so that we feel loved by someone. It's a mindset that was highlighted in February of 2008, when a former Secretary of Labor suggested that "the only lasting remedy of this economic sickness is to give middle- and lower-income Americans more buying power,"[21] a financial injection, if you will. Yet, since then we have witnessed this financial injection wear off. And, now, we require booster shot after booster shot of money to keep the positive effects on our economy going.

So, if we cannot buy our way out of this mess, surely the way we recover from Greed is to save our way out, forgoing the pleasures of this world. Not so, according to Rabbi Abba Hillel Silver, the 20th century American Reform Rabbi and Zionist. He writes, the answer to Greed is not found on the other side of the spectrum either as "not a single one of the 613 positive and negative commandments enjoins any form of asceticism…"[22] In fact, over a thousand years earlier, Rabbi Yitzhak interpreted such a lifestyle equally as selfish as consuming. And, he advised anyone who witnessed another individual taking a vow of abstinence – whether it be from drinking wine, cutting hair, even having sex – to say: "Are not all the restrictions in the Torah enough for you? Why do you restrain yourself from that which the Torah permits you to enjoy?"[23]

And one could add to his words, "to enjoy… *with others*." For the Jewish remedy to Greed is not found in consumption or in abstention, or even in time-tested, bubbie-approved chicken soup. No, the Jewish way to counter Greed, and to stay the trouble that is engulfing our world, is actually to share, to enjoy the pleasures of this world with others. Traditionally, this is done through sacrificing a portion – a *maaser* – to others. Specifically chosen, the word *maaser* means "a tenth" (from which we derive our modern word "tithe") and implies that the sacrifice is not and should not be one that results in the giver becoming a receiver of charity. Rather, the sacrifice should be just enough that we feel its loss in our world, so that we may better understand the gain it has in the lives of others.

Dealing with a little less, so that someone else might have a little more: this is the sacrifice our Torah is talking about when it says that we become holy through touch. It's not because we <u>touched</u> holy items, but by participating in a holy deed of generosity we <u>touch</u> the lives of others. In the Biblical world, sacrifice was our ancestors' way of confronting a similar societal sickness that we are experiencing right now. It was a vaccination of sorts from the perversion of our human nature which may at times – especially in difficult

---

[21] Robert B. Reich. "Totally Spent." *New York Times*: 13 February 2008.
[22] Abba Hillel Silver. *Where Judaism Differed*. Macmillan: New York, 1956. Pp. 195; 198-199.
[23] *Jerusalem Talmud, Nedarim* 9:1, 30:3

times – be more concerned about the self than about others. Therefore, if we ever hope to have a lasting economic recovery and return to a healthier society, we today must also sacrifice. Not because we were forced to by the stock markets or by our political leaders. Instead, we should sacrifice a portion of our blessings to others because that is what are hearts are moved to do.

Sacrifice, after all, is not a renegotiation of society's contract. Sacrifice, rather, is a recommitment ceremony to its original terms; terms that state we have a responsibility to care for one another, a responsibility to ensure that my success does not come at the cost of another's failure; terms that impress upon each of us to live and walk with God, who is – according to the book of Exodus (34:6) – "gracious and compassionate, patient, abounding in kindness and faithfulness, assuring love for a thousand generations." Through sacrifice, through giving a portion of our blessings so that others may be blessed themselves, we too can be gracious and compassionate, patient, abounding in kindness and faithfulness, assuring love for a thousand generations, so that Greed no longer has a foot-hold in our world.

Tzav // Command
Bite 2 – *It's a Thin Line Between Good and Evil*

On 25 March 2011, Jackson State University – in full cooperation with the Veterans of the MS Civil Rights Movement – hosted Minister Louis Farrakhan of the Nation of Islam, who delivered the keynote address at their annual Civil Rights Convention "to," states the press release, "inspire and empower today's youth."[24] To some this selection makes complete sense as Farrakhan is considered a recognizable and competent leader in many African American communities. He, in concert with the Nation of Islam, has fought successfully against crime and drug abuse in predominantly poor neighborhoods, facilitated important counseling programs for gang-members, prisoners, drug addicts and alcoholics, and has rightfully voiced opposition to a system of governance in America that spends much more on prisons than on education.[25]

However, to many others, his invitation to be the keynote speaker at a convention specifically commemorating the Civil Rights Movement and honoring one of its many enduring messages – "Respect for All" – is not only perplexing, it is downright offensive, especially to the diverse group of Americans who lived and died to fulfill the dream of equality for all people. For, Farrakhan has repeatedly and unapologetically distorted the facts of history in order to perpetuate stereotypes that create divisions in American society. To be clear, it is not just Jews who he has singled out as targets, calling them "bloodsuckers" and labeling Judaism as a "dirty/gutter religion."[26]

[24] "Min. Farrakhan, Shirley Sherrod, Myrlie Evers Williams to Speak at Civil Rights Veterans Conference." *Jackson Advocate: The Voice of Black Mississippians.* 11 March 2011
[25] William A. Henry III. "Louis Farrakhan: Pride and Prejudice." *Time Magazine*: 28 February 1994
[26] Louis Farrakhan. "Letter to the Editor." *Wall Street Journal*: 18 June 1997

Farrakhan has also spoken out against Catholics for "subjecting black people to a white-kind of theology"[27] and homosexuals, who he recently referred to as "swine."[28]

While these dueling perspectives regarding Farrakhan may confuse and shock many of us, it is likely they would have been comprehendible to and even expected by our Israelite ancestors. For, our ancestors seemed to have known well the complex nature of man. After outlining the rituals for each of the various sacrifices in the first portion of their priestly manual, known today as the book of Leviticus, we read in *Tzav* that the Lord spoke to Moses, saying, "Speak to Aaron and his sons regarding the ritual of the purification offering [to atone for his sins]. The purification offering," continued God, "shall be slaughtered before the Lord at the *same* spot that the burnt offering is slaughtered. This," adds God, "is most holy." (Leviticus 6:16-17)

But what, we may ask, "is most holy?" Is it the burnt offering, made to acknowledge the place God has in our lives and helps the giver to approach the Holy One in reverence and thanksgiving?[29] Or, could it be the purification offering, as we understand that there is tremendous value in reflecting upon the past, recognizing transgressions, and making a sincere act of atonement?[30] Well, according to my understanding of our sages' teachings, it would be neither. What is most holy are not the sacrifices, but the *place* of the offerings. For, it is there where we get a chance to perceive the true and full nature of man, who often contains dueling natures (in Hebrew: the *yeitzer hatov*/the good inclination as well as the *yeitzer hara*/the evil inclination) that cannot be so easily separated from one another.

Ah, but that has not stopped us from trying. Whether it's with Superman and Lex Luther or with Mordechai and Haman, whether it's within great works of fiction or the non-fiction of our reality, we are constantly attempting to draw a thick line, an unbreakable divide, between what we perceive are the forces of good in this world and the forces of evil. Observing this phenomenon within the comic book, Samuel L. Jackson (playing the character of Elijah in the motion picture *Unbreakable*) stated: "Notice the square jaw, common in most comic book heroes, and the slightly disproportionate size of the body to the head, common only to villains. Initially there were more realistic depictions of these figures. But, when the characters eventually made their way into the magazines, they were exaggerated."[31]

---

[27] Louis Farrakhan. "Meet the Press Interview" on *NBC* with Tim Russert: 13 April 1997.

[28] Louis Farrakhan. "Saviour's Day Address" at Allstate Arena. Rosemont, IL: 27 February 2011

[29] An earlier example of the burnt offering comes from Noah. After the flood, "Noah built an altar to the Lord and, taking of every pure animal and of every pure bird, he offered burnt offerings on the altar. The Lord smelled the odor and was pleased." (Gen. 8:20-21) Another early example comes from the story of Abraham. Rather than offering his son Isaac, "Abraham went and took the ram and offered it up as a burnt offering in place of his son." (Gen. 22:13). In both occasions, the burnt offering acknowledges the powerful and holy role God has in the course of human lives.

[30] There is a Chasidic teaching which expresses the value of an atonement offering. "Every individual is tied to God by a rope. When he/she commits a sin, the rope is broken. But, when he/she atones, the broken pieces are tied together, bringing that person even closer to God had there never been a break in the rope at all."

[31] M. Night Shyamalan. *Unbreakable*. Touchstone Pictures: 2000.

And, we continue to make these exaggerations, these distinctions between the holy good and the wholly evil, because we honestly believe that they help us to navigate our world by clarifying its complexities. But, frankly, that formula is too simplistic to actually work. We see this not only with recognizable leaders like Minister Farrakhan. We also observe the limitations of this perspective in reference to everyday individuals. For how many times have we been surprised by some news report of a supposedly "good" person acting badly or, the opposite, some supposedly "bad" person acting saintly? Likely, it is too often to count, as we are let down by a perspective that should have – we believe – supported us. "Oh, I never *imagined* that he/she could do something like that!" we say, stunned by the revelation.

But, not only should we have been able to imagine it; we should have – as our Israelite ancestors did – come to expect it. For, as we are reminded in this portion, we are all composite beings, struggling between a *yeitzer hatov* (a good inclination) and a *yeitzer hara* (an evil inclination). Sure, many of us correctly emphasize our *yeitzer hatov*, thank God. But, that does not mean that we do not still have the *yeitzer hara*. It will always be there, lingering, testing, trying our good inclination. And to recognize as much should allow us to reserve judgment against those whose *yeitzer hara* dominates. For they too have the other side, the *yeitzer hatov*, and to perceive as much may help them to see it as well. And, if not them, then – we pray – at least their children may, for the *midrash* tells us that even "the children of Haman went on to study Torah," doing justice, loving goodness, and walking humbly with God.[32]

That, my friends, is what this portion of *Tzav* is referring to when it stated that "this is most holy." It is not the sacrifices, but the place and time of the offering that allows us to continually perceive the complex nature of man and, even holier still, will be the ability to help others see it as well. For then, as we are commanded to do during the feast of Purim, may we all see that the line between good and evil is not as thick as we often make it out to be.[33] That, in truth, the line between good and evil is rather thin. This should not invoke within us worry or concern, but instill within us hope and courage. For then all those who were once regarded as "evil" may be seen as "potential good." And, all those regarded as "good" will not take their position for granted, as they work ever harder to "inspire and empower today's youth" to engage more thoughtfully and productively in the betterment of our collective future.

---

[32] BT Gittin 57b: "It is taught that Naaman [General of Syria who attacks Israel in the Book of Kings] becomes a resident convert, that Nebuzaradan [the Babylonian General who sacked Jerusalem in 586 B.C.E.] became a righteous convert, that the children of Haman [the vizier who attempted to kill the Jews in Persia] went on to study Torah in B'nai Barak, and that the children of Sisera [Canaanite General who oppressed the Israelites for 20 years in the time of Deborah], went on to study Torah a lot. Who, then, is not [worthy]?

[33] BT Megilah 7b: "Raba said, 'It is the duty of every person on Purim to drink on Purim until he cannot tell the difference between 'cursed be Haman' and 'blessed be Mordechai.'" Though opinions differ as to exactly how drunk that is, a person certainly should not become so drunk that he might violate other commandments or get seriously ill. In addition, recovering alcoholics or others who might suffer serious harm from alcohol are exempt from this obligation.

Tzav // Command
Bite 3 – *Masks and Ashes*

The festival of Purim is one of the most enthusiastically celebrated occasions in the Jewish calendar. *Megillat Esther*, our sacred text for the day, stands out as a curiosity, for on its surface it strikes us as being far from sacred: a violent and burlesque tale of intrigue, guile, and strange reversals of fortune—with never a mention of God! What kind of Biblical text is this?

One clue may be found in the name of the book and its heroine, Esther. Esther's Hebrew name, we learn, is *Hadassah*, meaning "myrtle tree," a symbol of victory. The name Esther means "star" in Persian; some say it is after Ishtar, the Babylonian goddess of fertility, love, and war. But the English "Esther" has a Hebrew meaning as well, as it contains the root S-T-R, which means "hidden," or "concealed" in Hebrew. We can interpret this hidden-ness to refer to Esther herself, who hides her Jewish identity during much of the story. In fact, Esther's hidden identity offers one inspiration for our tradition of Purim masquerading. Hidden identities abound in this story. Haman's role as an enemy of the queen is hidden from Ahashverosh; Mordecai's role as a champion of the king is hidden from Haman. On one level, the story is nothing but a comedy of mistaken identities.

But there is another, deeper (hidden!), level to this story. As we noted earlier, God is unseen in *Megillat Esther*—except that in the end, the Jewish people are miraculously saved from destruction. How? Esther removes her mask. Conquering her fears and risking her life, she steps out from behind the veils that conceal her true identity and, by so doing, Esther unleashes the story's Divine spark, the powerful secret of her courageous, God-given humanity. In our lives, as in *Megillat Esther*, God is often hidden. But like Esther, we have the ability to uncover God's place and power in our own lives. Very often, we achieve this best by removing our masks, by emerging from our own hiding places and holding true to who we are and what we believe.

Ellen Kushner, host of Public Radio's *Sound and Spirit*, has demonstrated this beautifully in her original radioplay, *Esther: The Feast of Masks*.[34] Woven throughout the familiar story of Vashti, Esther, Haman, and the rest, are four modern tales that demonstrate both the power and the pain of masks: Rita, a naive and devoted New York housewife, who discovers she wants more from life than her husband's worldly success; Ida, a light-skinned African American woman passing in the white world, hiding the truth even from her own husband; Natalie, an idealistic young American diplomat posted to Rwanda, compelled to speak out when her superiors would have her remain silent; and Nate, a high school big-man-on-campus who learns to stand up for the little guys when confronted with a homophobic friend. Each character encounters an opportunity to remove the mask; each one struggles with the consequences

---

[34] See http://www.sff.net/people/kushnerSherman/Kushner/esther.html for more information about the program and a link to a radio performance!

of his or her decision. In the end, only those who remove the mask are redeemed—we emerge from their stories exhilarated, hopeful, freed from old shackles. Those who choose to embrace their masks leave us feeling bruised, reminding us of all the brokenness and darkness that persist in our world.

Most of us wear masks from time to time. We are not always the same person at work that we are at home. We feel safer in some settings than others, more or less willing to "open up." In some circumstances it may be inappropriate to remove all pretense, to reveal our most inner selves. Like the priests in this Torah portion, *Tzav*, we put on our various roles and take them off like so many changes of clothing. The priest who cleans out the ashes from the alter dresses differently and performs a very different function than the priest who officiates over the Temple ritual. Yet both are recorded in the Torah. Only by looking at all the masks, all the versions of ourselves do we get the whole story, the holiest story of who we are. Whatever roles we choose to play, in earnest or in jest, let us never lose sight of the soul behind the mask.

PASSOVER:
Michele Schipper's Fried Matzah Balls with *T'shuvah* (a.k.a. Comeback) Dipping-Sauce

Ingredients (matzah balls):
2 tablespoons of vegetable oil
2 large eggs, slightly beaten
½ cup of Matzo Meal
2 tablespoons of water
1 teaspoon of Cajun season (or to taste)
Oil for frying

Ingredients (*t'shuvah* sauce):
1/3 cup of mayonnaise
1/3 cup of ketchup
Horseradish

Mix well the vegetable oil, eggs (slightly beaten), Matzo Meal, water, Cajun seasoning in a bowl. Place the bowl in refrigerator for 15 minutes to set.

While that mixture is cooling, begin to heat the oil for frying.

Next, make small balls from the dough mixture (make them smaller than regular size matzah balls done for soup). Fry them in the oil until light golden brown.

Finally, drain the oil and serve. Best while warm and incredibly delicious with *t'shuvah* (comeback) dipping-sauce below!

The dipping-sauce is simple. Mix 1/3 cup of mayonnaise and 1/3 cup of ketchup together. Then, gradually mix in grated horseradish. Continue to taste as you go along, so that you may flavor it per your personal or guests' taste.

Portion 3:
Sh'mini // Eighth
Torah Portion: Leviticus 9:1-11:47

"ON THE EIGHTH DAY MOSES CALLED AARON AND HIS SONS..." He called them in order to instruct Aaron to make a purification offering and a burnt offering to God, celebrating this new beginning for the people. It would be the first such officiation for these new priests of Israel.

After completing the sacrifice, Aaron blesses the people of Israel and the Presence of the Lord appears in front of the Tent of Meeting. Fire comes forth from the Lord and consumes Aaron's offerings. In response, the people "saw and shouted, then fell on their faces," affirming their authority as God's servants. (Leviticus 9:24)

Alas, this celebration is quickly marred by the tragic death of two of Aaron's sons: Nadav and Avihu. Having just begun their task as priests, they took it upon themselves to offer incense before the Lord. According to this portion, this was considered "alien fire, for which God had not enjoined upon them." As a result, "fire came forth from the Lord and consumed them." (Leviticus 10:1-2)

Aaron and his remaining sons, Eleazar and Itamar, are not given time to mourn over their loss. Instead, after Nadav and Avihu are carried out of the camp, they – by Moses' commanded – do not to bare their heads or rent their clothes, the traditional signs of mourning. Instead, it was the remainder of Israel who were charged to bare their grief.

After detailing more laws of the priesthood so that a similar fate would not befall Aaron, his sons, and any other priests to come, the Torah portion concludes by imparting the laws of *kashrut*: which animals are considered fit and which are prohibited from among the creatures of the field, those that swarm the earth, those that swim the waters, and those that fly the friendly or not-so-friendly skies.

Sh'mini // Eighth
Bite 1 – *Parental Advisory*

"WARNING: the following sermon may contain material of an adult nature; content which may be considered offensive to some listeners or inappropriate for young children. Parental discretion is advised." It's not just sermons. Parental warnings such as this have been plastered on everything from music to movies, from video-games to television, advising parents to take the necessary precautions to ensure the sanctity of our children. Sadly, for Aaron and two of his sons, no warning label had yet been affixed to fire-pans.

As a result, we read of an unfortunate tale in this portion of *Sh'mini*. It begins when two of Aaron's sons, "Nadav and Avihu each took a fire-pan, put fire and laid incense upon it. They offered before the Lord this strange-fire, which God had not enjoined upon them. Consequently, a fire came forth from the Lord and consumed them. Thus," the Bible tells us that "they died…and Aaron [contrary to expectations] was silent." (Leviticus 10:1-3)

But not Biblical scholars; they have – for generations – raised their voices, commenting on Aaron's silence, because it is rare for the Torah to draw attention to someone not speaking. Of note is RaSHBaM, grandson of RaSHI, who wrote: "Aaron was silent, unable to cry or mourn, because of his tremendous guilt," for as High Priest – and especially as a father – Aaron felt it was his responsibility to protect his children.[35] Regretting this failure, he was left to grieve in silence.

As parents, we know this responsibility all too well, for there is no holier task than protecting our children's sanctity. But, these days that sacred task seems overwhelming, if not impossible. It's no longer just 'fire-pans' with which we have to deal. Now, it's firearms. No longer is 'strange-fire' our sole concern. Now, it's strangers, who may pose a threat whether they are around the block or – thanks to the internet – around the world. Undoubtedly, we are inundated with what we perceive as ever-increasing new threats upon our children.

Yet, what do we do in the face of these new challenges? Well, we typically respond with an old, mother-tested and mother-approved method: the hand. Not in the 'I-will-save-you-from-flying-through-the-windshield' sort of way. Rather, as parents, we tend to use the almighty hand as a shield, covering the eyes of our children from seeing what should not be seen, covering the ears of our children from hearing what should not be heard, and covering the mouths of our children from saying what should not be said. We even use our hands to physically remove our children from experiences we feel they should not have.

But, despite our deepest desires, a 'speak to the hand' method to the world will only work so long. Eventually, our children will grow out of our protective reach. Eventually they will step beyond our shielding hand and be exposed to

---

[35] RaSHI commentary to Leviticus 10:3

the tough realities of our world. So it seems more advantageous during the years that they are within reach to not only protect them with the shield of our hand, but to provide them with a sword as well; a sword in the form of knowledge. Illustrations of this principle are frequent on the news. For example:

> In February of 2010, 4-year-old Joseph Lamoin woke in the very early morning hours in his home in Maine to the smell and sight of smoke. Having recently been exposed to a lesson on fire by a visiting fireman at his daycare, Joseph got out of his bed, and crawled on his hands and knees – as he was taught – to his mother's room. There, he woke his mother and his sister up just in the nick-of-time to save their lives before the house was consumed in flames.[36]

In other words, there will come a time when the shield of the parent's hand will not be around. And when it is not, when it is lowered, we must make sure our children can defend themselves. As we can see from the story, this cannot be done through the shield alone. Like the knights of old, every shield must come with a sword. And, what could be better than the sword of knowledge? For with it our children can pierce through the uncertainty of any moment. That is all Nadav and Avihu needed in this portion of *Sh'mini*, the knowledge of what fire could be offered and what fire could not. Thereby, they would have recognized the warning signs of life for themselves, using their own discretion – instead of relying upon that of their parent – to navigate the variables of that moment.

May this be the case for us and our children. May we, as parents, not cover our children's eyes. Rather, let us teach them to see the signs for themselves. May we, as parents, not cover our children's ears. Rather, let us teach them to hear the warnings for themselves. May we, as parents, not cover our children's mouths. Rather, let us teach them to speak the truth for themselves as well as others in any given moment. In that way, we can rest assured that they can ensure the sanctity of their own lives as well as the lives of their children.

Sh'mini // Eighth
Bite 2 – *Going Green: A Spiritual Approach*

It is with great sadness that I come to inform you of the anticipated passing of a very bright member in our community: the incandescent light bulb. Yes, his radiant presence, which has long illuminated the many dark places in our world, is slated to go out for the last time in 2012.[37] Though dimmed we may be when he joins his blessed creator (Thomas Edison), a glow of hope will remain, as his descendants – the halogen and the LED – will continue to shed a new and ever more energy efficient light on this world. For, as it has been the case many times before, it will be through this honorable and holy process of

---

[36] The Associated Press: 2/8/2010
[37] This requirement is part of the Energy Independence and Security Act, originally named Clean Energy Act, federally passed in 2007.

reducing, reusing, and recycling that the filament of the soul can transform into a *Neir Tamid*, an Eternal Flame.

One of those times, to be sure, is within the Bible. For example, in this portion of *Sh'mini*, we read of Aaron's two sons – Nadav and Avihu – who offered up a strange light before the Lord at the Tent of Meeting as "each one took his fire pan, put fire in it, and laid incense upon it." (Leviticus 10:1) But, notes the Bible, because this act "had not been enjoined upon them, a fire came forth from the Lord and consumed them." (Leviticus 10:2) A wasteful deed, one could say, that was repeated by Korach in the book of Numbers. As it is written there: Korach "took his fire pan, put fire in it, and laid incense upon it, taking his place at the entrance of the Tent of Meeting." (Numbers 16:17) And, as a result, the light of his life too was extinguished.

While not specifically mentioned in relation to Nadav and Avihu, God does instruct Moses later to "remove the fire pans that were used for sin at the cost of their lives. [Do not throw them away, but] let them be [reused] into hammered sheets as plating for the altar…they have become sacred." (Numbers 17:3) While RaSHI objects, stating: Moses "should be forbidden from deriving any benefit from the fire pans," RaMBaN insists that "RaSHI's language makes no sense… [The fire pans must be reused for] on Moses' command, the vessels became holy, as he dedicated them to God."[38] In other words, when we can see the Divine element inherent in all things, we can transform that which may have been regarded as wasteful into that which can be considered useful.

I think it is fair to say that there would be few among us today that would raise a fuss over Moses' deed, as "going green" has moved far beyond the ideal and even the trendy to enter into the practical. For, we have come to see that if we wish to leave a healthier world for our children, their children and their children's children, then we must embrace our responsibility to care for the earth. Although Schwarzeneggars's bio-fueled Hummer may be a stretch for many, everyday people are finding everyday solutions to help conserve energy and limit our impact on the environment, while – it's important to mention – encouraging growth both in nature as well as in our society. No longer does it have to be one verses the other, as business after business – for example – have come to see both the economic and environmental benefits of going green by going paperless.

We should not take this reality lightly. After all, it was not too long ago that the Greenhouse Effect, the Depletion of the Ozone, Global Warming, and other such ecological standards were considered merely unproven theories or, worse, myths. Sure, we can still argue whether the development of reusable resources is causing other strains on our society. But what cannot be argued is the importance of engaging in such acts. An importance, by the way, that is not only emphasized in God's command to Moses in this portion, instructing him

---

[38] RaSHI and RaMBaN commentaries on Numbers 17:3

to reuse the fire pans, but the eco-friendly pulse of Judaism can be felt time and time again in the values of our faith. For example, in the beginning, God entrusted his blessed creation – the world – and everything in it to man, saying: I "place him in the garden of Eden to work it (l'avdah) as well as to guard it (l'shamrah)."[39] Whence, later rabbinic sages rooted the eternal Jewish value of shomrei adamah, our sacred task to be "guardians of the earth." Later, a portion of this larger mandate was further defined, as God instructs the people "not to destroy [a city's] trees" when waging war, for that would be a waste from which we must refrain, according to the Jewish value of bal tashchit.[40]

But if we only see "going green" as eco-friendly, then we have missed their spiritual importance completely. For, God's command was meant to be people-friendly as well, as it sets up a powerful kal v'chomeir, meaning "a light to a heavy." It's a rabbinic tool that creates an analogy between something on a micro-level (the kal) to that on a macro-level (the chomeir). In these contexts, the kal v'chomeir would be: if this is the way that we are commanded to treat material items, seeing use in what was considered waste, then all the more so should we act this way with our fellow human beings, seeing the potential good in them where others may see only waste." Supporting this approach, Rabbi Nachman wrote: "Know that you must judge all people as worthy. Even if you meet someone completely evil, you must search and find the me'at tov (that little bit of good) in them. Through this process you can actually raise someone from unworthiness to the state of worthiness and cause them to be holy."[41]

This, my dear friends, is the spiritual implication of "going green" especially as it relates to this portion of Sh'mini. But, as clearly forewarned by the great sage Kermit HaFrog, "It's not easy being green."[42] There will remain constant challenges to seeing the potential use in the waste, the good in the evil, the light in the darkness. But, just as a new generation of bulbs is poised to come and shed a brighter and more energy efficient light unto the world, so may we – with each successive generation – do the same. May we get better and better at fulfilling the vision articulated by the Psalmist, who wrote: "Od me'at v'ein rasha v'hitbonantah el m'komo v'eineinu / Soon there will be no evil (i.e. no waste), for you'll look to its place and it will not be."

Sh'mini // Eighth
Bite 3 – Silence

Ours is a tradition of words: written words, spoken words, noisy prayer halls and noisy study halls. I remember when I first learned that silent libraries were a Christian invention, born in the whispering chambers of ancient

---

[39] Genesis 2:15
[40] Deuteronomy 20:19-20
[41] Likutey Moharan 282
[42] Jim Henson. "Bein' Green." Sesame Street: 1970

monasteries. It was an astonishing idea: I grew up on a steady diet of visits to the public library, and this sunny, civic-minded space was the last place I expected to find religious influence—much less Christian roots. On the other hand, it made perfect sense, given what I knew of Jewish etiquette surrounding book-learning. Traditionally, Jews always study in pairs, or groups, reading aloud to one another, talking out, sometimes arguing each point of law or prayer.

Silence does not always come easily for Jews. And, yet, it has its place in our tradition: time for silent prayer is built into the public service, at the end of the *Amidah* (the Standing Prayer), a visitor to a *shiva* house is instructed to remain silent until the mourner speaks, and in this portion of *Sh'mini*, we read: "*va-yiddom Aharon* / Aaron was silent.*" (Leviticus 10:3) His sons, Nadav and Avihu, have just died, consumed by God's fire on the altar. It is a mysterious and frightening episode, and tragic, followed by this enigmatic detail.

The commentators puzzle over the record of Aaron's silence. The Torah's terse narrative does not typically comment on silence. At times it seems scarcely to record speech. What, then, can Aaron's conspicuous silence mean? The tradition strains to fill the silence with words. Some suggest that it signifies his acceptance of God's harsh judgment, for he did not complain. Others say it shows his willingness to be comforted on his loss. But perhaps, as Rabbi Harold Kushner suggests, "the text is suggesting that there are more possibilities—and more power—in silence than in any words."[43] Aaron's silence communicates more than all our explanations can ever hold.

Most years, our reading of this Torah portion coincides very closely with Yom HaShoah, Holocaust Remembrance Day. There is no event in our history that more fully embodies the truth of Kushner's comments. As Holocaust survivor Elie Wiesel has said, "What we really wish to say, what we feel we must say cannot be said." There are events so unspeakable, emotions so terrible, that language fails us. There are circumstances in which words will always fall short. And yet, survivors have spoken, have written. And we thank God for that: the world benefits from their contributions to human history.

In Israel, on Yom HaShoah, all over the country at precisely the same moment, sirens sound—a deafening wail, air-raid sirens. Everything stops: cars, pedestrians, cash registers, conversation. Drivers get out of their cars and stand at attention in the street. For what seems an eternity, the sirens hover over an enormous silence. The only things that move in this scene are leaves on a breeze, a cat crossing the street. The sirens die down in waves, gradually, dropping in volume and pitch together. In the wake of the aural assault, silence rushes against our ears, amplifying the stillness for a swollen moment. And then it's over. The street, eerily transformed a moment ago, looks and sounds as if nothing has ever changed. Cars speed past; pedestrians scramble out of the way. Conversations continue where they left off. After the silence, life.

---

[43] Harold Kushner, ed. "D'rash Commentary." *Etz Hayyim Torah and Commentary*. Rabbinical Assembly: New York, 2001, p. 634.

This, I think, is the secret to silence. It is, as Kushner writes, so powerful. And yet, it is not enough. Its power can paralyze us, rob us of the opportunity or impetus to act. For some of us, silence can be habit-forming, difficult to break. But silence and stillness must give way to action and the noise of living. So Elie Wiesel mustered the great effort to produce his novels and essays. So *shiva* ends after seven days, and mourners are sent back into the world. So Aaron will eventually find his tongue again, and returns to his duties, his family, his life.

There is room for silence in Judaism. The growing popularity of Jewish meditation and mindfulness practice reminds us of the healing and even generative power of silence. It isn't only a response to trauma and loss. Silence contains truth, carries messages, which words cannot. But then, after the silence, there needs to be words: the moment of stillness and the busy street; the quiet library and the loud yeshiva hall; the acknowledgement from Aaron that anything we might say is sometimes inadequate and yet the attempt – nevertheless – to say something to record the moment and tell the story.

Double Portion 4 & 5:
Tazria-M'tzora // She Delivers-A Leper
Torah Portion: Leviticus 12:1-15:33

"The Lord spoke to Moses, saying, 'Speak to the Israelite people thus: when a woman delivers a boy...'" From these words comes a double Torah portion that will largely concern itself with the laws of ritual impurity for the people of Israel: how one comes to be included under this category and how one may be free of it.

For example, begins the portion of *Tazria*, when a woman gives birth to a child, she enters into a state of *tameih,* "ritual impurity." The specific amount of time she remains *tameih* varies upon the gender of the child she has delivered. However, what is of central concern here is the emission of bodily fluids, considered hazardous within the Israelite society. That is why it's not just birth that can render someone *tameih*; it's also skin conditions that leak bodily fluids like *tzara-at*, commonly translated as "leprosy."

This shall be the ritual for a leper..." begins the portion of *M'tzora*. And, what follows is a prescription of isolation, shaving the body, and sacrifices. *Tzara-at* can also occur in fabrics and the walls of houses. Thus, similar to the condition which afflicts people, this double portion provides purification rituals for these inanimate objects as well.

Finally, the double portion concludes with how discharges from sexual organs can likewise render a person ritually impure, and the process of purification for both the person as well as any objects that they have come in contact with, which entail sacrifices, washing, and waiting seven days until a state of purity can be re-attained.

In many ways, this portion is a guidebook, outlining safe protocols when handling potentially hazardous material. Thereby, the people of Israel could continue to progress through the wilderness in a safe and healthy manner.

Tazria-M'tzora // She Delivers-A Leper
Bite 1 – *Highway to Heaven*

As I drove down a highway, a passing billboard asked: "WHERE ARE YOU HEADED?" In my head, I responded: "Jackson, MS." This conversation continued on the next billboard, as it questioned: "HELL?" "I should think not!" I replied, offended at the assumption. Then perhaps, the third billboard inquired, it's "HEAVEN?" "Could be," I said, "but not quite yet." My answers must have befuddled the billboards, as I found the next one entirely blank. "Figures," I blurted out, as confusion is often the response I get from people too when I try to explain that Judaism does not maintain that same concept regarding Heaven and Hell.[44] There's confusion and even a little anxiety, because without a system of eternal reward and punishment, these people sincerely wonder: "What then keeps us on the Divine path?"

It's more than a fair question. For, as co-travelers of this highway to Heaven, we wish to have some assurance that others will be obeying the same rules of the road. Well, please rest assured we are or, at the very least, we are trying to. It's just that Judaism provides us different directions on how to get there, as is alluded to in this double portion of *Tazria-M'tzora*. Within this section, from the book of Leviticus, we read of a condition of ritual impurity, known as *tzara-at* (often translated as "leprosy"). Although it differs from today's medical diagnosis, *tzara-at* is nonetheless painful in both its condition as well as in its treatment. For the one inflicted with this skin abnormality "must dwell apart from the community" for a period of no less than seven days but "for as long as the disease lasts." (Leviticus 13:46)

Why? What could possibly justify this isolation? Playing on the linguistic similarity between the Hebrew for "leper/*metzora*" and the Hebrew for "the one who gossips/*motzi-ra*," the sages considered leprosy/*tzara-at* to be a punishment for the sin of slander as well as for other antisocial behaviors like perjury, lying, forbidden sexual relationships, arrogance, theft, and envy.[45] For example, Miriam – Moses' sister – is afflicted with *tzara-at* after she and Aaron criticize Moses' choice of a Kushite wife in Numbers 12. It therefore seemed reasonable for our ancestors in this cause-and-effect world created by God that an antisocial punishment ensued from an antisocial action. For, in Judaism, we understand that what brings us and keeps us close to God's community is not what we believe about the next life, but what we do in this one.

And, it's not just in Torah where this cause-and-effect relationship, inherent in God's order of this world, is painfully apparent. Likely, in our daily lives, we experience this phenomenon as well. Take driving for example. If we don't fill

---

[44] Often billboards like these, alongside the highway, are placed there by our Christian brothers and sisters, who maintain a concept of Heaven and Hell is oriented in the next life. Specifically, depending upon whether or not one believes in Jesus as the Messiah can determine whether one is destined for Heaven or Hell. As it is stated in the Gospel of John (3:36): "He who believes in the Son has eternal life; he who does not obey the Son shall not see life, but the wrath of God rests upon him." (RSV Edition)

[45] See *Leviticus Rabbah* 16:1; *Babylonian Talmud*, Arachin 16a

our cars with gas, they won't go. If we don't perform their regular maintenance, they'll break down. And, for the sake of argument, let's just say if a newlywed rabbi were to be distracted by his lovely wife and didn't pay attention to the speed limit, then it's more likely for him to be pulled over and – thank God – given only a warning to slow down. Clearly this Divine principle, which keeps the world in order, is so effective that we have emulated it in our own laws, as each and every one of them contains a reward and/or punishment to keep our society in good, working order as well.

If that is the case, then many of us may conclude that our society, this bridge which was designed to safely take us from our origin of birth to our destination of death, is on the verge of collapse. For every day, around the world, there are individuals who do great good but go unrewarded, and others who do great evil but go unpunished. On this bumpy road of our reality, whether presently or in the trials and tribulations of generations past, it is understandable then why some would choose to keep their focus forever forward on the world to come/*olam haba*, rather than perceiving the precarious present of this world/*olam hazeh*. Because, reasonably, if things seem "unfair" here, then there is – at the very least – hope and comfort that all will be smoothed out there, resolved either in a Heaven above or, consequently, in a Hell below.

But, those are neither the directions nor the exact destinations of Judaism. That is not to say that Judaism is without places of pleasure or pain, destinations of delight or discomfort, moments of contentment or torment. As this portion describes, by way of the *metzora*/leper, Judaism has these locales as well. But, they are always situated in *olam hazeh*/this world rather than *olam haba*/the next world. Therefore, rather than overlooking the bumps and bangs, the cracks and crashes on this road, the guidebook of Judaism – like an ol' AAA Triptik – draws our attention to them, encouraging us to slow down and even stop. For as God's road crew, it is up to us to smooth the road ahead, not just for our benefit, but for the betterment of all those travelers, all those generations, yet to come.

For, as the billboards remind us, we are all on a collective journey, one that can either be a highway to Heaven or a living Hell. Where are we headed? That will be up to each and every one of us. Not in some time to come, not at some distant point forever on the horizon. But, as the one-hit wonder Jesus Jones once taught us, that destination can happen at any point along the journey. It can happen, in fact, "right here, right now, [as we] watch the world wake up from history."[46] May we stay ever awake on this road we are traveling on, beholding not just the beauty that passes with every mile, but all the hazards therein. For only in this present focus can we arrive safely and speedily at a Heaven here on earth.

---

[46] Jesus Jones. Doubt. "Right Here, Right Now." SBK Records: 1990.

Tazria-M'tzora // She Delivers-A Leper
Bite 2 – *The Circulatory System of Judaism*

Somehow, somewhere religious bodies across the United States – including Judaism – have contracted a serious illness. With an onset occurring in the late teens and early twenties, this illness keeps a significant part of our religious body – our young adults – from reentering the synagogue and participating in Jewish communal life until their mid- to late-thirties. It's a development that has professionals (i.e. rabbis, cantors, Jewish educators) and laity alike concerned. What if this illness is contagious? What if it spreads to other parts of our religious body so that in the very near future our synagogues will be – as Rabbi Robert Gordis projected – "nothing more than a mortuary chapel where we recite *Kaddish* (mourner's prayer) and *Yizkor* (mourner's service)."[47]

It's a valid concern that thankfully comes with a traditional Jewish remedy, one by which my grandmother swears… chicken soup! Alright. Not exactly. But, the remedy for this illness is equally as simple and thus often overlooked. According to this double portion of *Tazria-M'tzora*, which addresses all sorts of ailments, "When one [such illness] is reported to the priest, the priest" as prescribed by the Torah, "shall go outside the camp, ordering two live birds, cedar wood, crimson stuff and hyssop to be brought to the one who is to be purified." (Leviticus 14:2-4) Then, by some manner of sacrifice performed by the priest, the illness shall be relieved and the person can reinsert him/herself into the community once more.

Now, admittedly, there is a slight chance that a sacrifice may not be as effective or nearly as appealing among today's young Jewish adults as it once was. But, what has not lost its potency, what remains a powerful prophylactic in addressing this problem, is the impact religious leaders and laity can have when they step outside their sacred camps, when they go outside the walls of their sacred institutions to reach and interact with their community. Modern commentator, Baruch Levine, called it a mandate: "For the priest is not to wait until people come to him with their concerns. [To effect positive and lasting change], he must go to them."[48]

And, this generation's Jewish leaders are doing just that. Whether it's with "Lunch and Learn" sessions at area businesses, "Tequila and Torah" parties at local pubs, or "Run with the Rabbi" programs at neighborhood parks, today's Jewish leaders are thinking about and implementing their Judaism outside the box. In fact, I know of one such rabbi, who – upon hearing that a young congregant has passed the driver's test – will go to his or her home, recite some prayers, and then affix a small mezuzah to the car. He says, "It's just his way to say *mazel tov* (congratulations) as well as to transmit the hope that Judaism will accompany this individual along every mile on the road of life, even when that road takes him or her far from the synagogue walls."

---

[47] Proceedings of the Rabbinical Assembly of America, vol. 10. 1946
[48] *Etz Hayim: Torah and Commentary*. Rabbinical Assembly of America Press: New York, 2001. p. 660

Surprisingly, though, these efforts do not blow out the fire of concern. For some, they only fan the flames, as these innovations are interpreted as an abrogation of that which has historically been central to Judaism: walls. Yes, walls… from the walls of the *Mishkan* (the Tabernacle) that were set up in the center of our ancestor's desert encampments, to the walls of the great Temple which were erected in the spiritual center of our people (Jerusalem). Walls have not only protected our people, they have defined our people. As the Zionist essayist Achad Ha-am once wrote: "Walls are the retaining element to the heart of the Jewish people. Because, [like today's synagogues], it is from within them that our people have drawn their strength and inspiration to overcome all difficulties and withstand all persecutions."[49]

But, what point is there in having a heart that is not connected to the body of the community? Or, for that matter, what point is there in having a body that is not connected to the heart of Judaism? Not much, as neither can really exist without the other (at least, not for long). That is why it is so important that the Torah, in *Tazria-M'tzora*, specifically commands the priest to go outside, beyond the borders of the camp. For – by his presence outside his sacred walls – he functions as an artery, connecting the life-force which is at the heart of Judaism (i.e. the synagogue and the spirit contained therein) to even the most remote of appendages of the Jewish community. This outreach presents the message that even those who may be far from the center of Judaism are still vital to the whole. And, equally as important, it establishes a connection through which the life-force – that was sent out by the priest – can one day return by way of the individual to revitalize the community.

As a priestly people, the responsibility to maintain the health of the circulatory system of Judaism is not for the priest, or the rabbi, alone. As a priestly people, this responsibility rests upon each of us. Each of us can be the veins and arteries in the body of our Jewish communities. So, as we step outside the walls of our sacred institutions this Sabbath and every Sabbath, let us continue the holy work that our priestly ancestors started so long ago. Let us not keep the spirit of our people contained and confined. Instead, let us take it with us, connecting this life-force to all who may be remote or removed from the heart of Judaism. For, through this personal connection, we open a pathway by which the individual may return the life-force that was sent out with an extra measure of energy and insight needed to restore the body of Judaism back to complete health.

---

[49] Leon Simon. Achad Ha-am: Essays, Letters, and Memoirs. 1946

Tazria-M'tzora // She Delivers-A Leper
Bite 3 – *Endangered: General Practitioner*

Like the polar bear, the black rhino, the giant panda, and the bengal tiger, another of God's blessed creations has recently joined the endangered species list: the general practitioner. Yes, as our minds have continued to venture farther and deeper into the frontiers of life, these magnificent creatures, who possess an array of knowledge and competency, have found their once sprawling habitat threatened and their once steady livelihood on the decline. And, according to the conservationists, who have spent countless hours observing these creatures in their natural habitat, the cause of the decline can be largely attributed to the rise of the specialist, a highly advanced being whose brilliance is sharply focused on understanding the inherent complexities of individual parts rather than addressing, more generally, the whole.

This supersession likely would have provoked concern amongst our Israelite forebears, particularly the priests, who – like their modern counterparts, the rabbis – were the general practitioners of their time. Whether it was during office hours at the Temple or on house-calls afterhours, the priests often addressed a wide range of matters in their community: from minor transgressions to great sins, from marital unease to structural disease. For example, in this double portion of *Tazria-M'tzora*, the priest – in addition to dealing with a stone wall plagued with lesions – is asked to aid an individual inflicted with *m'tzora*/leprosy. He does so, states the Bible, by "taking some of the blood of the reparation offering and placing it on the ridge of the leper's right ear, on the thumb of his right hand as well as on the big toe of his right foot." (Leviticus14:14)

Sages have long understood these priestly actions as a Biblical prescription of sorts, advising its patient readers, typically in hard-to-decipher script, that healing is a process best undertaken through both body and spirit. Though, such a perspective has often led to the unfavorable conclusion that one can suffer physically from some unrelated spiritual transgression. For example, playing here on the linguistic similarity between the Hebrew word for "the leper" (*hametzora*) and the Hebrew for "the one who gossips" (*hamotzi ra*), the sages considered leprosy as a direct punishment for the spiritual sins of slander and malicious gossip.[50] Today, such a conclusion is not only medically reckless; we have come to recognize it as also psychologically cruel. Though, that is not to say that the priest's actions lack meaning for our lives. On the contrary, as the great modern Biblical commentator Baruch Levine pointed out, there is still a great amount of significance in the priest's generalist approach. For only "when the person is treated literally from head (i.e. the

---

[50] Leviticus Rabbah 16:1. In addition to a lying tongue, the sages identified six other types of behavior punished by leprosy: haughty eyes, hands that shed innocent blood in secret, a mind that hatches evil, feet quick to do wrong, a witness who testifies falsely, and one who incites brothers to quarrel. (Proverbs 6:16-19)

leper's right ear) to foot (i.e. the leper's big toe)," says Levine, can a complete healing be achieved.[51]

But today we are steadily moving away from the generalist approach of our ancestors. And it's not just the doctors. From lawyers to librarians, from bankers to barbers, many areas of our society are jumping onto the specialization bandwagon. For they appreciate that our understanding of the world has grown with each successive generation and, as such, a division – or a specialization – of knowledge is needed to effectively process and apply the larger body of information in the advancement of our world. Playwright Charlie Kaufman, in his work *Adaptation*, understood this *tikkun olam* approach to specialization as: "To care passionately about something allows you to whittle down the world to a manageable size."[52]

Yet, others will say something valuable is lost in the whittled shavings. In demanding such a narrow focus on one thing, specialization can sometimes cause blindness to everything else. This was demonstrated in the case of little Joshua.

> Joshua was in the fifth grade. And, up until now, he had done fairly well in his studies. Though, for some reason, during this academic year he was failing. His teacher, after a failed attempt to align his teaching style with Joshua's learning style, finally recommended to Joshua's father that his son be tested for a learning disorder. Joshua was poised to enter middle school in a year and, thoughtfully, his teacher believed it important for him to be tested before that transition.

> Although Joshua's father initially protested, believing this was just his son's way of responding to his mother's military deployment, he nevertheless consented and sought out a childhood specialist. After briefing the specialist on Joshua's struggle, the specialist – relying upon his professional experience as well as a few tests – concluded that Joshua did have some sort of learning disorder; a diagnosis that did not sit well with his previous teachers, with whom Joshua had done well.

> Initiating an Individualized Education Program (IEP), these teachers in addition to Joshua's father, his present teacher, and the specialist met, as each one considered him/herself a specialist of Joshua. In this moment of sharing an interesting revelation came to light. In all other years, Joshua had sat up close, able to see the board clearly. But, in this year, he sat in the back. And upon further investigation, everyone saw what they had missed. Joshua did not have a learning problem. Joshua had a vision problem.

---

[51] Baruch Levine. "On the ridge of the right ear." *Etz Hayim: Torah and Commentary*. The Rabbinical Assembly: New York, 2004.
[52] Charlie Kaufman. *Adaptation*. Columbia Pictures: 2002.

Though, in some ways, one may say that it was those around him who truly had a vision problem. Because, by relying solely upon their own specialized perspectives, they became blind to the real issue: Joshua's father saw it as a parental issue, Joshua's teacher saw it as a teaching issue, and the specialist saw it as a diagnosable disorder. In fact, the real source of Joshua's struggle may have never come to light had it not been for the meeting, which created that sacred opportunity for knowledge sharing. In other words, when specialized knowledge is applied in a generalist way, seeing – as the priest did in this double portion of *Tazria-M'tzora* – the whole individual from head to toe, then and only then do we have a real chance to help people arrive at a healthy and successful future.

To be fair, that future is hard to predict. Will general practitioners move from the endangered species list to safety? Or, as our knowledge of the world continues to grow and specialists become ever more critical to our welfare, will they simply become extinct? Their fate remains uncertain. Nevertheless, in the here and now there is certainly something we can gain from their approach. And that is, through the sharing of specific knowledge, we can – like the general practitioner – begin to see the whole of a situation, gleaning, processing, and applying the Divine knowledge inherent in every moment. And thereby, we pray, help the world as well as everything and everyone therein to progress towards a healthier and happier future.

Double Portion 6 & 7:
Acharei Mot-K'doshim // After Death-Holy
Torah Portion: Leviticus 16:1-20:27

"THE LORD SPOKE TO MOSES AFTER THE DEATH OF AARON'S TWO SONS..." And, what God tells him is the Yom Kippur ritual, which Aaron shall perform. Namely, Aaron shall take two goats. Upon one shall he place the people's sins, letting it go into the wilderness (the original scapegoat); the other shall be the sin-offering, allowing Aaron and the Israelite nation to gain atonement before God.

What motivates this instruction is not theology but anxiety. God is concerned that Aaron may accidently suffer the same fate as his two sons: Nadav and Avihu. Thus, God instructs Moses to make sure Aaron knows explicitly that "he is not to come at will to the Shrine behind the curtain of the Tent of Meeting, lest he die too." (Leviticus 16:2)

It's not just Aaron whom God does not want to see removed from his people. Anyone who does not bring his offering before the Tent of Meeting or anyone who partakes of an offering with its blood still in it, may – God warns – be cut off from his people. Thus, God is putting everyone on notice.

In many ways these specific regulations and those yet to come are an outgrowth of a general principle laid out in *K'doshim*: "YOU SHALL BE HOLY, FOR I, THE LORD YOUR GOD, AM HOLY." As one may read there, holiness is not a condition confined to the Israelite relationship with God. It should pervade all human-to-human interactions as well, whether it's in casual business affairs or those intimate affairs of the heart, mind, body, and soul.

Their purpose, as this portion makes clear, is two-fold. One, these acts will distinguish the Israelites from the other people of the area. And, two, it will preserve their sanctity and stability, so that they may continue to progress soundly through the wilderness.

Acharei Mot-K'doshim // After Death-Holy
Bite 1 – *Food Revolution: A Jewish Movement*

Singer/song-writer Tracy Chapman once sang, "Don't you know. They're talkin' about a revolution. It sounds like a whisper."[53] But not all revolutions are so quiet. Some, like the current Food Revolution, are loudly reverberating their way around the U.S. From First Lady Michelle Obama to English nutritionist Jamie Oliver, influential people are picking up the bullhorn to trumpet a charge to free Americans from a mindless obedience to the will of their food. And, according to food revolutionists, the key to unlocking this multi-generational chain of unhealthy eating is education. "We have to change everything," stated food-activist Rachael Ray, "from the way we access our food to our attitudes about food. But, most importantly, we have to change our education regarding food. We have to become reacquainted with what we are eating."[54]

Because, as it is highlighted in this double portion of *Acharei Mot-K'doshim*, something happens when we know our food. With a sacrifice that began like any other, the sacrificial "kitchen" of the Shrine and altar were cleansed in Leviticus 16:20, as "a live goat was brought before [the Top Chef] Aaron." Yet, unlike other sacrifices, this sacrifice is not immediately slaughtered, roasted and then eaten by Aaron and his sons. First, Aaron is commanded to become acquainted with the offering, "laying both of his hands upon the head of the live goat and then confessing to it all the iniquities and transgressions of the people." No surprise, after playing and speaking with his potential food, Aaron takes a turn towards temporary vegetarianism. Instead of sacrificing the goat, he allows it "to go free into the wilderness." (Leviticus 16:21-22)

But, it must be said, that coming to know our food does not have to result in vegetarianism. Although, from the standpoint of Torah, a purely vegetarian diet was first ordered for us by our Divine partner in the Garden of Eden, and eating meat appears to be merely a concession to our human appetites after the flood.[55] Thus, comments Biblical scholar Baruch Levine, "To control our appetites, instead of our appetites controlling us, we must gain an intimate knowledge about our food – as Aaron did."[56] For "knowledge is power" and, if utilized effectively, we can free ourselves from anything, even a mindless obedience to the will of our food.[57] In other words, we can and should become empowered to think not only about what we don't put into our mouth, but – equally as important – is thinking about what we do put into our mouths.

In Judaism, we have always been thoughtful about what we eat. In addition to keeping kosher, this fundamental principle of our faith – which gives as much

---

[53] Tracy Chapman. "Talkin' 'bout a Revolution." *Tracy Chapman*. Elektra: 1988.
[54] J.M. Hirsch. *Celebrity Chefs Lead the Charge for Healthier Food*. Associated Press: 05 April 2010.
[55] See Genesis 1:30, 9:1-7
[56] *Etz Hayim: Torah and Commentary*. The Rabbinical Assembly: New York, 2001. p. 684
[57] "Knowledge is power" is a famous aphorism coined by Francis Bacon, a 16th century English philosopher, in his work: *Meditations*.

thought to food as it provides food for thought – manifests itself throughout our ritual year: from the *hamantashens* we devour on Purim (to symbolize the utter consumption of Haman's evil ways) to the *latkes* we enjoy on Chanukah (to remember the oil that sustained the flame of our faith), from the braided *challah* on Shabbat (which evokes the intertwined unity of all Jews) to the *matzah* we eat on Passover (recalling our rapid flight from Egypt to freedom). We understand that as much as food nourishes and sustains the body, it can also nourish and sustain the soul. Heck, we've basically said as much in our famous idiom: *"Ein keimach, ein Torah; ein Torah, ein keimach /* Without flour there is no Torah, and without Torah, there is no flour."[58]

Yet, somehow, in our secular diets this meaning doesn't translate. Every day, without thinking, many of us consume whatever offering is placed before us. Our food has gone from being familiar, to being friendly, to being an acquaintance which seems to pass so quickly from the plate to the stomach that it misses the warm greeting of our mouths altogether. And, as a result, the Stanford Medical School estimates that the U.S. spends over 150 billion dollars every year treating conditions related to unhealthy eating: high blood pressure, diabetes, heart disease, joint problems, even cancer. Sadly, even with the care, an estimated 300,000 people – including children – still die prematurely from making uninformed decisions about their diets.[59] In many ways, we are like the goat, who – without knowledge – eats without discretion.

But, as Rachael Ray challenges us, we can change. Like Aaron, we can send the goat away, casting off our unhealthy diets. Though, like Aaron, first we must become familiar, reacquainted with our food. Alright, we don't necessarily need to touch it, or play with it, or even talk to it. Minimally, all we need to do to make a positive and lasting change in our lives is to know from where our food comes and how it was processed. With this simple information, we have enough knowledge to make an informed decision about what food shall stay and what food shall go, what offering shall be consumed and which offering shall be allowed to pass into the wilderness.

Make no mistake. A revolution is afoot here in America. But, it is one that took its first steps thousands of years ago in the desert (not dessert) of the Middle East with our ancestors. And, now it is up to us. We must, as the great sage Bob Marley sang, "Get up! Stand up! Don't give up the fight!"[60] For this Food Revolution is inherently a Jewish movement, as it strives to improve our lives, the lives of our children, and the lives of our children's children through informed decision making. Let us embrace this lesson now, so that we may continue our revolutionary journey from being slaves to our food to being the master of our appetites, empowered to eat healthy and live healthy.

---

[58] Pirkei Avot 3:21. The statement is made in the name of Rabbi Elazar the son of Azariah.
[59] For more information please check out http://stanfordhospital.org
[60] Bob Marley and the Wailers. "Get up, Stand up." *Burnin'*. Tuff Gong Records/Island Records: Jamaica, 1973.

Acharei Mot-K'doshim // After Death-Holy
Bite 2 – *To Plant or Not to Plant Seed: Homosexuality in the Bible*

Ladies and gentleman of the jury, Your Honor – the Holy One, Blessed be God, I stand before you today to protest a great injustice and to defend the unalienable rights of fellow members of our human family. Every day, our brothers and sisters – people created in Your Divine image – are having their basic human liberties restricted or altogether stripped away. They are often harassed and tormented; they are often barred from supporting loved ones in times of great need; they are often prohibited from marriage; and, in some places, they are legally thrown out of public places like restaurants and theaters. Why? What supposed crime have they committed? Simply: falling in love with another human being of the same gender.

And, frankly, it deeply upsets me that this injustice is perpetrated and perpetuated by people of faith, who claim that such blatant discrimination and unabashed bigotry are justified by Your Holy Word. Specifically, contained within the Holiness Code, part of a special section in the book of Leviticus, they point to a group of laws dealing with inappropriate sexual relations. According to just two lines in the entire Hebrew Bible, both of which are found within the double portion of *Acharei Mot-K'doshim*, we are warned that "if a man lies with a man, as one lies with a woman, the two of them have done a *to-eivah*, an 'abhorrent thing;'[61] they shall be put to death – their blood guilt is upon them."[62] (Leviticus 18:22, 20:13)

So, no, I will not argue today whether or not homosexual sex is prohibited in the Bible.[63] Clearly, it is. However, I will attempt to answer the question that so often goes unasked in this debate, which is "*why* was it prohibited?" What about homosexual sex was abhorrent to our ancestors? To answer this pivotal question, which will dramatically change the course of the conversation, I call forward the expert testimony of Robert Alter, Professor of Hebrew Language, renown Biblical commentator. "The evident rationale for such a prohibition," explains Alter, "seems to be the wasting of seed in what the law envisages as a grotesque parody of heterosexual intercourse."[64]

---

[61] It is important to note that the Hebrew word *to-eivah* ("abhorrent," or sometimes translated as "abomination") occurs numerous times in the Bible. Taking stock of these, Rabbi Richard Friedman commented, "*to-eivah* is a relative term in the Bible, which varied according to human perceptions. For example, in Genesis, Joseph tells his brothers that 'any shepherd is a *to-eivah*/an abhorrent thing to Egypt' (46:34); but obviously shepherding is not a *to-eivah*/an abhorrent thing to the Israelites, as they proudly perform this role."

[62] Some would like to add Sodom and Gomorrah to this list. However, nowhere in that story does the Bible say anything about homosexual sex. It's merely inferred from: "Bring them (i.e. the men) out to us, that we may get to know them." (Gen. 19:5) It's true; occasionally "to know" is the Bible's way of saying "sex," but not always. Case in point: at the beginning of the book of Exodus, we are told "a new king arose over Egypt who did not *know* Joseph." (Ex. 1:8). If everywhere the word "to know/*yada'at*" means "sex," then we must conclude that the previous king of Egypt and Joseph were engaged in a homosexual relationship. And, because it did not continue with the new king, the Pharaoh became upset and enslaved our people.

[63] "Homosexual sex" not "homosexuals;" because, the Bible is not prohibiting a person nor calling them abhorrent. The text is specifically indicating an act as abhorrent.

[64] Robert Alter. *The Five Books of Moses: A Translation with Commentary*. W.W. Norton & Co.: New York, 2004. p. 623

Why? What's the problem with this parody? Well the problem, according to the Bible, is that heterosexual intercourse, wherein the seed of human life (i.e. sperm) is implanted in the fertile ground of the woman's womb, is meant for one purpose and one purpose only: to create life, to procreate, "to be fruitful and multiply." First issued as a blessing in Genesis 1:28, these words only became a Divine command to man upon the depopulation of the world after the flood in Genesis 9:6.[65] There, these words are found among others which deal with a case of homicide. This is intentional, writes the master commentator RaSHI, "for anyone who does not engage in reproduction should be compared to one who sheds blood," as both require a death penalty.[66]

Anyone, hum? Well then, based upon this rationale a lot of people would be slated for death.[67] Because, in addition to those who engage in homosexual sex, anyone – homosexual or heterosexual – who engages in sex using contraceptives (e.g. condoms), or anyone – homosexual or heterosexual – who masturbates, is likewise guilty of the same crime: wasting seed. What?! Don't believe me. Then please allow me to introduce into evidence the case of Onan, Judah's second eldest son. According to the Biblical testimony, "Whenever Onan went to join with Tamar, he let his seed go to waste. What he did," states the Bible, "was displeasing to the Lord, so God took his life."[68]

Given this precedent, some may wish to continue their prosecution and persecution of homosexuals. After all, they claim, "God instructed us, in this Holiness Code, 'to reprove our kinsman.'"[69] True, God did say we should "reprove our kinsman;" however that line ends with "but, we may not incur any guilt because of him." That is to say, when we see someone doing something we believe to be harmful, we are obligated to say something. However, as the second part of the verse implies, it has to be done in such a way as to not be disrespectful. For, we cannot resolve one sin by creating another. Besides, in God's law of nature, death eventually comes. Not in body, but in name, as one who does not procreate, has no one to carry it on.

With that, Your Honor, ladies and gentleman of the jury, I rest my case. Clearly, without any true Biblical basis, upon which to ground such injustices, I ask that you dismiss all grievances against these fellow human beings, our

---

[65] The prohibition addressed only men, because of our ancestors' limited knowledge about procreation. According to their understanding, all the material needed to reproduce life was contained in the *zerah*/the seed (i.e. the sperm), as a woman's egg is never mentioned in the Hebrew Bible. Hence, that's the reason why sex between two women was never prohibited in the Bible, but included later by the rabbinic sages.
[66] RaSHI commentary to Genesis 9:6
[67] Kinsey, Alfred C. et al. *Sexual Behavior in the Human Male*. Indiana University Press: Philadelphia. 1948 and 1998, p. 499. According to this study, Kinsey reported that 92% of men engage in masturbation. A similar study with women showed that 62% engage in masturbation.
[68] See Genesis 38:6-10. The *Mishnah*, written in the first century of the Common Era, makes reference to this act. As it is written: "The hand that oftentimes makes 'examinations' is – among woman – praiseworthy, but among men, let it (i.e. the hand) be cut off!" Just in case we were fooled by the euphemism "examination," tractate Niddah in the *Babylonian Talmud* makes it clear that "examination refers only to the emission of semen." (BT Niddah 13a).
[69] Leviticus 19:17

kinsmen in the family of God. For, as social psychologist Erich Fromm deduced, "In essence, all human beings are identical. We are all part of One; we are One. This being so, it should not make any difference whom we love," as long as we love with all of our hearts, all of our minds, all of our souls.[70] With this greater truth, may we go on to honor both God's Holy Words better, as well as all those who hold these Words near and dear: heterosexual and homosexual alike.

Acharei Mot-K'doshim // After Death-Holy
Bite 3 – *This Little Light of Mine, I'm Going to Let it Shine*

Diversity, as we know, is all around us. It pervades our world. In fact, some need only to look at their own families to see the beautiful tapestry that diversity can create. Such is the case within my own family, especially during the winter holidays. With the lights off in the dining room, those in my family who are Jewish light the lights of the Chanukah *menorah*. Those in my family who are Christian light the lights of the Christmas tree. Those in my family who are of African descent light the lights of the Kwanzaa *kinara*. And, those in my family who are atheist, well, they flip on the lights of the dining room and exclaim: "Man! It's dark in here!"

Regrettably, these same words could be used to describe the current state of tolerance in America: "It's dark in here." Yet wonderfully, to help bolster our attempts to shed light on this issue, God – in this double portion of *Acharei Mot-K'doshim* – provides all people of goodwill these enduring words of encouragement: "*K'doshim tih'yu ki kadosh ani Adonai eloheichem //* You all shall be holy, for I, the Lord your God, am holy." (Leviticus 19:2) Great! Now what does that mean?! Exactly, what does it mean to be holy? What does it mean to be, as holiness was understood by our Biblical prophets, "a light unto the nations?"

Commentators have struggled over this question for millennia. Some say holiness is simply following the guiding light of our Divine creator. "If holiness is the highest level of human behavior," as Rabbi Sampson Raphael Hirsch once wrote, "then human beings are at their most holy when a morally free human being has complete dominion over one's own energies and inclinations and the temptations associated with them, and places them [instead] at the service of God's will."[71] Hirsch's definition is not bad. After all, it certainly removes holiness from an attribute of things to an extension of our human deeds.

However, such a definition may also come to be counterproductive in terms of our diverse world, particularly if it is misinterpreted to mean that, in order to

---

[70] Erich Fromm. *The Art of Loving*. Harper and Row: 1956.
[71] See the d'rash commentary in "K'doshim" of the *Etz Hayim: Torah and Commentary*. The Rabbinical Assembly: New York, 2001. p. 693

become holy, one must raise themselves (i.e. their light) above others, rather than *with* others. Hence why modern Jewish theologian, Martin Buber, noting the plural context of our Levitical verse, chose to understand holiness as the ability to "recognize the latent light of divinity of other people, as God does with each one of us."[72] For, it is only together, through our diverse human interactions, that we can manifest that latent light of the Divine in our world, becoming holy as the Lord our God is holy.

Though, too often when we engaged in these interfaith, interreligious, intercultural, intergenerational exchanges, on our way to achieving holiness, we frankly do so incorrectly. Dismissing our differences, we tend to favor a focus on what we have in common. As the prize-winning poet Maya Angelou once wrote: "We are more alike, my friends, than we are unalike."[73] Sure, on the surface, this approach may seem appropriate, as then we come to understand that not only do we have a common past but also a shared future. But, when we whittle down our differences to some common singularity, then our function becomes singular as well, incapable of responding to the diverse needs of our time.

For, as many of us come to realize in our lives, diversity is an asset vital to our very survival. Like planning for retirement, an investment in one's future is made more secure by a diverse portfolio. Is it not? Acknowledging as much, the sages of our faith – in admiration of God's greatness – wrote long ago: "Praise the greatness of the Holy One! For, while man may stamp many coins with one seal and they are all alike, the King of kings, the Holy One, blessed be God, stamps every person with the same seal and yet none of them are the same."[74] In other words, the sages teach that the holiness of God, in which we are compelled to achieve, is manifest in our diversity.

Though, this is where the other common mistake related to diversity is made: not simply in belittling our difference, but in maintaining them. For when we choose, as has been done so often in the past, to reinforce our diversity by allowing one group to garner success at the expense of another's failure, then we ultimately put each and every person's welfare – including our own – in tremendous jeopardy. For, as those who put up holiday lights during the winter season will know well, when even just one, tiny, little bulb goes out, the whole string of lights goes out as well. The same goes for our society. If we stand idly by to watch another's light diminish, then ultimately our own light is diminished as well.

So how then do we allow our own light to shine without outshining another? How can we raise the light of holiness together, as encouraged by God in this double portion? It is by following those simple yet immortal words born to so many faiths and so many cultures: "Do unto others as you would have them

---

[72] *Ibid.*
[73] Dr. Maya Angelou. "Human Family." *The Complete Collected Poems of Maya Angelou.* Random House: 1994. p. 224
[74] *Mishnah* Sanhedrin 4:5

do unto you," as we have here in America; "choose for thy neighbor, what thou would choosest for thyself,"[75] as spoken by Bahaullah, founder of the Baha'i Faith; "love your neighbor as yourself,"[76] a Biblical quote found slightly later in this double Torah portion and subsequently shared by Jesus in the gospel of Matthew, and even "what is hateful to you, do not do to any person,"[77] as spoken by the Jewish sage Hillel.

For each of these expressions, whether framed positively or negatively, preserves the light of our neighbors, while allowing our own little light to shine. And, as the song goes, "Out in the dark, I'm going to let it shine. Oh, out in the dark, I'm going to let it shine. Out in the dark, I'm going to let it shine. Let it shine! Let it shine! Let it shine!" And, when we do this together, may this holy light, light up any room, illuminating a life of less hostility and more reasonability, less pain and more healing, less hate and more love, less war and more peace. Let us continue to be and become that beacon of holy light.

---

[75] From Bahaullah's *Epistle to the Son of the Wolf*, written to a Muslim cleric, who violently opposed him.
[76] Matthew 22:36-39. The author of Matthew places this quote, from Leviticus 19:18, in the mouth of Jesus.
[77] *Babylonian Talmud*, Shabbat 31a

Portion 8:

Emor // Speak
Torah Portion: Leviticus 21:1-24:23

"THE LORD SAID TO MOSES: SPEAK TO THE PRIESTS…" Detailing the duties of the priesthood has not been exhausted yet. There is more that God wishes Aaron and his sons to know, so that they may perform their many sacred tasks with precision. Thus, God calls upon Moses to deliver these instructions time and time again.

This time, God regulates not only their sacred duties but how they may or may not interact with their kin. Priests may not come into contact with the dead, except for the closest of relatives (mothers, fathers, sons, daughters, brothers, and sisters). Priests must be without blemish. Those with defects may eat of the holy food but not come near the altar. Special attention must be paid by priests in partaking of the sacred donations, eating them only when pure. And when a daughter of a priest defiles herself, she has defiled her father.

Having laid out some of the expected behaviors of the priests, the portion proceeds to impart the days of commemoration which are still celebrated by the Jewish people to this day: *Shabbat* (honored every week on the sixth day), *Pesach* (taking place on the fourteenth of the first month), *Shavuot* (occurring seven weeks later, with the offering of new grain), *Rosh HaShanah* (referred to then as the "sacred occasion commemorated with loud blasts"), Yom Kippur (the Day of Atonement, "on which expiation is made on your behalf before the Lord"), and finally *Sukkot* (the Feast of Booths).

At the end of the portion, God instructs Moses on how to properly light the seven-branch candelabra, known as the *menorah,* and how to present the loaves of bread for an offering. The portion concludes with a man – born from an Israelite mother and an Egyptian father – blaspheming God. In response, he is stoned to death, according to the laws of blasphemy that are explained to Moses.

Emor // Speak
Bite 1 – *The Handicap Advantage*

Many of us, if not most of us, by now are familiar with the story of Oscar Pistorius. Born without fibulas and becoming a double-amputee at the age of 11-months, Pistorius began running competitively with the help of prosthetics called "running blades" at the age of 18. In 2004, representing his country of South Africa at the Paralympics in Athens, Pistorius won a gold-medal in the 200-meter competition. But, that is not where his story ends. After battling for years on the track with fellow physically-challenged athletes, Pistorius began a fight off the track to compete in able-bodied events: the World Games, the Olympics, etc. And, in 2008, his battle was finally won. The Court of Arbitration for Sports overturned a ban against the double amputee by the International Association of Athletics Federation (IAAF), which was concerned that his prosthetics may confer an unfair advantage. Yes, surprisingly, in their words: "A physically-challenged athlete using a prosthetic has a demonstrable advantage when compared to an able-bodied athlete."[78]

This is surprising because ordinarily having some physical abnormality is not considered an advantage, but a disadvantage; a challenge which may limit one's ability to achieve at the same level as an able-bodied individual. Sadly, this is often the perception today, and – as we learn from this portion of *Emor* – it has been the perception for some time. According to Leviticus 21, our ancestors believed that "no offspring, throughout the ages, who has [what the Torah calls] a defect should be qualified to offer food to God: no person who is blind, lame, or has a limb too short or too long; no person who has a broken leg or broken arm; no one who is hunchback or a dwarf; no one who has a growth in his eye, a boil scar, scurvy, or crushed testes. No person, [just in case it wasn't clear by now, the Bible reiterates], who has a defect shall be qualified to offer the Lord's gift." (Leviticus 21:17-21)

Commentators throughout the ages have attempted to justify this rather harsh position which, on the surface, seems to exclude those with physical limitations from participating fully in the communal exercises of our faith. This is not just a surface reading, comments medieval sage RaSHI. This is *the* case, as "those who have a defect are disqualified from serving. But," with a glimmer of hope, he continues, "if the defect goes away, the person can be fit to serve once again."[79] And, if you think some slack on this position is going to come from modern commentators... well, think again. For example, modern Biblical scholar Baruch Levine suggests that "perhaps they are disqualified because their disfigurements would distract the [able-bodied] worshipers from concentrating on the ritual. Or," he continues, "like the offering of a blemished animal, [perhaps the blemished individual] would compromise the sanctuary's image as a place of perfection, reflecting God's perfection."[80]

---

[78] AP. "Blade Runner Barred from Olympics. 14 January 2008. See also AP. "Blade Runner Wins Olympic Appeal." 16 May 2008.

[79] RaSHI comment to 21:21

[80] Etz Hayim: Torah and Commentary. Rabbinical Assembly: New York, 2001. p. 719

With good reason, these antiquated resolutions and their interpretations may be met by modern aversion, if not complete repulsion. Informed by contemporary standards, outlined in documents like the Americans with Disabilities Act (1990), we justifiably question today the efficacy of these "throughout-the-ages" mandates of our Bible. For, who among us can say that he or she is without blemish? Who among us can say that he or she is wholly and holy perfect? If we are honest, we would say: "none... not even Aaron!" Although, don't tell Nachmanides that, for he wrote in the 14th century that "every part of Aaron was perfect. There was no blemish in or on him."[81] While that may have been the case, it's certainly the exception, not the rule. For, if there does not appear to be a blemish on a person, then it is statistically probable that there is some blemish within. In one form or another, a majority of Americans today struggle with mental, emotional, or even inconspicuous physical challenges.

And, like the Levitical priesthood, there are institutions throughout our country which then disqualify potential employees based upon these challenges. They consider them defects, blemishes, scars on one's resume. Although this discriminatory practice is prohibited, the Cornell University Law School notes that it can be justified if the employer determines that the inclusion of such an individual would, in some way, "pose a direct threat to the health or safety of other individuals in the workplace."[82] To say that this was of consideration within the priesthood's decision in this portion is only conjecture. But to say that this remains the case within the institution of the American military is not, for its recruiters are still forced – despite dwindling numbers – to reject some volunteers based upon the presence of mere physical or even mild mental challenges. As one recruiter, with great regret, told me: "They are simply not 'fit-to-fight,' and – if permitted – mission success may be compromised."[83]

Their perspective, while understandable, does not have to be the standard view. For a poignant example we need only look to our people in Israel. There, serving side-by-side with able-bodied soldiers of either gender and any sexual orientation are individuals with mental challenges (i.e Down Syndrome, Autism spectrum disorders, etc.). Limited only from serving in combat squadrons who are on the front lines, these soldiers fill vital roles in the machine of the Israeli Defense Forces working in logistics, supplies, services, and other instrumental roles. One of these new recruits, Gilad Rosdiel, happily told reporters that "ever since I was 18 [and saw all the other Israeli boys go off to fulfill their civic responsibility in service to their country, I] had dreamt of enlisting. And now, boast Gilad, "my dream is finally coming true!"[84] But, it is not just a dream come true for the individual recruit. It is a dream-come-true

---

[81] RaMBaN comment to Leviticus 21:17
[82] http://www.law.cornell.edu/uscode/42 (For more information see chapter 126, subchapter 1 of the Americans with Disabilities Act).
[83] Conversation occurred within my work within the military.
[84] Na'ama Rak. Equal Opportunities in the IDF. 24 March 2009 (For more information see http://dover.idf.il/IDF/English/News/today/09/03/2402.htm

for the entire community of Israel. For while some may have deemed them as not wholly fit for service, the IDF understands their service as fitting to make Israel whole and their forces stronger.

And that is really the message that we should take from this Biblical text. Alright, maybe not exactly from this portion, but even as close as the last portion we had the beautiful sentiment which stated: "You shall not insult the deaf, or place a stumbling block before the blind."[85] This provision was – in my opinion – not simply provided to insure justice for the individual. In addition, it was included to insure the greatest justice and success for the community. For the greatest resource any nation has is its people. And thus when we restrict this resource from the whole of the community, when we place these stumbling blocks and barriers before a portion of our people, we ultimately put ourselves at a disadvantage. So, let us not cripple ourselves. Let us remove the restrictions from our fellow, for when we do we will turn what – on the surface – appears to be a challenge for one into an advantage for all. "And that day," said the South African track star Oscar Pistorius, "that day will go down in history as the moment upon which we reached equality, wholeness of all [of God's] people."

Emor // Speak
Bite 2 – *Guardianship, Not Ownership*

Once there was a Catholic Priest, a Protestant Minister, and a Rabbi, who were all discussing how to deal with the charitable donations they received. That is to say, how much should reasonably be put aside for their own portion/livelihood and how much should go to the Lord? The Catholic Priest shared that he had devised a simple yet effective method for making this calculation.

> "I draw a circle on the ground and then toss all the charitable donations I receive into the air. Whatever lands inside the circle," explained the Priest, "that's for the Lord. And, anything outside, well that's for me."

> "Interesting," responded the Protestant Minister. "I also draw a circle and toss the charitable donations into the air. But, whatever lands in the circle, that's my portion. And, whatever falls outside, that's the Lord's."

> "Truly, friends, we are more alike than unalike," added the Rabbi. "For, I too use the circle method. Except, when I throw the charitable donations into the air I say – 'whatever God wants, let God keep' – and that which falls to the ground is mine."

---

[85] Leviticus 19:14

Well, if that were the case, then according to this portion of *Emor*, God – respectfully – should keep just about everything. Because, as we are making our way through the weekly readings of our ancient priestly manual, (known as the book of Leviticus), we hear of all matters of things being set aside for the Lord: from grain to goats, from flour to fowls. And just in case there is still some uncertainty on this matter, God instructs our ancestral priests "not to allow the Israelites to profane any sacred donations that are set aside for the Lord, or incur guilt requiring a penalty payment, by eating of the sacred donations. For," adds God, "it is I the Lord who makes them sacred." (Leviticus 22:15-16)

Clearly, this decree warns the average Israelite not to confuse their portion with God's portion, lest they incur a penalty (giving a power-play to the other side). However, the 11th century sage, Abraham Ibn Ezra posited that "the causative verb form [found in the Divine directive] of '*not allowing* the Israelites...to incur guilt' implies a secondary object: the priests," who were responsible for maintaining accurate accounts.[86] Particularly, elucidates modern Biblical scholar Baruch Levine, the verse focuses "on priests, who might be tempted to deal in the sacred donations for their own advantage."[87] Thus, like the circle, the command served as a simple yet effective guide at determining what part of a charitable donation went to people and what part belonged to God...with a clear point, here, that everything belongs to God.

But, this isn't necessarily correct. Not only did the priests regularly partake of the sacrificial offerings, as they had no land portion by which to make a living, but – on a larger scale – back in Genesis we were taught that the whole world is given to us as our portion. As it is written: "God blessed the human and said: 'Be fertile and increase, fill the earth and master it; rule the fish of the sea, the birds of the sky, and all the living things that creep on earth.'"[88] Furthermore, when someone wished to take the Nazerite vow, restricting their portion in life, dealing with a little less so that God could have a little more, the sages of old lambasted him, saying: "Are not all the restrictions and laws of the Torah enough for you? Why do you insist on restraining yourself from that portion which the Torah permits you to enjoy?"[89]

So it appears that, just as the Native American Obie Phillis deduced in his spiritual, we do indeed have "the whole world [or at least a great portion of it] in our hands," and are permitted to partake in the Divine sacredness of all life. While this feeling of personal ownership may productively lead to a developed sense of personal responsibility, if taken too far, it can actually become counterproductive. For example, just because it is in our hands, many feel that they rightfully "deserve" it. While not an irrational notion, this thought can lend itself to the erroneous conclusion that others, less fortunate, are also less deserving; a terrible judgment that inhibits charitable giving. Another

---

[86] Ibn Ezra commentary to Leviticus 22:15-16
[87] Baruch Levine. *The JPS Torah Commentary: Leviticus.* The Jewish Publication Society: Philadelphia, 1989. p.150
[88] Genesis 1: 27-28
[89] *Jerusalem Talmud, Nedarim* 9:1; 30:3

downside to this perspective, if taken too far, is what happens when what we feel we "deserve" is no longer there, taken by the hands of fate. Rather than responding to the change effectively, we respond with anger or, worse, immobilized dread.

That is why – despite the apparent contradictions – this portion teaches us that everything, even what we consider to be our portion, really belongs to the Lord. For when we see our role in life less as owners and more as guardians, less as inheritors and more as trustees of life's countless gifts and blessings, then we can come to appreciate those things in our hands every day, not just on that sad day when those things in our hands are taken away (whether gently or, as was the case unfortunately throughout the South recently, not so gently). And, beyond appreciating them for ourselves, when we come to understand that our blessings in life are not solely ours, but treasures entrusted to us by God, then we may be more inclined to pass them along to others, sharing in the bounty of our world. A far better reaction to navigate the unpredictable currents on life than anger or dread!

May we continue to embrace this perspective, especially at this time. As our neighbors sift through the rubble to find remnants of their lives before the storm, may we not waste time to sift our portion from that portion which should be given as a most holy offering to those in need. Those who survived the storms are amazing witnesses to the power of this teaching, as they began helping one another without delay. May those of us who have not been so immediately affected realize this valuable lesson as well. For truly, when we approach life as guardians rather than owners, passing on that portion which has been passed to us, then – as spoken by the prophet Ezekiel – we merit an even greater portion: God. When we hold nothing back from our neighbors, we can be assured that God will be our everlasting holding.[90]

Emor // Speak
Bite 3 – *The IKEA Sukkah: A Labor of Love*

Some months ago, I made a purchase of which I am particularly proud. It was a bookcase, not fancy or elegant. In fact, when I first brought it home, it was in pieces, some big, some small, each labeled with a letter or number which directed me on how they could be put together. It was like a little boy's dream: a giant jigsaw puzzle that you put together with a screwdriver! And though I love jigsaw puzzles, this one definitely tried my patience, as I inevitably put parts in the wrong place, inexplicably missed some critical steps along the way, and even went a little off script to get things to fit. After all, directions are merely suggestions, right? Because, just five little hours later, my tiny three-shelf bookcase was complete. I had not designed anything, measured anything, or cut anything (besides one of my fingers), but somehow I felt a great deal of pride, as I stood back and beheld my creation!

---

[90] Ezekiel 44:28

That sense of pride, we can imagine, was likely felt by our ancestors as well, as they put the finishing touches on the Divine's directions for the festival of Sukkot. After speaking about the gifts to be presented before the Lord, as well as the *lulav* and *etrog*, God instructs the people to "assemble booths and live therein for seven days… in order that future generations may know that I made the Israelite people live in booths when I brought them out of the land of Egypt." (Leviticus 23:42) And, we – the future generations – have certainly followed these instructions religiously, finding ever new and more efficient ways to invoke this remembrance. As one sukkah advertisement read: "Our new portable Sukkah snaps together in under five minutes with absolutely no tools necessary. It fits into any trunk, meets airline standards for check-in, and weighs only 18 pounds. Bag and shoulder strap sold separately."[91]

Even without the bag and shoulder strap, many will still assert that such innovations are blessings to our people. For, in their ease, they help people over the hurdle of the logistical to get into the meaningful, so that they may come to embrace the significance of these religious prescriptions. And, these innovations are not limited to the holiday of Sukkot. On Purim, there are ready-made costumes, featuring all the characters from the scroll of Esther. On Passover, there's ready-made matzah and matzah-ball mixes. And, on Chanukah, there are electric menorahs. Given this trend, it likely won't be long before we have the blessed ease of clap-on Shabbat candles, providing all the beauty of the original without the awkward difficulty of striking a match before a congregation… just beware of any further clapping in the service!

But, others insist, hand-clapping is not the only thing of which we should be aware in this gentle easing of our traditions. And surprisingly, this argument is not made on the grounds of simply adhering to what has been. Rather, this group is legitimately concerned that providing such an easy "in" may also, while unintentional, contain an easy "out," because it lacks the labor which makes for enduring love and thereby an enduring commitment. By the way, the unexpected consequence from making things too easy also became a concern for baking-mix companies over half-a-century ago.[92]

> In 1940, instant baking mixes of all kinds (from biscuits to brownies, from cookies to cakes) were introduced to the market. And, almost immediately, they had a strong presence in American grocery carts, pantries, and eventually at the table. That is with exception to cake mixes, which required only the addition of water. Marketers were baffled. Why were the mixes used to make biscuits and piecrusts – which were composed of pretty much the same basic ingredients – so popular, while cakes mixes were not?

---

[91] See http://www.sukkahonline.com/?gclid=CJCPhaaIzasCFZAs7AodVBFr5Q
[92] The following case example comes from Dan Ariely's *The Upside of Irrationality: The Unexpected Benefits of Defying Logic at Work and at Home.* HarperCollins Publishers: New York, 2010. pp. 84-89

An answer to this marketing perplexity was provided by psychologist Ernest Dichter, who theorized that the cake mixes simplified the process of baking to such an extent that the at-home bakers did not feel as though the cakes they made were "theirs." In other words, minimal effort meant minimal personal attachment. Thus, a baker could not in good faith receive a compliment on a dish that was "just a mix." For, as the food writer Laura Shapiro pointed out, biscuits and piecrusts are important, but they are not self-contained courses.[93]

So, Dichter speculated that if the companies complicated the cake recipe just a little, say by leaving out some ingredients so that the at-home bakers could add a little more themselves, this may resolve the issue. A speculation, by the way, which came to be known as the "egg theory," for once Pillsbury left out the dried eggs, requiring at-home bakers to add fresh ones themselves, sure enough, sales took off!

Many digest this slice of reality to mean that while we may desire ease, our souls actually have a hunger for more involvement. Sandra Lee, of the Semi-Homemade fame, has pinpointed the precise percentage of this personal involvement to 30. In using ready-made products for 70% of the process, states Lee, over-extended individuals can still feel the joy of creation through those little personal touches.[94] And that joy, that pride, of which Lee speaks, when one stands back to behold their completed creation with affection and appreciation results in prolonged attachment to the meaningful activity itself, whether it's baking or building, whether it's grilling or gardening, whether it's roasting or writing, whether it's pickling or painting. For, in adding something to the mix ourselves, we are – in fact – adding a little more *of* ourselves into the mix, a personal investment from which it is hard to withdraw.

That, speculates Ibn Ezra, was the feeling the Israelites were meant to experience in this portion when God commanded them to put on the final touches to this festival of Sukkot: making booths as a remembrance of their Exodus from Egypt. For although "that Exodus took place in the first month of Nisan, when the Lord hovered over their camp to shelter them," comments Ibn Ezra, "only on the seventh of Tishrei did God command them to build booths, so that they could participate in [the process of] protecting themselves."[95] Though more difficult, God knew that when we participate more in the Divine process of creation and protection, we can go beyond remembering the Divine shelter back then to providing Divine shelters right now. This is indeed a labor of love from which, we pray, all the world may one day stand back in pride. For "on that day," proclaims the prophet Zechariah, "the Lord [with our finishing touches] shall come to shelter the entire world."[96]

---

[93] Laura Shapiro. *Something from the Oven: Reinventing Dinner in 1950s America.* Penguin Group: New York, 2004.
[94] See http://www.foodnetwork.com/chefs/sandra-lee/index.html
[95] Ibn Ezra commentary to Leviticus 23:43
[96] Zechariah 14:9. A strict translation of this text says "rule" rather than "shelter." But, for sake of the theme of this Taste of Torah it was altered; though, not maliciously, as surely sheltering His kingdom is within the ruler's power, best interest, and responsibilities.

Double Portion 9 & 10:
B'har-B'chukotai //
On the Mountain-With My Laws
Torah Portion: Leviticus 25:1-27:34

"THE LORD SPOKE TO MOSES ON MOUNT SINAI…" The final section of the book of Leviticus outlines laws which shall come to pass after the possession of the land, cementing the concepts of the *Sh'mitah* year, when the land has a rest every seventh year, and the *Yovel*, the Jubilee year that occurs every 50 years, when all lands return to their original owners.

To provide guidance in the institution of these general principles, the portion includes hypothetical situations in which the rule of release applies. For example, there is guidance on what should transpire when a kinsman in straits has no one to redeem him, when a home is sold in a walled city versus a village, when exacting interest, and when an Israelite comes under the authority of his kin or a resident alien.

"IF YOU FOLLOW MY LAWS AND FAITHFULLY OBSERVE MY COMMANDMENTS…" then God promises blessings in their life within the Promised Land (rains in their season, peace, and plenty of fertile seeds). However, if they are not observed and God's ways are rejected, then curses will ensue (consumption and fever, dispersion and even cannibalism).

Leviticus concludes by outlining donations to the sanctuary for people of various ages and genders, and values are assigned to various vows that one can make to the Temple, including vows of property and animals. The first-born of ox and sheep must be given to God, and the firstborn of other impure animals may be redeemed. Tithes, of both the flocks and herds and of the seed of the ground and the fruit of the tree, are also owed to God.

Through these actions, the people of Israel will come to merit the blessings, and not the curses, laid out in this portion.

B'har-B'chukotai // On the Mountain-With My Laws
Bite 1 – *The Hands of God*

In the *Talmud*, Rav Assi said: "The mitzvah of *tzedakah* is more important than all the other commandments combined."[97] This is an incredible, if not – some may argue – a sensational claim! For Rav Assi appears to be saying the deed of helping others is not merely the most important of any other single commandment. He teaches that – after combining all the other commandments into one – the value of this one commandment out-weighs the others on the balance of our Jewish lives. "But," we may ask, "what's the basis for this extraordinary claim?" Surely God does not play favorites when it comes to the commandments. God, we believe, considers them all equally important.

Well, one possible Biblical location from which this rabbinic principle derives is in this double portion of *B'har-B'chukotai*. After discussing the sabbatical and jubilee years (in which the Israelites press life's little reset button), the first thing presented in the new societal game-plan are the words: "*ki yamuch achicha* / if your kinsman is reduced [to poverty]." (Leviticus 25:25) And, it is not just here. Four times our portion evokes those words, *ki yamuch achicha*: (1) when a kinsman is in dire straits and must sell his property,[98] (2) when a kinsman is in dire straits and must borrow money,[99] (3) when a kinsman is in dire straits and must become an indentured servant,[100] and (4) when a kinsman is in dire straits and must sell himself to a resident alien.[101]

According to our rabbis, we are made aware of our kinsman's plight so as not to be by-standers. Rather, the Torah commands us to be the remedy, as it is our responsibility to help our kinsmen rise from their reduction. Yet, despite our efforts, we are not the ones who are thanked. Instead, after we complete the righteous deed, the Torah credits God. As it is stated: thanks are due unto God for "it is the Lord your God, who brought you out of the land of Egypt to be your God." (Leviticus 25:38 & 55) It figures. Not because we erroneously understand God as a show boat, stealing the spot-light from our worthy endeavors. Rather, from this statement, we understand that when we provide for one another, when we are able to answer another's prayers, our deeds become an extension of God's hands. Such is the case in the story of Chayim and Yankel:

> Once – many years ago – in a small village, there lived an extremely wealthy man named Chayim and an extremely poor man named Yankel. Every Friday evening, Chayim would come to the synagogue in the finest Shabbat clothes and sit in the most cherished seat near the ark in the synagogue. After the service, Chayim would regularly

---

[97] BT Baba Batra 9a
[98] Leviticus 25:25
[99] Leviticus 25:35
[100] Leviticus 25:39
[101] Leviticus 25:47

rise and – without saying a word – leave, returning to his magnificent mansion on a hill, overlooking the town. Meeting him at his door, a butler would show Chayim into his regal dining room, where a table fit for a king awaited. Chayim would sit surrounded by the finest china, flatware, and crystal. He would be served the most remarkable meal, accompanied by the sweetest, most heavenly of challahs. But, none of it brought Chayim joy. For, he was alone. Chayim had no family and no one he called a friend.

On one particular Sabbath, as Chayim stared at the golden platters and the wonderful array of dishes set before him, he suddenly realized what he needed. He needed to share Shabbat with someone. "But with whom?" Chayim questioned. "Who is worthy of sharing Shabbat with me? Then it hit him: "God. Yes, God! Let God share my wonderful Sabbath feast!" And with those words, a plan began to take shape in his mind. According to the plan, on the following Shabbat, Chayim would not leave the sanctuary to run off to his mansion. Instead he would wait around until everyone had gone back to their homes and – with no one looking – he would place two of the most delectable challahs in the ark. "In this way," Chayim thought, "God can share with me the sweet delights of Shabbat. For there is no way God has ever tasted something so good." When the next Friday evening service came and went, Chayim did just as he had planned. He placed two warm challahs into the ark, whispering 'Shabbat Shalom,' before returning home.

But something happened that Friday night that Chayim didn't plan. After leaving the synagogue, Yankel entered the sanctuary. Being the poorest man in town, Yankel always arrived late as he tried to squeeze every last bit of work into his week. "Besides," he thought, "this was best, as then no one has to see me in my dirty clothes or smell my sweaty stench." So, alone in the synagogue, Yankel would pray to God. "Master of the universe, it's *Shabbos*! How can You let me go home once again with nothing to bring to my family? You know how hard I work. And You know that I have nothing. Without Your help, dear God, I will not have the strength to go home and watch my family suffer!" With those impassioned words, Yankel slammed his hands on the doors of the holy ark. The doors jolted open and out rolled two beautiful, golden, warm challahs. "It's a miracle!" shrieked Yankel. "Thank You, dear God! Thank you!"

Yankel returned home to share with his family the miracle and to celebrate the joy of Shabbat with his family like they had never done before. And, just as he did, Chayim was sitting down for his own Shabbat meal. Although he was still alone, he ate and drank with a new spirit. Never before had he felt such joy wrapped around this moment. And, this joy continued for each of them for almost an entire year. Each week Chayim filled the ark with his gifts for God and each week Yankel accepted God's miracles.

But all that came to an end on one Shabbat. After an unusually long service, Yankel entered the sanctuary to see Chayim in the middle of his weekly routine: placing the challahs into the ark. As Chayim turned to leave, he saw Yankel standing in the doorway. The two men stared at one another, understanding immediately what had been happening over the last year. Feeling utterly humiliated, they began to ridicule one another for impersonating God. Their raised voices caught the ear of the rabbi, who had been in his study. Coming out to the sanctuary to calm the two men down, the rabbi spoke: "Neither of you are God. But, Chayim, your gifts did in fact reach God. And, Yankel, your gifts did indeed come from God. For where your hands end, Chayim, and where your hands begin, Yankel, that is where God exists."

With those words, Chayim and Yankel looked at each other and knew what needed to be done. Instead of opening the doors of the ark for his challah, the following Friday night Chayim opened the doors of his home to Yankel and his family. In return, Yankel and his family filled Chayim's lonely and cold mansion with the warmth and joys of Shabbat. Having met God where their two hands united, they relished together in the joys of Shabbat, singing long into the night: "*Hinei mah tov umah-nayim shevet achim gam yachad //* How good and pleasant it is for kinsmen to dwell in unity."[102]

So, it is that the mitzvah of *tzedakah* is more cherished than all the other commandments combined; for in its fulfillment God becomes present in our daily lives. Maybe that is the reason the words – "*ki yamuch achicha /* if your kinsman is reduced [to poverty]" – is repeated four times in this portion. For the number four calls to mind the four seasons of our year, as if to say that this commandment of connecting with our kinsmen is not just for our set-times alone (i.e. Shabbat, sabbatical, or jubilee year). No, this Biblical injunction – which our rabbis so highly praised – rests upon us each and every day. Therefore, let us continue these efforts with a renewed spirit. Because through our human connections we have the opportunity to act divinely: raising up those who are lowly, bringing joy to those in strife, creating harmony where there is discord, and opening eyes to the extraordinary for those blinded by the ordinary.

---

[102] Adapted from Rabbi Edward M. Feinstein's "Challahs in the Ark", contained in a collection of Jewish stories called *Three Times Chai: 54 Rabbis Tell Their Favorite Stories*. Laney Katz Becker, ed. Behrman House, Inc.: New Jersey, 2007. pp. 71-77.

B'har-B'chukotai // On the Mountain-With My Laws
Bite 2 – *High Heel Hell: Walking a Mile in Someone Else's Shoes*

I hate high heels! And no, as a vertically challenged man, it's not out of jealousy for the stylized life afforded to woman, which allows them – despite a similar challenge – to grab things off top shelves with ease. If that were the case, I would have no justification whatsoever to use such a strong word as "hate." No, my justification to voice this intense feeling comes from experience. Yes, even I have worn high heels. Not to get onto an amusement park ride prematurely, but I put them on to raise additional funds for the American Cancer Society (ACS).

During its 2nd Annual Celebrity Waiter Dinner in Jackson, MS, I was tasked to get as many tips from my table as possible. Without thinking, I asked a fellow waiter, a local female DJ, if I might borrow her 6" heels. As this would raise additional dollars for ACS, she agreed. In spite of some tense moments pouring hot coffee, everything went well for my guests. My feet, on the other hand, were a different story. Days afterwards, they were still in pain. Having literally walked a mile or so in someone else's shoes, I can say accurately and assuredly that high heels are hell!

But, is walking a mile in someone else's shoes enough to know how they truly feel? Maybe we should do it longer: perhaps a day, a week, or even a full month? "Try an entire year," suggests this double portion of *B'har-B'chukotai*. "For though you may sow your field and prune your vineyard, as well as gather its yield for six straight years, in the seventh year," warns the Bible, "the land shall observe a Sabbath of complete rest, a Sabbath of the Lord…" During its Sabbatical, clarifies the texts, "you may eat only what the land will produce." (Leviticus 25:3-7)

It's unequivocal; from the land owner to those who work the land, all shall observe this rite. As such, comments Rabbi Harold Kushner, the Sabbatical year – in addition to being good for the land – was instituted to help the people. "Because sometimes," writes Rabbi Kushner, "the wealthy people in society don't believe poor people are actually suffering; they suspect that they are just too lazy to provide for themselves." Therefore, the Bible imposes this Sabbatical, as to "let the wealthy undergo the experience of the poor, not knowing whether there will be enough to eat [throughout the year]. For then," writes Rabbi Kushner, "their attitudes will change."[103]

It's not just with the poor that we make these grand conclusions from such quick observations and so little information. When we see someone who is overweight, we may think, "he or she just needs to get off the couch a little more and eat better." When we see someone in a wheelchair, we may assume that "they cannot do anything for themselves and obviously need our help." And, when we see a baby cry unrelentingly, we may start raising serious

---

[103] Harold Kushner, ed. *Etz Hayim: Torah and Commentary*. Rabbinical Assembly: New York, 2001. p. 739

questions about his or her parental care as well as to "thank God our child is not like that." Judgments like these happen all the time.

And, according to the TV reality show "What Would You Do?," they should. Because, as this hidden-camera, ethical drama shows, there are times when and where these premature and amateur analyses and interventions are not only appropriate, but essential to keep our society functioning at its best. Yes, unlike the three monkeys that hear no evil, see no evil, and speak no evil, we are encouraged to be ever aware and responsive to all the good and all the bad occurring in and around us. For, as the great German-Israeli-American sociologist Amitai Etzioni wrote, "Responsiveness is the cardinal feature of any and all authentic and effective communities."[104]

However, we cannot achieve this effective society from just hearing, seeing, or speaking to those around us who are experiencing challenges. We must, as this portion prescribes, allow ourselves to experience it with them firsthand. The military calls this "providing ministry of presence," for it allows people to relate better with one another, laying the ground work for real and lasting change. This, we see, from the life of Moses. Though raised in a home of privilege, Moses walks out to witness the harsh labor of his kinfolk.[105] Only then did his attitude change; only then did God enlist his service of helping to change this world for the better.

This is the true service we are called upon to provide. And, sure, we can continue to perform such a service in comfort, as we have often done before, wearing the figurative flat or loafer, the symbolic slipper or sandal. Though, as this portion presents, we can and should do more. Therefore, may we voluntarily step into places of discomfort (such as high heels). There, may we find new feelings, new attitudes, new perspectives, which will allow us to walk not just a mile or two in someone else's shoes, but walk with them, hand-in-hand. For, then, our feet become more than a means of individual transportation. They become tools of community transformation!

B'har-B'chukotai // On the Mountain-With My Laws
Bite 3 – "Girls Rule;" "Boys Drool!"

"Girls rule! Boys drool." "Nah uh, boys are cool! Girls are fools." "Oh yeah! Girls rock and boys just wear dirty socks." "Okay, but boys are still rad, while girls are just plain sad." As demonstrated by these super sophisticated school-yard chants, practically from the time we are born we begin to value males and females differently. This valuation happens today as much as it appears to have occurred amongst our Israelite ancestors, with Moses stating to his sister, Miriam: "Girls are strange mammals, who ride on camels." "Oh, yeah, Moses!" retorts Miriam. "Well, boys are *schmonkies*, who ride on donkeys."

---

[104] Amitai Etzioni. "The Responsive Community: A Communitarian Perspective." *American Sociological Review.* Volume 61 (No. 1): 1996. pp. 1-11
[105] Exodus 2:11

Alright, this little gender tit-for-tat is not exactly how the appraisal of males and females went down in antiquity. Rather, the exact valuation of genders occurred as part of the fundraising efforts for the sanctuary. In these final two Torah portions of Leviticus, *B'har-B'chukotai*, we learn that one may pledge a value equivalent to that of a person. Specifically, "if one vows a male, age twenty to sixty, the equivalent value is 50 shekels. But, if it is a female [at the same age], the equivalent is 30 shekels." Furthermore, the Bible continues, "if it is a male from age five to twenty, his value is equivalent to 20 shekels, while a female's value [at the same age] is equivalent to 10 shekels." (Leviticus 27:2-5)

While this gender valuation – at various age brackets – continues for another couple of verses, men are always valued higher than women, with exception that both are considered of equal value before the age of one month.[106] Some commentators attempt to benign the growing disparity between the genders with statements like "at least women could participate freely in the votive system."[107] Though, such a pill may be a little hard to swallow, particularly in light of other statements. For example, in his commentary on the verses in question, the 11th century sage Ibn Ezra states: "This text should be taken at face value. At times in life, a female's value will be worth 50%, 60% or 67% of her male equivalent," for men and women are inherently different.[108]

Despite our progress over the centuries towards greater gender equality, some in our faith tradition continue to maintain a gender disparity. This is particularly evident among some Orthodox groups, who delineate distinct roles for males and females for the "proper functioning of society."[109] But, it is not just them. Even God, they profess, appreciates such delineation. According to one *midrash*, God selected Moses as leader of the Israelites based upon his ability to comprehend the differences between men and women. As the story goes, "When Moses went out to witness the labors of his brethren, he saw men's burdens on women and women's burdens on men. Moses, thereupon, rearranged them according to gender. As such, God said, 'Since you have ordered the burden of My children respectfully, so should you continue to order them (i.e. lead them) into the future.'"[110]

But, for many others, there is still a subtle yet important difference between *appreciating* gender differences and *appraising* gender differences by saying "men are *better* than women" or "women are *better* than men." For in valuing gender differences we actually decrease our overall value as a society. As Margaret Thatcher acknowledged in her book, *Statecraft: Strategies for a*

---

[106] See Lev. 27:6. There it states that the valuation system only begins after the age of one month.
[107] Baruch Levine. *The JPS Torah Commentary: Leviticus.* The Jewish Publication Society: Philadelphia, 1989. p. 193
[108] Abraham ibn Ezra (1089-1164), commentary on Leviticus 27:3.
[109] For example, maintaining that certain clothes or settings are inappropriate for women, the ultra-orthodox Yiddish paper of *Der Tzeitung* (The Time) recently removed the images of Secretary of State Hillary Clinton and another female White House staffer from a White House photo of the Situation Room during the operation to kill or capture Osama bin Laden. http://www.jpost.com/International/Article.aspx?id=219660
[110] Leviticus Rabbah 37:2

Changing World, "the greatest resource of all is human beings."[111] This does not mean, as the motion-picture *The Matrix* depicted, that machines will one day harvest the resource of people for energy. Rather, Thatcher meant that when we weed anyone out of society based upon external factors like gender, age, race, religion, or sexual orientation, then we not only do an injustice to them, we also do an injustice to ourselves.

And that is the point which is so often overlooked by Biblical commentators with regard to the verses stated above. When we move beyond appreciating gender differences to appraising them, we actually perpetuate an injustice upon ourselves. For, as the portion acknowledged, before the age of one month old we are all equal in value. Only as we progress through life do we – as a society – begin to make the mistake of placing a subjective value on those differences. For objectively, in the sight of God, we were created equal, each reflecting an equally valued part of the Divine image. And, if we wish to see the whole of the Divine image in this world, then we must begin to perceive each and every one of equal worth, whether male or female, whether young or old, whether black or white, whether heterosexual or homosexual.

Instead of giving voice to such divisive value statements as "girls rule and boys drool" or "boys are rad, while girls are just plain sad," (as hard, I am sure, as that might be for us adults), let us embrace this teaching by embracing one another as equals. In doing so, may we come to build – as was the inspiration of our Israelite ancestors – a stronger and more caring society united under God. For, on that day, we will lift our varying voices in perfect harmony, singing with one another: "*Hinei mah tov umah-nayim shevet achim gam yachad /* how good it is for men and women to dwell together in harmony."

Chazak, chazak, v'nitchazeik!
From strength to strength, we are strengthened!

---

[111] Margaret Thatcher. *Statecraft: Strategies for a Changing World.* HarperColins: New York, 2002. p. 118

NUMBERS

B'midbar

Portion 1:
B'midbar // In the Wilderness
Torah Portion: Numbers 1:1-4:20

"IN THE WILDERNESS OF SINAI..." God commands Moses to take a census of the whole Israelite community, initiating the book of Numbers. Moses tallies the Israelites by ancestral tribe, recording only males, age twenty years and up, who are able to bear arms. The final count comes to 603,550.

However, not all the Israelites are counted. The Levites are left out, receiving a "draft exemption" so to speak, since they alone are placed in charge of the Tent of Meeting and the *Mishkan* (Tabernacle). When the Israelites set out on their way, the Levites pack up the Tabernacle, and when the Israelites pitch camp, the Levites set it back up.

Anyone who encroaches upon the *Mishkan* or the Tent of Meeting uninvited shall be put to death. To ensure this doesn't happen, the Levites camp around the Tabernacle, thereby guarding the holy sanctuary. The other tribes' encampment encompasses them, thereby forming a second-tier perimeter with the *Mishkan* in the direct center.

Furthermore, the Levites bear the responsibility of serving the priests of Israel: the High Priest Aaron and his priestly sons Eleazar and Itamar. Because, after God smote every firstborn in Egypt, God consecrated every first born in Israel unto the Eternal. However, so as not to take every firstborn from their family, God declares that the Eternal will take the Levites in place of all Israelite firstborns.

After these instructions, God tells Moses to assign the Levite clans separate tasks, further delegating the spiritual responsibilities of the community. The Kohathite go first, as they are tasked with the duties of the Tent of Meeting, the Holy of Holies. When the Israelites are on the move, the Kohathites come and lift the Tent of Meeting to its next destination. Talk about heavy lifting for God!

B'midbar // In the Wilderness
Bite 1 – *The Internet: Our Children's New Playground*

Before entering a playground, most have signs advising their visitors how to behave correctly in this communal space. Some rules are framed in the positive, like: "treat others with respect;" "mind your property;" "use the equipment appropriately." Some rules are framed in the negative, such as: "no unaccompanied children allowed;" "no horseplay;" "no littering." And, still others are framed in the just-plain-weird: "don't pick-up sticks and swing them around; they are branches, not light-sabers;" "no animal here can be taken home as a pet, no matter how cute or alone it may appear;" and "for the love of God, if you find – what you think is – a Tootsie-roll in the sandbox, don't put it into your mouth." After all, we are warned, we "play at our own risk."

One wonders if that was the unspoken warning God gave the Israelites after He outlined all the dos and don'ts in the book of Leviticus. For, as we know, shortly after our ancestors departed Egypt, the wilderness narrative of Exodus is interrupted by many positive blessings and negative curses which may ensue from our interactions with others on the playground of this world. Having then heard them all, we can now enter the sandbox of the wilderness in this portion of *B'midbar*, beginning the book of Numbers. There, we read that "on the first day of the second month, in the second year, following the exodus from the land of Egypt, the Lord spoke to Moses in the wilderness of Sinai." (Numbers 1:1)

Despite these Divinely articulated rules, the children of Israel – we know – will refuse to play nice. At times, they will be rambunctious, rancorous and rebellious. On occasion, they will be rude and sometimes crude. Had the Israelites acted like this in any of our public parks or playgrounds, surely they would have been removed. But, not in the Bible. "Even under extreme provocation," writes commentator Jacob Milgrom, "God keeps His Covenant with the Israelites. God guides them through the wilderness. God provides for their needs."[1] Why? Because, God understands that – in many ways – the Israelites are children. And, like children, it is natural for them to test the boundaries of their new sandbox, to explore every inch of their new playground.

That's not necessarily bad when the playground has defined borders, whether it's in the backyard of a school or on a small lot near one's home. But, there is a new playground out there where the boundary between safe and suspicious space is not so clearly laid out. I'm speaking of the Internet. To be fair, the Internet provides many blessings: it fosters innovation, allowing entrepreneurs to pop-up anywhere; it can cut carbon footprints through less paper waste; and it connects people from around the world to share ideas and disseminate knowledge, which may one day upgrade the entire world. Such was the case

---

[1] Jacob Milgrom. *Etz Hayim: Torah and Commentary*. Rabbinical Assembly: New York, 2001. p.768

with the recent pro-democracy movements in the Middle East, which continue to make positive waves through many Muslim nations there.

We know that these movements would not have been possible without the Internet and its social networking sites like Twitter and Facebook. Facebook alone boasts 900 million users. "If it were a nation," reports NPR's Michel Martin, "it would be the third most populous nation in the world."[2] Such a populous playground has great power; but it's also paved with plenty of risk. Even the most watchful of parents know that it's not a matter of "if" our children will get lost in the Internet, but "when:" stumbling upon bad sites, posting private things to a public world, even cyber-bullying. For, as our Israelite ancestors prove, even the ever-watchful eye of God was not enough to keep the children of Israel from messing around in the sandbox.

In that realization, many communities near and far would like to keep their members safely inside their walls, limiting the Internet or outlawing it all together.[3] Yet, depriving that opportunity to stretch one's mind is tantamount to slavery. And, as we know, God doesn't look so kindly upon slavery, despite whatever dangers may lay along the road to freedom. So, rather than attempting to ensure our children's safety by limiting choice, we must – as God did – educate choice. We have done this successfully on the physical playground; now it's time to socialize our kids for success in the virtual playground, laying out what is appropriate and what is not, what is holy and what is profane, what is a blessing and what is a curse.[4]

Even then, we know, there are no guarantees, as our children will continue to explore the ever-expanding boundaries of the Internet at their own risk. But, in their explorations, let us equip them to mitigate the risks with the most useful tool imaginable: an inquisitive and self-reflecting mind, which will beg them to question how their every action and interaction on the Net may affect them and their relationships with others. Because more than a list of dos and don'ts posted on a wall, they will need a guiding list in their own minds. For then, come what may, they may continue to make safe, smart, ethical decisions in the digital playground, just as they have done in the real playground.

B'midbar // In the Wilderness
Bite 2 – *Unlocking the Drawer of our Souls*

There was once a very successful businessman, who had a peculiar habit. Every morning his co-workers would observe him going to his desk, opening a

---

[2] Michel Martin. "Don't Trip Over Your Digital Footprint." NPR: 21 May 2012.
[3] This approach has been articulated within the Jewish community, evident in the gathering of 60,000 Orthodox Jews in Queens, NY. According to the article, "'The speakers at Citi Field said that if improperly used, the Internet can destroy families, with gambling, pornography and other addictions." Read more: http://www.nydailynews.com/new-york/internet-leads-60-000-ultra-orthodox-jewish-men-citi-field-arthur-ashe-stadium-warn-dangers-internet-article-1.1082281#ixzz1vhoKZau7
[4] Recently, many groups have been advancing curriculum on this topic. In addition to the ISJL, Common Sense Media offers free curriculum on-line: http://www.commonsensemedia.org/educators.

locked drawer, looking inside, before closing it a few seconds later. This occurred every day, with his coworkers growing ever curious about the secret of his success that was locked away. "Perhaps it was the first dollar he ever made," hypothesized one co-worker. "Or a fantasy wish-list for motivation," speculated another. "Or even a tiny fortune teller telling him today's fate," fantasized a third. Finally, curiosity got the better of them. While the successful businessman was out of the office at a meeting one day, his colleagues broke into the drawer. And, what did they see? Themselves, staring back at them, for all the drawer contained was a simple, ordinary mirror.

Just to be clear, this mirror was not a sign of obsessive vanity possessed by the businessman. Rather, the mirror symbolized a valuable look into one's life; a perspective, coincidently, that was key to unlocking the drawer of success in the lives of our Israelite ancestors, as the story of their Exodus resumes in this Torah portion of B'midbar. After each and every Israelite clocked in for work through the census, which begins the book of Numbers, the Lord spoke to Moses and Aaron, saying: "The Israelites shall camp each with his standard, under the banner of their ancestral house. They shall camp around the Tent of Meeting," the dwelling place for God, setting the Eternal One at the center of their lives in the wilderness. (Numbers 2:1-2)

Unlocking the text and identifying the secret to the Israelites' eventual success in the wilderness is modern Biblical commentator Jacob Milgrom, who – according to his commentary – wrote: "The key to the successful deployment of the Israelites as they camped and as they marched was the setting of the Ark at the center of the camp. Every individual Israelite," as Milgrom understood it, "was located in relation to the Ark and the Tabernacle. The Tabernacle was the first thing one saw on leaving home and the first thing one looked for on returning home. Gradually," concludes Milgrom, "this physical centrality must have led to the Ark gaining a central place in the Israelite soul."[5] For, an inward perspective is essential to one's outward projection of success in life.

Yet, paradoxically, that is not where one often looks to gauge one's progress while wandering in the wilderness of this world. Rather than looking inward, we often gauge our level of success, our sense of fulfillment and happiness in this life, on external factors like the amount printed on our paychecks, the title placed next to our name, or the size of our place of residence in relation to the place of others. And, some argue that may have even transpired amongst our Israelite ancestors in the desert. Whether it was when they were encamped or while marching, it is likely that the various tribes and the individual members therein perceived the progress of their own standard or ancestral banner based upon where it stood in relation to the standard or banner of the others.

This is certainly a fair interpretation, particularly from anyone who has ever been part of a military formation, where one's position is based upon the position of others. However, these same individuals would also be keenly

---

[5] Jacob Milgrom. *Etz Hayim: Torah and Commentary*. The Rabbinical Assembly: New York, 2001. p. 774

aware of two major problems inherent in this outward perspective. For starters, external factors are not always reliable. Salaries can be altered, titles can be stripped away, living situations can change. And, if we gauge our success based on them, we may feel like a failure when they change for the worse. Secondly, even if we were able to keep pace with others, who's to say the direction in which we are gradually marching is correct, meaningful, or most fitting for our lives?

Truthfully, no dependable answers can be found from such unreliable external factors. That is why, in this Torah portion of *B'midbar*, the people are commanded to center their lives around the Tent of Meeting. Because, with the desert sands ever changing around them, looking inward rather than outward, maintaining an internal perspective rather than an external one, just proved to be a more reliable gauge for determining progress. For God's central Presence in the wilderness encampment, which we now understand as infused within the sanctuary of our souls, is and remains constant, a steady reminder that our success comes not from outside, but from inside, discovering the role that fulfills our soul. What is the internal constant in your life?

For the businessman, it was neither the title placed next to his name nor the money that came with it. For he knew, in business, no matter how successful you may be, you can always be replaced. But, where he was irreplaceable was in his cherished role as a husband and as a father. By looking into the mirror each and every morning, he was able to keep these cherished constants in view, maintaining a perspective that not only brought him a great amount of fulfillment throughout his day, but also a sense of direction which guided each and every one of his steps to success. May we too take the time to unlock the drawers of our own souls this day and every day, to see – God willing – what it would take to keep them constantly full. For then, we pray, success may accompany each and every one of our steps as well.

B'midbar // In the Wilderness
Bite 3 – *The Earlier the Better*

Concerned with whether or not our children will grow to be spiritually strong, it seems – as parents – that we start our kids on a healthy regimen of Jewish knowledge earlier and earlier. For example, the Jewish Theological Seminary (JTS--which has long and honorably trained this nation's Conservative spiritual leaders) began training this nation's three and four year-olds as of 2006. Called *Ma'alah*, the JTS program – which immerses our toddlers in an all-Hebrew learning environment – was designed "to build strong Jewish identities and connections to Israel."[6] For Rabbi Natan taught in the second century C.E.: "*Vatikach hatzipor hamukdemet et hatola'at*," which translates into

---

[6] For more information regarding early childhood education initiatives in Judaism, please see www.jecei.org/documents/ and click on "vogelstein early childhood education pdf."

'the early bird catches the worm.' Alright, those weren't his actual words. More accurately, he said, "What is learned early in life is absorbed into the blood."[7]

The long-term benefits of this early academic infusion into our children's tender lives were already attested to in the earliest writings of our faith. While all other Israelites were recorded from age 20 years and up for military service, God commands Moses in this Torah portion of B'midbar to start earlier with the tribe of Levi. According to the book of Numbers, chapter three: "The Lord commanded Moses in the wilderness of Sinai, saying: 'Record the Levites by ancestral house and by clan;'" but not from age 20 years and up. Instead, the Lord commanded Moses to "record every male among them (i.e. Levites) from the [tender] age of one month and up." (Numbers 3:14-15)

Why the distinction? Surely God would not be playing favorites among His children, for it is taught that "each is a valued jewel in the crown of God."[8] Some Biblical scholars and sages therefore suggest that the distinction made in the Bible was likely based upon the divergent roles of each tribe. In his commentary on the book of Numbers, modern Biblical commentator Jacob Milgrom writes: "The Israelites were only counted from age 20 and up for the purpose of military readiness (i.e. physical training). Spiritual training, on the other hand," Milgrom goes on to say, "must begin virtually at birth."[9]

Because, as contemporary research has demonstrated, "the earlier the better" when it comes to educating our children in faith.[10] Not only do their tender minds make it easier for the information to enter, but – more importantly – it is believed that what is learned early stays late. Reaching a similar conclusion, Rabbi Elisha ben Avuyah stated in the Ethics of our Ancestors: "One who studies Torah, while still a child, to what can this be likened?" His answer, "To ink written on clean paper," for the ink is absorbed with clarity, leaving an indelible impression on the heart and mind. And, he goes on to ask, "One who studies Torah, while older in age, to what can this be likened?" His answer, "To ink written on smudged paper," for later in life our minds are crowded with a life-time of information, making it difficult to absorb new material.[11]

These astute observations are not meant to discourage those more advanced in years from becoming stronger in faith by continuing their religious education. For, as we have witnessed, even these early efforts come with no guarantee that our children will grow to be spiritually strong. In fact, recent statistics show that despite the rise of early childhood education programs in our religious schools, our nation (not just Judaism) is losing faith with each passing generation. Based on interviews with more than 35,000 Americans age 18 and

---

[7] Avot d'Rabbi Natan 24
[8] RaMBaM. Hilchot De'ot 6:1
[9] Jacob Milgrom. "Numbers." Etz Hayim: Torah and Commentary. The Rabbinical Assembly of America: New York, 2001. p. 779
[10] Beck, P. (2002). Jewish preschools as gateways to Jewish life: A survey of Jewish parents in three cities. New York: Ukeles, Inc. (Retrieved January, 2006) and Kotler-Berkowitz, L. The Jewish Education of Jewish Children: United Jewish Communities Series on the NJPS 2000–01 Report 11. New York. United Jewish Communities. (2005).
[11] Pirkei Avot 4:25

older, the Pew Research Center found that "the number of people who say they are unaffiliated with any particular faith today (16.1%) is more than double the number who say they were not affiliated with any particular religion as children."[12]

How then are we to explain these observations, which – on the one hand – have shown that there is a demonstrable advantage to educating our children early, but – on the other hand – have demonstrated that the early gains are lost over time? One possible explanation comes from what happens in our children's lives from the time when they are one-month old to the time they reach 20 years of age. During this time, our children learn from us of an artificial separation between the spirit and the body, between spiritual readiness and physical readiness. Like our ancestors in this portion, we begin to educate our children in a variety of topics (i.e. faith) virtually from birth. But, when it comes to physical education we are less demanding. We overlook the sugar treats they eat, instead of presenting them with healthy options. We ignore the prolonged TV-watching and video-game playing sessions, instead of taking them by the hand and playing a game with them outdoors. And as a result, our waistlines have increased just as our faith in this country has decreased. Or, to put it another way, as our physical strength has decreased, so too has our spiritual strength.[13]

I am not suggesting causation. Because as the great sage, Dennis Quaid, stated in the movie, *The Rookie*: "In life, it is never one thing."[14] Rather, what I am proposing is correlation; I am suggesting that there is a link between the body and the spirit. I know this may make some Jewish theologians nervous, as Judaism has strictly divided the Divine spirit and mortal body from one another as to not confuse the mortal body as Divine. Yet, in the book of Genesis, this correlation between the body and spirit was already made explicit. In the second account of creation, from the second chapter of that book, we read: "And God formed man from the dust of the earth and blew into his nostrils the spirit (the *nefesh*) of life. Thus," the Bible states, "man became a living being."[15] And from these words we are taught that in order to manifest the condition we call 'life' we have to have both a spirit (a *nefesh*) as well as a vessel (i.e. a body) into which it is contained. It would then stand to reason, if we wish to strengthen one, we must remember to work on strengthening the other.

A great example of this comes from the Ben-Gurion University of the Negev (BGU). A researcher there conducted the first study of hand-clapping songs (i.e. physical exercise), which revealed "a direct link between those activities

---

[12] Pew Research Center. *U.S. Religious Landscape Survey: Religious Affiliation - Diverse and Dynamic*. February 2008.
[13] Among pre-school age children 2-5 years of age, obesity increased from 5% to 10.4% between 1976 and 2008 and among 6-11 year olds obesity increased from 6.5% to 19.6% in that same period. Adolescents aged 12-19 also saw an increase in obesity between 1976-2008, from 5% to 18.1%. (See www.cdc.gov/obesity/childhood/index for more information).
[14] *The Rookie* is a 2002 motion picture directed by John Lee Hancock. It is inspired by the true story of Jim Morris, who had a brief but famous Major League Baseball career.
[15] Genesis 2:7

and the development of important skills in children and young adults," including spiritual growth. According to Dr. Idit Sulkin, "We found that children in the first, second and third grades who sing these songs with hand-clapping demonstrate skills absent in children who don't take part in similar activities." Conversely, reports Dr. Warren Brodsky, who supervised the study: "Children who don't participate in such games may be more at risk for developmental problems," including – one may presume – in the area of faith development. "There's no doubt," states Dr. Brodsky, "that such activities train the brain and influence development in other areas" such as the soul.[16]

So, let us take a cue from the research as well as this Torah portion of *B'midbar* and start our children's training early. For as the great idiom goes: "the earlier the better." But, let us not consider this Divine mandate one that is solely directed at the soul of our children. In addition to preparing their souls and minds virtually from birth, let us also – at that time – start to prepare our children's bodies. For then – we pray – they will grow to be truly strong in mind, in body, and in soul, ready and able to endure all the bumps and bruises (whether experienced internally or externally) on the precarious journey through the wilderness (in Hebrew: the *midbar*) of life.

---

[16] "Research Confirms That Hand-Clapping Songs Improve Motor and Cognitive Skills." Beersheva, ISRAEL: 28 April 2010 (See www.aabgu.org/media-center/news-releases/ben-gurion-research-handclapping.html for more information).

SHAVUOT:

Shirley Eriksen's Pimento Cheese Potato Kugel

Ingredients:
2 – 10 oz. packages of extra sharp cheddar cheese (grated)
5 tablespoons Durkee's Famous Sauce
1 – 4 oz. jar pimentos (drained)   ½ teaspoon of yellow mustard
1 tablespoon of lemon juice   ¼ teaspoon of garlic powder
½ teaspoon of Worcestershire sauce   1 cup mayonnaise

3 pounds potatoes (peeled & shredded)   4 eggs
1 onion (chopped)   5 tablespoons olive oil
Salt, pepper, and TABASCO sauce – to taste

Preheat oven to 350 degrees. Grease a 9x13 inch pan. Mix cheddar cheese, Durkee's Famous Sauce, pimentos, mustard, lemon juice, garlic powder, Worcestershire sauce, mayonnaise together for a homemade pimento cheese (or you can purchase already made). Chill.

Place potatoes in a colander and squeeze out moisture. In a large bowl, combine eggs, salt, pepper, TABASCO sauce, oil and onion. Place potatoes and cheese mixture in the bowl and mix well. Pour the potato and cheese mixture into the prepared pan.

Bake at 350 degrees for 1 hour. Raise heat to 450 degrees and bake for 5 to 10 minutes until browned, serve hot.

Betsy Samuels' Sweet Tea Noodle Kugel

Ingredients:
2 tea bags   ¾ cup of sugar
½ pound of egg noodles   4 eggs
½ cup of sour cream   ¼ pound of cream cheese
½ cup of sugar   1 stick of melted margarine
1 cup of cottage cheese   ½ cup of golden raisins

Boil water, add sugar and tea bags. Let tea steep. Use the tea to cook the noodles. Drain well.

Next, beat eggs, add sour cream, cream cheese, and sugar. Mix well. Add egg mixture, melted margarine, cottage cheese and raisins to noodles. Blend well.

Bake in 2 quart greased casserole dish at 350 degrees for 45 min. Serves 8.

Portion 2:
Naso // Take
Torah Portion: Numbers 4:21-7:89

"TAKE A CENSUS OF THE GERSHONITES..." At the end of the previous portion, Moses was instructed to take a separate census of the Kohathites, another clan of Levites. But, more than divvying up the spiritual responsibilities of the budding Israelite nation, *Naso* describes ways by which all Israelites can come closer to God.

Namely, it is through our personal relationships. "When a man or woman commits any wrong toward a fellow man, thus breaking faith with the Eternal, s/he shall confess the wrong that s/he has done." (Numbers 5:6) Wrongs to our fellow man are wrongs to God. By Biblical law, the perpetrator must then make restitution by compensating the victim for the principal physical loss plus one-fifth.

But, what happens when the loss is not physical, but emotional, like jealousy? Then, as the portion describes, there is still something that can be done to bring the relationship back to Divine harmony: a ritual performed by a priest. In these times, sadly, it was the woman (whether she did something or not) who is put through the ordeal.

The portion then lays out rules for Nazirites, who are akin to Jewish monks, for one's relationship with oneself can also be considered Divine. Solely dedicated to God, the Nazirite vows not to consume wine, approach a dead person, or shave his hair, as his "consecrated hair" is an outward sign of his commitment to his community.

Finally, Aaron and his sons confirm the holiness of these relationships by linking God's Name with the people Israel through the famous priestly benediction: "May God bless you and protect you! May God deal kindly and graciously with you! May God bestow favor upon you and grant you peace!" Moses consecrates the Tabernacle to end the portion.

Naso // Take
Bite 1 – *The Con-census is "Never Count Us Out!"*

There's an illustrated map out there of the U.S. that is truly unique. It shows the grand cities along our Eastern shore, like New York City, Boston, Washington D.C, and Miami. As well, it brilliantly depicts all the beautiful sites along the West coast, including: San Francisco, Los Angeles, Seattle. Though, in between appears to be nothing more than a hollow wasteland, a wilderness, as not a single thing is detailed, depicted, or described. Why? Well, some say, "It's because those places in the middle are so small that they are of little consequence to the larger fabric of American life." Little consequence, huh? Well, I don't mean to burst anyone's bubble, but I know of another group of people who too were small, who too occupied the wilderness, but who went on to reshape and redefine our entire world: our fabulous ancestors, those pesky little Israelites!

In fact, it is there – in the wilderness – where we find our ancestors. After participating in a detailed counting of most of their meager numbers as well as prescribing their positions in the procession of the people through the wilderness in the prior portion of *B'midbar*, the calculations continue in this portion of *Naso*.[17] "The Lord spoke to Moses," begins the Bible, saying, "Take a census of the Gershonites (a sub-group of Levites), by their ancestral house and clans… Also," adds the Lord, a few verses later, "record the Merarites (another sub-group of Levites) by the clans of their ancestral house." Finally, the counting culminates with the remarkable words, "Each one was given responsibility, each one was given his service, each one was given his burden, at the command of the Lord through Moses." (Numbers 4:49)

Specifically, elucidates the sages of the *midrash*, "Moses, at the command of the Lord, counted off the people 1, 2, 3, 4 and so on, before proceeding to connect them to specific pieces of the community's camp, labeled *aleph*, *bet*, *gimmel*, *dalet*, etc."[18] In this IKEA-like fashion, which begs us to take notice of each and every small piece, the late 11th century/early 12th century Biblical commentator Ibn Ezra remarked that our counting appears to be more a function of community efficiency than an evaluation tool to later demean, dismiss, or delete any one group therein.[19] For, though small, no one was ever counted out by God. God, in fact, appreciated – despite our small size – that each of us has a part to play, each a sacred responsibility to shoulder, when managing to lift the collective burden of the Jewish community higher and higher.

Nonetheless, long has our focus been – in the Jewish world – on large congregations. When people wish to know how we are addressing the major

---

[17] In part, the census taking continues from the previous Torah portion because of God's insistence that the tribe of Levi be counted separately. As it is written: "Do not, on any account, enroll the tribe of Levi or take a census of them with the Israelites." (Numbers 1:47)
[18] Adapted from B'midbar Rabbah 6:11
[19] See Ibn Ezra commentary to Numbers 4:49. There he wrote: "'Each was recorded.' These words should be read as 'each was assigned' to his task of service or burden."

challenge facing all Jewish communities today, our dwindling numbers,[20] they do not look to the wonderful small towns of Tupelo, MS,[21] Dahlonega, GA,[22] or Lake Charles and Lafayette, LA,[23] who are innovatively tackling this problem as we speak. No, they turn to the behemoth congregations of New York and California, who boast memberships in the thousands. Such a "bigger is better" mentality has sadly led many congregations to mistaken quantity (i.e. their size) with quality (i.e. their value). And, it's not just some large congregations who do this; some small ones do it as well. "Why do you waste your time with us?" they ask me. "Surely, you're good enough to play with the big boys up in NY."

Perhaps, but even they know that more members doesn't necessarily mean more action. Because, as a congregation grows so too does its sacred responsibilities, its sacred services, its sacred burdens, as spoken of in this Torah portion. And, that ever-growing weight is exacerbated by the psychology of man, who tends to engage less the more people there are. We see this clearly in emergencies. In such instances, people often stand around and do nothing, assuming someone else has called for help. This phenomenon is occurring in our congregations as well. As they grow, people begin to think: "Well, I don't need to go to services, someone else will be there to pray;" "I don't need to go to the social action project, someone else will be there to work;" "I don't need to do this or that, because surely," they think, "there will always be someone else."

Not in small towns. Without large financial resources to secure some of the Jewish basics like Torah scrolls, updated prayer books, education material, and a full-time rabbi, these small Jewish communities certainly cannot afford such complacency. In fact, to make up for the deficit, each and every member of the community – regardless of their size, their age, their knowledge, their wealth – invests more than their fair-share of time and energy to lift and carry forward their Jewish community. For, they understand very intimately the distinction being made in this Torah portion: the difference between simply being counted and being able to be counted on. If they don't stand up to do their individual part in the Jewish community, then Judaism – in these small towns – simply does not get done. And, they're not about to let that happen!

That message rings loud and clear from just about every small Jewish congregation throughout the world, including Ft. Smith, AR's United Hebrew Congregation. There, up front, directly in the center of their

---

[20] According to the National Jewish Population Survey 2000-01, the total Jewish population in America went from 5.5 million in 1990 to 5.2 million individuals in 2000. Although I have no definitive statistics on hand, all signs point to these numbers continuing to fall steadily.

[21] The notion that the burden of the community falls upon each and every member of the community led B'nai Israel in Tupelo, MS to hand every member a key to their temple. It empowers each and every member to be a leader within the community, which allows this congregation to continue to survive and thrive.

[22] Shalom B'Harim is a small, dynamic congregation in the foothills of Georgia. Rather than using their limited financial resources to build a building, they invest their funds instead in people and programs to great success!

[23] Thanks to working together to share resources and time, these two congregations are still blessed by a steady presence of an ordained rabbi, Rabbi Barry Weinstein, in spite of very limited financial resources.

sanctuary sits an extraordinary and unique table, where the Torah is read during Sabbath services.

What makes this table so special is its center. Encompassed by wood, there is an extremely large and completely solid stone with a Star of David on it. The stone once rested above the front archway of their old, historic building, which stood as a beacon of Jewish values in the American frontier since 1892.

Unfortunately, as the congregation dwindled in size and they moved to a new building, the old one was razed to the ground. At that time, a member of the congregation – Mr. Mort Marks – came walking by the demolition site. There he saw the stone, atop a heap of rubble, slated to be thrown away.

Mr. Marks would not have this. Something had to be done. So, Mr. Marks went to his store (a few blocks away), grabbed a wheelbarrow and headed back to the site. Standing only 5'5" tall, weighing only 120 pounds, and no longer a young man, Mr. Marks – beyond comprehension – managed to lift the stone all by himself and cart it back to his store.

Unbelievably, no one would discover what he did until after his passing. Only then did Mr. Mark's action to save a piece of their old building, to preserve a piece of their heritage, come to light. In his name, the present congregants made it into a table to honor the past and give expression to their hopes for a future.[24]

Hopes… because, given the present counting of our numbers, our future is far from guaranteed. Nonetheless, we shall not be distressed, dismayed, or discouraged. Because, from this Torah portion, we understand that numbers – in and of themselves – are not meaningful. They merely represent that which is: the potential which rests within each and every one of us, whether we are small or large. So, may we take a cue from our Israelite ancestors, who too were small, who too occupied the wilderness. Rather than overlooking and writing off any portion of our American Jewish landscape, which limits our future potential, may we turn our attentions there. For there, like our ancestors, they are innovatively addressing today's challenges, so that we may – as a people – forge ahead to reshape and redefine our world for a better tomorrow.

---

[24] For more information and pictures of the United Hebrew Congregation, check out the online Encyclopedia of Southern Jewish Communities at http://www.isjl.org/history/archive/. This story varies from the history (as is often the case in Judaism). By historical accounts, in 1955 the keystone was with a local historian. When she passed, it passed to Mort Marks. Being of no real use, Barbara Turner made sketches of the keystone as a Shabbat table. The congregation resisted; so its Sisterhood took over, engaging James Kahlaen, a carpenter. Early 2000's, it was installed. Others involved were: Bea and Bob Zemansky, Isabel Marks, Wade Turner, Rhonda Viehmyer, Mary and Manny Jaye, and Joel Rafkin.

Naso // Take
Bite 2 – *Dealing with the Bitter Taste of Jealousy*

Jealousy. It is a secondary emotion that typically stems from the initial feelings of insecurity or inadequacy, fear or anxiety, over an anticipated loss of something that a person values, particularly some much appreciated human connection. And, as such, jealousy has wreaked havoc on countless relationships whether they occurred a millennia ago or a minute ago. Though long-lived and observed among various cultures and ages, since no two human beings seemingly express jealousy in the same way, professionals of all types (from theologians to scientists) have an extraordinarily difficult time defining it and an even more difficult time attempting to treat it.

But, apparently, not our Israelite ancestors! No, by an account contained in this Torah portion of *Naso*, the *Kohanim* (the priests) advanced an approach to put the Green-eyed Monster of Jealousy to rest in their society. As it is written in the book of Numbers: "If a fit of jealousy comes over a man regarding his wife [whether she has had sexual relations with another or not], the man shall bring his wife to the priest." (Numbers 5:13-15) Thereupon, the woman - commonly known as the *sotah* (the deviant) in rabbinic texts - is put through an ordeal which includes having to drink the water of bitterness and accept a curse articulated by the priest should the feeling of her husband be substantiated. "This," the Bible reiterates at the end of the ordeal, "is the ritual in cases of jealousy." (Numbers 5:29)

Yet, despite this Biblical emphasis that the ritual was about treating the husband's jealousy, rabbinic commentaries tend to redirect our attentions onto the wife, after all it is the woman (not the man) who is the one going through the ordeal. Some do so by pointing out the very apparent misogynistic structure of the ritual by which the woman is completely vulnerable to the privileged position of men, whether it's the husband or the priest. Others, however, believe that this ritual actually works to protect the woman. As Bible Professor, Amy Kalmanofsky of the Women's Commentary on the Torah stated, "In Biblical law, the crime of adultery warranted death. Therefore this ritual, which does not result in death even of a guilty woman, may reflect a more compassionate form of punishment."[25]

Whether its misogynistic or compassionate, whether one argues it's appropriate or not, there tends today to be a consensus that this Biblical ordeal was nothing more than a relationship placebo pill, which only had effect on believers despite the lack of any real treatment.[26] Why? Because, today we have come to appreciate that a person's feelings – such as jealousy – cannot adequately be dealt with by simply looking at the object of those feelings. In many ways, this would be like trying to cure an insatiable appetite by getting

---

[25] Dr. Tamara Cohn Eskenazi, ed. *The Torah: A Women's Commentary*. URJ Press: New York, 2008. p. 822
[26] *Mishnah* Sotah 9:9 - Observing the ineffectual treatment, the sages stated: "When adulterers became many, the rite of the bitter waters ceased; and Rabbi Yochanan ben Zakkai brought it to an end."

rid of food, or impatience during rush-hour by getting rid of cars. While a smirk-provoking thought to be sure, as these so-called solutions – like the Biblical ordeal of the *sotah* – may provide some temporary relief, they are really impractical and even unsustainable in the long-run.

Hence why – to deal more adequately with jealousy or any difficult feeling – there has been a push to halt the redirection, which misplaces our attentions on the object of those feelings rather than on the subject (in this Biblical case... the husband). And, this push isn't just from contemporary women attempting to bring balance to a male-dominated view of the past, nor is it from psychologists who understand that the subject holds the power to either maintain or let go of the feeling. Even our sages recognized an inherent deficit in the Biblical approach to jealousy, as it practically leaves the man out. So, to counter this, RaSHI includes the man, stating: "this deviant/*sotah* course is a result of the spirit of *shoteh*/foolishness entering them [both]."

Both, says RaSHI, the man and the woman, because jealousy cannot be adequately addressed – as it so often has been in the past – by looking at one party (whether it's the male or female) in the relationship and not the other. As jealousy stems from an anticipated loss (i.e. one without proof, as was the case between the husband and wife in the Bible), it really necessitates both parties to lift the psychological barrier of jealousy between them in order to reaffirm that much appreciated human connection. As Rabbi Harvey Fields wrote, "The feelings of the husband as well as the wife must be expressed. Unless they care enough about each other to articulate what bothers them, and agree upon what is acceptable behavior (which will be different from couple to couple), suspicions will eventually drive husband and wife apart."[27]

This we cannot allow. For even the best of relationships, whether they are with our spouses, our life-long friends, or even our coworkers, are laden with fragility that stressors like jealousy, suspicion, and even simple misunderstandings can expose. Therefore, to remove these stressors and thereby strengthen our relationships, we must abstain from committing the errors of the past: placing blame solely on one party and not the other. Rather, in all such moments of stress, let us do better by thoughtfully exploring and accepting our part in the folly, as bitter as it may be. For when each person drinks their portion of "the water of bitterness," processing it with one another, the bitterness of that moment can pass much quicker, restoring the love and trust which originally characterized that relationship once more.

Naso // Take
Bite 3 – *The Silver Lining*

Undoubtedly, one of the oldest, most popular, and most powerful prayers in all of Judaism is the Priestly Benediction. Its words have been used for

---

[27] Harvey Fields. *A Torah Commentary for Our Times: Numbers/Deuteronomy*. UAHC Press: New York, 1993. p. 20

practically every occasion under Heaven: from the *brit-milah* to the *b'nai mitzvah*, from conversions to marriages, from decorating jewelry back in the year 600 B.C.E. to stopping an asteroid from striking the earth in 1998.[28] Alright. That last one was fictional (a scene from the Dreamworks film *Deep Impact*). Nevertheless, you'll be hard pressed to find many – if any – who believe that the words of the Priestly Benediction don't truly convey some sense of strength at the most opportune moments of life.

Whether it is from the lips of God (as we read in this Torah portion of *Naso*) or Morgan Freeman (who recited the prayer in the movie *Deep Impact*), these words seem to have real efficacy in our lives. Originally written in the book of Numbers, we read that the Lord spoke to Moses, commanding Aaron to bless the people Israel with these eternal words: "*Y'varech'cha Adonai v'yishm'recha* / May the Lord bless you and keep you. *Ya-eir Adonai panav eilecha vichuneka* / May the Lord deal kindly with you and be gracious unto you. [And,] *yisa Adonai panav eilecha v'yaseim l'cha shalom* / may the Lord bestow his favor unto you, granting you peace." (Numbers 6:23-26)

As powerful as these words were, are, and – God willing – will remain, we often don't hear them as they were originally written. After reciting the first two blessings – 'may the Lord bless you and keep you' as well as 'may the Lord deal kindly with you and be gracious unto you' – almost verbatim, many of our contemporary priests (i.e. our rabbis) suddenly become improvisational artists, rifting away at the last blessing with ease. Instead of simply stating 'granting you peace,' they add other blessings like 'health,' 'happiness,' and 'prosperity.' Other times, the officiating body ends the Priestly Benediction with: "granting you, *life's most precious blessing*, peace."

Look. I'm not disagreeing. Surely, one of life's most precious blessings is peace. Yet, some of us may still ask, "why change a classic?" as there is no guarantee that changing a classic will work. For example, when Coca-Cola changed its classic formula in 1985, introducing New Coke, the company was forced to go back to the original formula just three months later due to a dramatic drop in sales. Ever since, thirsts around the world have been quenched by Coca-Cola Classic. Many rabbis, therefore, assert that the improvisations are not really changes to the classic prayer. They are, as one of my rabbinic mentors once explained to me: "highlights, emphasizing the importance of the classic value of peace in our lives and our role in achieving it."

In many ways, my mentor is right. As a priestly people it is our mission to continue the work of our priestly forefather Aaron, who – according to the 15th century Rebbe, Yitzhak Arama – "had a skill for weaving together the threads of discord into a harmonious fabric. His tool," writes Rabbi Arama,

---

[28] In 1979, Israeli archeologist Gabriel Barkay discovered silver amulets in a burial chamber while excavating in Ketef Hinnom, a section of the Hinnom Valley, south of Jerusalem's Old City. Etched into the silver, in ancient Hebrew script, were the words of the Priestly Benediction. The amulet was roughly dated to 600 B.C.E., making it the oldest extant extra-Biblical manuscript.

"was a silver thread."[29] But why silver? Surely gold is more precious, and thus a more fitting thread to create our precious blessing of peace. It's not because Aaron suffered from a rare allergy to yellow gold, just in case that was what you were thinking. Nor, is it because silver matched Aaron's priestly vestments better. Rather, writes Rabbi Norman Patz (rabbi emeritus from Temple Shalom in New Jersey), silver was selected as Aaron's thread of peace because unlike gold "silver needs polishing. It needs to be burnished."[30]

In other words, in order for peace to prevail we cannot simply wait for God to grant it to us, despite whatever the prayer says. Instead, as it is taught through our rabbis' emphasis, peace needs our attention; we must work at creating it. For example, on 13 September 1993 – after nearly a half-century of fighting – Prime Minister Yitzhak Rabin of Israel and Chairman Yasser Arafat of the PLO sat down together for direct negotiations. It was hoped that these first-of-their-kind talks would initiate a series of discussions that would eventually lead to peaceful relations between the Israelis and the Palestinians. As former Prime Minister Rabin (*z"l*) stated on the eve of the Oslo Accords in Washington: "It is dusk in our homes in the Middle East right now and soon darkness will set it. But, it will not prevail. By the will of the Israelis and Palestinians alike, we will once again see the shimmering of light."[31]

But, unfortunately, that shimmer has not come. And, it's not because we have not prayed enough. For, as we learn from *Naso*, no matter how much we pray God does not provide peace. God simply provides the raw materials (opportunity, communication, healthy leadership, etc.) for us to create peace for ourselves. So, whether it's the *shalom* we wish to create and maintain in the world, or the *shalom* we wish to create and maintain in our homes, we have to do something more productive with our hands than pointing fingers. We have to start using our hands to transform the raw materials alluded to in the words of the Priestly Benediction into something tangible, something useful, like a shining, shimmering thread. For by this thread we – like our priestly forefather Aaron – can weave the clamoring discord of this world into a harmonious fabric by which to blanket everyone in peace. As the wise Hillel charged us so many centuries ago: "Let us be among the disciples of Aaron, loving peace and pursuing peace by loving people and bringing them closer together."[32]

---

[29] Yitzhak Arama. Aqaydat Yitzhaq; Eliyahu Munk, trans. Rubin Mass, Ltd.: Jerusalem, 1986. pp. 726-727
[30] Norman Patz. "Silver Threads: Ties that Bind." *Living Torah*; Elaine Glickman, ed. URJ Press: New York, 2005. p.330
[31] Alfred Kolatch. *Great Jewish Quotations*. Jonathan David Publishers. Inc.: New York, 1996. p. 370
[32] Pirkei Avot 1:12

Portion 3:
B'ha-alotecha // When You Set Up
Torah Portion: Numbers 8:1-12:16

"WHEN YOU SET UP THE LAMPS…" Having dedicated the Tabernacle, this instruction from God to Moses then to Aaron, sets the stage for the dedication of the Levites at the start of the portion *B'ha-alotecha*.

B'ha-alotecha elaborates on God's presence in the Israelite community… literally! God's cloud covered the Tabernacle during the day and a cloud of fire hovered over it at night. The Israelites would break camp when the cloud lifted, and encamp wherever the cloud settled.

The portion describes the position of each tribe as the people marched. The Ark of the Covenant traveled in front. As the Ark was carried forth, Moses would say, "Advance, O Lord! May your enemies be scattered, and may your foes flee before You!" (Numbers 10:35) These very words are found in the Torah service to this day.

Despite God's presence among them, the people of Israel continue to complain. Frustrated, Moses turns to God, "I cannot carry this people all by myself…kill me rather, I beg You, and let me see no more of my wretchedness!" (Numbers 11:15) God responds by assigning 70 elders to assist Moses in ruling the people. God also brings in quail from the sea, and then strikes the people with a terrible plague for their defiance.

The portion concludes with Aaron and Miriam speaking against Moses because of the Cushite woman Moses married. Jealous of Moses, they ask "Has God not spoken through us as well?" God chastises Aaron and Miriam for speaking against Moses and affirms that only with Moses does God speak directly. Miriam is stricken with "snow-white scales" on her skin, and Moses cries out to God in our very first prayer for healing, "O God, pray heal her!" (Numbers 12:13)

B'ha-alotecha // When You Set Up
Bite 1 – *Branches of Study: The Menorah's Illumination*

For some reason, as children, we often imagine our rabbis as something more powerful than your average being: a community superhero, God, or even Alex Trebek. Yes, as a child, I imagined my rabbi as none other than the illustrious host of Jeopardy. Standing before a live studio audience (i.e. the congregation), near the end of a Shabbat service, I would often imagine 'Alex' presenting the Final Jeopardy answer in perfect Hebrew: "*Etz Chayim hi lamachazikim ba v'tomcheha m'ushar* / It is a Tree of Life for those who hold it fast and all of its supporters are happy."[33] Pondering this answer for a moment, during a musical interlude of do-da-do, dada do-da-do (played, of course, by our organist and sung by the choir) my response, phrased in the form of a question, would be: "What is Torah?"

But, based on this Torah portion of *B'ha-alotecha*, that response may not have been correct. For, according to the eighth chapter in the book of Numbers, the religious item to which our Israelite ancestors were holding fast, at this point in their transformative journey to find happiness in the Promised Land, was none other than the *menorah*, "a seven-branch lamp stand... hammered from base to petal from pure gold, according to the pattern that the Lord had shown Moses." (Numbers 8:2-4) That pattern, as it was first laid out in the book of Exodus, required "three branches [to be made] on one side and three branches on the other," leaving one branch as a center stalk. (Exodus 25:32, 37:18)

And, it's not just the ancient Israelites who held fast to the *menorah*. According to historical records, the *menorah* came to represent the descendants of Aaron, the Hasmoneans, during the First Temple period. It was the symbol of the Jews during the Second Temple period, as depicted on the Arch of Titus. As well, it continues to stand as the sign of our people today, as it was selected as the symbol for the modern Jewish State of Israel. One reason, teaches the mystic Isaac Luria, for the *menorah*'s historical relevance is "its six peripheral branches, which represent several scientific and academic disciplines" vital to understanding the world. Yet, because they are connected to "the center stalk, which represents the light of Torah," continued Luria, secular disciplines work not against but *with* the Torah to help illuminate this world.[34]

Now, to some, this teaching may sound radical. Not because of its mystic origins, rather this teaching creates unease because of a long standing assumption that religious and secular teachings must be rivals. After all, if one believes that God gave the exclusive rights to record the Divine work to specific "chosen ones," then all other attempts to disclose the blueprint of this world

---

[33] Proverbs 3:18. In their original Biblical context, this verse refers to wisdom and understanding. Tradition interprets them as speaking of the Torah, which is why this verse is recited as part of the Torah service on Monday, Thursday, and Shabbat.
[34] This summary of Isaac Luria's commentary is found in *Etz Hayim: Torah and Commentary*. The Rabbinical Assembly: New York, 2001. p. 816

are forgeries, deemed of little worth in both product and any additional efforts to understand them. This perspective was laid out humorously in the *midrash*:

> In response to a line in Deuteronomy, the people asked Shmuel: "What does it mean that *the Torah is not found in Heaven*?"[35] To which Shmuel answered: "The word of God is not to be found amongst the astrologers whose work is to gaze at the Heavens." But, the people said to Shmuel, "Lo, you are an astrologer and yet you are also great in Torah." Whereupon he replied: "I only engage in astrology when I am free from studying Torah." "What?!" responded the people in astonishment. "God forbid, when are you free from studying Torah?!" To which Shmuel answered: "When I am in the bathroom."[36]

While some, like Shmuel, may deem the paper upon which secular teachings are written as worthless as toilet paper, not all members of the Jewish community are willing to live without it, as – I am sure many of us will agree – even toilet paper has an important purpose! For example, within these contexts, we can understand that pursuing the academic discipline of biology can be useful for a successful *sh'chitah* (ritual slaughtering), arithmetic for constructing a sound *sukkah* (a temporary shelter during the festival of *Sukkot*), and chemistry for producing that perfect shade of *techelet* (blue) for a *tallit* (prayer shawl). In fact, one could even argue that the pursuit of secular subjects is a natural outgrowth of studying Torah, which – as it is articulated in our morning liturgy – "is equal to them all, because the study of Torah leads to them all."[37]

But, if we only see secular subjects as a tool by which to fulfill the commandments of God, then we greatly limit their full and intended purpose: understanding God, the Eternal-self. As Rabbi Yehoshua ben Levi taught, "If anyone has a talent for understanding astrology and does not pursue it, then Scripture regards that person as 'thoughtless in the ways of the Lord, having taken no note of what God is designing.'"[38] For, just as Torah can connect us to secular subjects, secular subjects can connect us to Torah. That is what the branches of the menorah relate; and, it's what the distinguished physicist Albert Einstein imparted when he stated: "While I long deemed religion without science blind, I now understand science without religion as lame."[39]

We can no longer afford this deficit, which the sages of each generation acknowledge is created by the reliance upon any one branch of study alone (whether religious or secular). Rather than assuming that these teachings are rivals, each competing for their interpretation of Truth, let us instead see them – as our ancestors did – as connected branches on the menorah of Eternal

---

[35] Deuteronomy 30:12
[36] Deuteronomy Rabbah 8:6
[37] Birchot HaShachar; after the blessing for being able to engage in the study of Torah
[38] BT Tractate Shabbat 75a
[39] Albert Einstein. *Science, Philosophy, and Religion: A Symposium*. Conference on Science, Philosophy, and Religion in Their Relation to the Democratic Way of Life, Inc.: New York, 1941.

truth that together help us illuminate all the mysteries of this world. In that way, we pray, next time Alex Trebek (a.k.a. our rabbi) presents us with the answer, "It is a Tree of Life for those who hold it fast and all of its supporters are happy," we can answer confidently: "What is Torah along _with_ any other discipline of study?" For when we utilize them together, we truly win, as we come to know God fully with all our hearts, with all our minds, and with all our souls.

B'ha-alotecha // When You Set Up
Bite 2 – _The "Second Chance" Off Ramp_

As an ISJL team, we rack up countless miles on our nation's highways, crisscrossing the South in order to visit many of our smaller – but no less valued – Jewish communities. And, every once in a while, for some reason or another, we may miss our appointed exit. Maybe it was bad signage; maybe it was poor navigational efforts by our GPS units; or maybe it was – dare I say – even a human foible, as we often become the passionate lead-singers of whatever band is playing on the radio.

No matter the reason, this missed opportunity often proves rather costly in terms of time, as we are forced to drive on, waiting and waiting until the next exit to turn around. In these moments, some may offer a prayer to God, beseeching the Omnipotent One to manifest a new off-ramp. Sure, there are obviously more important things for which to pray. Yet, it's fun to imagine that in the 5773rd year after God created the Heaven and the earth, the sky and the sea, the sun, the moon and the stars, God created an off-ramp and called it 'Second Chance.' There was evening and there was morning, a 2,107,145th day."[40]

As comical as this may appear, it is not without precedent. In this portion of _B'ha-alotecha_ there was a group of Israelites who too missed an important off-ramp, one which led to the holiday of Passover. They claimed, while on their journey through the wilderness, that they were distracted while in performance of another _mitzvah_ (such as caring for the dead) or had 'zoned-out' while along the long journey. And not wanting to walk on, in order to wait and wait for the next off-ramp to Passover a year later, they offered a prayer to God.

They beseeched God, through Moses, for a second chance. And, miraculously, God granted it to them, stating: "If any person shall become defiled by a corpse or shall be on a distant road, [and thus missed the first Passover], that person shall be permitted to make a Passover offering [exactly one month later] in the second month on the 14th day of the month, at twilight." (Numbers 9:10-11) This unusual permit, known by the later rabbis as _Pesach Sheini_ (the 'Second Passover') shall last one day, as God ordered the individuals to eat this

---

[40] This count of days in merely meant to be a humorous estimation, not an exact calculation.

alternative Passover sacrifice "with unleavened bread and bitter herbs, leaving nothing over for morning." (Numbers 9:12)

To many, this alternative is not only unusual, it's shocking as "it illustrates a capacity [of God or the Israelite leadership] to modify time-bound obligations."[41] And not for the whole community, as if the First Passover had been rained out, creating a justifiable need for a make-up game. No, this leniency for a Second Passover is even more exceptional as it was made on account of only a few; teaching – writes Biblical commentator Jacob Milgrom – that "to the individual, life will often offer a second chance for fulfillment that may have been missed when the opportunity first presented itself."[42]

But that is where agreement on this interpretation ends, as there are those who maintain that a second chance should only be granted to those who justifiably deserve it. A second chance, they portend, is only for those who have a good excuse for missing the first like: "my dog ate my *matzah*," "I must have left the shank bone in my other pants," or – would you believe – "a funny thing happened to me on the way to the Temple." These excuses are clearly in jest. Nonetheless, there are those who would require substantial evidence, verifying – beyond reproach – one's innocence before determining whether one was truly deserving of a second chance.

Yet, rationally, we understand that there are few – if any – among us who could say that he/she is all together pure, that he/she has not erred, that he/she is without blame. Even so, there is still an impetus within our human hearts to judge. I believe we do so mostly out of fear. We fear having our hearts broken, our good natures taken advantage of, our power to forgive returned upon us in spite. And, so, we judge. We judge who is worthy and who is not, who we believe should be given a second chance and who should not, hoping, praying that this assessment guarantees our safety.

However, in life there are no guarantees and in Judaism there is only one who has the power to judge: God. Thus, there are others – like Rabbi Yosef Yitzchak Schneersohn (1880-1950) – who maintain that "even if a person has failed to fulfill a certain aspect of his or her mission in life, whether accidently or even deliberately, there should always be a Second Passover, [a second chance] to make good on what he or she has missed out on."[43] In other words, this perspective asserts that no one is ever lost simply because they missed their off-ramp. A second chance should always be presented to them as an opportunity to turn around.

Recognizing and utilizing the second chances we get in life to correct the past and transform our futures is indeed living up to our human potential. But, presenting the opportunity for a second chance to others – as it is taught in this

[41] Dr. Tamara Cohn Eskenazi, ed. *The Torah: A Women's Commentary*. URJ Press: New York, 2008. p. 849

[42] Jacob Milgrom. "Numbers." *Etz Hayim: Torah and Commentary*. Rabbinical Assembly: New York, 2001. p. 820

[43] For further information please check out *Pesach Sheini: A Second Chance for Spiritual Progress* at www.chabad.org

Torah portion – is living up to our Divine potential. May we continue, then, to live up to this Divine potential, opening up the off-ramps of second chances to others… not merely to those we believe deserve it, but equally as important to those we believe do not.

B'ha-alotecha // When You Set Up
Bite 3 – *Nostalgia: Yesterday's Gefilte, Today's Savory Salmon*

Have you ever heard someone talk about "the good old days," where and when everything was magically better than today? If so, did ya' find it odd, upon hearing more about those "good old days," that they didn't always seem so good: jobs were few, times were tough, money didn't stretch far, but one was mighty glad the elastic waistband in pants did, as one would wear the same clothes year after year after year. In these "good old days," there always seemed to be so many who had so little. Yet, somehow they made it work, whether it was during the Great War, the Great Depression, or the Great Pandemic which set the world on the verge of collapse. Okay, I may have exaggerated that last one. "But, that's what made it," they say, "the 'good old days!'"

In that case, it's finally understandable why our Israelite ancestors looked back on those 427 years of slavery with such fondness. Yes, upon leaving Egypt, "the people [actually] took to complaining bitterly before the Lord." Why? Given the Divine gift of freedom, what could the Israelites possibly have to complain about (as if they needed a reason)? Food, of course! In the good old days, recalled the people in the Torah portion of *B'ha-alotecha*, "we remember the fish we used to eat free in Egypt." Not only that, but we remember "the melons, the leeks, the onions, and the garlic!" *Oy vey is mir*, who could forget the garlic! "Now our gullets are shriveled. There is nothing at all. Nothing," they admit, "but this manna to look to!" (Numbers 11:1, 5-6)

To be fair, notes the Bible, "the manna tasted like rich cream."[44] So then, why did the people become such an Oscar the Grouch or Moishe Oofnik (for fans of the Israeli Sesame Street)? Because, comments Rabbi Jacob Weinstein, "Whenever the present changes," for good or not, "we tend to cast a retroactive glow of delight over the past, suffusing old woes, muting old indignities."[45] Such was the case with our ancestors, adds Rabbi Pinchas Peli. "Too demoralized to look to the future, they turned to the past. Yet, their memory is very selective. They do not recall the humiliation of slavery or the joys of liberation. All they remember is the fish they supposedly ate free in Egypt," which keeps them so rooted in the past they have trouble moving forward.[46]

---

[44] Numbers 11:8
[45] Rabbi Jacob Joseph Weinstein. *The Place of Understanding: Comments on the Portions of the Week and the Holiday Cycle*. Bloch Publishing Company: New York, 1959. p. 103
[46] Rabbi Pinchas Peli. *Jerusalem Post*: 15 June 1985. Noted in Rabbi Harvey Field's *A Torah Commentary for Our Times*, Vol. 3. UAHC Press: New York, 1993. p. 30

And, like a genetic trait passed down from generation to generation, we too often glow over difficult days long passed. We don't recall the homesickness we first felt at summer camp; we merely remember the fun we had with our bunkmates and counselors. We don't recall the errors made on the field of play; we just remember that one spectacular game which set everything right. Wearing those rose-colored glasses, country singer Mark Wills once looked at his past and sang: "It was 1980-something, in the world that I grew up in: skating rinks and Black Trans Ams, big hair and parachute pants. Lookin' back now, I can see me. Oh man, did I look cheesy! But," he admits, "I wouldn't trade those days for nothin', it was 1980-something."[47]

No, no one should trade in those memories. Because, there's nothing wrong about recalling the past, even if slightly distorted, as so many of us do this on a daily basis. In part, we make these alterations to the past due to the inability of the human mind to have total recall. Though, to be fair, most changes are more conscious, as we willfully spice up old stories to provide extra meaning or entertainment value therein. Take that fish we caught yesterday; today it's a whale. Or, to put it another way, yesterday's gefilte becomes today's savory salmon, calling our ancestors back to last night's Egyptian dinner. If anything, that's Jewish tradition: drawing upon the power of memory to drive us forward, particularly through present predicaments.

"A-oh, oh-a," speaks up Arthur Herbert Fonzarelli, a.k.a. "the Fonz," asking: "So, what's the problem here?"[48] Well Fonz, the problem here – in this Torah portion – lies in the Israelites exaggerating the past to such a degree that it glows in light of their present difficulties, enticing them to not only forgo today, but tomorrow as well, for some misunderstood sense of yesterday. Nowadays, we see this with: past loves reunited on the Net, who abandon their present families for another chance; former-athletes, who – despite the pain – reenter the game to experience once again their glory days; and parents, who dress and behave like their teenage children, just to relive parts of their youth. But, all too often, these voyages to the past end only in capsizing.

Why? It's because "the good old days," as previously mentioned, are rarely, if ever, as good as we have made them out to be. Though, some sadly only realize this after squandering precious time, energy, and relationships. For, in perverting the past, we prevent the present from moving forward towards a prosperous future. That shall not be our fate. While we are encouraged to revisit the past, let us do so in a more open and honest way, unpacking both the good clothes as well as the dirty laundry. Not only will this honest view temper the past from calling us backward, but it will provide a better guide to the present in moving forward, as we learn to repeat the good while avoiding the bad. For then, may we be blessed to say with each passing day that the one ahead is magically better than the one behind.

---

[47] Mark Wills, singer. David Lee and Chris DuBios. "19 Something." Greatest Hits. Mercury Nashville Records: 2002.
[48] Arthur Herbet Fonzarelli (also Fonzie, The Fonz) is a fictional character played by Henry Winkler in the sitcom *Happy Days*, which ran from 1974 to 1984.

Portion 4:
Sh'lach-l'cha // Send for Yourself
Torah Portion: Numbers 13:1-15:41

"SEND FOR YOURSELF MEN TO SCOUT THE LAND OF CANAAN…" commands God at the beginning of this portion. To fulfill the command, Moses selects one scout from each tribe. The scouts set out through the Negev and reach Wadi Eshcol, where they cut down a branch with a huge cluster of grapes. After 40 days, they report that the land indeed flows with milk and honey, but the people who inhabit the country are like giants, too large to be defeated by the Israelites, who must appear like grasshoppers to these people.

Caleb and Joshua, however, urge the people to have faith, as God is with them and will ensure their victory. The community does not listen. The Israelites rail against Moses and Aaron, "If only we had died in the land of Egypt!" (Numbers 14:2)

God, beset with anger at this lack of faith, is poised to strike the people down and make - from Moses - a new nation. Moses, however, convinces God that it would be better to let them live lest the Egyptians think God weak, unable to bring the Eternal's people to the land as promised. Seeing wisdom in his words, God concedes to Moses' plea.

Even so, God proclaims that none of this generation will see the land of Israel, save Caleb and Joshua. The Israelites are to wander in the desert for 40 years. Overcome with grief, the Israelites make a last ditch effort to follow God's command and enter the land. As it was too little, too late, they were decidedly defeated and forced back at Hormah.

The portion concludes with the commandment to make *tzitzit*, or fringes with a cord of blue attached to the corners of garments, to remind the Israelites to follow the commandments of God, as they were to be a nation of priests.

Sh'lach-l'cha // Send for Yourself
Bite 1 – *From Selfishness to Selflessness*

A married couple, in their early 60s, was out celebrating their 35th wedding anniversary in a quiet, romantic little restaurant. Suddenly, a tiny fairy appeared on their table and said, "For being such an exemplary married couple, faithful to each other all this time, I will grant you *each* a wish." "Ooh," cooed the wife, "I would like to travel around the world with my darling husband." The fairy moved her magic wand and – *abracadabra!* – two around-the-world tickets on a luxury cruise liner appeared in her hands.

Now, it was the husband's turn. He thought for a moment and said, "Well, this is all very romantic, but an opportunity like this only occurs once in a lifetime. So, I'm sorry my love, but my wish is to have a wife 30 years younger than me." The wife and the fairy were deeply disappointed. But, a wish is a wish after all. So the fairy made a circle with her magic wand and – *abracadabra!* – the husband became 92 years old.

Although humorous here, the consequences of selfishness are rarely amusing, as the Israelites found out in this portion of *Sh'lach-l'cha*, which literally means "Send for Yourself." According to the Bible, after finally reaching the borders of the Promised Land, the Lord spoke to Moses, saying: "'Send for yourself men to scout the land of Canaan, which I am giving to the Israelite people; send one man from each of their ancestral tribes, each one a chieftain among them.' So Moses, by the Lord's command, sent them out from the wilderness of Paran, all the men being leaders of the Israelites." (Numbers 13:1-3) But, at the end of 40 days, 10 out of these 12 leaders returned with bad news, a report which precipitated the Divine punishment to wander the wilderness for 40 years.

Why? What was the proverbial straw that broke the "slow-to-anger, abundantly kind, forgiving iniquity and transgression" back of God?[49] Answers to this question abound. But, according to the well-known Jewish mystic Isaac Luria, the 40-year wandering of the Israelites was a consequence of abundant selfishness. As Luria suggests in the *Zohar*, "These leaders took for themselves evil advice, saying: 'If Israel enters the land, we will be removed from our leadership positions. For Moses appointed us leaders in the desert, but he won't appoint us as leaders in the Land.'"[50] Thereupon, a selfish decision was made that – like any selfish decision – kept us wandering in the wilderness of this world, delaying our Divine Promise.

But, it's not just wasted time. History has shown that the consequences of selfishness can be devastating: careers are often destroyed, friendships obliterated, and families torn. Nevertheless, as the country sage Toby Keith pointed out, there are still many in this generation who only "wanna talk about

---

[49] Numbers 14:18 -- These Divine attributes are repeated in the High Holy Day liturgy.
[50] Targum Zohar 3:158

me, wanna talk about I, wanna talk about number one, oh me oh my."[51] And, as a result, the news – both in print and on television – is littered with terrible, heart-wrenching aftermaths of decisions based on the flimsy calculations: assessing one's immediate desires without considering the long-term cost on others. In fact, I think it is fair to say that most of us have likely experienced these consequences firsthand, whether directly (due to our own selfish actions) or indirectly (due to the selfish actions of others).

Still, some of us may defend selfishness, believing – to some degree – it has a legitimate place in a healthy society. In support of this perspective is the "oxygen mask rule," which states that one must think of oneself first (securing one's own mask) before thinking of others (helping to secure the masks of our travel companions). For, it is argued, how can you help someone else, if you are in need of help yourself? It's a fair argument, to be sure, that is not only reinforced through the social courtesies of I-statements, but one legitimized by our sages. For example, noting the superfluous use of "for yourself" in this Torah portion as well as others, like the famous *Lech-l'cha* ("Go for Yourself"), RaSHI comments that while it was a Divine command, one must also go "for your own pleasure and benefit."[52]

For our faith recognizes that one must have a personal stake in a communal endeavor in order for the journey to be successful. It's a conclusion, by the way, codified in the first century B.C.E., by the sage Hillel, who said: "If I am not for myself, who will be for me?"[53] But, what Hillel perceived immediately after recognizing the value of selfishness was: "If I am only for myself, then what am I?"[54] The answer, as presented in this portion, is a wandering Israelite without a home, slated to be lost among the sands than to stand out in the Promised Land. For Hillel understood that selfishness is not in and of itself an evil inclination. However, he concluded, it can lead to evil – both for ourselves and those with whom we are in a relationship – if taken to the extreme.

Therefore, let us not be led astray by selfishness. Instead, may we see this inclination as merely the motivation to begin a journey with others, one that leads us to think as much for them as we do ourselves. For while our relationships may be born from selfishness (expressed in such statements as *I* need you, *I* want you, *I* love you, *I* miss you), they are only nurtured and strengthened by selflessness. In this manner, may we make our way out of the wilderness of this world and into the Promised Land. In this manner, may we grow old together, as we transition from strangers to neighbors, from friends to family. In this manner, may we come to be at home and at peace – together – under God's shelter.

---

[51] Toby Keith. "I Wanna Talk About Me." *Pull My Chain*. Dreamworks: 2001.
[52] RaSHI commentary to *Lech L'cha* - Genesis 12:1
[53] Pirkei Avot 1:14
[54] *Ibid.*

Sh'lach-l'cha // Send for Yourself
Bite 2 – *The Epithet of our Lives*

Daniel was a little over three years old when he was diagnosed with cancer. Thankfully, though, after two years of treatment and several surgeries, Daniel's physical health was secure. However, due to the aggressive treatment, Daniel's learning ability had been stunted...but happily not deterred! With the help of the Cancer Institute and its personnel, Daniel was able to enter into a special-education class at his local school. But, his teacher soon realized there was a small problem. Two little boys in her class now shared the same name: 'Daniel.' And, every time she called that name, both little boys would answer. To solve this challenge, the teacher decided to ask each one what his mother called him at home, hoping that they would be different. And different, they were. The first little boy answered, "Danny," while the other little boy, recovering from cancer, said: "Sweetheart!"

In this Torah portion of *Sh'lach-l'cha*, we too read of a poignant time in which one's given name is replaced with another. Just as the scouts are about to depart on their infamous reconnaissance mission into the Promised Land to gather vital intel for Moses and the community, we read in the book of Numbers that, "Moses changed the name of [one of the scouts] Hoshea son of Nun to Yehoshua (Joshua)." (Numbers 13:16) This apparently inexplicable alteration, believes RaSHI, is a result of poignant timing. In his commentary on the book of Numbers, RaSHI explains that Hoshea's name was changed to Yehoshua at this particular moment because Moses saw that he was poised to embark upon a new and potentially challenging course. So according to RaSHI, Hoshea's name-change is really Moses' prayer, as if to say that Moses prayed: "May Hoshea be Yehoshua," meaning 'may Hoshea be saved.'[55]

I love this! Because, unbeknownst to him, RaSHI just re-envisioned Moses *rabbeinu*, (Moses our teacher), into Moses our charismatic preacher, who lays his shaking hands upon Hoshea and exclaims triumphantly: "Yehoshua...may he be saved!" And saved he was. As this portion later informs us, Yehoshua (Joshua) along with Caleb would be the only ones to live beyond this generation, able to enter the Promised Land. Similarly, as we embark on different courses in our lives, we too are given new names, titles, designations. And, similar to what RaSHI implies, it is not the name that is important, but what we do to fulfill its meaning at life's poignant moments that will determine whether or not we will find success along the journey.

This phenomenon of receiving new names happens continually throughout our lives, whether realized or not. For example, within our families, we often acquire new names as we mature, going from 'son' or 'daughter' to 'brother' or 'sister,' growing from 'husband' and 'wife' to 'father' and 'mother,' and – God willing – experiencing the moment when we will be forced to decide whether to be called 'grandma' and 'grandpa,' 'mima' and 'papa,' or 'bubbie' and

---

[55] RaSHI commentary to Numbers 13:16

'zaydie.' In addition to our families, we may also be given new names in the workplace, especially as we climb the corporate ladder. In fact, every year, the ISJL is blessed to bestow upon recent college graduates the name 'education fellow,' as these young adults join our team to make a difference in the lives of our southern Jewish communities.

As grateful as we undoubtedly are for these new names by which we are called, we must understand that power is not necessarily bestowed with them. By whatever name we may be given, we should not feel entitled by our title. For as William Shakespeare rhetorically questioned in his romantic tragedy *Romeo and Juliet*: "What's in a name? That which we call a rose by any other name would [still] smell as sweet. So Romeo would, were he not Romeo call'd, retain that dear perfection which he owes without that title." In other words, names are merely labels to be pressed and passed by the hands of time, until - that is - one provides substance to the signature, depth to the designation, texture to the title, or – to put it another way – character to the name.

This is where the true power of one's name resides. Not from the name itself, but from the actions we do to fulfill their intended meaning. For even with Hoshea's name change, there was no guarantee that he would indeed be saved. Like the other scouts, Joshua too could have easily been overcome by what he saw. This is, after all, a natural condition of our humanity as noted in another great Shakespeare play: *Julius Caesar*. In a striking comparison to this Torah portion, in which the scouts compare the 'others' to giants and themselves to grasshoppers, Shakespeare wrote: Other men may "bestride the world like a Colossus and we – petty men – walk under his huge legs and peep about [only] to find ourselves dishonorable graves."[56] Therefore, Shakespeare advises, "Men must become masters of their fates. For the fault is not in our stars, but in ourselves, that we [see ourselves] as underlings."

And he is right. Unlike the other scouts, Joshua did not see himself as an underling. In fact, he saw himself standing tall in a world that was majestic and holy, and then engaged in a process to help others see it as so.[57] Through this and other righteous deeds, we all can emerge as masters of our fate, leaders of our lives, as we bring both meaning and power to our names. For it is by our actions, not by our words, that we make a name for ourselves. As the rabbis taught, "Every person has three names: the one his/her parents give him/her, the one his/her friends call him/her, and one he/she makes for him/herself."[58] It is this last one that is not only the hardest to acquire, but it is ultimately the one that our Torah portion teaches us how to achieve. Therefore, let us – at this poignant moment – recommit ourselves to these ends, engaging in meaningful actions, thereby creating meaning-filled names: the epithet of our lives.

---

[56] See the parallel in Numbers 13:33

[57] While the other scouts (save Caleb) spread calumnies upon their return, Joshua reports: "The land that we traversed and scouted is an exceedingly good land... Have no fear then of the people of the country, for they are our prey: their protection has departed them, but the Lord is with us. Have no fear of them!" (Numbers 14:7-9)

[58] Kohelet Rabbah 7:3

Sh'lach-l'cha // Send for Yourself
Bite 3 – *Regrets… I've had a Few*

"Regrets… I've had a few."[59] Sure, Ol' Blue Eyes, but what you're likely not referring to are tattoos, or singing "It Ain't Easy Bein' Green" at a karaoke bar, or even drinking recently expired milk – believing it was still safe – only to wake up the next morning nauseous.[60] Because, although there are a lot of sources of regret out there in the world, what most provokes this emotional response – according to a recent survey – is not something we did and wish we would not have. Rather, what we regret the most are those things we did not do, but later think we should have. Topping that list are romantic relationships we did not pursue, family members we did not reach out to, and professional roles we did not assume.[61]

Had this survey been taken by our Israelite ancestors, surely another regret would have been added to that list, namely "…the God we did not listen to." Because, when the people stood on the border of the Promised Land, and heard the Divine command to enter, they refused. "Let's head back to Egypt!" they cried. "Better to die there or here in the wilderness…than to fall by the sword attempting to enter that land." Very well, responded the Eternal. "I will do just as you have urged Me. In this very wilderness your carcasses shall drop… while your children are left to roam the desert for forty years." When Moses repeated all these words to the Israelites, states the Bible, "the people became overcome with *avel*, with regret." (Numbers 14)

What's incredibly interesting here is this Hebrew word *avel*, because – as many Hebrew speakers will know – besides "regret" *avel* can also mean "grief" or "mourning." Recognizing this connection, Rabbi Harold Kushner teaches that when the Israelites – full of regret – "leave this place, they leave it sullenly, reluctantly, and without enthusiasm."[62] It's as if the people are not simply regretting one bad decision; they are grieving, mourning a life – their lives – prematurely, forsaking what remaining time they had left. It is from them that we learn that whenever we stand on the border of Promise, we must take on some risks and step forward, thereby leaving regret behind and greeting the potential for a life more fully lived.

Unfortunately, many of us don't live that way. Practically, in nearly every second of every day, we become consumed or – to put it more Biblically, plagued – by the three stooges of regret: could've, would've, and should've. We think, "What if I had only responded in that crucial moment rather than

---

[59] Paul Anka. "My Way." *My Way*. Reprise: 1969. "My Way" was sung by Francis Albert "Frank" Sinatra and set to music based on the French song *"Comme d'habitude"* composed in 1967 by Claude François and Jacques Revaux. *"Comme d'habitude,"* interestingly, had in turn originally been written in English, titled "For Me." Anka's English lyrics are unrelated to the original French song or the earlier English version.

[60] Also known as "Bein' Green." The song was written by Joe Raposo and was originally performed by Kermit the Frog on the *Sesame Street Book & Record* in 1970 . However, as an interesting connection, it was then covered by many artists, including Frank Sinatra in 1971 in his *Sinatra and Company* album.

[61] John Tesh Radio Show. *Intelligence for Your Life*: 28 September 2012.

[62] Harold Kushner, ed. *Etz Hayim: Torah and Commentary*. Rabbinical Association: New York, 2001. p. 849

remaining silent; what if I had been the one to step forward as opposed to simply standing still; what if I had tried just a little harder instead of letting go so easily; what if…?" In fact, notes the fictional advice columnist Juliet in the 2010 motion picture *Letters to Juliet*, "'What' and 'if' are as non-threatening as two words can possibly be. But, put them together, side-by-side, and they have the power to haunt you the rest of your life."[63]

And, what haunts us really are not the potential losses we could have incurred from taking on the risks. For, honestly, what would we be losing: a little time, a little money, a little pride? No, what truly keeps us awake at night are those forsaken gains we gave away by deciding not to risk at all. That misfortune (and missed-fortune) is one of our own doing. Because, every time we stand on the border of what is certain and what is merely a promise, we are confronted with a question: "what can be gained versus what can be lost?" And, more times than not, we err on the side of safety. "Better safe than sorry," right? Well…wrong. For, in this safe-mode, life has a way of dulling to dust, grains of sand which – like our ancestors – become lost in the wilderness.

Therefore, we are encouraged to take on some risks. Not simply for the sake of standing out, being counted among the brave and faithful of our people; rather, we – in Judaism – are encouraged to step into that yet-to-be realized Promise, because we know that any potential loss will surely be mitigated by our Insurance Policy: God. As it is written: "Have no fear then…for though their protection has left, the Lord remains with you."[64] And, what is the sign of that protective policy? None other than the Sukkah, that temporary dwelling in the desert. With its thatched roof, it reminds each successive generation of one simple truth: even in loss, we hold our heads high, for in looking up we see all we still have learned with the Eternal by our side.[65]

So, from that second generation in the wilderness, who eventually risked settling the land, to those in today's generation who continue to do the same, from the dispersed of Israel, who risked bringing God's word to the four corners of the earth, to Israeli astronaut Ilan Ramon (*z"l*) who risked bringing them far beyond it, from the young, who are just now risking their first steps, to those who continue to risk one more down life's long road, may we all continue to take their lead and implement this valuable lesson. For then we will not live some half-life full of regret. Rather, by setting down our regrets and picking up some risks, we come to live a life more filled with peace and with Promise.

---

[63] José Rivera and Tim Sullivan. *Letters to Juliet*. Summit Entertainment: 2010.
[64] Numbers 14:9
[65] It is customary to allow some sky to show through the roof of the Sukkah, as to remind its inhabitants of God's heavenly protection that sheltered our people through their precarious desert wanderings.

Portion 5:
Korach // Korach
Torah Portion: Numbers 16:1-18:32

"Now Korach...betook himself...to rise up against Moses." Dramatically, the portion of *Korach* opens, as Korach, Dathan and Abiram, along with 250 Israelite chieftains, combine against Moses and Aaron, asserting: "You have gone too far! For all in the community are holy... Why then do you raise yourselves above the Lord's congregation?" (Numbers 16:3)

His accusation comes on the heels of the people donning *tzitzit* (fringes), reminding them that they are a priestly people. But, there is only one High Priest: Aaron. Thus, to determine the legitimate Israelite leader, Moses arranges a test, inviting Korach and his band to place incense before God along with Aaron and himself. Whoever's offering is accepted by God will be considered the true leaders of Israel.

Moses, thereupon, warns the community to move away from the tents of Korach, Dathan and Abiram, suggesting that these men will die a miraculous death for spurning God. Soon enough, the ground underneath the feet of these men opens up and swallows them with their entire households. They go down shrieking into Sheol, and the earth closes over them. Then a fire from God consumes their 250 compatriots.

God instructs Moses to remove their fire pans and hammer them into plating for the altar, as a reminder that only Aaron's offspring are to offer incense before God. Furthermore, God decides to settle once and for all the question of leadership. Each tribal chieftain is to bring one staff to the Tent of Meeting. Aaron's staff sprouts blossoms and almonds, thus indicating that God chooses Aaron.

The portion concludes by listing the special responsibilities and privileges of the priesthood and of the Levites, possibly to strengthen Aaron after this challenge to his authority.

Korach // Korach
Bite 1 – *"Having it Made" vs. "Having Made it"*

At this point in the year, many recent college and university graduates are standing in line to receive a small dose of reality. The slightly painful injection is typically administered during the first few weeks of work (that is, if they were fortunate enough to find a job at all!). Rather than stepping into their dreamy, cushy corner offices, with large windows, idyllic panoramic views, and perhaps their own mini-fridge, these starry-eyed individuals, filled with euphoria for having finally "made it," are often guided by some senior colleague down a dark hallway to a tiny cubical with the only view being that of the bathroom and a communal refrigerator, which resembles the Bermuda Triangle, for anything that goes in is very likely never to come out again.

Understandably, such a rude awakening is bound to arouse disappointment, if not outright anger. That may help explain the outburst of Korach in this Torah portion by the same name. Having left the harsh schooling of Egypt, the relatively young and inexperienced Korach – eager to make his mark on the world   experiences a less than ideal work environment in the wilderness. Already, there had been two incidents involving mass casualties and a failed scouting mission into the Land.[66] Banding together with other disgruntled Israelites, Korach yells at Moses: "You have gone too far! Is not the whole community holy, all of [us], as the Lord resides in [our] midst?! Why then do you raise yourself above the Lord's congregation?!" (Numbers 16:3)

As we know, it is not Moses who raises himself up. As Korach and his band are swallowed whole by the earth, it is clear that the real Mover-and-Shaker in this company is none other than God. But, why? Was Korach not correct when he insinuated that the whole community was holy? And, thereby, was he not justified – despite his tender age and inexperience – to demand some equal compensation from the Divine? Not quite, comments 20th century Israeli intellectual Yeshayahu Leibowitz. "Israel, in fact, is not holy, at least not yet. At Sinai, we were simply charged 'to become holy.'"[67] Not understanding, then, the difference between a status to be gained and one that is granted, Korach's fall becomes unavoidable.

Clearly, he is not the only one to make this mistake, not then and certainly not today. What took previous generations years of hard work to achieve is often seen by successive generations as a "gimme," an entitlement based solely upon reaching their title of "Being." Think about it. It's not just cushy corner offices we expect after graduation; it's the new car after earning our driver's license, new clothes after each yearly academic matriculation, and the latest and greatest tech upon our disembarkation from the womb. Yes, today, it seems that even babies are born with smart-phones in hand, allowing them to update

---

[66] Numbers 11:1-3; 11:10-34 and Numbers 13-14

[67] Leibowitz commentary is noted in *Etz Hayim: Torah and Commentary*. Rabbinical Association: New York, 2001. p. 861. Leibowitz is referencing Leviticus 19:2, in which God charges the people: "You shall be holy, for I – the Lord, your God – am holy."

their status from 'in utero' to 'in the world' in seconds. "Sure, the trip in was a bit bumpy," says the tiny Tweet. "But I've finally arrived!"

These aspirations 'to arrive,' 'to have' or 'to be' something, aren't necessarily unhealthy, particularly not if they drive us to work harder to achieve them. The problem arises when we, like Korach, misinterpret a 40-year trek towards success as a quick stroll in the park. For though a few may go the short-route (like Mark Zuckerberg, who became a multi-billionaire at age 26), the vast majority of us are headed to the Promised Land the long way.[68] Unwilling to wait, some will attempt to reach these lofty heights artificially, propping themselves up through a distorted self-image or by extending lines of credit well beyond their means. Ultimately, like Korach, this path leads only to a flimsy ground, upon which one may be swallowed whole at any minute.

Not Moses. When God approached him with a special job offer, to free the Eternal's people, Moses did not respond with: "It's about time! Given my resume and qualifications, I had expected your call much earlier!" Rather, with great humility, Moses said to God: "Who me? Who am I to go to Pharaoh and free the Israelites from slavery? Oh please, O Lord, I have never been a man of words, not now nor in times past… Please make someone else your agent."[69] That, writes Rabbi Harold Kushner, is the deciding difference. "A true messenger, like Moses, presents themselves as unworthy of the task, not deserving of it, like Korach."[70] For a true messenger understands the difference between having it made, and having to work hard to make it.

Knowing that, it is then clear why the Lord stood at Moses' side, for he was continually working to stand on ever more solid ground. May we recommit ourselves to doing the same. May we, like our forefather Moses, never mistake any of our steps as our final step, thereby feeling entitled to all the benefits inherent in having completed the journey, in having arrived, in having it made. Rather, may we be humble enough to see, understand, and appreciate that each step merely presents us with a new opportunity to make it happen. For, as Theodore Herzl poignantly stated: "If you will it," if you willfully work towards it, "it is no dream."[71] May that be the case for us and all our recent college grads as they venture on their next step of life.

Korach // Korach
Bite 2 – *The More We Talk, the Less We Say*

Radio…television…cell phones…the Internet…cell phones with Internet. And, now, Apple has showcased its new iPhone which will allow for hand-held

---

[68] Mark Zuckerberg is the founder of Facebook. Forbes keeps track of his net worth, which you can see via the following link: http://www.forbes.com/profile/mark-zuckerberg/. At last check, at age 28, Zuckerberg's net worth is 17.5 billion.

[69] Exodus 3:11; 4:10-13

[70] Harold Kushner. *Etz Hayim: Torah and Commentary*. Rabbinical Association: New York, 2001. p.861

[71] Herzl. *Altneuland*. 1902

video calls. With every piece of new technology we are gifted with a chance to communicate more. Yet, even with this opportunity to talk more, it actually seems that a lot less is being said; for, rhetoric runs rampant over the airwaves. There is more hyperbole and less substance, more rambling and less focus. Responding to this growing phenomenon in 1956, the legendary author and cartoonist of the New Yorker, James Thurber, stated: "Most men lead lives of noisy desperation."[72] And since that time, some will argue, the desperate noise – often in the form of inflammatory speech – has only grown, threatening to burn our very society down to the ground.

Inflammatory language and the threat it presents is nothing new. Using words to wage war is a tradition as old as the Bible itself. For example, in this portion of Korach there is an incendiary exchange initiated by the title character: Korach. He barks at Moses, saying, "You have gone too far... Why do you raise yourself above the Lord's congregation?!" (Numbers 16:3) In response, Moses fights back: "[No, it's] you who have gone too far, sons of Levi... Is it not enough for you that the God of Israel has set you apart from the community of Israel?!" (Numbers 16:7-9) [73] After another round of back-and-forth anger, God puts the fire out by smothering Korach and his band with earth. As it is written: "The earth opened its mouth and swallowed them up with their households: Korach's people and their possessions." (Numbers 16:32)

Now, there is a wealth of commentary that comes to legitimize this event, seeing truth in both sides of the argument. On the one hand, commentators suggest that Korach is saintly, merely attempting to become closer to God.[74] On the other hand, there are commentators who suggest that Moses' leadership, which had successfully guided the people out of slavery, is needed – at least at this point – because the people were not ready to engage in such leadership matters for themselves.[75] Yet, by debating which side of the argument has more legitimacy than the other, we fan the flames, perpetuate the rhetoric, and miss the larger lesson. It is a lesson which comes to teach that the threat to our society is not merely born from a malicious message, it can also be materialized in the manner in which the message is being made.[76]

Indeed, there is some value to putting on a show. It grabs people's attention, a legitimate goal for anyone who feels that they have something worthwhile to

---

[72] James Thurber (1894-1961). This quote comes from his book entitled *Further Fables from Our Time*, based on the famous quote from American author and poet Henry David Thoreau: "Most men lead lives of quiet desperation and go to the grave with the song still in them."

[73] Korach, as a member of the priestly tribe of Levi, had already been given privileges greater than the rest of the Israelite community. Yet, Aaron's lineage - within the tribe of Levi - is about to be promoted above the other Levite to a special place as the High Priests, called the Kohanim. This act is the inciting factor for Korach's rebellion.

[74] Ha'amen Davar; noted in Leibowitz. *Studies in Bamidbar (Numbers)*. Maor Wallach Press: Israel. p. 221-222.

[75] Isaac Arama, better known as the Akedat Yizhak, argues that the whole incident was part of a larger lesson for the community showing the victory over evil, and teaching them to distinguish between the worthy and unworthy, the good and the evil (adapted from Nechama Leibowitz. *Studies in Bamidbar (Numbers)*. p. 222-223).

[76] Based upon Rabbi Harvey J. Fields. *A Torah Commentary for Our Time: Volume Three: Numbers and Deuteronomy*. UAHC Press: New York. 1993. p. 51: "Will it be a community ruled by the loudest voice with the most might or by the laws of Torah, publicly open to all?"

say. For, good thoughts retained within one individual maintain little power or significance to the world. As Martin Luther King, Jr. so poignantly stated, "History will have to record that the greatest tragedy of this period of social transition was not the strident clamor of the bad people, but the appalling silence of the good." In other words, in order for good ideas to really impact the world they must be heard. And a little flair, a little overreacting, may be just the way to open the door, encouraging people to enter. But, what about getting them to stay and listen to the speaker's message?

"Ah there's the rub," said Shakespeare.[77] Without that credible message at the heart of our presentation, then all the showy stuff is merely "sound and fury, signifying nothing."[78] When something is said in an overly ostentatious way we lose the message, even if it is a good one. For example, take Richard Simmons. Even though he speaks of something very important – health and exercise, the bombastic manner in which he broadcasts that message is almost enough to turn us off (or, more correctly, to turn him off). As it is argued, anyone with more style than substance is nothing more than a "player that struts and frets his hour upon the stage and is heard no more."[79]

So, how then do we get the message to last longer than an hour? How do we speak with a fiery passion, drawing people into our warmth, without creating cause for concern that they may get burned? A possible resolution may be found in the *Talmud*. In tractate *Chullin*, we read that "the world exists on account of people who are able to restrain themselves during a quarrel."[80] This is not to say we should be quiet, that we should roll over and play dead in the face of threatening words or actions. Just the opposite! These words of our tradition encourage us to confront our accusers, our critics, our cynics: not with the language of fire and brimstone, but with a language that is grounded in reason and commanded by respect. In this way, the message is not lost in the smoke of inflammatory rhetoric. Instead it permeates our lives.

And this, I believe, is where Korach as well as Moses failed. Their responses lacked restraint. Indeed, like them, we want to engage in our conversations, readily and excitedly. After all, these exchanges – which we establish with our neighbors – are the foundation of our society. However, only with words marked by restraint and respect will we lay a firm foundation. Sure, this may result in saying less as we choose our words more consciously whether it be on the radio, the television, the cell phone, the Internet, or most importantly, in the face-to-face conversations we are blessed to have. But, the impact of those words will be more. As the knight in *Indiana Jones and the Last Crusade* warned, "Choose [your words] wisely," for while respectful words will bring you life, disrespectful ones will take it from you.[81] May our words lack the flames that burn, but contain the warmth that brings us together.

---

[77] Shakespeare. *Hamlet*: Act III, scene 1 as part of his famous "to be or not to be" speech.
[78] Shakespeare. *Macbeth*: Act V, scene 5 as part of Macbeth's most famous soliloquy.
[79] Ibid.
[80] BT Chullin 89a
[81] Jeffrey Boam and George Lucas. *Indiana Jones and the Last Crusade*. Paramount Pictures: 1989.

Korach // Korach
Bite 3 – *Destructive History, Constructive Memory*

It starts out like any other museum. You walk into the welcome center. You peruse the first images on the wall, which are presented as a way to prepare you for what is to come. Yet, the truth is that nothing can prepare you for the physical and emotional drain that comes from walking the grounds of Majdanek [pronounced My-don-ic], a concentration camp, just outside the city limits of Lublin, Poland. Just standing on its ground is enough to rip the very breath from your lungs. The magnitude of this place weighs on you, as you enter barrack after barrack, attempting to glean an answer to the question: "Why?"

The gas chamber and crematorium both chill the mind, but nothing can compare to the horror of what comes next. On the outskirts of the camp there is a monument, a dome-shaped stone structure that covers a cavernous pit. And, housed in that pit are thousands upon thousands of pounds of human ash. How is it that something so horrific can be used as a means of remembering? How is it that something so awful can be transformed into something so meaningful?

The truth is, Judaism has built a tradition on constructing memories from dark horrific moments. This Torah portion of *Korach* is no exception. Named for the main antagonist of the scene, Korach approaches Moses with a gang of rabble-rousers to contest Moses' leadership. To settle the matter, a test of legitimacy is made by use of incense in fire-pans. Thereby, God will be the One to accept or reject the leader by the acceptance or rejection of their offering.

As Korach and his band of not-so-merry men are swallowed whole by the earth, it is fair to say that the matter is settled. Though the Torah tells us that "the fire pans of those who have sinned at the cost of their lives [i.e., Korach and his group, should] be made into hammered sheets as plating for the altar – for once they have been used for an offering to the Lord, they have become sacred." Furthermore, the Torah adds, "let them serve as a warning to the people of Israel." (Numbers 17:3)

There are volumes of commentary dealing with Korach: was he justified in demanding a "democratically elected leader," did his punishment fit the crime, and were his motives even sincere? But, what is often given little or no attention is the reuse of the fire-pans. RaSHI comments briefly on them, considering the fire-pans as a "sign" to the people.[82] Specifically, he says, "they shall be a sign for commemoration."[83] As RaSHI alludes to, tradition asks us to approach tragic and destructive moments with the power and conviction to transform them into sources of strength and sacredness.

---

[82] Rabbi Solomon ben Isaac (1040-1105), renowned commentator on Hebrew Bible and *Babylonian Talmud*.
[83] RaSHI commentary to Numbers 17:3

Naturally, this is not just a one-time occurrence in the historical course of our people. Taking moments we would rather forget and transforming them into meaningful memory markers occurs in several other instances: God using the destructive water of the flood to fashion a rainbow as a sign of the protective Covenant,[84] the horn from the ram sacrificed in Isaac's stead being used as a symbol by which to herald the coming of the Messiah,[85] and Moses – in the next portion – using a snake which inflicted the people as a sign of healing.[86] The examples from our tradition are not solely contained in the Torah; they permeate our lives. For example, even in a moment such as a wedding, where one is expected to be lifted high in jubilation, a memorial is attached to the situation, as a glass is smashed under the groom's heel in remembrance of the Temple's destruction.

Transforming hardships, such as these and others, into daily reminders is not an easy task. There will be many who will just want to move on. They don't want to be reminded of the horrors of the past. After all, was it not Albert Einstein who claimed that all of "life is like riding a bicycle. To keep your balance you must keep moving"?[87] So, why then would one forcefully pause to relive a moment of hardship? Why force these individuals to shape a reminder from the ever present scar left behind? One might as well poke a finger through the stitches and pour in some salt. As for this portion, it is fair to assume that some of the Israelites may have felt this way as well, particularly when they saw the fire-pans of the agitator Korach used as plating for the *Aron haKodesh* ("the holy ark").

Recognizing then how difficult and even painful it is to create these memorial markers, why then does the tradition insist they be made? What value is there in having them? What purpose do they serve? It has to be beyond evoking a memory. For after all, anyone can put up a sign saying, "such-and-such happened here on such-and-such a day." That just becomes factual information. Rather, these memorials are significant because their physical nature, beyond creating an emotional response, should also evoke an intellectual and physical change.

Imagine, for a moment, the Israelites simply packing up and moving on after Korach was swallowed. How quickly would another "Korach-type" rise up in his place? How soon after would this or another similar scenario transpire? It is very likely, especially without some preventative warning sign, we would be doomed to repeat the transgression. These fire-pans were the warning sign. Each time the people turned to face the ark, there was a physical reminder instructing them in their actions. "Choose the path of righteousness," warn the pans. "Be wary of the deeds of Korach."

---

[84] Genesis 9:13
[85] Pirke de Rabbi Eliezer 31
[86] Numbers 21:8-9
[87] http://quotes-aboutmovingon.com/

That is the same message presented at the Majdanek mausoleum. Much more than a marker of the Holocaust, a symbol of hardship and tragedy that should never have happened, it is both a reminder of the past and a guide to the future. In addition to feeling the sins of the past, one is compelled to rise above them. Much like the fire pans of Korach, hardship, strife and conflict can and should be transformed into the meaningful and the sacred. Let us take ownership over the difficult moments in our own lives and shape them into our vision of the future. In that way, we pray, we will be able to face the hardships head on, constantly striving for a better world.

Portion 6:
Chukkat // The Law
Torah Portion: Numbers 19:1-22:1

"THIS IS THE RITUAL LAW THAT THE LORD HAS COMMANDED..." The law, in which God is instructing Moses and Aaron at the opening of this portion, is the perplexing ritual of the "red heifer." Eleazar the priest is to slaughter and burn a red cow without blemish, and its ashes are to be gathered up and deposited in a pure place for purification of corpse-contaminated individuals. Some commentators hold that this ritual defies rational explanation, while the *midrash* views the red heifer as a symbolic rebuttal of the Golden Calf.

The narrative continues with the people of Israel railing against Moses and Aaron for lack of water in the desert. God instructs Moses and Aaron to assemble the people and to order a particular rock to produce water. Moses angrily exclaims, "Listen, you rebels, shall we get water for you out of this rock?" (Numbers 20:10) Moses then strikes the rock twice with his rod, disobeying the word of God, thereby failing to affirm the Eternal in the eyes of the people.

While water does flow, God punishes Moses and Aaron for this act of disobedience and prohibits them both from entering the land of Israel. God instructs Moses to strip Aaron of his vestments and put them on his son Eleazar on Mount Hor. Moses appoints Eleazar High Priest and Aaron dies on the summit of the mountain.

The people yet again complain against God and Moses about leaving Egypt for the barren wilderness. God sends *seraphs* (winged serpents) against the people. Many die when they are bitten. The people repent and God instructs Moses to make a *seraph* figure, which heals the people who are bitten when they gaze upon it. The Israelites march on through the desert, defeating the king of Arad, the Amorites, and the king of Bashan. They arrive at the steppes of Moab across the Jordan from Jericho.

Chukkat // The Law
Bite 1 – *Standing Firmly in Mystery*

A little over a month ago, I stood – as so many rabbis have done before me and as so many rabbis did this year in seminaries across America – in front of an assembled community to wait for a designated rabbi to perform the ritual: "laying of hands." It is a ritual by which the authority of the rabbinate is miraculously transferred from a senior rabbi to a student rabbi through a movement of the hands and the words of the Priestly Benediction found in Numbers 6:22: "*Y'va-rech-echa Adonai v'yish-m'recha/May the Lord bless you and keep you…*"

At this long-awaited and highly-anticipated moment I was overwhelmed…*but* not how you may expect. During the Ordination service, at the moment of "laying of hands," I began to feel a tension between my mind and my heart, between the rational and emotional states of my being. How can I grasp an experience as meaningful when it so obviously defies reason? Such may be the reaction whenever we stand in moments of mystery, whether they are rituals of religion or daily life, whether they are acts of nature or man.

To navigate this tension, we turn to this portion of *Chukkat*, which is flooded with moments of mystery. Beginning with the purification ritual of the red heifer, the Torah portion completes a three-ring circus of sorts with miraculous tales of a serpent staff which has the ability to heal and a donkey which can speak the words of God. In the *midrash*, even the great wisdom of King Solomon could not crack one of these mysteries. According to the story, Solomon states, "I have labored to understand the word of God and have understood it all, except…" he adds, "the ritual of the red heifer."[88] So what is a wise man to do? Does he choose to abandon the ritual because no rationale could be found within it? Or, maybe, a wise man performs the ritual anyway, motivated by: "because God said so."

Either decision, however, would result in Solomon as well as the wise amongst us today standing precariously, confining our feet to a narrow position on one side or the other. Instead, to truly stand firm on a foundation of Judaism, it may be advisable to take a wider stance which encompasses both positions: an intellectual pursuit of meaning in mystery and – at the same time – acceptance that the mystery is in and of itself meaningful.

For some, this will be a difficult task, as these miraculous stories appear irrational and thus –by literally no stretch of the imagination – could or should one find meaning in them. In fact, the early Jewish American Reformers espoused a complete abandonment of such spectacular stories along with any and all practices related to them. As it was articulated in the Declaration of Reform Principles (a.k.a. "The Pittsburg Platform") of 1885:

---

[88] Numbers Rabbah 19:3

"We hold that all such Mosaic and rabbinical laws as regulate diet, priestly purity, and dress originated in ages and under the influence of ideas entirely foreign to our present mental and spiritual state. They fail to impress the modern Jew with a spirit of priestly holiness; their observance in our days is apt rather to obstruct than to further modern spiritual elevation."

In other words, this position beseeches our <u>mind</u> to avoid practices without rational underpinnings for they are nothing more than vestiges of a primitive religion from which we have evolved.

The supposition that these mysterious rituals lack, or even worse, take away meaning from one's life rather than bringing meaning to it is not held by everyone. Others, both within the Reform Movement and beyond, insist that no matter how irrational a ritual, the ritual is *not* irrelevant. A wonderful classic rabbinic tale highlights this perspective as the students of Rabbi Yochanan ben Zakkai demand to know the meaning of the red heifer:

"There is no explanation," replied Rabbi Yochanan. "The ritual is commanded by God. It is set out in Torah law. That is what justifies its observance, not some rational interpretation."[89]

For Rabbi Yochanan and others who share his view sometimes it is enough to do something simply because "God said so." While similar, this perspective is more than parental hopes that a child will later – as an adult – find meaning in childhood lessons. Rather, this perspective beseeches the <u>heart</u> to allow the infinite oneness of God's presence to move and awe the finite of us so that we feel meaning in that moment of mystery.

In my opinion, both responses to the question – "What is a wise man to do in the face of the unknown?" – are unsatisfactory because they limit our engagement to God to one mode of expression: either via the mind or the heart. This all-or-nothing stance seems antithetical to Judaism, for we are commanded to love God with all our being. As we recite in prayer: "You shall love God with all your mind, with all your heart, and with all your soul."[90] It does not read like a menu from which we can choose what suits us best at any given moment: "Hi, welcome to Judaism. Can I take your order? Today you can choose to love God with all your mind, *or* with all your heart, *or* with all your soul." No. To be a Jew requires the full engagement of our mind, heart, and soul; a soul which is created when the mind and the heart wrestle. For in that moment of tension we truly fulfill the Torah's mandate to be *Yisrael*, literally "wrestler(s) with God."

It seems appropriate, therefore, that in all moments of mystery – those found in this portion or those which occur as part of our living Judaism, such as the "laying of hands" – that we neither blindly accept them as meaningful nor turn a blind eye to them as meaningless. Rather, in order to stand firmly in that moment of mystery as Jews let us straddle both sides: intellectually pursuing meaning in mystery and allowing the mystery to be meaningful.

---

[89] *Pesikta de-Rav Kahnana* 4:7
[90] Deuteronomy 6:5

Chukkat // The Law
Bite 2 – *Retelling Our Story of Survival*

Defiance, *The Pianist*, *Schindler's List*, *The Boy in the Striped Pajamas*. The list of movies about the Holocaust could go on and on. But, some wish it wouldn't. This desire is not by Holocaust-deniers or neo-Nazis per se, nor is it solely by individuals who simply wish to move on from such a dark moment in history. Rather, the desire to stop producing Holocaust films strikingly comes from those who wish to remember it... though not as a piece of dramatic entertainment but as a real event which scarred the lives of millions. Others, however, argue that such dramatic means actually help keep the event and its enduring lessons alive for the next generation. For soon, they acknowledge, there will be none left who experienced the Holocaust firsthand.

Notably, it is the transition of a generation that created a similar concern for our Israelite ancestors in this Torah portion of *Chukkat*. After being told that the generation who left Egypt will not live to enter the Promised Land because of their lack of faith in God (save Caleb and Joshua), Moses and Aaron learn – on the heels of Miriam's passing – that their fate shall be the same.[91] Because, rather than fulfilling the word of God by speaking to the rock to issue its water, Moses (with Aaron standing idly by) struck it, not once but twice. And, as a result of not affirming God in word or deed, the Lord informs Moses and Aaron that "you shall not lead this congregation into the land that I have given to them." (Numbers 20:1-13)

Like our beloved Holocaust survivors, the passing of this generation in the wilderness presents the people with a serious challenge. How do you keep the momentum of the people going without a deeply personal experience? That is to say, without having experienced slavery firsthand, where will the next generation find the strength needed to overcome the obstacles encountered on their way to achieving peace and freedom for all? According to modern Biblical commentator, Jacob Milgrom, it is to be found in the retelling of the story of the Exodus. Upon his reflection of the passage, Milgrom wrote: "Soon there will be no Israelites left who actually stood at Sinai." Nevertheless, their journey of freedom will continue through those "Israelites who have heard about [the struggles] from parents and grandparents."[92]

As both parents and teachers, we can appreciate Milgrom's lesson as so much more than ensuring the survival of a story. It is, in fact, a story of survival: ours, as we have come to appreciate intergenerational story telling as a tactic for our continued existence as a people. After all, does not the *yeshiva* (school) of Crosby, Stills, Nash, and Young say: "Teach your children well, their father's hell did slowly go by."[93] Okay, while not Biblical in origin, this statement might as well be. For as we are reminded every year at Passover, four times

---

[91] Numbers 14:22-23
[92] Jacob Milgrom. *Etz Hayim: Torah and Commentary*. The Rabbinical Assembly: New York, 2001. p. 880
[93] Crosby, Stills, Nash and Young. "Teach Your Children." *Déjà Vu*. Atlantic Records: 1970.

does the Bible instruct us to teach our children the story of the Exodus. As it is written: "You shall say to your children, 'We were slaves to Pharaoh in Egypt and the Lord freed us from there with a mighty hand.'"

Why four? Well, according to tradition, it is because there are four types of learners: the eager student, the reluctant student, the passive student and the shy student. And, as teachers, we are encouraged to adapt our teaching styles to reach each of them. But, that is not the only reason we repeat the story so many times. It is also because something is always, as writer and director Sofia Coppola would say, "lost in translation."[94] I mean, how many times has some supposedly hilarious story been met by an awkward silence, which is then broken by the words: "Well, I suppose you had to be there." To make up for our absence at such events, some maintain that is why we repeat the story. For then, potentially, one can comprehend what was missed the first time through.

Though, even in retelling the story, it is unlikely to evoke the emotional response desired. This is true particularly if the story is retold in the same exact way. Because, as we know intimately well as parents and teachers, we are competing with a whole new level of technology that is more interactive and engaging than the mere sound of a voice. But rather than throwing in the *tallit* in defeat, we can and should see this and all moments of transition not as challenges, but as moments of opportunity. Specifically, here, we can take the technology which is drowning out our voices and use it to amplify our message.

This, for example, has wonderfully transpired at the ISJL. In addition to our Webinar series, I – as the ISJL Rabbi – am blessed to officiate over B'nai Mitzvah ceremonies. Though, before these events, I very rarely have an in-person lesson with any one of them. This feat, which is now taking place all over the world, was accomplished through the use of Skype, a handy computer program which – in addition to hearing the student – allows me to see the student and the student to see me. In his Bar Mitzvah speech, one student remarked: "Thank you Skype... when you actually worked!"

Yes. As with most forms of advanced technology, some bugs always remain. The same can be said with regards to challenges: with every one overcome, there will remain more ahead. But, we have the capacity to address this challenge presented by the soon-to-be departure of our survivors, whether from the Exodus in Egypt or the Holocaust in Europe. Through the media of movies and mobile technology, we can breathe new life into old stories. Through iTunes, YouTube, Skype and other advances yet to be dreamt of, future generations will not merely come to hear these stories of our survival. They will engage and interact with them, making some past moment presently and personally meaningful. And, as a result – we pray – the enduring lessons of these real events will be lived, that our journey from slavery to freedom will endure, that the story of our people will continue.

---

[94] Sofia Coppola. *Lost in Translation*. Focus Features: 2003.

Chukkat // The Law
Bite 3 – *Stand-by to Stand-up*

In the finale of the sitcom *Seinfeld*, Jerry Seinfeld and George Costanza are faced with having to leave New York for California after finally striking a deal with NBC. Before leaving, they decide to take NBC's private jet to Paris with their friends – Elaine and Kramer – for one last hurrah. Unfortunately, due to Kramer's antics, the plane veers wildly out of control, nearly killing the four friends in a crash. Stranded in Massachusetts, waiting for the plane to be repaired, they witness an overweight man getting carjacked at gunpoint. Instead of helping him, they crack jokes about his size as Kramer – with camcorder in hand – films the entire encounter. The victim of the event notices their apathy and reports this to the responding officer. Immediately, the four friends are taken into custody. Their crime, fitting for this sitcom about nothing, was for "doing nothing."[95]

As unique as this charge may be, it is not without precedent. After Miriam dies and the community is left without water in this Torah portion of *Chukkat*, God commands Moses to "take the rod and assemble the community. And, before their very eyes, speak to the rock to yield its water. Thus you shall produce water for them, providing drink for the congregation and their beasts." (Numbers 20:8) But Moses, with Aaron standing idly by, did not do as God had asked. Instead of speaking to the stone, "Moses raised his hand and struck the stone [not once, but] twice with his staff." (Numbers 20:11) As a result of his failure to affirm "God's sanctity in the sight of the Israelite people," God tells Moses, "you shall not lead this congregation into the land that I have given them... [As well,] Aaron shall be gathered with his kin. He too shall not enter the land that I have assigned to the people of Israel, because you [Moses] disobeyed My command." (Numbers 20:12 & 24)

"Wait a moment!" as I imagine tennis star John McEnroe yelling: "You cannot be serious!" This punishment, doled out by God, hardly seems fair... especially not for Aaron! Sure, one could argue – as it has been argued by the rabbis – that Moses' punishment was just, as he lost his temper and lessened the miracle set up by God.[96] But why is Aaron punished? Why must he also die? After all, he did absolutely nothing! "Acha!" states modern Biblical commentator Jacob Milgrom. He did nothing. "After the first strike, Aaron could [and should] have stopped Moses from repeating his error, but," says Milgrom, "he did not."[97] Thus, it is concluded, that Aaron was as guilty as Moses, for it is not always what we do that can get us into trouble. Sometimes, it is what we don't do that can put our very lives in jeopardy.

---

[95] *Seinfeld*. "The Finale: Part 1" Season 9: Episode 179. 14 May 1998
[96] BT Pesachim 66b, "When a prophet loses his temper, his gift of prophecy abandons him." See also RaMBaN's extended commentary on Numbers 20:1and 20:8-10.
[97] Jacob Milgrom. "Numbers." *Etz Hayim: Torah and Commentary*. The Rabbinical Assembly: New York, 2001. p. 885

Like...standing by when God would have us stand up. This isn't just a work of fiction, as it was in Seinfeld. Sadly, there are a plethora of real life circumstances from which these fictional stories are based. Some are obvious. Yet others – like the one in this Torah portion – are more subtle; scenarios in which only after they pass do we turn back to ask: Why didn't I do something? Why didn't I speak up against that hateful word or offensive joke? Why didn't I act when I saw someone in need or someone being accosted? And often, the answer we give is "...because I was afraid." I was afraid that it wasn't my place. I was afraid that I would fail. I was afraid that I too would be hurt. I was afraid for myself.

And while these responses are saturated with selfishness, the great sage Hillel comes to teach that being selfish isn't always sinful. It's only sinful if – in addition to asking "if I am not for me, who will be" – we don't also ask: "If I am only for myself, then what am I?"[98] For, as this portion presents, we are communal creatures. We should not live by the primal principle of the 'survival of the fittest,' because when one of us falls, we all stand to fall. When we allow another's life to pass us by, we also permit others to pass us by. And the consequences of this inaction are disastrous, as presented in the famous poem, *First They Came*, by Martin Neimoller. Written in 1946, the poem states:

> First they came for the Communists, and I didn't speak up because I was not a Communist. Then they came for the Trade Unionists, and I didn't speak up because I was not a Trade Unionist. Then they came for the Jews, and I did not speak up, because I was not a Jew. Then they came for me, but – by that time – there was no one left to speak up.

But, it's not too late for us. There is still time to have our voices heard, still time to have our actions counted as a blessing in the lives of others. And, that time is none other than now, as Hillel rhetorically concluded his three fold teaching: "If not now, then when?"[99] In his way, Hillel recognized that there will never be a moment when all our personal fears will be fettered, no moment when all our apprehension will be annihilated. There will never be a moment we can affect that won't have an effect upon us. And if we were to wait, then – as the White Rabbit from *Alice in Wonderland* stated – we would indeed miss a very important date; a moment to stand up and affirm our Divine potential. Not merely as we attempt to help and save one life, but – as the rabbis of the *Jerusalem Talmud* understood it – "he/she who helps save even one life, it is as if he/she has helped save the entire world."[100]

This may explain why both Aaron and Seinfeld (along with his friends) are punished so severely. Whether it was God or the responding police officer, the dramatic reaction made was not because these key characters in our stories

---

[98] Pirkei Avot 1:14
[99] *Ibid.*
[100] *Jerusalem Talmud*, Sanhedrin 4:1 (22a). See also: Pirkei deRabbi Eliezer, ch. 47; Eliyahu Rabbah 11; Yalkut Shimoni on Exodus 166; and *Babylonian Talmud*, Sanhedrin 37a

simply did nothing, as another individual faltered. But, because they did nothing, they put our entire world in jeopardy of faltering...a crime worthy of punishment. We shall not make the same mistake. Through this portion of *Chukkat*, God is putting us on stand-by, warning us that at any moment we could be called upon to stand-up to help another in need. May we be ready and willing to face that moment with courage. For by helping to support one another, we ultimately help support our entire world. May we never be by-standers, but people standing-by ready; willing, and able to lend a helping hand.

Portion 7:
Balak // Balak
Torah Portion: Numbers 22:2-25:9

"BALAK...SAW ALL THAT ISRAEL HAD DONE TO THE AMORITES." It was not pretty. Thus Balak, king of Moab, feared the Israelites. Attempting to make a preemptive strike, Balak sends messengers to the prophet Bilam, asking him to curse this nation that dwells apart. Initially he refused. But, when Balak's messengers beseech him a second time, Bilam agrees and goes with God's blessings.

Traveling to Moab on his donkey, Bilam's path becomes blocked by a sword-bearing angel. Bilam cannot see this Divine messenger though his donkey can, halting her motion. Frustrated, Bilam beats his donkey. In a humorous scene, the donkey asks Bilam, "What have I done to you that you have beaten me?" (Numbers 22:28) God then uncovers Bilam's eyes and he sees the angel, who instructs Bilam to prophesy only what God tells him.

Balak brings Bilam to a mountain peak overlooking the Israelite encampment. Expecting a curse, Balak instead hears Bilam give Israel God's blessing. Surprised and angry, Balak brings Bilam closer to the people, where again Bilam blesses them! Balak tries once more, bringing Bilam even closer to the Israelites. Standing on the peak of Peor, Bilam views them encamped tribe-by-tribe. There he blesses them with the famous words, "How fair are your tents, O Jacob, Your dwellings, O Israel!" (Numbers 24:5)

The Israelite encampment, however, is not as idyllic as Bilam portrays. The Israelites profane themselves by whoring with Moabite women, who invite the people to sacrifice to their false deities. God instructs Moses to publicly impale the ringleaders and slay the idolaters. The portion ends with Pinchas, son of Eleazar, arising to impale an Israelite man and a Midianite woman, thereby stopping the plague that had ravaged the people on account of their sins.

Balak // Balak
Bite 1 – *My Foe is My Friend*

"It has been said that if you do not know your enemy nor do you know yourself, you will be imperiled in every single battle." It has been said that "if you do not know your enemy, but you do know yourself, you will win one out of every two battles." And, it has been said that "if you know both your enemy and you know yourself, you will not be imperiled even in a hundred battles," for then these battles may not be.[101] These wise words of war were written in the 6th century before the Common Era by the Chinese military strategist Sun Tzu in his book, *The Art of War*, which – one may surmise – must have been nightly reading for Michael Corleone from the movie *The Godfather - Part II*, as he poignantly summarized Sun Tzu's teaching in the now infamous line: "You should keep your friends close, but your enemies even closer."[102]

Gradually getting closer and closer to your enemy is exactly what transpires in this Torah portion of *Balak*. Accompanied by a certain talking donkey (not the one from *Shrek*), this Torah portion tells of the non-Israelite prophet Bilam's infamous ride from Petorah to the frontier of Moab to curse the people Israel after the King of Moab perceived them as a threat, thereby making Israel his enemy. As the story goes, each time Bilam approached closer and closer to Israel and opened his mouth to curse the people, a blessing issued forth: "*Mah tovu ohalecha Yaakov, mishk'notecha Yisrael* / How good are your tents, O Jacob; your dwellings, O Israel!" (Numbers 24:5) Enraged, the King of Moab raised his voice to Bilam, saying: "I called you to damn my enemies, and instead you have blessed them three times!" (Numbers 24:10)

How could this be? How could Bilam go from standing against Israel to standing with them? According to the Bible, the divergent forces of Israel and Bilam were brought together by an external pressure: God. As Bilam explained to the King of Moab, "I could not on my own accord do anything good or bad....Only what the Lord says, that I must say!"[103] In fact, from his testimony, the *midrashic* sages concluded that Bilam had not really changed at all. He remained an oppositional force to Israel, even as he blessed them, for "it was the Lord who put those words into Bilam's mouth, like a rider who puts a bit into the mouth of a stubborn horse, directing him where he pleases."[104] For the Lord understood, what Michael Corleone understood, that while we should "keep our friends close, [it is wiser to steer our] enemies even closer."

Why? What purpose does this intimacy serve? The most common answer given to this question is "to gain valuable intelligence," as intimacy fosters a feeling of relative safety whereby our enemies' guard is lowered and thereby we can study and understand them in relation to ourselves with ample opportunity; a response, by the way, which is entirely correct. But, then we

---

[101] Sun Tzu. *The Art of War*. Chapter 3
[102] Francis Ford Coppola and Mario Puzo. *The Godfather - Part 2*. Paramount Pictures: 1974.
[103] Numbers 24:13
[104] Numbers Rabbah 20:20

make a mistake. All too often, out of fear or frustration, we misuse the insights gained from our enemies to exploit their weaknesses and defend ourselves against their strengths. In other words, we use it to tear down, tear apart and destroy, when – according to Judaism – we should use the intelligence gained in these close-encounters with our enemies to repair, to build and even to grow... together! It's a lesson brilliantly highlighted in the following story from our tradition.

> Shimon ben Lakish, better known as Resh Lakish (one of the most prominent sages of the 2nd century) had a questionable past. Abandoned at an early age, some say he became a Roman gladiator.[105] Others profess he was a thief.[106] In either case, one day – along a narrow road – his threatening presence confronted the famed master sage of the second century C.E., the gentle Rabbi Yochanan.
>
> "My brother, where are you going?" asked Rabbi Yochanan. "To kill or to be killed?" Resh Lakish responded. "What does it matter? Life is fleeting. But in death there is life and glory eternal."
>
> Resh Lakish's response startled Rabbi Yochanan. He sensed something soft behind the tough exterior, a keen intelligence and perhaps even a longing to be loved. "Come, my brother," said Rabbi Yochanan. "There is another way to life eternal." Although hesitant, Resh Lakish too saw something unexpected in Rabbi Yochanan. Rather than fear, he saw in the Torah scholar's eyes a strength and serenity unlike any maintained by even his fiercest opponents.
>
> Though they never stopped opposing one another, in that instance, these two divergent forces on the path of life became intertwined, joining one another in the study of Torah. Every time Rabbi Yochanan would offer up an interpretation, Resh Lakish would challenge him. And, when Resh Lakish would offer up an interpretation, Rabbi Yochanan would challenge him.
>
> Until one day, Resh Lakish died. So grieved was Rabbi Yochanan over the loss of his opposing friend that he could not bring himself to study in the assembly. Other scholars from near and far were brought in to rekindle Rabbi Yochanan's spirit. But, none succeeded.
>
> Finally, Rabbi Yochanan's grief and frustration overcame him. He yelled: "Is there anyone like Resh Lakish?! When I would state a matter, Resh Lakish used to raise twenty-four objections, which I would then respond with twenty-four rebuttals, forming a debate that led to further comprehension of our traditions. But all y'all could

---

[105] BT Gittin 47a

[106] BT Bava Mitzia 84a; See also *Sefer Ha-Aggadah*, edited by Bialik and Ravnitzky, which notes that "this was quoted only proverbially [in a *midrash*], though in later times it was taken literally." p. 284

offer in response was "there is a *baraita* (a teaching) that supports you."

Thereupon, Rabbi Yochanan burst into tears, rent his garments, and sat on the floor, mourning another loss on top of his foe, who he saw as friend.

"What additional loss?" you may ask. The one that will undoubtedly come to our people without oppositional force. For like the resistance of weight which builds muscle, the muscle of our minds, hearts and souls are similarly strengthened when challenged. Therefore, let us bring hope and strength to Rabbi Yochanan and all our people. Rather than waiting for some external force to bring us together, let us – on our own accord – actively seek out people with whom we don't see eye-to-eye. For, in forming these types of oppositional, yet respectful relationships, we can gain a wider perspective on our world and a deeper appreciation of our place therein. When we bring our enemies close, seeing the foe and friend, then – like Bilam – may all our curses in life become blessings, which issue forth unrestrained.

Balak // Balak
Bite 2 – *The Ripple Effect*

"Water, water everywhere, and not a drop to drink."[107] "Like a bridge over troubled waters..."[108] "Don't go chasing waterfalls. Please stick to the rivers and the lakes that you're used to."[109] Today, through our music, through our poetry, through our art, we are drowning in water imagery. Even in our common speech this imagery is everywhere; for example – we often avoid "getting into hot water" and attempt to "keep our heads above water." We use this and other such metaphors to paint our emotions in sparkling blue language, whetting listeners' and readers' appetites for more.

But, it's not just us. The sorcerer Bilam uses similar imagery in this portion of *Balak*. Originally sent by King Balak to curse the budding Israelite nation, Bilam is inspired by God to bless them instead. As part of his third blessing of the Israelites, Bilam compares them to "palm trees [saying that they] stretch out / like gardens beside a river / like aloes planted by the Lord / like cedars beside the water. Their boughs drip with moisture / their roots have abundant water." (Numbers 24:6-7) These poetic lines are ripe with repetitive similes commenting on the Israelites' growth and, more importantly, their potential to grow even further.

Commentators from the classic period to the modern period read these poetic verses and expanded on their symbolic meaning. For example, Sforno (1475-

---

[107] Samuel Taylor Coleridge. "Rhyme of the Ancient Mariner." *Lyrical Ballads.* 1798
[108] Simon and Garfunkel. "Bridge Over Troubled Waters." *Bridge Over Troubled Waters.* Columbia Rec.: 1969
[109] TLC. "Waterfalls." *CrazySexyCool.* LaFace Records: 1995

1550) understood the winding of the water and streams to be illustrative of how prayer and study expand far beyond their source; that both prayer and study flow through the people, giving life and inspiration to whomever they touch.[110] But, this life-giving current is not just with prayer and study. It is also with acts of loving-kindness. For even the smallest good deed can have a huge impact, making a world of difference.

Unfortunately, this is not how we typically view our actions. We often think that one small act will make no difference. Either we are waiting for that one impossible moment to change the whole world, or – more likely – we don't see our own actions as having an impact. We choose to pass up the small opportunities to do good. It could be as simple as ignoring a piece of trash we find on the ground. After all, when forest fires and oil spills dirty our natural world, that little garbage seems insignificant in the end, right? Perhaps, it is easier to look unhappily at a problem than it is to correct it.

In either case, we are more likely to ask, "What can *I* do?" than to say "I need to do what I can." In the opening scenes of *Peter Pan*, Wendy does all that she can, sewing Peter's shadow onto his feet. Although Peter thanks her for her generosity, she dismisses him, saying: "I did nothing…" But, Peter is quick to respond: "No. You did a little."[111] That little action, seemingly small and insignificant, did have the power to create change. While it may not be immediately evident in the story of Peter, it is clearly recognizable in the deed of Rosa Parks.

On December 1, 1955, Ms. Parks refused to give up her seat on a segregated bus in Montgomery, AL. She was arrested and charged with disorderly conduct. Thereupon, the black American community rallied behind her with a boycott of the Montgomery Bus Line; an act which eventually blossomed into the Civil Rights Movement. Upon Rosa Park's death in 2005, U.S. Representative John Lewis said in an interview on NPR: "A very simple act was an act of civil disobedience, non-violent resistance that carried a very powerful and very strong message…not only in Montgomery, but all across the South and all across America."[112]

Although we may not believe so, any little act has the power to do the same, for within it is the potential to set everything into motion. Like the flap of a butterfly's wings which can create a windstorm around the world, or a drop of water that can ripple across an ocean as a mighty wave, our good deeds will inspire others to act. From one, will come another, which will lead to another, to another, to another, until the whole ocean is brewing with excitement. From that one small first deed will swell a tour de force of positive actions. If everyone created their own little drop, the world would be overwhelmed with positive change. May we be the small but significant drop of water that creates

---

[110] Sforno's comment to Numbers 24:6
[111] From J. M. Barrie's *Peter and Wendy*, first published in 1911
[112] *All Things Considered* from NPR News, hosted by Richard Siegel and Melissa Block, October 25, 2005

ripples in the ocean. May we constantly do the little actions because they can have a big impact. For drop by drop we can and will change the world.

Balak // Balak
Bite 3 – *The Others in our Midst*

I loved watching the television show *Lost*. Each twist and turn excited me, and I often found myself shouting warnings at the fictional characters on screen. In my own living room I would yell, "Watch out Hurley! Others! The Others are behind you!" "The Others," for those that haven't seen *Lost*, was a name coined by the protagonists of the show to refer to a different group of people who also dwelled on the island where the show is set. Their name alone makes it clear that this group of people was not accepted. They were mysterious, secretive, and therefore should not be trusted. However, like all good plot twists, The Others eventually played a crucial role in helping to understand the mysteries of the island as well as the protagonists' place therein.

Our ancestors dealt with Others as well. In this Torah portion of *Balak,* we learn of various encounters between the Israelites and other peoples. Balak, the Moabite king, feels threatened by the power of the neighboring Israelite tribes and summons a non-Israelite sorcerer Bilam to enter their tents and curse them. Viewing the camp of the Israelites three different times, Bilam tries to curse the people but instead bestows the familiar blessing: "*Mah tovu ohalecha Yaakov, mishk'notecha, Yisrael,* How fair are your tents, O Jacob, your dwelling places O Israel." (Numbers 24:5)

There is a tension in this portion about the role of insider and outsider. After all, King Balak is threatened by the strange group of outsiders: the Israelites, a people "who dwell apart."[113] Bilam is both an outsider to Balak, coming from Pethor, and a visitor to the Israelite's camp. In fact, Balak insists that Bilam view the Israelite camp only from the outside, the summit of Pisgah, in order that his view is partial, making the camp seem less remarkable. Even the blessing that Bilam bestows is a play on what is inside and outside. The Ba'al Shem Tov teaches that when Bilam describes "Your tents," it is a comment only about the external appearance of the camp, however, "your dwelling places" refer to the interior.[114] The blessing of Bilam and the role of insider and outsider makes us think about those who are considered "in" and "out" of the Jewish community. We learn from Bilam that it is often the "outsiders" who are welcomed in, that have the potential to shed new perspectives on how we think about ourselves as a Jewish community.

---

[113] Numbers 23:9

[114] The Ba'al Shem Tov also compares the wording of Jacob to Israel, implying that the interior dwelling places are worthy of more blessing by being called Israel. (Ba'al Shem Tov, cited in Aharon Yaakov Greenberg, *Torah Gems*, vol. 3 [Tel Aviv: Y. Orenstein, Yavneh Publishing House, 1998], p. 128) from Leslie Silverstone "Curses and Blessings" www.urj.org

The Jewish community has benefited from allowing outsiders to be insiders. Forty years ago, The Hebrew Union College-Jewish Institute of Religion opened its doors to the first female rabbinic student named Sally Priesand.[115] And now, walking through the hallways of rabbinical schools, sitting on organizational boards, and holding down synagogue leadership positions, one can see many more females in Jewish life. And opening the door to one group, helped open the gates for others – people who have chosen Judaism, Jews of color, Jews from different countries, and Jews with varying sexual orientations – everyone who has the dedication and desire to serve the Jewish people are affirmed. These new "insiders" have brought with them new perspectives to Judaism. Jewish Feminists have added scholarly perspectives that incorporate women's experiences and history into our text tradition, while the lesbian, gay, bisexual, and transgender Jewish Community has offered creative and insightful "queer" takes on our Torah.[116] Broadening the access into Judaism gives more education to all and gives all individuals more power over their own Jewish choices. The more we welcome into our community those who have been previously marginalized, the more we are able to gain new insights about our ancient tradition and what it means to be Jewish today. Our job as Jews is to make the "Other" an "Us," affirming that variety is the spice of Jewish life.

Of course, there will always be naysayers. There will be those members of our communities who feel that preserving the "status-quo" of our communities is equivalent to preserving some kind of "more authentic" Jewish tradition. We see this in our portion to the extreme. At the end of *Balak* we encounter Pinchas, a man who is unnerved when he sees an Israelite man in public with a Moabite woman. He was so unnerved in fact that he acts as a vigilante for the Israelite cause and violently murders the man and woman. RaSHI, expounding on this story, tells us that Pinchas approached Moses when he saw this man and woman together. Pinchas asked Moses, "Is this woman forbidden or permitted?"[117] In essence, Pinchas articulates our own human need to know who is "in" and who is "out." Insider and outsider boundaries help us define our own group identities but we must be careful not to be like Pinchas. In a contemporary world where identities are more fluid, it is all the more important that we keep those boundaries fluid as well.

I too am experiencing life as an outsider turned insider. For those of you that don't know, I am interning with the ISJL for the summer, but I'm a northerner, having lived in New York for my entire life. Spending the summer in Jackson, Mississippi has taken me out of my comfort zone and allowed me to meet many new people and expand my own personal understanding of Judaism and the Jewish community. In New York City, "everyone is Jewish, even if they are not." It is not uncommon for me to hear a non-Jew "schlep" to Brooklyn or order their bagel with lox and "shmear." Down here, meeting

---

[115] In the Conservative movement, Amy Eilberg, In the Reconstructionist movement, Sandy Eisenberg Sasso
[116] Gregg Drinkwater, Joshua Lesser, David Shneer. *Torah Queeries: Weekly Commentaries on the Hebrew Bible.* New York: New York University Press, 2009.
[117] RaSHI commentary to Numbers 25:6

another Jew is like entering a club that has a secret password. Connecting with other Jews in the South makes me feel like I have insider knowledge to a special culture and group of people. It has made me reaffirm the privilege and pride it is to be Jewish.

Like the characters from the TV show, *Lost*, we need the Other to know how to identify as a group. But also like the show, we eventually need to open ourselves up and welcome others in order to learn and grow as a group. The RaMBAN teaches that God's purpose in guiding Bilam was to promote brotherhood and friendship between peoples and displace hatred and rivalry.[118] By better understanding the role of the "other" in the Jewish world, we redefine what it means to be a Jewish community. May we all find the ability to welcome others into the open tent of Judaism.

---

[118] Nehama Leibowitz. *Studies in Bamidbar*. Israel: Maor Wallach Press P. 310

Portion 8:
Pinchas // Phineas
Torah Portion: Numbers 25:10-30:1

"PINCHAS…HAS TURNED BACK MY WRATH FROM THE ISRAELITES…" This portion picks up where the last one left off, with the fatal spearing by Pinchas of an Israelite man and the Midianite woman. By this act, Pinchas is credited as stemming God's plague against the Israelites for his display of passion against mixing with non-Israelite peoples.

Though, with the community decimated, God instructs Moses and Eleazar to take a new census of the Israelite community, so that they may know how many men remain who can bear arms. Oddly, one woman is mentioned in this census: Serach bat Asher. She, along with Caleb and Joshua, are the only individuals left from the Egyptian exodus. Looking forward, God then instructs that the land of Israel be apportioned to each tribe according to that tribe's size.

Picking up on the theme of land allotments, the daughters of Zelophechad make an appeal before Moses. Their father had passed, leaving no sons to inherit his portion. Therefore, they asked that their father's inheritance be passed onto them. Moses brings their case to God, who decrees that their plea is just. God decrees that if a man dies without leaving a son, the property shall go to his daughter.

As the Israelites camp on the far side of the Jordan, God instructs Moses to ascend the heights of Abirim and view the land of Israel from afar. When Moses has seen it, he will pass away. Though, before he departs, Moses appeals to God to appoint his successor, so that God's community "may not be like sheep that have no shepherd." (Numbers 27:17) God singles out Joshua son of Nun. Thereby, a peaceful transition of leadership commences.

The portion concludes by describing the various daily, Shabbat, new moon, and festival sacrificial offerings.

Pinchas // Phineas
Bite 1 – *United We Stand*

Upon celebrating the birthday of these United States, it is apt to point out that one sentence – above all others – gave our American patriarchs the impetus to bore this land of the free and this home of the brave. As it is stated in the Declaration of Independence, "When a long train of abuses and usurpations, pursuing invariably the same Object evinces a design to reduce them under absolute Despotism, it is their right, it is their duty, to throw off such Government, and to provide new Guards for their future security." In other words, our founding fathers believed that those who have the ability to act also have the responsibility to act.

That is certainly the message the story of Pinchas presents at the very beginning of this portion, as he violently throws off the old guard and ascends as the new leader of the priesthood. At the end of the previous portion, Pinchas – seeing an Israelite man take a Midianite woman as a companion – left Moses and left the assembly of Israel to act on his own and stab both the Israelite man and Midianite woman to death. For God had warned not to cohabitate with the Midianite women. Now, a portion later, we read that Pinchas is rewarded with the Covenant of Peace and the priesthood, "because he took zealous action for his God." (Numbers 25:23)

There is a lot that is intriguing about this episode in our Biblical text. Not least among them is part of the statement which includes the words: "for *his* God." Why not say, 'for *their* God,' or 'for *our* God,' or simpler yet 'for God.' According to Rabbi Menachem Esh in his early 20th century commentary *Homat Esh*, "It does not say 'for God' but 'for *his* God' because Pinchas at that moment felt it was his personal responsibility – and that he alone had – to sanctify God's name, even though those greater than he stood by his side." But, just because we have the *ability* to act, and thus feel the personal *responsibility* to act, does not mean that we have the personal *right* to act. For, as we are all well aware, to be a Jew is to be part of a Jewish community which guides us to temper our personal convictions and inclinations with communal expectations.

From David versus Goliath to Daniel Larusso versus the Cobra Kai in the 80's movie *The Karate Kid*, we have reveled in the stories where and when the heart and soul of the little guy triumphs over the physical might of the giant. Such stories – whether in the written word or in film – not only move our hearts, they also have the ability to move our bodies as we are inspired to stand up and take responsibility for our own histories. For example on December 1, 1955 the then 42 year-old Rosa Parks refused to move from her seat on the Montgomery City bus, igniting the Civil Rights Movement. And even now, half way around the world, Iranian protesters who, in the face of horrific violence and harsh prison time, continue to stand up for Democracy.

It's no wonder why we get caught up in these David and Goliath stories, since we, the Jewish people, epitomize – at least in number – history's small guy. The simple fact that we are still here today is considered by many people, Jews and non-Jews alike, a miracle and the clearest evidence of God's existence in this world. A fact that is not lost in the prayers of our people as we praise God for the "miraculous" victories which occurred on Purim, Chanukah, and Yom Ha'atzmaut (Israel Independence Day) with the words: "You delivered the strong into the hands of the weak, the many into the hands of the few, the impure into the hands of the pure, the wicked into the hands of the righteous, and the sluggard into the hands of those engaged in Torah."

Yet, while Judaism preserves such stories in the Biblical and liturgical texts of our people to inspire us in the face of the larger nations which have continued to surround us, our tradition cautions us from acting as Pinchas acted. According to Rabbi Y. L. Maimon, a mid-20th century religious Zionist, "The law is that a person who asks whether he can act as Pinchas did is told that he may not follow that example." How is this conclusion made? The lesson actually comes from two unique apparitions in the hand-writing of our portion in the Torah scroll. The first is the *yod* in Pinchas' name, which is written smaller than other *yod*'s in the Scroll (25:11). This is to teach us that a person who takes it upon him/herself to sanctify God's name without consulting or working with his/her community actually decreases the *yod* (standing for the name of God and/or *yehudut*, meaning 'Judaism') in him/herself. Additionally, we know not to follow Pinchas' example, because the *vav* in the word *shalom* (meaning 'peace' – 25:12) is purposefully written with a break in the stem. It is as if to say that when we work alone the job can never be complete.

These lessons should come as no surprise. As Bob Marley sang in his song, *Exodus*, Judaism has and will always be about "the movement of a people." Maybe that is why we do not call the different communities of Judaism 'denominations,' but rather 'Movements,' emphasizing that while we may have different paths we are collectively moving in the same direction: towards God and the sanctification of God's name on earth. Because, from the Exodus until today, our very survival has been based upon our uncanny ability to come together and create community in the most unlikely of places: from the sands of the Middle East to the deep rural south of America. There is no place, no outside force, that could break the bonds of our collective Jewish community. Let us not break these bonds from the inside either by choosing to act alone. It is not that we belong to the community, per se, but the community *does* belong to us and we have not only the *ability* and thus the *responsibility* to protect it, but we also have the indelible *right* to protect it. Let us, as our American forefathers stood up for their rights, stand up for ours as well.

Pinchas // Phineas
Bite 2 – *Up, Up and Oy Vey: The Adventures of Serach bat Asher*

It's a bird! It's a plane! No, it's Superbubbie![119] Yes, ladies and gentleman, she's faster than a speeding shopping cart; she's more powerful than the most potent of chicken soups; she's smarter than a TI-82 graphics calculator; and she is capable of leaping tall piles of dirty laundry in a single bound.[120] She is none other than Superbubbie; rowdy toddlers, everywhere, beware! Although the analogy drawn here may seem humorous, this super wise old woman has a lot in common with one of the most elusive Jewish superheroes of the Bible, whose secret identity is finally revealed in this Torah portion of *Pinchas*.

Yes, attempting to conceal herself within a part of the portion that is often overlooked, we find this ancient superhero's real name hidden among others as part of a census, which comes just after the shocking actions of Pinchas, who kills an Israelite man and a Moabite woman, and just before the exciting exchange between Zelophechad's daughters and Moses. Upon counting the descendants of Jacob's sons Reuben, Simeon, Gad, Judah, Issachar, Zebulun, Joseph, Benjamin, and Dan, we finally get to "the descendants of Asher: the clan of Yimnites, the clan of Yishvites, the clan of Beri-ites… and," adds the Bible, "Asher's daughter, Serach." (Numbers 26:46)

Now, what's exciting about this revelation isn't simply that a woman's name is mentioned. On the rare occasion, women were included in such accountings.[121] No, what's really exciting is that Serach's name appears twice, in two separate censuses, which occur over 400 years apart! As it is written back in the book of Genesis, Serach, daughter of Asher, was one of the "70 souls of Jacob's household who came to Egypt."[122] As such, the sages transformed Serach bat Asher into one of the longest living individuals in *midrashic* literature, as a wise old superhero, who helps the children of Israel time and time again, embodying values we may wish to emulate.[123]

Like all good superheroes, Serach bat Asher has a cool origin story. It all started when her uncles received word that their brother Joseph was alive and well in Egypt. Yet, none of them – out of fear – would tell their father Jacob. Serach, however, could not allow her grandfather to remain in mourning for a son who was not dead. At a very tender age, she decided to break the difficult news to Jacob in song. Rather than sending him into a fit, her comforting tone brought him hope and joy. And for that, state the sages, Jacob blessed her with

---

[119] Bubbie is a Yiddish word for "grandmother." Zaydie is Yiddish for "grandfather."
[120] This wording is adapted from a phrase about Superman's character, first coined by Jay Morton and first used in the *Superman* radio series of the 1940s.
[121] For example, in Genesis 46:15, Jacob's daughter Dinah is mentioned.
[122] Genesis 46:8-27; specifically she is noted in Genesis 46:17 – "Asher's sons: Yimnah, Yishvah, Yishvi, Beriah and their sister Serach."
[123] *Midrash* is a general title given to a large body of various rabbinic texts, which attempt to explain provocative parts of the Bible via story telling.

longevity. "My child," conveyed Jacob, "may death never rule over you, for you brought my spirit back to life."[124]

With the blessing of long-life and the amazing powers of compassion, Serach bat Asher's status as a superhero for her people would be solidified in our great struggle for freedom in Egypt. According to the legend, the spirits of Abraham, Isaac, Jacob and her own father Asher visited her one night, bestowing upon her superhuman wisdom, known as "The Secret of Redemption."[125] She and she alone would know how to identify the true redeemer of Israel. So that, when Moses announced to the people that "God will surely visit you," as opposed to "redeem you," it was Serach who confirmed their suspicions, saying: "This indeed is the man who visits us to redeem us, so taught my fathers."[126]

Ah, the clear voice of reason! How many of our bubbies are like that! And like them, the task of Superbubbie, Serach bat Asher, never seems complete. Before departing Egypt, she is attributed as having shown Moses where the Egyptians hid the bones of Joseph.[127] Serach is also identified as the "old wise woman" during the time of King David who saved the town of Avel from attacks, for she came forward as "one of the peaceful and faithful of Israel."[128] And, amazingly, the sages also explain how Serach appeared in their own day, correcting an influential rabbi's misconception about how the sea parted. "Listen to me," she said bluntly, "I was there."[129]

Because of her great compassion, because of her unrivaled wisdom, and because of her bravery to stand up for truth, justice, and the Jewish way, the sages say that she is among the very few (like Elijah the Prophet) who "never tasted death," but rather "entered Paradise alive."[130] In essence, what they are saying is that by demonstrating these eternal values of compassion, wisdom and bravery, we – like Serach bat Asher – can live eternally through how we positively impact the lives of others. May we, like our own bubbies and zaydies, do the same. Thereby, not only will we be a nation of priests, but a nation of superheroes.[131] "Up, up and oy vey!"[132]

---

[124] Sefer HaYashar, VaYigash, 109b-110a
[125] This term was coined by Dr. Marc Bregman, professor of Rabbinic Literature at the Hebrew Union College-Jewish Institute of Religion.
[126] Exodus Rabbah 5:13
[127] Mekhilta de-Rabbi Ishmael, Beshallach. Jacob Z. Lauterbach, ed. Vol. 1. Jewish Publication Society: Philadelphia, 2004. p. 120.
[128] Midrash Samuel 32 on II Samuel 20. Also found in Pesikta de-Rav Kahana 11:12. William Braude and Israel Kapstein, eds. Jewish Publication Society of America: Philadelphia, 2002. pp. 283-284.
[129] Pesikta de-Rav Kahana 11:13 William Braude and Israel Kapstein, eds. Jewish Publication Society of America: Philadelphia, 2002. pp. 284-286. According to the story, it was Rabbi Yochanan of the 3rd century of the Common Era.
[130] Yalqut Shimoni 2:367, Derekh Eretz 1:18
[131] This reference to a "nation of priests" comes from the book of Exodus, when God told the people: "If you obey Me faithfully and keep My Covenant, you shall be My treasured possession among all the peoples. Indeed, all the earth is Mine, but you shall be to Me a kingdom of priests and a holy nation." (Exodus 19:5-6)
[132] Up, Up, and Oy Vey is originally the title of a book on Jews and comic books written by Simcha Weinstein.

Pinchas // Phineas
Bite 3 – *Change: The Gold Standard*

What is the most common human emotion? Happiness... perhaps. Sadness... maybe. But, according to my own limited experiences as a rabbi, I would conclude that it is neither. To me, the most common emotion exhibited in humanity seems to come from that strange place in the middle called anxiety, as we worry which direction our life is headed: towards the heights of happiness or the depths of depression. Indeed, this continuous up-and-down motion of life in general, or the constant flux of the stock-market in particular, has been noted by prophets and poets alike, leading to the conclusion that "life is like a roller-coaster baby, baby."[133] But unlike the alternative-rock group, The Red Hot Chili Peppers, many of us may not "wanna ride."[134] In fact, we may actually scream to get off in the hopes of finding a stable place along the course, which surely would be interpreted as a God-send.

If so, then we may be shocked to learn – by way of Zelophechad's daughters – that God not only embraces change, but may actually prefer it. With no male heir, the daughters of Zelophechad drew near to the leaders of Israel, in this portion of *Pinchas*. "Let not our father's name be lost to his clan just because he had no sons!" protested the daughters Machla, Noah, Hoglah, Milkah and Tirtzah. "[Embrace change by] allowing us a holding among our father's kinsmen!" Upon hearing their words, Moses went before God, who responded: "The plea of the Zelophechad's daughters is just; you shall give them a hereditary holding among their father's kinsmen... Furthermore," added God, "this now shall be the law of procedure for all Israelites." (Numbers 27:1-11)

God's apparent willingness to change the laws of Israel so soon after Sinai arouses considerable debate among the sages of Torah. For example, Rabbi Samson Raphael Hirsch suggests the claim of Zelophechad's daughters was just because of a concern for their father's name.[135] For, it was written: "Honor your father and mother."[136] Rabbi Harold Kushner, however, contends that their concern was accepted out of ultimate conviction to God's plan. For, "while men had been unwilling to enter the land, it was the women who drew near, asking for their inheritance."[137] In either case, Kushner concludes, "God honored the daughters of Zelophechad [thus encouraging change] by arranging for them to cause a new law to be added to Torah, which was not included in the original revelation at Sinai."[138] For, in our willingness to encourage and embrace change, we become agents in God's plan for our people's continued welfare.

---

[133] Red Hot Chili Peppers. "Love Rollercoaster". Geffen Records: 1996
[134] Ibid.
[135] Rabbi Samson Raphael Hirsch commentary on Numbers 27:1-4
[136] Exodus 20:12 - The full line is an even better proof text for Rabbi Hirsch's interpretation: "Honor your father and your mother, that you may long endure on the land that the Lord your God is assigning you."
[137] Numbers Rabbah 21:10
[138] Harold Kushner. *Etz Hayim: Torah and Commentary*. Rabbinical Assembly: New York, 2001. p. 927

In other words, there is a tradition of change in Judaism, which is – as Mrs. Potts from Disney's *Beauty and the Beast* once sang – "a tale as old as time. True as it can be. Barely even friends, then somebody bends (in this case: God), unexpectedly."[139] And, as either the Beauty or the Beast in this affair, we have emulated God's willingness to bend and change, particularly with a daughter's inheritance. Originally written in the Torah to exclude daughters from inheriting when a son was present, the law was modified by the sages so that, even in the presence of a son, fathers could give their daughters an inheritance up to half of whatever the son would receive.[140] Then later, when the then Chief Rabbinate of Palestine issued a *takkanah* (a rabbinic injunction) in 1943, daughters were finally granted the right to inherit equally with sons.[141]

But wait a Biblical moment! While beneficial, does not this tradition of change conflict with another great tradition of Judaism: the drive to keep things the same?! After all, "Tradition!" with a capital "T" is not only the basis for one of the great modern musicals, the idea that "there is nothing new under the sun" is also a cornerstone of our Biblical texts.[142] As it was laid out in the nook of Deuteronomy, "You shall not add anything to what I (the Lord) command you or take anything away from it." For, as it was understood by the great sage RaMBaM, consistency and stability in the law provides a reliable standard to guide people in an ever-changing world.[143] And, surely, he has a point. Whether it's in the changing sands of the wilderness or in today's rapidly changing economic landscape, any semblance of stability – as previously mentioned – would seem like a God-send.

That is, unless the standard we are holding onto becomes antiquated, ill-equipped to address the challenges posed by the new environment. This seemingly was as true for the standard of Biblical law spoken of in this portion as it was for the economic standard of gold:

> Faced with a new and depressed economic reality in the early 1930's, a low man on the governmental totem pole, an agricultural economist by the name of George Warren recognized a problem with the current economic standard of gold. Yes the gold-standard, as it was called, had long provided a feeling of stability even with the typical instabilities of the market. But now it was not only unresponsive to the problem, the gold-standard was contributing to its perpetuation. For the infusion of money needed to make the economy healthy once again was severely limited by the fixed amount of gold maintained in the various banks.

> Even so, most people – including many of President Roosevelt's top advisors – believed that the gold-standard was the only thing holding

---

[139] Howard Ashman and Alan Menken, music. "Beauty and the Beast." *Beauty and the Beast.* Walt Disney Pictures: 1991
[140] Moshe Isserles. *Shulchan Aruch,* Choshen Mishpat 281:7 gloss
[141] Elliot Dorff, ed. *Etz Hayim: Torah and Commentary.* p. 926
[142] Ecclesiastes 1:9
[143] RaMBaM (Maimonides) Foundations of Torah 9:1-2

America together, which makes Warren's ability to recognize and address the problem ever more remarkable. Drawing close to Roosevelt, Warren expressed his grievances, asking FDR to depart from the accepted standard. Surprisingly, the President found his petition just, informing his advisors of the change. One advisor – the then assistant secretary of Treasury – resigned in disgust. Another, in fear, exclaimed: "This will be the end of Western Civilization!"[144]

Likely, similar human emotions were experienced and expressed by the people of Israel when they heard the daughter of Zelophechad's call for change in the established standard of Sinai's Law: "This will be the end of Israelite Civilization." For, as we are well aware, anxiety or fear is the most common human emotion exhibited in the face of change. And while we may want things to remain the same, that semblance of stability can provide no real guarantee. For, as it has been shown in this Torah portion, God's plan includes a tradition of change. And by embracing that tradition, we participate more fully in God's ultimate plan for our people's continued welfare. Therefore, let us in all moments of instability demonstrate the bravery of the daughters of Zelophechad. Thereby, we pray, we may be steered away from the depths of depression and directed instead to the heights of future happiness and success.

---

[144] This is a condensed version of the story, "Why We Left The Gold Standard," which was reported by Jacob Goldstein and David Kestenbaum on NPR: 21 April 2011.

Double Portion 9 & 10:
Matot-Masei // Tribes-Marches
Torah Portion: Numbers 30:2-36:13

"MOSES SPOKE TO THE HEADS OF THE ISRAELITE TRIBES…"
And, what he stresses to them is the importance of following
through on one's oaths and promises. This is right before
God instructs Moses to wage war on the Midianites.

After a victorious war, the Reubenites and Gadites appeal to
Moses to remain in the lands of Jazer and Gilead on the
eastern bank of the Jordan River. These tribes are cattle
herders, and the lands they request are primed for good
grazing. Moses agrees to allow the tribes of Gad, Reuben, and
the half-tribe of Menasseh to settle on the eastern bank as
long as these tribes send warriors to help settle the land of
Canaan for their Israelite brethren.

Thus, "THESE WERE THE MARCHES OF THE ISRAELITES," so
begins the final portion of the book of Numbers. Stage-by-
stage, it reviews the route the Israelites marched from Egypt
to the banks of the Jordan, before their final march into the
land of Israel. It also delineates the precise boundaries of the
land, so they can make their final preparations.

But, before initiating that confrontation, some expectations
are expressed regarding what will happen in that land once it
is settled. Within the land, there shall be six cities of refuge to
which a manslayer, who has unintentionally killed a person,
may flee. Additionally, the manslayer may only be executed
for murder on the testimony of multiple witnesses.

The portion concludes with the sequel to the saga of
Zelophechad's daughters, who inherited their father's land.
Menassite clan leaders worried that if Zelophechad's
daughters marry men from another Israelite tribe, those clans
may lose some of their land. As a result, Zelophechad's
daughters could marry only into a clan of their father's tribe.
No ancestral land may pass from one tribe to another.

Matot-Masei // Tribes-Marches
Bite 1 – *Let's Keep the Boat Afloat!*

Once again, in this double Torah portion of *Matot-Masei*, the people of Israel find themselves on the border of the Promised Land. Last time, due to insufficient paperwork (i.e. those bad reports) spawned by either a lack of confidence or selfishness, the Divine's border-security prevented the people from entering. So it begs the question: After observing the 40-year waiting period, did Israel return with lessons learned and would they be permitted entrance? At first, it seems unlikely, as the Gadites and Reubenites approach the leaders of Israel saying: "Favor us by giving us this land [outside Israel]; do not move us across the Jordan." (Numbers 32:5)

Moses is flabbergasted: "[Really?!] Are your brothers to go to war while you stay here? Why do you turn the minds of the Israelites from crossing into the land?" Gaining some composure, Moses then attempts to reason with them by reminding them: "That is what your fathers did...after going up to the wadi Eshcol and surveying the land; they turned the minds of the Israelites... And now you, a breed of sinful men, have replaced your fathers... If you turn away from God," warns Moses, "God will abandon them (i.e. Israel) once more in the wilderness, bringing calamity upon all the people." (Numbers 32:6-15)

How? How exactly does this decision by the individual tribes of Reuben and Gad cause calamity for an entire people? From deduction, we can infer that the Gadites and Reubenites would have provided additional might essential to settle the land. Thus, when they volunteered to withdraw from the blessings of the land, others – as an indirect consequence – risked missing out on them as well. Additionally, notes Biblical commentator Jacob Milgrom, it is not just the Reubenites and Gadites who would harness the blame. According to his commentary, "Calamity would be brought upon all the people if the other tribes tolerated their rebellion."[145] In other words, when any of us maintain the mindset that 'it is not my problem,' we ultimately put everyone's lives at risk.

> Such was the case in the little kingdom of Eden. Once considered a small slice of paradise, the kingdom of Eden began to deteriorate, especially under the rule of its new king. When a famine would arise, the king would say simply: "I'm sorry. But, I didn't cause the problem." When a drought occurred, the king stated: "I'm sorry. But, I didn't cause the problem." And, when storms ravaged the towns of the kingdom, leaving ruin, again the king responded: "I'm sorry. But, I didn't cause the problem."
>
> The people of the kingdom of Eden looked up to their king and began to emulate his example. When a neighbor was in need of assistance, the people – rather than helping – got in the habit of saying: "I'm sorry. But, it's not my problem." When strangers and wayfarers

---

[145] Jacob Milgrom. *The JPS Torah Commentary: Numbers.* JPS: Philadelphia: 1990. p.270

would pass through the kingdom in need of respite, its people – rather than being welcoming – would respond: "I'm sorry. But, it is not my problem." And, when pollution began to spoil the land, the people again responded: "I'm sorry. But, it's not my problem."

But, for one fisherman – who relied upon the river – it was a problem, his problem. His paradise was slowly becoming a wilderness. But, rather than dismissing or tolerating the problem, as so many others had in the face of such waste, the fisherman began to think about what he could do. Then, suddenly, a solution hit him! He would fix up his ol' boat and show the king the problem firsthand. "Maybe then," thought the fisherman, "the king would see it as his problem too."

It took some time to complete the work. The wood needed refinishing, the keel needed to be replaced, and the rudder mechanism needed serious tweaking. And, although costly in terms of time and money, the fisherman was undeterred. He finished the work, confirmed the king's visit, and invited the entire kingdom to observe and celebrate the maiden voyage of the new boat.

That day was splendid! Clear, the sun shone warmly on the milky-brown water, while a large crowd gathered on shore. The fisherman guided the boat into the middle of the lake, where he dropped a small anchor into the water, handed a pole to the king and another to his servant, and began drilling a hole in the bottom of the boat, directly underneath his seat.

"What are you doing?!" yelled the king.

"Drilling a hole," calmly responded the fisherman.

"Why, fisherman?" inquired the king, panic stricken.

"To drop my line in, of course," explained the fisherman nonchalantly.

"But, if you drill a hole in the bottom of the boat," worriedly retorted the king's servant, "water will rush in, the boat will sink and the king will…"

"Yes," said the fisherman. "Spit it out already. You're blocking my light. The king will… what?"

"He will drown," said the servant, adding, "for the king has never learned how to swim."

"I'm sorry," said the fisherman. "But, it's not my problem. After all," he added, "I'm only drilling underneath my seat."

"But fisherman!" yelled the king. "We are all in the same boat. If you go down, I'll go down. If I go down, you'll go down."

With those words, the fisherman smiled. "We can return home now and now our home can be returned to us." For once the king arrived safely back on shore, he began to impart the lesson learned on the boat to his people. No longer would his kingdom simply say "I'm sorry. But, it's not my problem." Instead, wherever there was a need, the people of Eden would respond in both word and deed.[146]

That was the reply the Gadites and Reubenites eventually gave to Moses in response to his claim of calamities in this double Torah portion. "Let us build here [outside the land]... and we will hasten shock-troops in the van of Israelites... We will not return to our homes," they emphasized, "until we have helped establish every Israelite in possession of his portion." (Numbers 32:17-18) Seeing that this generation of Israelites had indeed learned the lesson presented by both the previous generation and the fisherman in this story, the Lord finally permitted the people entrance into the land. May we too see all humanity as residing in the same boat. So that, as we secure our portion in life, may we also help to secure the portion of others. Thereby, we pray, all of our holdings shall be secure under the watchful protection of the Lord.

Matot-Masei // Tribes-Marches
Bite 2 – *Israel: A Vacation Nation*

Many of us may have been caught off guard by a recent headline. And, no, I'm not referring to the sudden departure of Jennifer Lopez from American Idol. Sure, that's sad; but what I'm referring to is even more depressing: Americans are afraid to take vacations. Yes, it's almost unbelievable! But, according to recent studies, Americans already have fewer paid vacation days than nearly all of their European counterparts; and now comes the news that only 57 percent of us actually take all of our allotted time off work, leaving – on average – 11 days on the table... or should I say, "on the desk!"[147]

Kathleen Christensen, author of the book *Workplace Flexibility: Realigning 20th-Century Jobs for a 21st-Century Workforce*, says a lot of this is cultural. "Within different countries there is just a clear cultural norm that people take vacations. Virtually the entire country of France closes down during the month of

---

[146] This story was adapted from "It's Not My Problem," found in *Capturing the Moon: Classic and Modern Jewish Tales* as retold by Rabbi Edward M. Feinstein. Behrman House, Inc.: New Jersey, 2008. pp. 41-46
[147] According to the World Tourism Organization, Italy has the most vacation days with the average worker receiving 42 paid days off; next was France with 37 days, Germany with 35, Brazil at 34, the United Kingdom at 28 , Canada with 26 and South Korea and Japan both with 25. The United States was near the bottom of the list with the average worker getting 13 days off.

August. But," Christensen adds, "in the United States we don't have any kind of prevailing cultural norm that is so dominant, that defines any month as a vacation month."[148] As such, America often earns the dubious title of "no-vacation nation."[149]

Certainly, that is not the distinction God wished the nation of Israel to earn, as they – in this double Torah portion of *Matot-Masei* – stand poised to build the Promised Land. Yet, before entering that land and engaging in that work, a considerable amount of space in the Torah is given to recount all forty-one stops the Israelites made, along the way, from Egypt until the steppes of Moab on the other side of the Jordan River. Standing there, we hear: "From Rameses, the Israelites set out and encamped at Sukkot. From Sukkot, they set out and encamped at Eitam... From Eitam, they set out and turned toward Pi-hachirot...encamping before Migdol," until finally "they encamped by the Jordan...in the steppes of Moab." (Numbers 33:5-49)

What may come across as a dry list of place-names was, for the sages, a fertile ground from which their imaginations could blossom. Thus, according to the *midrash*, it was God who dictated this list to Moses, saying unto him: "Write down the stages by which Israel journeyed in the wilderness." Why? Because, continued the *midrash*, "they shall need to know what miracles I produced for them."[150] Hence, contained in the list is the wilderness of Sin, where manna first appeared;[151] Rephidim, where the rock brought forth its water;[152] Kibrot-hataavah, where wind swept in quail from the sea,[153] and so many others. In other words, by recounting these miraculous places, God reminds us that life's journey is measured not by the number of breaths we take to reach each place, but by those miraculous moments along the way that can truly take our breath away.

If only we allowed for that to happen! Because, as the news report indicated, it's not our bosses who are to blame; it's ourselves. We are the relentless taskmasters, rarely allowing ourselves to take anything more than a quick breather from work. As a result, the miraculous moments of daily life transform into the mundane: spousal conversations are reduced from passion to information; playtime with children goes from electrifying to attention occupying, and often a moment of silence turns from a great teacher to loathsome bother, especially given all we still have left to do. And that's the rationale we give, even as we recognize these consequences. "There is simply too much time and too little to do. Wait a minute. Strike that. Reverse it," said Willy Wonka, as he rushed to show the children his magnificent Chocolate Factory.[154]

---

[148] Scott Mayerowitz. "Americans Afraid to Take Full Vacations." ABC New: 10 August 2012.
[149] Annalyn Censky. "Vacation? No Thanks, Boss." CNN Money: 18 May 2012.
[150] Numbers Rabbah 23:1
[151] Exodus 16
[152] Exodus 17
[153] Numbers 11
[154] Mel Stuart, director. *Charlie and the Chocolate Factory*. Paramount Pictures: 1971. For an example, not from fiction, you may turn to Emily Harley, a marketing and media relations manager (based in Helena, AL). She put these feelings like this: "I can't afford to do anything when I do take time off. Therefore, it just doesn't

It's not that we need to slow down, as slowing down would be like putting a Band-Aid on a broken back. What we need to do is allow ourselves a complete break in order to recuperate. If not, we may become like the Biblical wood-gatherer.[155] As we may recall, the company of Israel was given a day off (i.e. Shabbat) by the Boss (and I am not referring to Bruce Springsteen). Yet, the man would not stop his work of gathering wood. As a result, states the story, it was ironically the wood-gatherer who was gathered to his death. Thus, the sages have long questioned: "How much wood could a wood-gatherer gather, if a wood-gatherer could gather no wood?" The answer: none. And, very likely, that would be our fate as well. For when we work incessantly, "death" is certain, whether personally or professionally, as we ultimately become unproductive.

Bart Lorang, an entrepreneur in Denver, understands this all too well. In starting up his newest company, FullContact API (a contact management company), Lorang wished to have a more productive workforce than ever before. To accomplish this, he not only provides his employees a paid vacation, but he also gives them $7,500 cash to spend on that vacation. There is, however, a catch: employees must disconnect completely from all work: no phone calls, no texts, no emails. Nothing. If you do this, research says, not only will you benefit, but the work does as well, as you become more productive in your job.[156] "It's a real break for your brain," FullContact API employee Robbie Jack said. "You come back refreshed and reinvigorated and more excited about the stuff you were working on when you left."[157]

That's the feeling, taught our sages, which God wanted the people to have as they approached their work to build the Promise Land. God wanted them to be excited, enthusiastic, and ever eager for the work ahead, as it was not going to be easy. So the Eternal took the time to detail each and every one of the forty-one places where miracles transpired in the Israelite journey through the wilderness. It was not to boast or brag. Rather, it was to remind us to similarly take the time to revel in the miraculous. For only through recreation do we get the inspiration for truly innovative creation. We needed it then, as we stood poised to enter the Promised Land. And, we need it now in this land of Promise. Thereby, we pray, we may fulfill that promise contained within each one of us.

---

seem worth the trade-off to let work back up and cause myself stress within my work environment, if the only thing I could do with my time off was clean house!" (Censky. "Vacation? No Thanks, Boss.")
[155] Numbers 15:32-26
[156] M. J. Grawitch and L. K. Barber. "Work Flexibility or Nonwork Support? Theoretical and Empirical Distinctions for Work-Life Initiatives." *Consulting Psychology Journal: Practice and Research* 62 (2010): 169–188.
[157] Alyssa Newcomb. "Boss Gives Employees $7500 for Vacations." ABC News: 14 July 2012.

Matot-Masei // Tribes-Marches
Bite 3 – *"Sanctuary! Sanctuary!"*

"Sanctuary! Sanctuary!" Wrongly accused of murder, the lovely Esmeralda – in Victor Hugo's *The Hunchback of Notre Dame*[158] - is about to be hung by the lustful Archdeacon. Quasimodo, having seen the injustice done unto his love, knows that something must be done to correct this egregious error. The law of the land allows for cathedrals to be used as asylums for those fleeing revengeful retribution and seeking genuine justice. So, in heroic fashion, Quasimodo swings down to snatch Esmeralda from the hands of the hangman, screaming – on her behalf – "sanctuary, sanctuary;" which, spares her life temporarily.

The idea of safe space for accused murderers in Hugo's epic novel is not a novel notion. Places of refuge for suspected criminals are a much older concept, dating back to ancient times. This double Torah portion of *Matot-Masei* details the command of God unto the Israelites to establish such a system. As it is written: "When you cross the Jordan into the land of Canaan, you shall provide yourselves with places to serve you as cities of refuge to which a manslayer who has killed a person unintentionally may flee. The cities shall serve you as a refuge from the avenger, so that the manslayer may not die unless he has stood trial before the assembly." (Numbers 35:11-12)

As to the exact societal function of these cities of refuge, the rabbis are in disagreement. Some see them purely as places of punishment, large-scale prisons in which criminals are confined.[159] Others, however, understand these cities as models for human decency. Rabbi Samson Raphael Hirsch, for example, writes that these cities provide opportunities for forgiveness and rebirth. He continues, these cities are not prisons, but rather "nurturing places for the human [soul, in order that it may]...grow both spiritually and intellectually."[160] And yet this nurturing and growth is not limited only to those inside the city. One may understand that both the one indicted, the accused, and also the one who was incited, the accuser, benefit from the safe space – this time and place apart.

Without a doubt, the cities of refuge provide a safe space for the accused. Mentally, the city is a place where the accused, tormented by the whirlwind experience, can sift through the details in peace. Emotionally, it is a place of healing to recover from the stress and chaos of the painful incident. Spiritually, this divinely ordained city is a sign of God's unconditional love and presence.[161] In many ways, as Hirsch wrote, it's like group therapy "where

---

[158] Victor Hugo. *The Hunchback of Notre Dame*. Gosselin. 1831.
[159] Medieval commentator Aharon Halevi, for example, stressed that asylum cities were meant to exile these criminals from the rest of the society. From his perspective, being exiled was equivalent to being put to death. (Fields. *A Torah Commentary for Our Times:: Numbers/Deuteronomy*. New York: UAHC Press. 1993. p. 91.)
[160] Harvey J. Fields. *A Torah Commentary for Our Times: Volume Three: Numbers and Deuteronomy*. New York: UAHC Press. 1993. p. 90-91.
[161] Rabbi Neal J. Loevinger. "Cities or Sanctuaries." Kolel: The Adult Centre for Liberal Jewish Learning. http://www.kolel.org/pages/5760/matot_masei.html. 2000.

human beings can enjoy the company of others."[162] But, there is another benefit. The most obvious is that this safe space also provides the accused – whether he/she actually committed the crime or not – physical safety; for the accused is in a period of vulnerability, exposed to any residual anger from the accuser.

We know this feeling well. It's the adrenaline that keeps our hearts beating fast well after a harrowing moment has passed, while the lingering tension remains. The resolution may be as simple as the time-tested "time-out." While our children may have a more recent experience with a "time-out," we, as adults, may have forgotten the benefits that come from this period of forced cool-down. A "time-out" can be a way to catch our breath, to collect our composure, to gain perspective in order to know how to approach the moment more wisely. As Victor Hugo expands on the idea of sanctuary, "Amnesty is as good for those who give it as for those who receive it. It has the admirable quality of bestowing mercy on both sides."[163] And so – as we can hear – these opportunities, these "time-outs," these safe spaces are not just for the accused, but also for the one who is accusing.

And with that Hugo hits the nail directly on the head. When both sides, the accused and the accuser, seek mercy then justice can be established. The relationship between *rachamim* (mercy) and *din* (justice) is intrinsically part of Judaism. The *midrash* of *Genesis Rabbah* states: "Happy are the righteous who turn the attribute of judgment into mercy."[164] The *Zohar*, the Jewish book of mysticism, teaches: "There is no true justice unless mercy is part of it."[165] And so, it's fitting that only after these safe spaces have been established, allowing mercy to be present on both sides, our portion testifies that the manslayer is brought to justice, "standing trial before the assembly." This is to teach that a society functions best when justice is balanced on the scale with mercy.

This balancing act upholds for our society the humanity and the morality that makes us a godly people. The safe spaces we create together are beneficial to both the accuser and the accused alike, because of the values we inspire through them. Safe spaces are really opportunities for mercy to be present, which in turn invites genuine justice to dwell therein. May the accuser and accused alike, whichever we may be during different times in our lives, take the moment to gain control over our instincts in order to reflect on the situation. Then mercy and justice, good sense and sound reason, will prevail, and our safe spaces will be the holy sanctuaries of our community.

Chazak, chazak, v'nitchazeik!
From strength to strength, we are strengthened!

---

[162] Fields. *A Torah Commentary for Our Times:: Numbers/Deuteronomy*. New York: UAHC Press. 1993. p. 90-91.
[163] This quote from Victor Hugo, while similar in theme to his novel, *The Hunchback of Notre Dame*, was said independently from the book.
[164] Genesis Rabbah 73:3
[165] Zohar, iv, 146b

DEUTERONOMY

D'varim

Portion 1:
D'varim // Words
Torah Portion: Deuteronomy 1:1-3:22

"THESE ARE THE WORDS…" which Moses speaks to the people of Israel on the first day of the Hebrew month of Sh'vat, a mere twenty-seven days before his death. This ability for Moses to speak directly to the people, as opposed to recapitulating the words of God, is one of the striking differences in the book of Deuteronomy.

Moses begins by reviewing the events that have occurred in the people's forty-year desert wandering, emphasizing their lack of faith and fidelity time and time again. Their constant complaining and bickering has made an already difficult journey ever more arduous. Unable to handle it alone, we read once again about the appointment of judges, who help Moses with the strain and stress of leadership. This delegation of authority is also a proactive response to his approaching death, as the people will surely need a structure of leadership if they hope to continue to move forward and upward into the Promised Land.

The reader is then brought along for the retelling of the military battles at the end of the book of Numbers. Some of the people of the land were not to be disturbed: the people of Seir, the people of Moab, and the Ammonites because it was not within God's plan to give the Israelites even a square foot of that land to stand on. However, the same could not be said of the Amorites, as the people – by God's command and help – defeated the kingdoms of Sichon and Og.

These victories leave the people as well as the reader with an enduring message as the portion comes to the end: "You have seen with your own eyes all that the Lord your God has done to these two kings; so shall the Lord do to all the kingdoms into which you shall cross over. Do not fear them, for it is the Lord your God who will battle for you." (Deuteronomy 3:21-22)

D'varim // Words
Bite 1 – *"Like a Bee:" The Sweet Sting of Words*

We are a people of words. So, naturally, Jews should make great athletes, right? For, in the great world of sports, it is not just the action that grabs our attention. It is also the words. In addition to those issued by the players in and around the field of play, one can also hear the clever and supportive calls from charismatic cheerleaders or the amusing (and oftentimes harsh) critiques of the sports critics. But, the words that should really garner most of our attentions are those of the manager of the mayhem, the guide of the grid-iron, the director of the diamond, the commander of the court, the supervisor of the swimming pool, the boss of the boxer, the one and only: Coach, for upon his/her shoulders rests the greatest responsibility for the athlete's or team's success.

Appropriately, then, the final playbook of the Torah is called: *D'varim*/Words. Named so for the first major word in its opening address: "These are the *words* that [the coach] Moses addressed to all Israel on the other side of the Jordan." (Deuteronomy 1:1) What thereupon ensues throughout this address of *d'varim*/words are five retrospective discourses and poems that chronicle the events of the Israelite team as they crossed the field of play from their encampment in Moab to shortly before Moses' death just outside the Promised Land; discourses and poems which – at times – berate the Israelites for their abhorrent behavior ("bad Israelites"), as well as discourses and poems which – at other times – provide comfort and reassurance along life's difficult path ("ra-ra sis boom ba...go Israelites!").

This dual approach, claims Rabbi Shmuel ben Nachman, is appropriate. Noting the similarity between the Hebrew *d'varim*/words and *d'vorim*/bees, Rabbi Shmuel states, "God's children have been guided through the world by righteous prophets like a swarm of bees."[1] For, as it is further explained, "Just as a bee's honey is sweet and its sting sharp, so too are the words of Torah. Anyone who transgresses them receives a punishment, as it is written, 'Anyone who profanes it shall surely be put to death.' But, anyone who fulfills the Torah merits life, as it is said: 'so that your days may be long.'"[2] Thus, we are taught from *D'varim* that one's words can only be considered true guidance when they include both supportive as well as critical elements.

Yet, far too often, people tend to emphasize one side of this balanced equation over the other. For example, how many of us have someone in our lives who – no matter how much trouble we are in, no matter what we did wrong – will still be there with supportive and encouraging words? "Although you came in last, honey, your technique was perfect." Or, "yours was the best belly-flop in the entire diving competition." These individuals are our cheerleaders, people in our lives who will consistently highlight our strengths even to the exclusion

---

[1] Deuteronomy Rabbah 1:6
[2] Ibid. Rabbi Shmuel's quotes Exodus 31 and Exodus 20.

of our weaknesses. And, frankly, we should all be so lucky to have such people in our lives, as their relentless positive reinforcement is oftentimes the encouragement needed to get us back into the game of life and score!

Though, there are others who tend to over-emphasize the other side of this equation: the sports critic. Unlike the cheerleader, it is the job of the critic to be emotionally objective when examining the finished product. If it is good, then so be it. But, if it is bad... watch out! For mercy, typically, is not in the sports critic's vocabulary, as was highlighted in this real critique about an athlete who will go nameless: "[He] has a fake smile covered by me-first makeup. Instead of commanding respect, he demands it, making a win over the locker room a real struggle." While clearly harsh, the role of critic in our lives is not necessarily bad. For sometimes we tend to be unaware of our faults, particularly if we are solely surrounded by cheerleaders. And, therefore, the sports critic comes in to point out our deficits so that we may – hopefully – fill them in.

I say, hopefully, because while they point out our faults, critics do not typically provide any further words of guidance on how to get better. Though, to be fair, neither do cheerleaders. That is where our coaches in life come in. Like Moses, God's prophet, a good coach provides guidance through a balanced approach with words. With concern and care, the coach will not hesitate to offer criticism, pointing out areas of improvement. But, rather than leaving us to our own devices, a good coach remains at our sides, enabling us to get better through insightful *and* supportive words. Summarizing this dual approach, Walter Scott wrote, "When Israel, of the Lord belov'd, out of the land of bondage came, [needed was] her father's God in [both gentle] smoke and [harsh] flame."[3]

These are the words to which we should really pay attention. Yet, that is not to say the balanced words of the coach are easy, particularly in light of the one-sided approach of the critic or cheerleader. As Rabbi Harold Kushner commented, just as a bee's sting hurts the deliverer more than the recipient, so too is this the case when a coach must deliver a stinging response. It hurts him/her as much as, if not more, than his/her players.[4] Yet, like the bee's honey, the sweet supportive words of a coach may come to soothe the pain. May we do the same. Whether as coaches or parents, whether as teachers or managers, may we provide ample guidance to the next generation through a balanced approached, using both words of support and words of critique. Thereby, we pray, we may all – after rounding the bases of life – come home to our Promised Land in safety and peace!

---

[3] Sir Walter Scott. "Ivanhoe." *Waverley Novels: Ivanhoe*. Nabu Press: 2010. p. 356
[4] Harold Kushner, ed. *Etz Hayim: Torah and Commentary*. Rabbinical Assembly: New York, 2001. p. 981. In his exact words: "Moses' criticisms of the people are like the sting of the bee. A bee's sting hurts the person stung but it hurts the bee more, causing its death."

D'varim // Words
Bite 2 – *To Judge and To Be Judged*

To judge and to be judged – two notions which may leave a sour taste in the mouths of many. Nonetheless, judicial matters are, at least in their formal capacity, something we must swallow in order for society to function. Articulating this point, Justice Stephen Breyer said during his difficult confirmation hearings in 1994 for the U.S. Supreme Court: "Law is not theoretical. It is a set of opinions and rules that judges have to understand in order for everyone in a society, where different views are held, to know how to live together. [It is necessary] so that people can work productively together." Such judicial necessity was understood by Moses very early in his efforts to manage the fledgling society of Israel.

From their days of captivity in Egypt to their flight towards freedom in the Promised Land, Moses quickly grew frustrated with the large burden (i.e. the constant bickering of the people), which he felt he carried alone. In an attempt to offset that burden, Moses appointed judges over a 1,000, judges over a 100, judges over 50, and judges over 10, instructing them as follows: "Hear out your fellow and decide justly between any person: an Israelite or a stranger. You shall be impartial in judgment, hearing out low and high alike, fearing no person for the judgment is God's. Only if a matter is too difficult for you, shall you bring it to me and I will hear it." (Deuteronomy 1:16-17)

Moses, for all intents and purposes, was the Supreme Court of his day… and even then – alone as he was – deliberations took hours! Yet, his appointment of the lower judges seems almost instantaneous, as within a few verses a system of judges is in place. The same, however, cannot be said of our judicial system today. Today, particularly in confirmation hearings, judicial appointments at almost every level become long, drawn out affairs, as our duly elected representatives try to sort out who will most fulfill the ancient mandate of our people: to "be impartial in judgment" and to "hear out low and high alike." However, to answer this question, we must first ask another: "What truly makes for a proficient judge?"

According to this portion, it is one with a superior intellect. As Moses states in Deuteronomy 1:13: "Pick from each of your tribes people who are wise, discerning, and knowing and they will be appointed as your judges [lit. heads]." I suppose it comes as no surprise for a people whose very survival has been linked to intellect (i.e. the ability to read, understand, and apply the laws and lessons of Torah) that we would desire the same intellectual conviction from our judges. In a way, this standard may serve as a cultural safeguard of sorts as judicial opinions would surely be based upon a common body of knowledge, ensuring that the eventual ruling would be in accord with precedent (or, in another word: tradition!).

But, from time to time the cord of judicial history must be broken in order for justice to be upheld. We need only to recall the Women's Suffrage Movement of the 20's and the Civil Rights Movement of the 60's to realize the truth of this statement. At these moments the book of Exodus, through the words of Moses' father-in-law Jethro, guides us not to pick a judge with a superior intellectual capacity, as does Deuteronomy. Rather, in Exodus, we are advised to "seek out from among the people able ones who fear God, trustworthy people who spurn ill-gotten gain…let them judge the people at all times."[5] In other words, the type of judge we should seek is one whose allegiance is pledged to morality rather than strict legality; a judge who will regard the spirit of the law of equal, if not of greater, consequence than the letter of the law.

Yet, in the book of Numbers neither superior intellect as proposed by Moses in Deuteronomy nor a strong moral fiber as advised by Jethro in Exodus is recorded as the essential standard by which to pick a new judge. What God demands in Numbers is an individual with experience. As God commands there: "Gather for Me…Israel's elders of whom you have experienced as elders…they shall share the burden of the people with you (Moses), and you shall not bear it alone."[6] The condition of experience, in light of the other two standards, exists as an intermediary. So that when our intellectual capacity is challenged by our emotional one, when strict adherence to the letter of the law contends with the unwavering devotion to its spirit, when legality bumps heads with morality, it is there where we should have a judge with significant life experience to help navigate the precarious moment and return our society to homeostasis.

These three: intellect, moral integrity, and life experience are the essential standards by which we must vet any and all judicial nominees, and find the one who will have the awesome responsibility of judging among us. Reflecting on his own nomination process, Justice Breyer said: "It's appropriate in an era when people can find out about you so quickly through the media that millions of people would like to have a look at you." So, at these moments, when we take a close look at our judicial nominees, let us look and (make no mistake about it) judge him/her appropriately. According to RaSHI, this is not by "saying that such-and-such a person is handsome, so let's appoint him as judge," for we are not to base this decision on such external factors as race, ethnicity or gender.[7] These external factors are insufficient standards in assessing whether or not an individual will be a successful judge. Rather, as our Torah instructs, the standards which prove reliable are internal: wisdom, moral integrity, and life experience. For when we judge judicial nominees in such a manner, so too is it our hope that they will judge others the same, allowing our society to truly function at its best.

---

[5] Exodus 18:21
[6] Numbers 11:16-17
[7] RaSHI comment to Deuteronomy 1:17

D'varim // Words
Bite 3 – *Putting the Present Distress to Rest*

Already late due to an early-morning power-outage, a young businessman rushes to work only to be pulled over by a police officer. At work, the day's calamities continue to mount as the man accidently spills coffee on his shirt minutes before a big presentation. This, however, is the least of his troubles, for soon he realizes – in his rush to work – that he left his presentation at home. Many of us can likely empathize with this man and his distress. For who among us has not experienced at least one day in which it appeared as if anything that could go wrong, went wrong? And, while we may be hesitant to admit it, a thought – even if fleeting – often comes to mind in these moments: "God must hate me!" This response is not radical. In fact, one could almost say it's traditional, as old as when our people first wandered through the desert on their way to the Promised Land.

Recapitulated at the beginning of the book of Deuteronomy, we once again read of the troubled steps of our people from the land of Egypt to the valley of Aravah, from the mountain of Horeb to the wilderness of Kadesh-barnea, where the people heard the reports of the spies who scouted the Promised Land. And, although this version of the report differs from the previous one in Numbers, the outcome is similar.[8] The people still refuse to go up and "take possession of the land that the Lord [our] God had sworn to [our] forefathers: Abraham, Isaac, and Jacob."[9] Nevertheless, for the first time here in *D'varim*, we hear of what the people did instead. Rather than pursuing their Divine path by entering the Promised Land, the people entered their tents and sulked, saying: "It is because the Lord *hates* us! [Why else would] He bring us out of the land of Egypt, to be handed over to the Amorites, who will wipe us out?!" (Deuteronomy 1:27)

What's more, says RaSHI, is that the people in their sullen states continued sulking well into the night, stating: "If God really loved us and not hated us, God would have given us the land of Egypt and sent the Egyptians into the wilderness."[10] This notion may seem humorous, if not ridiculous, but it's not without logic; because – from an Israelite perspective – an endless wandering through the wilderness would reasonably appear as a punishment from God. However, suggests modern commentator Jeffrey Tigay, these morose remarks, whether posited Biblically or rabbinically, actually say little with regards to God and God's feelings towards the Israelites. Rather, Tigay insinuates, "they are more indicative of the feelings of the people," people who could not see outside their present moment.

It's not just the Israelites. Many today continue to live and espouse a life based solely in the present. Motivated by such cultural statements as '*carpe diem*/seize

---

[8] Numbers 13
[9] Deuteronomy 1:8
[10] See RaSHI's commentary on Deuteronomy 1:27, where he speaks of a *midrash* on the value of the land of Israel verses the land of Egypt.

the day' and 'no time like the present,' these individuals exist in a state of what the first Buddha, 2500 years ago, called *samma-sati* (meaning, 'mindfulness'), identifying it as *the* critical factor to true liberation and subsequent enlightenment.[11] It was understood, as many understand it today, that a present mind – unbridled by the restraints of the past and unencumbered by the pressures of the future – is free to be fully attuned to the ever-changing here and now. And, if fortunate, this hyper-awareness may elicit a glimpse of the Infinite Power behind those changes: God.

That is the glimpse, some would say, the Israelites perceived in the desert. Others, however, argue that such a perception could be nothing more than a mirage; a skewed image of reality manifested in the mind. For, if our reality extends only as far as the eye could see, if our here and now exists only as far as the arms can reach, then our perception of the present is no greater than that of an infant, who turns to tears and fears when a loving parent is no longer in view. And, that is what happened to our Israelite ancestors. God, out of view, also became out of mind. And, in this near-sighted view of reality with calamities mounting with every step, the Israelites distressed, expressing: "God [must] hate us!"

Thus, in an attempt to alleviate their distress, Moses endeavors to open their eyes to a larger world. As it is written: "Have no dread or fear [in this moment]... For, just as a parent carries a child, the Lord your God has carried you all the way to this place...and will continue to do so, guiding you on the route you have left to follow."[12] These words, as Tigay commented, are not limited to the people's theology. In addition, Moses is also addressing their psychology, reminding the people that past circumstances as well as future hopes must be calculated into the equation of their present. For by their presence in the present, the Israelites may garner a fuller more accurate view of reality. And thereby, it was hoped, that the people would be able to navigate the present challenges without fear and trepidation, without dread and apprehension, without… him.

Yes, as we know, Moses will soon be gathered to his kin. Yet, even in his absence, his guidance can still be felt. Because undoubtedly a day will come in all our lives when the calamities will mount, when everything that could go wrong, will go wrong, when the challenges of the hour lend their weight to our distress as we express – even if momentarily – that 'God hates us!' But, before we give into that impulse, before we give up on our Divine path, let us heed Moses' instruction. Let us factor in the present equation the essential variables of the past as well as our aspirations of the future. For when they are brought into the picture, we gain a wider perspective of our world, allowing a more balanced response to the challenges in our lives.

---

[11] The phrase 'carpe diem' is part of the larger Latin phrase, written by Horace in 23 BCE, '*carpe diem quam minime credula postero,*' meaning: "Seize the day, trusting as little as possible in the future." [Horace. Odes 1:11] For more information on Buddhism, please refer to *The Origin of Buddhist Meditation* by Alexander Wynne and published by Routledge in 2007.
[12] Deuteronomy 1:29-31

Portion 2:
Va-etchanan // I Pleaded
Torah Portion: Deuteronomy 3:23-7:11

"I PLEADED…" with God, says Moses, at the start of this portion. And, who could blame him? After affirming God's power to fight on behalf of all Israel at the end of the last portion, Moses asks God to fight on his behalf, allowing him to enter the Promised Land with the people. Of course, God is not persuaded, and informs Moses that he shall instead ascend a mountain and view the land from afar.

On that solemn note, the first part of Moses' long discourse in Deuteronomy comes to an end. What follows in this portion and later ones is largely legalistic, as Moses exhorts: "And now, O Israel, give heed to the laws and rules that I am instructing you to observe, so that you may live to enter and occupy the land that the Lord, the God of your fathers, is giving you." (Deuteronomy 4:1) Highlighted among those first laws was the prohibition against creating any sculpted images, whether it was of God, man, or beast. As well, Moses reminds the people about the necessity to create cities of refuge upon entering the land. These two laws encapsulate a whole new model of faith in the world: ethical monotheism.

To guide the people in its formation, Moses reprises the Decalogue. By these simple rules the people of Israel could manifest the best within themselves, in their community, and in their world. "Be careful then," states Moses, "to do as the Lord your God has commanded you. Do not turn aside to the right or the left: follow only the path that the Lord your God has enjoined upon you, so that you may thrive and that it may go well with you." (Deuteronomy 5:29-30)

The portion ends with what comes to be known as the declaration of faith in Judaism, the *Shema*. Its words declare the fundamental essence of the Israelite cult then and the faith culture their descendants hold fast to this very day: the unity of God and the obligation to study and live Torah.

Va-etchanan // I Pleaded
Bite 1 – *Sensing the Divine*

"Oh, that's divine!" These words are often spoken in response to an outside stimulus which overloads one, if not more, of our senses. Think about it. We may have said these words ourselves while enjoying a remarkable meal or when a pleasant aroma such as that from a bakery or confectionary crosses our path. "Oh, that's divine," is also an expression heard equally among concert goers during an extraordinary performance as it is uttered by visitors to a surprisingly astonishing view.

Experiencing Divine moments through our senses is a theme of this Torah portion of *Va-etchanan*. We are told by Moses: "[Use your sense of sight to] see the laws and rules which I am imparting to you…" as well as "[use your sense of hearing to] hear the laws and rules that I am instructing you to observe." (Deuteronomy 4:1-5) Not to mention, this portion also contains those immortal words: "*Shema Yisrael Adonai Eloheinu Adonai Echad* / Hear O' Israel, the Lord is our God, the Lord is One." (Deuteronomy 6:4) "Why," we may ask, "does this portion contain such an unusual emphasis on our senses?"

In a way (and excuse the pun) it makes sense, as we primarily experience and understand our world through our senses. Our senses function like scientific equipment gathering measurements from the outside environment and inputting them into the laboratories of our bodies, where technicians, our various systems and organs, begin the work of synthesizing, processing, and analyzing the information, eventually sending the results to our mind. It is there and then that some make the rational conclusion that they have experienced God in our world. For example, the 11th century Jewish philosopher, Bachya ibn Paquda theorized this in his work *Chovot haLevavot*. He said that if the world is seen as a text and one is able to hear a message from it, then one must rationally conclude a Divine author was behind the arrangement. Otherwise, that which occurs in the world is just scribble, void of any real inherent meaning.

While ibn Paquda argues "such infallible proofs and explanations for the truths of Torah and our faith are necessary [in order] for the nations to recognize us as being wise and understanding people" as spoken of in this portion (Deuteronomy 4:6), others will argue not only are such proofs not needed, they actual demonstrate a lack of faith. To these individuals, faith in God's existence and influence in our lives needs no external validation. Faith is, by its very definition, internal, sustained and supported solely by a sixth sense: intuition. As a contemporary illustration, it is similar to a child who inherently trusts the validity of a parent's teachings even though the child lacks sufficient external reason to do so.

By focusing on our senses, this portion is not denying that one could contain faith like a child, born into the heart and soul of a person. After all, Moses comforts the people with the words: "You will find God as long as you seek

God with all your heart and soul." (Deuteronomy 4:29) But, what our Torah portion is attempting to convey is that such faith from a Jewish perspective cannot be sustained. That is, unless it is nurtured and strengthened through our senses. For just as a child matures from infancy to adolescence to eventual adulthood through observations of his/her world, so too should a faith based in Judaism mature from a state of blindness to that of sight (not to mention our other senses of hearing, taste, and smell). Abraham Joshua Heschel wrote: Israel is not a nation which closes its eyes to the world. No. "Israel is a nation of witnesses."

We have the opportunity to witness and experience God everyday through our senses, save one: touch. Amazingly, it is also the one sense which today is rarely accompanied by the words: "Oh, that's divine!" According to *Deuteronomy Rabbah*, this is because the ability for a mortal to touch the Divine is associated with idolatry. As it is stated in the *midrash*: "Idols may be physically close to their worshippers, but they are emotionally distant, incapable of responding. Our God, on the other hand, while physically removed (i.e. incapable of being touched), is [we sense] emotionally close."[13] In other words, while we cannot touch God, God can touch us by way of our other senses. Let us, during our Sabbaths of internal reflection, when our hearts and souls are turned towards God, turn our external sensors towards the Divine direction as well. In this way, may we experience in the fullest sense possible God's presence in our lives, exclaiming with complete faith: "Oh, that's Divine!"

Va-etchanan // I Pleaded
Bite 2 – *Sustainable Salvation*

What a year it has been so far: earthquakes in New Zealand, a tsunami in Japan, catastrophic floods in Australia and around the Mississippi River, an economic situation still in turmoil, tornadoes that ripped through the American South and Midwest, volcanic eruptions in Iceland and Chile, a dreadful drought in Africa, civil unrest throughout the Middle East. And, then – some months ago – there was that rift heard around the globe: Maria Shriver's separation from Arnold Schwarzenegger, which one news agency actually called "the End of Days!" And, they are not alone. Stringing these events together, many conclude that we have now reached that critical end moment in which God, in the nick-of-time, will emerge from the fires to save the Divine's chosen ones with salvation.

While we may disagree, it is a belief – from a certain perspective – based in Hebrew Scriptures. Besides the orations of our prophets like Zechariah, Isaiah and Amos, who speak of the Day of the Lord being one of "darkness rather than light," we are reminded – in the Torah portion of *Va-etchanan* – that God's salvation can indeed emerge from fire.[14] As this notion was introduced

---

[13] Deuteronomy Rabbah 2:10
[14] See Zechariah 14, Amos 5:18-20, and Isaiah 66:15-21 for examples.

by Moses in the book of Deuteronomy, chapter four, "You (the people of Israel) came forward and stood at the foot of the mountain. The mountain was ablaze with flames to the very skies, dark with dense clouds. And the Lord spoke to you out of the fire; you heard the sound of words, but perceived no shape –nothing but a voice. And, God declared to you His *Brit* (His Covenant), in the form of the Ten Commandments." (Deuteronomy 4:11-13)

This fiery moment, as many of us may recall, is not the first time God emerged from flames. As it was written in the book of Exodus: "The Lord appeared to [Moses] in a blazing fire out of a bush. [Moses] gazed and there was a bush all aflame, yet the bush was not consumed."[15] So, if Moses met God through the burning of a little bush, and the people of Israel met God through the burning of a large mountain, then it would stand to reason – based upon this Biblical pattern – that all life on this planet will come to know God through an even larger burning: the burning of the world. Examining this information, the sages in the *Talmud* surmised: "We really look forward to the Messiah's arrival, but we fear his coming."[16]

Sadly, reality seems to validate their point to a degree. I mean, think about it. What happens immediately after these fear-filled moments of flame and fire? What happened immediately after the earthquake in Haiti? What happened after the tsunami in Japan? What happened around the United States after 9-11? That's right! Ordinary people came together in aid of their neighbors and strangers alike. As David Myers of the U.S. Department of Homeland Security reported to the White House, after tornadoes devastated parts of Alabama, "Disasters [may] blow down fences, [but they also] make for good neighbors; they bring us to the center of what we believe rather than the boundaries."[17]

But, we must ask, "for how long?" How long does this collective response of goodwill last? How long does the Presence of God – manifest in the helping hands of others – remain? We ask, because likely reality has also shown us that – whether it's with large communal disasters like floods or deeply personal ones like the loss of a loved one – sooner or later people go back behind their private fences, back to their own little worlds, managing the constant challenges of everyday life. Why? Why is this response of solidarity not sustained? Very simply, it is because that slice of salvation is based upon a single moment of suspense. So that, when the awe of that fiery moment passes (whether it is truly gone or has simply passed from our consciousness), so too does the motivation to unite and fight the flames.

That is not to say that these temporary responses are not appreciated. Indeed, they are. However, if we wish to have a lasting salvation, temporary responses in times of emergency just won't do. Hence the reason why God, out of flames, produced the Ten Commandments. For this *Brit*, this Covenant, is a guide towards prolonged investment, not just in God, but in ourselves and more

---

[15] Exodus 3:2
[16] Sanhedrin 97a-b
[17] Birmingham Jewish Federation. "Disasters Make Good Neighbors." *BJF Updates*: 10 June 2011.

importantly in the lives of our neighbors. God understood, more than fire, we would need friendship. More than woe, we would need wisdom. More than disasters, we would need discernment. More than punishment or pain, we would need progress. Because, through these care-filled efforts, we actually become more invested in the final product of peace. So that, when it arrives through our Divinely driven efforts, we won't be so careless as to let it pass.

Right now, a fire is burning; one that's been burning – as the great musical sage Billy Joel once sang – "since the world's been turning. We didn't start the fire. No," adds Joel, "we didn't light it, but we [must] try to fight it."[18] Because, that is our sacred task in this *brit*, this Covenant, with God. As it is stated in this portion: "Has any other people heard the voice of God speaking out of the fire and survived?"[19] The answer, given our complex history, is clearly: no. Yet, we are not dismayed. For, from that history, we have come to embrace our responsibility – in partnership with God – to pass along the wisdom and discernment gained in those trying times. Namely, there is a better way to salvation. So let us clear away the brush that stands between us and our neighbors. For when we remove this kindling that makes for strong fires, we make room for sustained acts of solidarity that make for lasting peace.

Va-etchanan // I Pleaded
Bite 3 – *A Symbol to Live By*

On January 27, 2002, the nationally syndicated comic strip *Non-Sequitur* surprised morning readers with a startlingly piece.[20] In this strip, one of the main characters – a young girl named Danae – is sitting on a park bench with an elderly man. She innocently comments to him, "I've gotta tell ya, mister… that's an awfully boring tattoo on your arm. It's just a bunch of numbers." He calmly replies, "Well I was about your age when I got it, and kept it as a reminder." He then proceeds to tell her of the horrors of the Holocaust. The young Danae begins to softly cry and then asks the elderly man, "So, do you keep it to remind yourself about the dangers of political extremism?" "No, my dear," he answers. "[I keep it] to remind you."

While the Holocaust tattoo on the arm of a survivor may dig deep into the well of our emotions, the nature of physical reminders is an ever-present concept in Judaism. The Jewish people have long used objects to remind us of spiritual, ritual, and theological concepts. The most obvious example is found in this Torah portion, *Va'etchanan*. Famous for including our declaration of faith (the *Shema*) as well as the *V'ahavta*, we read in these unforgettable verses from the book of Deuteronomy: "Bind them as a sign upon your hand and let them serve as a symbol before your eyes; inscribe them on the doorposts of your house and on your gates." (Deuteronomy 6:8-9)

---

[18] Billy Joel. "We Didn't Start the Fire." *Storm Front.* Columbia: 1989
[19] Deuteronomy 4:33
[20] Wiley Miller, *Non Sequitur*. Universal Press Syndicate. January 27, 2002.

Long have most rabbis understood these Biblical verses as God's command upon our people to wrap *t'fillin* during morning prayers and affix a *mezuzah* to the doorposts of our homes. For example, RaMBaN in the 14th century wrote: "'Binding them as a sign' means that these words shall be placed upon the arm and head through tying. And, furthermore, the knot in the strap of the *t'fillin* is symbolic of Moses at Sinai, [for it was there where he bound us with our people to God]." Yet, as we can hear, these symbols are not as simple as physical manifestations. Indeed, they come to symbolize so much more... a sign, some would say, directing us to manifest the ideas these items represent.

Truly, it is not uncommon to have physical items as reminders. Many of us do it more often than we think. A string on the finger or a rubber band on the wrist reminds us of what needs to get done that day. Alarms and Post-It notes stuck on the wall keep us on task. And, for many people, the physical token takes on much greater depth than a mere reminder. Many of us wear necklaces and other forms of jewelry to publicly as well as personally acknowledge our connection to our religion, our families, and our friends. While somewhat abrasive to some of our faith's traditions, some people even choose to permanently mark the body as a way to continually call to mind people, ideas, thoughts, and memories that hold deep significance to them.

And, it is a near guarantee that – for many people – we don't affix these physical reminders simply as a memory. But, more so, we keep these physical items close in order to aspire to achieve a piece of what they represent: a locket from our mother, reminding us to be as loving as she was; a pendant from a lost friend, encouraging us to live every moment of life to the fullest; a black box with leather straps or a small rectangle affixed to the door, inspiring us to walk in God's ways as we go about our day. In regards to this topic, Rabbi and author Hayim Halevy Donin poignantly wrote, "These physical symbols are not meant to encourage just sentiments or abstract feelings. [Additionally, through these symbols,] we are called upon to demonstrate...ethical and moral standards of the highest caliber."[21]

Why? Because, *we* can become the symbols. For example, when you think of pacifism, you think of Gandhi; when you think of Civil Rights, you think of Dr. King; when you think of Democracy, you think of Jefferson; and, when someone, anyone, thinks of a Jew, they should think of...you! For "people need these dramatic examples [more than they need items] to shake them out of apathy. And," according to Bruce Wayne (a.k.a. Batman), "[we] cannot do this as simple as human beings, for as humans [we] are just flesh and blood. [We] can be ignored. [We] can be destroyed. But as a symbol, as a symbol [we] can be incorruptible. [We] can be everlasting."[22] Because no longer is the message contained within a fragile trinket or confined to brittle four-walls.

---

[21] Rabbi Hayim Halevy Donin. *To Be a Jew: A Guide to Jewish Observance in Contemporary Life.* New York: Basic Books. 1972. p. 144.
[22] Christopher Nolan. *Batman Begins.* Warner Bros. Studios: 2005.

Rather, through us and our actions, it is mobile and contagious, inspiring the world to live up to a higher ideal.

So, it's time to take the next step. Instead of merely wearing these symbols, we must become these symbols, mobile markers leading others to a nobler way of life. Because what good is a message if we have no one to share it with? What good is the desire to improve our world if no one will do it with us? As the old man in the comic strip spoke to the young girl, the symbol is not meant to remind ourselves. Rather, it is to remind others... except, he was only half right. These symbols we own, these symbols we are, will be more than reminders; they will be inspiration for others. Let us then, in our daily actions, be these daily symbols, directing others toward that higher ethical and moral standard of which we are capable.

Eikev // As a Result
Torah Portion: Deuteronomy 7:12-11:25

"AS A RESULT OF LISTENING TO THESE RULES AND OBSERVING THEM CAREFULLY…" All good laws and rules must have a set of consequences attached to them, whether positive or negative, to ensure that they will be followed. That is where this portion begins. It starts with detailing some of the blessings that will ensue as a result of the faithful observance of God's laws: maintenance of the Divine Covenant, multiplication of our seed, good health, and secure dwellings.

Thereby, the people understood that the way forward is found through faithful action – in addition to belief – guided by law. To ensure the message was delivered clearly, Moses speaks of the rough road they have already traveled, a subtle reminder that if they do not follow these ordinances from God, Moses will turn the proverbial car around – as was done before – to face all these hardships once more.

Yet, in reminding the people of the difficulties they have overcome, Moses expresses concern. Given this exceptional history, will the people start to think that they too are exceptional, somehow inherently better than others? Full of themselves, will they leave room for God? To address this concern, much of the portion that remains includes reminders and strategies for the Israelites to maintain their humility.

The portion concludes with a simple guide. Only this does the Lord require: "Revere the Lord your God, walk only in the Eternal's paths, and love God, serving the Lord with all your heart and soul." (Deuteronomy 10:12) In these ways, the Israelites may merit the blessings found within God's Covenant: a long and healthy life, progeny, and a secure portion in the Promised Land.

Eikev // As a Result
Bite 1 – *Our Chosen-ness Uncovered*

"You know... you are God's chosen ones." Not itchy T-shirt tags or six-inch heels, not indigestion or emotional consternation, not even those hard little bicycle seats can compare to the discomfort we may feel when – with the noblest of intentions – a person of another faith refers to Jews exclusively as God's "chosen people." Yet, like the fabled pea under the stack of mattresses, the exact source of this discomfort may be challenging to pinpoint.[23]

That is, until we take a good look under the cover of this portion of *Eikev*. Because, in addition to the books of Malachi and Psalms (which speak of God choosing Israel as an *am segulah* – a "treasured people"), we read here that the "Lord our God will maintain the Covenant God made with [our] ancestors."[24] Specifically, it is written, "God will favor [us] and bless [us]... as [we] are blessed *m'kol ha-amim*." (Deuteronomy 7:14)

Frequently, it is from within this Hebrew phrase that our discomfort lies. For all too often *m'kol* is understood as "above all others." As it is written in the 1999 Jewish Publication Society's translation: "God will favor [us] and bless [us]... as [we] are blessed above all other people."[25] Likely meant to be complimentary, we can nevertheless hear, within this translation, tones of superiority and – worse – separation from our fellow man.

Possibly provoked by this discomforting thought, our sages began a process of removing some of its textual layers. What they uncovered was *m'kol*, rather than meaning "above all others," could also be understood as "from/by all others," thus rendering the verse as: "God will favor [us] and bless [us]... as [we] are blessed _by_ all other people." Rabbi Chiyya expounded: "A noble lady feels herself flattered when she is praised not by her relatives, but by her rivals."[26]

With an aroma of animosity still apparent, this nuance may bring little relief to our discomfort. Though, it's certainly a step in the right direction. Because, by understanding *m'kol* as "from/by," then these "others" do not necessarily have to be rivals. They can be simply the benefactors of our blessings. As such, we are not in a position of superiority, but humility that behooves us to act kindly. For in blessing others by kind deeds, truly then we merit blessings for ourselves.

Indeed, blessings like being "God's chosen ones" may be uncomfortable to rest upon, particularly when we feel we did nothing to deserve them. Yet, when we act in such a manner as to pass along such blessings to others, then these

---

[23] Hans Christian Anderson. *The Princess and the Pea*. C.A. Reitzel: Copenhagen, 1835.
[24] Malachi 3:17 and Psalm 135:4. Also see Ex. 19:5, Deut. 7:6, 14:2, and 26:18 as well as Isaiah 41:8, 42:1, and 44:1-2.
[25] See *JPS Hebrew-English TaNaKH*. The Jewish Publication Society: Philadelphia: 2000.
[26] Deuteronomy Rabbah 3:6

discomforts begin to wane. For, in performance of *g'milut chasadim* (acts of loving-kindness), we are not merely meriting blessings for ourselves, we are – in fact – blessing others, helping them to see that they are uniquely chosen too!

Eikev // As a Result
Bite 2 – *A Patient Process*

One year ago, I almost died. The Crohn's Disease I was born with came out of a decade-long remission in dramatic fashion. Without a cure, a group of doctors assembled in my hospital room and stood around me as if I was a war table and they, the leading generals, strategized a plan of attack. After a series of exchanges, with grunts of pain as my sole input, it was decided that my only option was a surgery that would remove the diseased and collapsed part of my intestine. Hoping, praying, and even expecting that this bold and decisive act would solve my problem once and for all, I consented. The plan was enacted with precision, but the war over my health – I would soon realize – was far from being won, as months later recovery would continue to be a daily battle.

I suppose I should have taken a closer look at the battle plans enacted by these competent medical warriors before giving my consent. Although this information would not have changed my ultimate decision, the added intel would have prepared me more thoroughly to effectively confront the challenge, providing me with something very valuable, something very helpful: insight. It's an insight already spoken of in the battle plans enacted by God as our people prepared for their own return to wholeness in the Promised Land. According to Moses, in this portion of *Eikev*, "The Lord your God plans on dislodging [your opposition] little by little. You will not be able to put an end to the struggle all at once, lest wild beasts will multiply to your hurt." (Deuteronomy 7:22)

In their original context, these words acknowledged a limitation of the budding Israelite nation. As Biblical scholar, Jeffrey Tigay comments, "There were just too few Israelites to subdue and fill the land [all at once]...Therefore, God planned on giving the Israelites only as much territory as they could occupy. If they did alright with this, then God would give them the rest."[27] Rabbinic tradition, however, has applied these words more broadly. According to our sages, no matter what type of confrontation – whether it be military or medical – we must establish realistic expectations prior to our engagement. Namely, that no war can be won in a single battle.

Yet that is not what many of us would like to believe. Caught up in the message of Hollywood (as opposed to the message of the Holy Word), we would like to believe that one bold act, one decisive moment can dramatically change the course of history. Take the movie *The Patriot*, for example.[28] With the real

---

[27] Jeffrey Tigay. *Etz Hayim: Torah and Commentary*. The Rabbinical Assembly: New York, 2001. p. 1038
[28] Robert Rodat, writer. *The Patriot*. Mutual Film Company: 2000

complexities of the Revolutionary War as a backdrop, many viewers still swallowed the unbelievable premise that Mel Gibson (more correctly, his character Benjamin Martin), in one pivotal battle, single handedly repelled the British army, thereby freeing the American colonies.

And it's not just in war. In this Burger King era, we have convinced ourselves that any wrong can be righted, any break can be fixed, any sickness can be healed "our way, right away." And, coincidently, this approach is as healthy for our bodies as a fast-food diet. Speaking to the adverse effects of this aggressive approach, Moses says: "You will not be able to put an end to your struggle all at once, lest wild beast will multiply to your hurt." (Deuteronomy 7:22) In other words, taking this verse metaphorically, it was understood that when we push the natural process, the natural process may push back.

Therefore, the Divine doctor reminds us that in order to truly arrive at a moment of wholeness, a moment of *r'fuah shleimah* (meaning, 'a complete healing'), we can't expect fast-acting solutions. Rather, it is written, a more advantageous path is the long path, advancing towards healing "little by little." (Deuteronomy 7:22) After all, as it is often pointed out, "Rome was not built in a day," nor – one could add – did our people advance from Egypt to arrive in the Promised Land in one fell-swoop (although that would certainly make our Passover seders shorter). No. Our advance to the wholeness we sought in the Promised Land was measured. For, in measuring our steps, we ensured that one was steady and stable before taking on another, making our eventual arrival more sound.

This insight, presented by Moses in *Eikev*, is commonsense. Yet, it now serves me well, as I continue to battle Crohn's Disease. For while I would – at times – like to hop, skip and jump my way through the steps of life, especially when those steps become laid with challenges, I am reminded that such an aggressive and rushed approach could lead "to my own hurt." (Deuteronomy 7:22) But, by embracing this teaching, establishing more realistic expectations, I become more patient in my approach to the process of life. Ultimately, then, I am able to confront its challenges with less worry and more confidence, with less angst and more composure, with less frustration and more assurance, with less chances for failure and more opportunities for success. For being a patient patient is, as Abraham Lincoln so spoke, "the key to the war," allying us with the natural process, instead of the natural process working against us.[29] May we all overcome our challenges, so that we may one day, soon, in our day – we pray – stand firmly in a Promised Land of wholeness and peace.

---

[29] Abraham Lincoln speaking about the Civil War battle of Vicksburg, MS

Eikev // As a Result
Bite 3 – *Back to the Basics*

As the lazy days of summer inundate our minds, we may feel as Sam Cooke did in 1958 when he sang: "Don't know much about history; don't know much biology; don't know much about a science book; don't know much about the French I took." Then, it's a good thing the beginning of another academic year is soon upon us, so that once again we can get back to the basics. Coincidently, many of our youth tend to misinterpret that phrase: "back to the basics." To them, it means "basically, what do I need to know in order to pass?"

It is a minimalistic approach to education which has never been coveted in our culture. Nonetheless, in *Eikev*, Moses our Teacher does whittle the Torah down to a set of four basic teachings. According to Deuteronomy 10:12, you need to know "only this: (1) revere the Lord your God, (2) walk only in God's paths, (3) love God, and (4) serve the Lord your God with all your heart and soul." Evidently, the exercise of reducing a vast amount of information down to a smaller, more manageable form did not start with Cliff Notes.

In fact, this exercise was entertained by many of the first rabbis at the beginning of the Common Era. The famous writings of Pirkei Avot, written sometime before the year 200 C.E., preserve many of these early formulations. One of the most famous from this period is from Hillel, who stated to a potential Jew-by-Choice: "What is hateful to you, do not do to another. The rest [of Torah] is commentary. Go and learn."[30] Yet, shouldn't we question: if one could reduce the whole Torah to this or any other summary, why then should we need or feel motivated to go and learn the entire thing?

As you know, some have neither the motivation nor feel the need to study the whole Torah. These individuals, whether religious or not, simply believe it is a waste of time to engage in a task themselves when someone more qualified, experienced, and knowledgeable has already done the work for them. To dispel this myth, RaMBaM wrote: "Every person is obligated to study Torah, be s/he: poor or rich, healthy or suffering, young or very old and weak in strength… Husband, wife, and children [are all obligated to the study of Torah]."[31]

But quoting an obligation is a weak strategy to convince anyone to do anything… just ask parents. In this case, it is especially difficult to persuade one to fulfill the obligation of pursuing the full breadth and depth of Torah, because a summary of its contents (provided by the hard work of another) appears to be in hand. But, as the adage goes: appearances can be deceiving. Even though these basic teachings come in the last of the five Books of Moses, they are not to be understood as conclusions as most modern commentators would have us believe. For example, Jeffrey Tigay writes: "Moses summarizes

---

[30] BT Shabbat 31a
[31] *Mishneh Torah*, Hilchot Talmud Torah 1:8

these principles that must guide the people's behavior if they are to avoid further acts of rebellion."[32] Summaries, however, are not motivational addresses. Full of general information, they lack the specifics to inspire lasting change. Think about it. How inspirational is the infamous one-line summary of Jewish history: "they attempted to destroy us; we survived; let's eat!"

Therefore, rather than imparting a summary to one day be printed on the back cover of the "Good Book," we can understand that Moses is using his remaining time with the people for something a little more advantageous: a primer. Yes! These basic teachings are not an end to a course of study. They are a beginning, handed to the people in the hopes that they will initiate for themselves the sacred task of combining these teachings with others in order to reconstruct the valuable lessons of Torah; lessons which will successfully guide and sustain the people throughout the generations. In a way, they may be likened to the basic elements on the periodic table. As the elements are the building blocks for all other matter, so too are these basic teachings the building blocks upon which the whole Torah stands. Alone they are important, but of little consequence. Combined, they provide something of substance.

However, Sam Cooke would know little about such things in science books (not to mention the valuable lessons of history, biology, or French). Yet, he was confident that "one and one is two. And, if this one could be with you, what a wonderful world this would be." Similarly, in our lives we may need to start off with what we are sure of, i.e. "the basics." But, in order to sustain and guide our people as Moses had hoped, we cannot and must not stop there, figuring that is all we need to know to pass. To be satisfied with the bare minimum is to consign our people to the pages of history. We, however, are the people who make history! Not through resting on another's conclusion. Rather, we make history when we see within another's conclusion an invitation for further study. May we continue to explore all the pages in the book of life, finding within them meaning and inspiration.

---

[32] Jeffrey Tigay. "Deuteronomy." *JPS Torah Commentary*. JPS: Philadelphia, 1996. p. 107

Portion 4:
R'eih // See
Torah Portion: Deuteronomy 11:26-16:17

"SEE, THIS DAY I SET BEFORE YOU BLESSING AND CURSE..." This portion, as the opening verse makes clear, picks up just where the last one ended… deep within the second part of Moses' discourse concerning the laws and rules (along with their consequences) that the people shall institute upon their entrance into the Promised Land.

However, there is a special focus that comes out within this portion: a central sanctuary place to be designated by God, serving as the only legitimate site for the sacrificial offerings. As it is written, "Look only to the site that the Lord your God will choose amidst all your tribes as the Eternal's habitation, to establish the Divine Name there. There you will go and there you are to bring burnt offerings and other sacrifices." (Deuteronomy 12:5)

The reason is clear. There is concern that if the people worship God in places that were designated as sites of worship by the people who previously possessed the land then the people of Israel may come to worship God in that same abhorrent manner. Thus, Moses commands, "You must destroy all the sites at which the nations you are to dispossess worshiped their gods, whether on lofty mountains, on hills, or under any luxuriant tree." (Deuteronomy 12:2)

The sacrificial focus of the portion continues by extending its guidance from the place of the offering to the offering itself, detailing the procedural where, when and how. Included in these details are the the proper authorities (who will not lead the people astray), the food fit for slaughter, tithes given to the needy, and the three pilgrimage festival offerings.

There, the portion ends with the people seeing one central focus for their faithful observance to the God of Israel.

R'eih // See
Bite 1 – *Do you see what I see?*

Nuclear fission and fast food, what do they have in common? It's more than quantum "Mc"chanics. The fact is that both nuclear fission and fast food have the capacity to provide fuel, whether it is for a machine or the engine of the human body. Nevertheless, both means have been perverted toward destructive ends. How these potential gifts went from blessings to curses in a blink-of-an-eye is understood better through this Torah portion of *R'eih* (which coincidently means, "see"). According to the first verse: God "sets before [us] this day blessing and curse." (Deuteronomy 11:26). Sound familiar? It should. Every year, just before Rosh HaShanah, we read: "I have put before you life and death, blessing and curse. Choose…"[33] However, given the choice between these two extremes, blessing and curse, doesn't the decision seem obvious?

So, sensing there was something deeper at work, Rabbi Yonatan ben Uziel issues an interesting commentary through his Aramaic translation of the Hebrew Bible. Instead of translating *k'lalah* as "curse," Rabbi Yonatan uses the word, *chilufah*, meaning: "transmutation."[34] Thus, the Biblical verse is rendered: God "sets before [us] this day" not blessing and curse, but "blessing and its transmutation." This isn't just a crafty spin from one of Judaism's brightest PR men, trying to avoid the unsavory term "curse." Had that been the case, it is likely that Rabbi Yonatan would have just said, "blessing and its opposite" or "blessing and you know that pesky other thing." Rather, Rabbi Yonatan is under the assumption that everything in life is a blessing or a mutation thereof.

This is not simply a side effect of wearing rose-colored glasses. Individuals who espouse the belief that all of life is a blessing are actually stating a valid point from a perspective of Judaism. To explain, it's a lot like the trivia game Six Degrees of Kevin Bacon, which is based upon the idea that any actor in history can be linked through a series of film roles to Kevin Bacon. For example, Elvis Presley has a "Bacon number" of two since Elvis starred in Change of Habit (1969) with Ed Asner and Ed Asner starred in JFK (1991) with Kevin Bacon. Similarly, in Judaism's version of the game, Six Degrees of God, everything in life – through a series of rational deductions – can be traced back to God. While the "God number" may differ depending on the item, everything – as a result of that Divine connection – is considered a blessing. For, as the *midrash* states, "no evil can come from Heaven," only blessings.[35]

Yet everyday our eyes are flooded with images of suffering, some we have experienced personally and others we learn of through word of mouth or through the news media. So, are we to see these events too through the

---

[33] Deuteronomy 30:19
[34] Targum Yonatan, Devarim 11:26
[35] Yalkut Shimoni Va'era 186

optimistic lens of Judaism and consider them blessings as well? Surprisingly, based upon a Biblical passage describing our suffering in Egypt, the answer could be 'yes.' As it is stated in Deuteronomy 4:20: "The Lord took you and brought you out of Egypt, that iron furnace, to be God's very own people." According to the 11th century sage, RaSHI, the "iron furnace is a vessel used to purify gold."[36] It is used here to teach us that just as gold is refined through fire, we are perfected and enriched through our suffering. You have to give Judaism credit. After all the suffering our people have endured throughout the centuries, we still have the impulse to remain positive.

Hindsight, however, is always 20/20. For that reason our Torah portion focuses not on what's behind us. Its message is how to see what is presented before us at any given moment. As it is written: "I set before you…" (Deuteronomy 11:26) And, what is set before us is neither blessing nor curse, for everything in life is inherently ambiguous. This could be said of people as well as for such taboo things as sex, drugs, and alcohol. While some may consider these latter items the wish-list of some seedy subculture of society, we must be reminded that sex produces children, drugs cure diseases, and alcohol is used to bless the Sabbath day. The character of a thing, whether it is a blessing or a curse, emerges not by what it is, but how it is used.

Rabbi Yonatan was right. Like a Hasbro Transformer, there is more to this choice than meets the eye. At this moment when we are to see what God has placed before us, it is not a matter of having the sight to distinguish between blessing and curse. That is as obvious as distinguishing day from night. Instead, this moment is about having the insight to understand that everything in life, from nuclear fission to fast food, has the potential to be both: a blessing or a curse. "Curse," it is worth noting, has many synonyms in the Hebrew language: *k'lalah*, as it was written in our Torah portion as well as *arar*, *me'erah*, *kavav*, etc. On the other hand, there is only one word in Hebrew for blessing: *b'rachah*. May we devise more, by choosing to see the potential good which resides within everything and every moment of our lives.

R'eih // See
Bite 2 – *Breaking Bad*

A lady walked up to a little, wrinkled man rocking in a chair on a porch. She said, "I couldn't help noticing how happy you look. What's the secret for a long and happy life?" "Well, I don't know," he replied. "But, for me, I smoke three packs of cigarettes a day. I drink a case of whiskey a week. I eat fried foods regularly. And, I never, ever exercise." "Wow! That's amazing!" she exclaimed. "How old are you?" He answered, "Twenty-three." Truly, it seems, the more we pour into our urges the quicker life pours out of us. Maybe that's why in this portion of *R'eih* our ancestors introduced a stopper of sorts, a cork

---

[36] RaSHI commentary on Deuteronomy 4:20

to keep the elixir of life from draining from the vessel of our bodies, namely… regulations.

Yes, in the book of Deuteronomy, we read about some of the detailed dietary laws of our people. For example, it is written that "you may not partake in your settlements of the tithes of your new grain, wine, or oil, [nor may you partake in your settlements] of the firstlings of your herds and flocks…" (Deuteronomy 12:17) Yet, it goes on to say, "When…you have the urge to eat meat, you may eat meat whenever you wish. If the place where the Lord has chosen to establish His Name (i.e. the Temple) is too far from you, you may slaughter any of the cattle or sheep that the Lord gives you…and you may eat to your heart's content in your settlements." (Deuteronomy 12:20-21)

Now, these verses are unique. Typically when the Bible speaks of the laws of our people, they rarely mention the desires of the individual. Imagine, if you will, the response of the people of Israel had God consulted us before decreeing circumcision! Yet, here, the Bible makes explicit the individual's "urge." Rabbi Abraham Chill suggests this inclusion amidst the laws of our people indicates that a society's laws can mitigate personal urges. Commenting on these verses, he writes, "Perhaps because of the bother and annoyance of the whole [regulatory] procedure, people will be restrained from such a strong and uncontrollable desire for meat."[37] That is to say that the complexity of the laws will frustrate the people to such a degree that they throw up their hands and say before their next Israelite hamburger, "Forget it! It's not worth the trouble!"

Although today it is debated whether eating meat is such a bad habit, Rabbi Chill's approach of finding ways to make the bad habit more difficult to perform is generally accepted. As Benjamin Franklin once quipped, "It is easier to prevent bad habits than to break them." In this vein, our society has – for example – raised the price of cigarettes and the age limit for drinking alcohol (going from 18 to 21 in 1984). The rabbis have a term for this procedure. They call it si'ag l'Torah (meaning "a fence for the Torah"). For, it was believed that by putting up a fence around the rules, one could be prevented from breaking the rules; and, according to the great sage RaMBaM, "these fences [even have a way] of perfecting us."[38]

Indeed, these fences keep us away from the bad habits. However, it is hard to argue that genuine perfection, genuine change is reached. High prices may stop us from smoking for a bit, but what if the prices are lowered or we win the lottery? And, higher age limits on alcohol may slow our drinking for a moment, but ask anyone what happened on their 21st birthday… if they can remember it at all! In other words, if we remove the barrier, take down the fence, or have the means to overcome them, many people will likely return to

---

[37] Rabbi Abraham Chill. "The Mitzvot: The Commandments & Their Rationale." Jerusalem: Urim Publications. 2000. p. 400.
[38] Harvey J. Fields. *A Torah Commentary for Our Times: Volume Three: Numbers and Deuteronomy*. New York: UAHC Press. 1993. p. 130.

their bad habits. This is because genuine change cannot be imposed upon us from the outside. Genuine change must be generated internally.

Psychologists recommend a wide range of tools and techniques to help us change from the inside out, thus defeating our bad habits, including: (1) admitting the error of our ways – called *vidui* in Hebrew, (2) making a conscious effort to correct the error – *tikkun* in Hebrew, and finally (3) setting our minds, hearts, and souls on positive action – *t'shuvah*, "the answer" in Hebrew.[39] According to our faith culture, it is this last technique that is most critical in changing our behavior, for *t'shuvah* targets the origin of our actions: our internal dialogue, those unrelenting and unending questions and resulting answers that direct our behavior in this world. All one has to do to change oneself, it is believed, is to change the course of that internal conversation between the heart, mind, and soul. Or, to put it another way, positive thoughts will eventually translate into sustained positive action.

The philosopher Aristotle once taught, those sustained actions are the essence of the individual. "We are what we repeatedly do," he stated. Interestingly, he did not say, "We are what society would have us do." Why? Because of what God taught our people in *R'eih*. That is to say, the rules and regulations of society alone will not and cannot be the lasting motivations that cause us to change our behavior. Rather, the only effective and meaningful path towards change starts within. As such, may we come to be more conscious of our unconscious internal discourse. Thereby, we pray, we may come to change the course of the conversation, breaking the bad by replacing them with good.

R'eih // See
Bite 3 – *There Will Always be Needy*

This portion of *R'eih* presents an apparent contradiction. First, we read, "There shall be no needy among you." (Deuteronomy 15:4) Then, only a few verses later, we have: "There will never cease to be needy ones in your land." (Deuteronomy 15:11) How should we understand this?

Perhaps, rather than a promise, the first verse expresses an exhortation, a prayer: "Let there be no needy among you, may all have their needs met by a just and compassionate society." And, the second — a statement of realism, a reminder that just as the need will never cease, never shall our efforts. But, how overwhelming! Where do we begin? Anywhere, instructs the *Mishnah*: "It's not for you to complete the task; but neither are you free to desist from it." In other words, life is not an all-or-nothing proposition. First we do what we can, then – after that – if we can do more, so much the better!

---

[39] Denise Mann and Dr. Louise Chang. "3 Easy Steps to Breaking Bad Habits." WebMD. http://www.webmd.com/balance/features/3-easy-steps-to-breaking-bad-habits. November 17, 2007.

These instructional words for immediate action from Torah and *Mishnah* struck with particular force when we arrived at this portion in late summer of 2005. In the aftermath of Hurricane Katrina, we tasted the bitter truth of Deuteronomy 15:11: "There will never cease to be needy ones in your land." Even if we lived in a society that addressed the basic needs of all its inhabitants, we would still face moments like that, moments when survivors slip further into distress, moments when basic needs – water, food, shelter, medicine – go unmet.

If any of us, then, had felt personally obligated to clean up the entire mess, we might have never begun. But, we did. Following the *Mishnah*, we did what we could. Communities throughout our nation and the world loaded up trucks with supplies, buses with volunteers, making their way to those in need with whatever they could get their hands on: from diapers to drywall. The ISJL helped coordinate the efforts of many, a legacy of which we are reasonably proud. In simply doing what we could, we showed we can do a whole lot!

To enact this principle, we need not think back to Katrina. Every week, a new catastrophe or tragedy seems to hit the human inhabitants of our little planet. This reality has motivated many of us to become first responders to members of our human family, whether they live near or far. Yet, just as it was for the verses of this portion, that resolute position also contains a prayer. In sharing our blessings with others, we are hoping to create an environment where one day such blessings may be revisited upon us, when life's challenges knock on our door.

By this collective effort, we get ever closer to fulfilling God's vision for our people: "There shall be no needy among you." For need anywhere, should impassion a response from all of us, everywhere. Let us not stand idly by. By simply doing what we can, states the Bible, "the Lord your God will bless you in your efforts and all your undertakings."

Portion 5:

Shoftim // Judges
Torah Portion: Deuteronomy 16:18-21:9

"YOU SHALL APPOINT JUDGES AND OFFICIALS…" It's not just judges and officials that this portion concerns itself with; it's also kings, priests, and prophets which occupy Moses in his continued discourse to the people. Specially, Moses focuses his words on limiting their power. For, the well-being of the Israelite society would not be predicated on the goodwill of its leaders, but on justice rooted in law.

"Justice, justice shall you pursue." (Deuteronomy 16:20) Arguably nowhere else in the Bible is the theme of justice more emphasized than in this portion. It begins by ensuring that the judges treat everyone equally under the law, showing no partiality or taking bribes which only blind the eye. Additional instructions are provided regarding how judges are to handle cases of capital punishment.

Following this, the portion turns to a potential king, as the people may opt to have one upon entering the land. However, cautions Moses, "Be sure he is one of your own people… Moreover, he shall not keep many horses... or many wives, etc." (Deuteronomy 17:15-17) As opposed to helping himself, his power was meant to help the people. To help him remember this charge, Moses ordered that a copy of this teaching be kept beside him at all times.

To write it, Moses had the priests, whose power Moses also limited. Owning no portion in the land, they were dependent on the people (not the other way around). From the priests Moses moved on to the prophets, guiding the people on how to tell a true prophet from a false prophet.

The remainder of the portion redirects its focus from the administrators of justice to the application of justice: distinguishing manslaughter from murder and how to preserve justice while waging war.

Shoftim // Judges
Bite 1 – *A Guide to Pursue Justice*

Our tradition is filled with amazing stories, meant to transmit enduring lessons that can soundly guide one generation to the next. This is particularly true of the following *midrash*: God – when speaking to Moses of social justice – showed him a coin of fire, saying: "A coin such as this the people of Israel shall give."[40] Why specifically, it was asked, a coin of fire? Because, stated Noam Elimelech of Lyzhansk, "This is to teach that money is like fire. Fire can be very useful, supplying heat and power. But, it can also be very damaging, as it consumes and destroys. By the same token," continues Elimelech, "money can be used for the most worthwhile causes, establishing *tzedek* (justice). But, it can also be used to cause damage, as the source of every type of wrong."[41]

Money's potential to be a double-agent in the fight for social justice was first exposed in this Torah portion of *Shoftim*. Devoted almost entirely to the theme of protecting the most vulnerable in society from those who would exploit them, we read of God's command to "not judge unfairly." Specifically, it was elucidated, "you shall not show partiality; you shall not take bribes, for bribes blind the eyes of the discerning and upset the plea of the just." Instead of using money to damage our ever fragile social system, God insists on another path. In a call that has been trumpeted and echoed throughout the generations, we further read of the unforgettable charge: "*Tzedek, tzedek tirdof //* Justice, justice shall you pursue!" (Deuteronomy 16:19-20)

Although of primary importance throughout the Torah, nowhere is the theme of social justice emphasized more than right here. In fact, these words serve as the traditional basis for the Jewish law regarding the respect and adherence to matters of social justice, as well as the mandate to actively pursue them (which may be the reason why Jews repeatedly, throughout history, have been at the forefront of such struggles).[42] But, the sages of blessed memory, knew that these pursuits – while worthy in whatever form they take – are ultimately served better with direction, so that our efforts build rather than unintentionally destroy, warm rather than inadvertently chill. Thus, more than a mere emphasis, the sages read within these three words – *tzedek, tzedek tirdof* – a Divine guide to help us engage more productively in matters of social justice.

Tzedek, the first in this guide to social justice, is often decoded as a passive step. Illustrated in the book of Leviticus, we read, "When you reap the harvest of your land, you shall not reap all the way to the edges of your field, or gather the gleanings of your harvest. You shall not pick your vineyard bare, or gather its fallen fruit. You shall leave them for the poor and the stranger."[43] Admittedly,

---

[40] RaSHI commentary on Exodus 30:13
[41] Aharon Yaakov Greenberg, ed. *Torah Gems.* Vol. II. Chemed Books and Co., Inc.: New York, 1998. pp.206-207
[42] Harold Kushner, Elliot Dorff, and Susan Grossman, ed. *Etz Hayim: Torah and Commentary.* Rabbinical Assembly, 2001. pp.1088-1089.
[43] Leviticus 19:9-10

this first step of *tzedek* may appear cold and unkind. But, let us not mistake passiveness for insensitivity. In this act of passive *tzedakah* (charitable giving), the receiver is enabled to participate in the process of *tzedek* (justice). As a result of participating in the act, any stigma felt by the receiver from being in a position of need may be reduced or completely eliminated.

Even so, the first *tzedek* seems to lack the heart many will argue is needed for social justice to endure. Hence, the second *tzedek* is more active. As it was spelled-out in the prior portion, "If there is a needy person among you...do not harden your heart and shut your hand. Rather, whatever is needed to meet the need, you must open your hand and lend."[44] "Lend" and not "give"... why? Because in addition to the sensitivities mentioned above, lending – as opposed to giving – maintains a relationship between the two parties. And, as my friend Rev. Phil Reed taught in his work for greater justice in Jackson, MS: "More than giving, it is the relationships between people of various socio-economic strata that lay the groundwork for true social justice."[45]

While *tzedek*, *tzedek* may lay the groundwork, the establishment of social justice takes place in the *tirdof*, the pursuit. As RaSHI acknowledged, "We shall not wait until a person declines or falls, for then it will be more difficult to raise him up. Rather, we must [pursue him,] strengthening him from the time it first appears as if he might falter."[46] To highlight his point, RaSHI uses the illustration of a donkey's burden. "While a donkey is standing and his load begins to slip, one person can easily grab hold of it and set it back into place. But, once it has fallen, not even five people may be able to lift it." Though an unfortunate comparison, RaSHI has a point. If we merely rely on passive and active approaches to social justice, eventually we will exhaust our abilities with much work left to be done. But, if we employ those same energies proactively, then we can ensure a just and upright society endures.

Indeed, it has been said that "since the time of Abraham, justice has been spoken with a Hebrew accent."[47] Yet, understanding that accent has proven quite difficult, as many of our well-intended efforts have fallen short: destroying rather than building, cooling rather than warming. That is why we are provided a guide to better navigate our pursuits of social justice. May we follow this guide as we continue with the first step of *tzedek*, engaging passively in deeds of social justice. May we continue to take the second step of *tzedek*, engaging actively in efforts of social justice. But, even more than that, may we *tirdof*, pursue proactive ways to make our world a more just and upright place. For truly then we can continue to move soundly from one generation to the next.

---

[44] Deuteronomy 15:7-8; also check out Leviticus 25:35-38
[45] Reverend Phil Reed is the Director for the Voice of Calvary Ministries' *Circle Initiative: An Innovative Model to End Poverty*. In addition to incorporating effective social justice strategies like providing basic assistance and professional services on an individual and community level, the program also creates a mentoring situation between individuals of various socio-economic strata. http://www.vocm.org/aboutus.htm
[46] RaSHI commentary on Leviticus 25:35; see also *Torat Kohanim, parshata* 5:1
[47] Heinrich Heine, German poet (1797-1856).

Shoftim // Judges
Bite 2 – *Capital Conditions: Judaism and the Death Penalty*

Forty-three. No, that's not my highest word-point total in the game, *Words with Friends*. Nor is forty-three the vague title of some book or movie, which then must be entertained to discover its significance. As a point of fact, the number forty-three is significant all by itself, as it was the number of people put to death by the criminal court system in the United States in 2011. Thirty-one of those forty-three individuals were sentenced to death in the South, which means that nearly three out of every four capital punishment cases were carried out to their conclusions in our region that year.[48] Given this prevalence, we may be asked how we, as Jews, feel about the death penalty. And, like many, it's a difficult question to answer.

Because, from their early vantage point, our Israelite ancestors would say that the Torah condones the use of capital punishment. We see this, for example, in this portion of *Shoftim*, which means "judges" or "magistrates," as the portion begins with their appointment. Afterwards, it is said, "if there is found among you, in one of the settlements that the Lord your God is giving you, a man or a woman who has affronted the Lord your God and transgressed the Eternal's Covenant… and you have been informed or have learned of it, then you shall make a thorough inquiry. If it is true… then you all shall take that man or woman to the public place and stone him/her to death." (Deuteronomy 17:2-6)

According to Professor of Law, and Classical and Near Eastern Studies, Dr. Bernard Levinson, "Upon establishing a professional judiciary, this law granted local courts maximal autonomy, enabling them to try even capital cases. Just one essential condition was imposed: trials must be conducted according to strictly rational standards that assured empirical proof for the verdict. Thus, vague rumors ('you have been informed') were put to a test ('a thorough inquiry') in order to verify its truth."[49] For, as Rabbi Shimon ben Gamliel taught, "By three things the world is sustained: by truth, by judgment, and by peace."[50] Once truth is established, judgment must be carried out, for peace to reign.

That virtue of capital punishment, as well as others, is extolled throughout this portion. For example, proponents of the death penalty believe it acts as a deterrent, dissuading other would-be criminals from committing their crime. As it is written, "In this way, you will sweep out evil from Israel. The people will hear and be afraid, so that they will not act presumptuously again."[51] Others, holding the death penalty as a crucial piece in the always befuddling

---

[48] This information comes from the Death Penalty Information Center at http://www.deathpenaltyinfo.org/documents/FactSheet.pdf. This year there have already been 27 individuals who have undergone the death penalty (19 in the South).
[49] Dr. Bernard Levinson. *The Jewish Study Bible*. Adele Berlin and Marc Zvi Brettler, eds. Jewish Publication Society: Oxford University Press, 2004. p. 404.
[50] Pirkei Avot 1:18
[51] Deuteronomy 17:12-13

puzzle of justice, lean on the Bible's advice to "show no pity," as pity may lead to complacency, complacency to noncompliance, and noncompliance to outright chaos. Rather, to bring order to the puzzle of justice, continues the verse, be ready to take "life for life, eye for eye, tooth for tooth, etc."[52]

Over the course of Jewish history, these words have come to mean that "one may be charged the equivalent value of the physical loss," as opposed to undergoing the physical loss itself.[53] Nonetheless, it seems in a perfect system (like the one depicted in the Bible) capital punishments are encouraged. But, as every child comes to learn early in life, we don't live in a perfect system. Not because, as parents often say, "life just isn't fair." Bad things happen to good people, as Harold Kushner will tell you, because there really aren't any bad or good people; we're merely variant shades of imperfection, reflecting the One Perfection: God.[54] In our imperfect states, innocent people are found guilty and guilty people are proclaimed innocent every single year.

Recognizing this, a legal process began in Rabbinic Judaism long ago to define the preconditions of capital punishment cases so narrowly as to virtually do away with death penalties entirely. In the case of a man, for example, who has "a wayward and defiant son," the Bible says "the men of his town can stone him to death."[55] But, state the Sages in great assurance to our youth, it cannot happen before the boy (i.e. not girl) can produce two hairs on his lip, has both eaten copious amounts of meat and drunk at least a half a log of Italian wine, stolen from both his father and mother, and both agree unreservedly to this course of action, etc. etc. etc.[56] So tight were these regulations that the *Talmud* tells us that no children ever "qualified" as wayward and defiant.[57]

Unfortunately, the same cannot be said for adults. Once, there was a rabbinical court that came to be known as the "Bloody Sanhedrin." How did it earn this dubious designation? Because, taught Rabbi Eliezar, "in seventy years, they sentenced one man to death."[58] Clearly, then, the course of the conversation on capital punishment has changed. No longer is it simply a question about "how do we feel about the death penalty;" rather, it's "how do we make sure it is never applied." Our Sages of blessed memory worked on the backend of this discussion. It's time we started on the frontend, by putting in place the proper

---

[52] Deuteronomy 19:21
[53] RaSHI commentary to Exodus 21:24
[54] Reference to Harold Kushner's book: *When Bad Things Happen to Good People.* Avon Pub.: 1983. RaMBaM wrote: "Human reason cannot fully conceive God in His true essence, because of the perfection of God's essence and the imperfection of our own reason." (*Mishnah*, Avot, Eight Chapters, VIII)
[55] Deuteronomy 21:18-21
[56] *Mishnah* Sanhedrin 8:1-5, BT Sanhedrin 68b–72a
[57] BT Sanhedrin 71a, "There never was, nor will there ever be, a child who meets all of the legal qualifications of the 'wayward and rebellious son.' Why then was this law written? That you may study it and receive reward."
[58] *Mishnah* Makkot 1:10. There is a Rabbinic dispute within the texts. Others argue that the stigma of a "bloody Sanhedrin" should be applied if it convicts a person of death once in every seven years. The proliferation of brutal terrorist acts, and the imposition of life sentences instead of capital punishment, led the military courts of the State of Israel to say that though the death penalty may be a more appropriate punishment, they were bound "to uphold principles of the State of Israel, the moral concepts of Jewish tradition, in which a Sanhedrin that passed a death sentence was considered to be a 'a bloody Sanhedrin.'" (cf. *Ram 3009/89 Army Pros. v. Ahmed Gibril Ottrrzan Takrzrru*)

conditions for a society of truth, of justice and of peace. Thereby, though all crime may not stop, surely the numbers will come down.

Shoftim // Judges
Bite 3 – *In the Same Boat*

Once upon a time, three men went fishing in a boat; not one of them could swim. Yet, the best fish were always found in the middle of the lake. So, despite their lack of aquatic training, the three men paddled out to cast their lines. Once in the middle of the lake, the man in the front of the boat cast his line forward. The man, in the rear of the boat, cast his line backward. And, the man in the middle of the boat, well, he started to drill a hole for his line beneath his seat. "Wait!" yelled the man at the front of the boat. "You can't drill a hole!" screamed the second man. Responding to their cries, the man in the middle stated: "What concern is it of yours? The hole," he insisted, "is underneath *my* seat!"

Many of us have likely come across individuals who epitomize this mentality; individuals who forget that we are all in the same boat: the business person who ruthlessly climbs the corporate ladder, the pro-athlete who boasts of his/her achievements in spite of the team effort, and even the child who has yet to learn to share his/her toys. So, rather than perpetuating this mentality through more examples, I would like to share with you a story that highlights a more constructive mentality. It is a story that reminds us – whether we are Jewish, Christian, or Muslim; whether we are Black, White, or Hispanic; whether we are Republicans, Democrats, or Independents – that we reside, at all times, in the same boat. And, because of that reality, we have a responsibility to care for one another. For, by doing so, we truly keep ourselves as well as others afloat.

It was a cold and icy winter night in the middle of the Atlantic Ocean. In the black-out conditions, the once cruise-liner now transport ship, the U.S.S. Dorchester slowly made the treacherous journey through 'torpedo alley' loaded with its precious cargo, 900 young American soldiers and 4 chaplains: Father John Washington, Reverend Clark Poling, Reverend George Fox, and Rabbi Alexander Goode. Together, these four men of faith brought comfort and levity in a moment that was drenched with tension and fear. But, they could not prevent the inevitable.

In the early morning hours of February 3, 1943 a German U-boat made a direct hit on the Dorchester, crippling it with one massive torpedo. The ship was lost. Those that survived the initial hit frantically scurried from the lower chambers up to the main deck, struggling for their very survival. Amidst the chaotic storm of fear stood firm these four men of faith, who had, throughout the journey, provided comfort. Now, in this harrowing moment, their resolve to fulfill the mandate directed to them by the ultimate Commander-in-Chief, our God above, did not waiver.

Noticing that one young man was without gloves, a chaplain handed him his. "But Chaplain, what about you?" Reassuring the young man, the chaplain said, "Do not worry, my son. I have another pair."

Another man approached, "Chaplain what am I to do? I do not have a jacket. I'm going to freeze to death." Taking off his, a chaplain said, "Here, take this one. It'll keep you warm, my son." "But Chaplain," asked the young soldier, "won't you need it?" "Do not worry about that. Go on. I have another one."

Rapidly, bit by bit, the Four Chaplains were saving lives, but at the cost of their own; for there were no other jackets, no other gloves. And even after all the extra life-jackets were divvied out, the chaplains took off theirs and gave them to others who were still without one. According to the testimony of one survivor, he was saved when Rabbi Goode, bent down, took out the laces of his own boot, and secured a broken life-jacket around the frightened young man, stating, "Do not worry, my son. God is with you. Go on. Live!"

Without concern for race or religion, these four men made the ultimate sacrifice. They made the fateful decision to give up their space on a life-boat to others, choosing instead to minister to those who remained. Survivors testify to the last unforgettable image of these Four Chaplains. With unshaken faith, the Four Chaplains linked arm-to-arm, each reciting a prayer in his own liturgical tongue. Father Washington said one in Latin. Reverends Poling and Fox recited a prayer in English. And, from Rabbi Goode, the ancient call of our people rang out like a beacon of hope, "*Shema Yisrael Adonai Eloheinu Adonai Echad* / Hear O' Israel, the Lord is our God, the Lord is One."[59]

While tragic, this inspiring story is a true example of the role of the chaplain first spoken of in this Torah portion of *Shoftim*. "Before you join in battle, the priest shall come forward and address the troops. He shall say to them, '*Shema Yisrael*/Hear O Israel! You, who are about to join in battle against your enemy, let not your courage falter. Do not fear, panic, or be in dread of them. For, it is the Lord your God who marches with you.'" (Deuteronomy 20:2-4).

This priestly act is nothing new. Narratives about the wars of Israel from the time of Moses to David indicate that priests often accompanied the army. For like today's modern priest, the chaplain's presence is understood as a physical reminder of the holy. His/her presence is, in a word, a prayer. But, not a prayer

---

[59] For more information on this story please read Dan *Kurzman's No Greater Glory: The Four Chaplains and the Sinking of the Dorchester in World War II*. Random House: New York, 2004.

- as it may be assumed – petitioning the Holy One to be in our vessel rather than theirs, thereby securing our victory and ensuring their defeat. For, what is unique here is that the priest – unlike all other accounts in the Bible- carries no vessel with him (particularly: the Ark of the Covenant).[60]

Therefore, it is to be understood that his prayerful presence is meant to acknowledge this difficult reality: right now we are fighting, fighting one another as if we believed we sat in separate boats. But, we pray, that this will not always be the case. We pray for a day "when swords will be turned into plowshares, spears into pruning hooks; a day when nation shall not lift up sword against nation, nor shall they study war anymore." (Isaiah 2:4) For, on that day, we will have learned well – what was demonstrated by the Four Chaplains – that we all exist in the same boat. And, thus, when we help keep another afloat, we keep ourselves afloat as well.

---

[60] As pointed out in Jeffrey Tigay's commentary to Deuteronomy 20:2. See *Etz Hayim: Torah and Commentary*. Rabbinical Assembly: New York, 2001.

Portion 6:
Ki Teitzei // When You Go Out
Torah Portion: Deuteronomy 21:10-25:19

"When you go out to war against your enemies…" Understandably, this portion begins where the last one ended: how to engage in war justly. However, it very quickly jumps from laws concerning large public affairs to containing a diverse assemblage of laws addressing individuals, their families, and their neighbors. Primarily, the focus of each will be on preserving the dignity and worth of every human being as well as the integrity of the community.

Within the family, the portion begins with issues of rivalry that may erupt in a family that has multiple wives as well as the tricky dynamics that may result with their children. Also, there is legislation for parents on how to deal with a wayward and defiant son. Finally, nowhere is the value of human dignity more apparent than in the command to immediately bury an individual put to death because of a capital offense, and not let him linger on a stake overnight.

From there, the portion addresses individual action in relationship with neighbors. Specifically, Moses speaks on dealing with another person's property: actively returning another person's lost goods, refraining from wearing another's clothing, along with various scenarios dealing with sexual relations with another man's woman, whether she is married or betrothed. Additionally, Moses provides guidelines on who shall be permitted to enter the community of Israel and who shall not. As well, guidance is to be found in this portion in all matters of business affairs: exacting interest, making vows and taking pledges, gleaning produce from one's own land or another's land, providing wages, etc.

Concluding this vast array of legislation is the law regarding corporal punishment and the Levirate marriage, as well as an eternal charge to wipe out the memory of Amalek from under Heaven.

Ki Teitzei // When You Go Out
Bite 1 – *Live Long and Prosper*

Lord Voldemort. Wolverine. King Aragorn. What do these three characters have in common? And please, do not say that they are all works of fiction. The hearts of little boys and girls everywhere (including a few adults) couldn't bear it. So, then, what is it? Well, according to my extensive "research" on the topic, I can tell you that all three of these characters lived exceptionally long lives, whether it's through the act of splitting one's soul, or a genetic mutation that constantly causes human cells to regenerate, or simply because of a connection to the Dúnedain people of middle earth, who were blessed with long life.[61]

In light of this "research," we may wonder how we can be similarly blessed. How can we ensure that our days are long and filled with meaning on *this* earth? It's a question we have likely asked ourselves numerous times, a question whose answer is presented in this Torah portion of *Ki Teitzei*. As it is written, "If, along the road, you chance upon a bird's nest in any tree or on the ground with fledglings or eggs and there is a mother sitting over them," first you must chase the mother bird away. "Do not take her with her young. Let the mother go and take only the young," emphasizes the Bible. "In that way, you may fare well and have a long life." (Deuteronomy 22:6-7)

A heck of a lot easier than splitting one's soul, obtaining a genetic mutation, or becoming a part of the Dúnedain people, isn't it?! Yet, before we hurry out onto a road, hoping that – by chance – we may come across a nest and achieve long life, I am obliged to remind you of a Talmudic tale of a young man who attempted just that.[62] But, rather than receiving long life, he sadly fell to his death. Not so eager anymore, are we? Neither were the sages, who surmised that something deeper must be at play, for this was just one of only three specific commandments in the whole of Torah which contains the detailed promise of long life.[63] But, rather than encouraging something fanciful, each of these commanded deeds can occur within our daily routines.

This is apparent in the last of these three commands, which – coincidently – comes within this Torah portion as well. As it is written, "You must maintain completely honest weights and measures, so that your life may be long."[64] While the specific reference here is to good business practices, the sages have

---

[61] Lord Voldemort is prime villain from J.K. Rowling's *Harry Potter* series. He extends his life unnaturally by splitting his soul through evil acts. On the positive side, Wolverine is a superhero from *Marvel Comics*, who possesses - among other abilities - the mutation to heal from just about anything. King Aragorn is one of the main protagonists in J.R.R. Tolkein's *The Lord of the Rings* series. Aragorn is a descendant of Numenor, a Dunedain, blessed with long life.

[62] BT Chulin 142a

[63] The story led one of the sages, Elisha ben Abuyah, to despair of God's goodness and even God's existence. In light of the story, Rabbi Akiva interpreted the promise of long life as referring to "life in the world to come." See commentary by Rabbi Harold Kushner in *Etz Hayim: Torah and Commentary*. The Rabbinical Assembly: New York, 2001. p. 1117

[64] Deuteronomy 25:15

long applied the measure of honesty to all our social interactions.[65] For just as honest weights and measures ensure a stable commerce system, honesty in our relationships helps ensure a stable social system, which allows everyone therein to live a healthier and more meaningful life. In other words, the parental teaching of "honesty is the best policy" was understood by our sages as specifically a life insurance policy.

That is, unless the policy of honesty confronts another policy of long life: compassion. Based upon the command not to take a mother bird with her young, the rabbis formulated a general principle, forbidding any unnecessary pain to be inflicted upon God's creations.[66] As the American abolitionist writer, Harriet Beecher Stowe once wrote: "The laws of Moses, if carefully examined, are a perfect phenomenon; an exception to the laws of either ancient or modern nations in the care they exercised over women and widows, orphans and paupers, foreigners and servants, as well as dumb animals."[67] And, through these laws of compassion, the Jewish people have endured.

Then, what are we to do? Because, if we are completely honest, then we may – on occasion – hurt feelings and forgo the blessing of a long life. And yet, if we are only compassionate, we may – on occasion – temper honesty and likewise forgo the blessing of a long life. To aid us in this daily policy debate, God presents the third command related to long life: "honor your father and mother...so that you may live long and fare well." Because, more than pleasing one's parents, this command is rooted in respect. For, it is by the respect/honor we show others that we will come to gauge more accurately how to strike the balance between justice and mercy, between honesty and compassion.

Upon finally striking this balance, it may be disappointing for some of us to hear that we do not actually become a Wolverine, or a King Aragorn, or – thankfully not – a Lord Voldemort. We do however, to quote another unforgettable character, go on – with God's blessing – to "live long and prosper," as we engage every day in deeds of honesty, compassion, and respect.[68] May we, by embracing these eternal values in our culture, become daily superheroes, helping all the world to live long and meaningful lives.

Ki Teitzei // When You Go Out
Bite 2 – *Family Pressure*

Cartoonist, Mark Parisi, has a way of satirically depicting how we as human-beings relate to one another, especially with those closest to us. In one of his

---

[65] RaSHI commentary to Deuteronomy 25:15: "If you were untruthful about measures and about weights, be worried about provocation by the enemy for, as the Proverb has it: 'dishonest scales are an abomination of the Lord,' and afterwards it is written: 'iniquity comes and disgrace follows.'"

[66] BT Bava Meitziah 31a-33a; see also Deuteronomy 22:10 and 25:4 as well as Exodus 23:5

[67] From Harriet Beecher Stowe's "Moses and His Laws," quoted in Simon Wolf's *American Jew as Patriot, Soldier, and Citizen*: 1895.

[68] Spoken by the Star Trek character, Captain Spock.

drawings, he presents a particular restaurant from the outside. This restaurant, however, is not just *any* restaurant. Peering through the front window, we see a cook as well as a waiter screaming at a couple as they try to enjoy a meal. Meanwhile, another couple – who apparently just finished – steps out the front door in a wretched state: the man is hunched over as if he had just received 50 lashes and the woman is in tears. On the roof, the name of the restaurant reads, "Fizby's: Where You're Treated like Family!"[69]

It seems within our nature to be toughest on those closest to us; a nature brought to light in the collection of laws presented in this Torah portion of *Ki Teitzei*. According to Deuteronomy 23:3: We shall "not permit a misbegotten [son or daughter of Israelites]…even into the tenth generation, to be admitted into the congregation of the Lord." This standard however is not universal, as six verses later we read, "Though, the children born unto them [referring to the Egyptians from a previous verse] may be admitted into the congregation of the Lord in three generations." (Deuteronomy 23:8)

According to the *Sifrie* (a work of legal Biblical exegesis) on this verse, the reason different standards are held for different groups is because after the Exodus, the Israelites looked back and saw that "the sins of Egypt only threatened their physical survival," whereas the sins of Israel continued to endanger the community both in body and soul.[70] Through the words of the *Sifrie*, we learn that we are often toughest on those closest to us because we perceive them as the greatest threat to our own survival.

Ask any child, with a sibling, and they will readily testify to the absolute truth of this statement: those closest to us pose the greatest threat. As evidence, they can produce upon demand a litany of moments in which a brother or sister knew just what to do to provoke a raging fit or a down-pour of tears. It took Jacob, after all, very little to provoke his older brother Esau, convincing him to sell his birthright in Genesis 25:29-34. It is as if, upon entry into this world, siblings are given a blue-print of each other's souls, detailing the exact location of each and every "personal button" which may then be pushed and prodded at will by the other, typically for their own amusement.

But, as we later come to understand, this knowledge is not given; it is earned. Through observation and direct interaction, we learn a lot about those closest to us, including seeing within them things they cannot even see within themselves. It is, at these moments, that we can and should embrace our role as a "button pusher." Not as a threat. Rather, as adults (especially those of us who are parents), we understand that it is our responsibility to apply pressure which may push a close-one to success, bringing out of them the potential we see within. As it is stated by our rabbis, "Just as a diamond is produced through pressure, so too is the precious gem of the soul brought to its brilliance."

---

[69] Mark Parisi. Restaurant Cartoon # 2005-01-25. http://www.offthemark.com/cartoons/restaurant/pg/8/
[70] Noted by Rabbi Harold Kushner in *Etz Hayim: Torah and Commentary*, Rabbinical Assembly: New York, 2001. p. 1123

Where, however, our good intentions often go awry is in our application of pressure. Feeling that a close-one's potential was not realized, when in truth it is *our* own expectations that have gone unfulfilled, we respond with raised voices, hostile language, and sadly at times even physical violence. These responses are inappropriate. And even more, they are a mistake if we think the solution to our frustration lies in the application of more pressure. For, as we know, while the right amount of pressure over time can transform a lump of coal into a precious diamond, too much pressure too quickly turns that same lump of coal into dust.

Those close to us are not lumps of coal.[71] But, within them does reside something precious… the secret to our survival. For when they fail, we fail. And, when they succeed, we succeed. Thus, it is in our interest to help them be, in the words of the U.S. Army, "all that they can be." While some may argue this is best achieved by being tough, *Ki Teitzei* encourages us to take a different approach: stepping back and applying only the right amount of pressure at the right time. This is not an easy task, not for any of us who care for another. But, once achieved, we will be happy to enter any place where "you are treated like family."

Ki Teitzei // When You Go Out
Bite 3 – *A Discipline Problem*

At the beginning of any academic year, we are likely to find many a parent frantic. In addition to all the other preparations needed to ensure our children's success in school, we – as parents – are busy completing our own required summer-assignments of sorts: updating our child's emergency contact form, updating our child's health form, and – lest we forget – updating our child's corporal punishment form. Yes, in many school districts in Mississippi and elsewhere around the nation, corporal punishment is considered a potential part of a child's proper education. Though, as parents, we are at least provided a form, granting us the option to opt-out.

By Biblical standards this would have seemed ridiculous! No, surprisingly, not the idea of corporal punishment; rather, what would have been regarded as foolish is the option to opt out, as that would have appeared as nothing less than uncaring. For, in the wisdom of King Solomon, recorded in the book of Proverbs, we are taught: "He who spares the rod hates his son. But, he who loves him disciplines him early." (13:24) This does not mean that the 'breakfast-of-champions' for an Israelite child included a healthy dose of spanking. God forbid! Instead, our ancestors understood that a parent's

---

[71] This is in contrast to the 1970s lyrics of Billy Joe Shaver, who originally wrote and sang "I'm just an old chunk of coal." American country music artist John Anderson released it again in 1981, as the first single from the album *John Anderson 2*.

involvement in the discipline of their child is an essential part of their education, ensuring their future success.

Nevertheless, taken out of its greater Biblical contexts, this line has often been used to support corporal punishment to all-sorts of excess both in public-schools as well as in private-homes. But, within its proper contexts, we see that Jewish tradition was not entirely comfortable with its use, gradually attempting to limit its employment. Starting with *Ki Teizei*, we read that "one may be given up to forty lashes, but no more." (25:3) Then, approximately in the year 70 C.E., rabbinic tradition tried to further abrogate the law by restricting the number to "forty lashes, minus one."[72] For, the Bible informs us, these limitations are necessary in order to prevent "one from being degraded before another's eyes." (Deuteronomy 25:3)

Reasonably, many argue, these efforts by our predecessors do not go far enough. Opponents of corporal punishment argue that such practices are barbaric, as no credible scientific evidence can be brought to bear which proves beyond a reasonable doubt or beyond a responsible margin of error that the potential benefit in hitting a child outweighs the obvious harm. And that harm, argues opponents of corporal punishment, goes well beyond the physical. By witnessing their adult role models (teachers, coaches, parents, etc.) hit, well – it is argued – our children in effect learn through observation that hitting and similar violent activity is okay.

"And, isn't it?" rhetorically question the proponents. After all, they will point out, limited corporal punishment is not just supported by some of our textual traditions, it is also found to be "okay" through our secular courts. For example, in 1977, the U.S. Supreme Court ruled in Ingraham v. Wright that school corporal punishment does not constitute cruel and unusual punishment under the Eighth Amendment. Furthermore, proponents of corporal punishment argue, this form of discipline provides an immediate response, allowing the student to return to the learning environment with his/her better-behaving peers in short order, rather than being suspended from school and/or sequestered in a separate classroom where the negative behavior is only likely to continue.

But, what these advocates don't realize is that corporal punishment does exactly that. Rather than being the deterrent many hope that it will be, this form of discipline actually compounds the potential for our child to repeat the offensive act. For, when an adult hits a child – especially when it is done, as it was so often done in the past, in front of his/her peers – one risks, as the Torah portion put it, irreversibly "degrading [the child] in the eyes of [his/her] fellow." (Deuteronomy 25:3) In other words, through this form of discipline – by a respected authority figure – not only is the child's act marked as unwanted and undesired, so is the child. In turn, comments Bible scholar Jeffrey Tigay,

---

[72] *Mishnah* Makkot 3:10-11

the child "will be further alienated from [his/her] society, [thereby] making [him/her] more likely to repeat the [undesired] behavior."[73]

So, if we truly wish to address this discipline problem we must not abandon the trend initiated by our ancestors, which sought to limit the use of corporal punishment. This does not mean that, in opting-out, we are taking a hands-off approach. Quite the opposite; we are encouraged to be more hands-on, opting-in – both as parents and teachers – becoming more involved in all aspects of our children's education, including their discipline. For when we are involved in the discipline of our children – not through force, but through the gentle hand reinforced by the strength of our caring relationships – all our children stand a better chance at success both now and in the future.

---

[73] Jeffrey Tigay. *Etz Hayim: Torah and Commentary*. Rabbinical Assembly: New York, 2001. p. 1133

Portion 7:
Ki Tavo // When You Come Into
Torah Portion: Deuteronomy 26:1-29:8

"WHEN YOU COME INTO THE LAND…" These words initiate the last part of Moses' long discourse. Having first reviewed the history of the people's wanderings, followed by a lengthy legislative address, Moses climatically ends his discourse by invoking the blessings of faithful adherence to those laws and calling down curses on those who will depart from them.

All of this, though, is conditional upon entering the Land. When that happens, one must "take some of every first fruit of the soil," and give it to God as thanks for the fulfillment of the Divine promise. This ritual is known as *bikurim* and it is accompanied with the first guided recitation in Jewish history, which is still recited on Passover today: "My father was a wandering Aramean, etc." (Deuteronomy 26:5-9)

This would not be the only ceremony to mark their entrance into the Land, nor would it be the only ritual to recognize the reciprocal relationship which exists between God and the people of Israel. The portion continues to describe other rituals the people must engage in upon their arrival: erecting an altar of stones, plastering other stones and writing the words of God upon them, as well as calling forth the blessings and curses that are attached to these words.

Some of these blessings and curses are pithy, like "cursed be he who subverts the rights of the stranger" or "blessed shall you be in your comings and goings." However, other parts of the portion spell out the details of these blessings and curses, some sounding like the plagues visited upon Egypt.

As a summary note, the portion makes clear that "these are the terms of the Covenant which the Lord commanded Moses to conclude with the Israelites in the land of Moab, in addition to the Covenant which God had made with them at Horeb." (Deuteronomy 28:69)

Ki Tavo // When You Come Into
Bite 1 – *Shattered Hearts and Souls*

Sometimes the biggest challenge when teaching is getting everyone's attention, regardless of the students' ages. And, the size of this challenge increases as the size of the group increases. Some of the very best teachers deal with this challenge through silence. They will become so quiet at the front of the room that everyone stops talking and pays attention. But, there is a great measure of patience required for this method, a willingness to wait until everyone is ready. Frequently people in the room will try to help by shushing each other, which sometimes makes the situation worse, as the sound of *shuuussssshhh* becomes louder than the idle chatter. Though, once everyone is quiet, the next challenge arises: how to be sure that they are really paying attention, so that they may absorb what is taught.

One can only imagine how Moses faced this challenge, given the sheer number of people he faced. There were so many things that he wanted the Israelites to hear, absorb, and internalize. So, how does he get their attention? Throughout the book of Deuteronomy he used storytelling, promises, threats, poetry and yes… even silence. As it is written in this portion of *Ki Tavo*, "Moses and the Levitical priests spoke to all Israel, saying: 'Silence/*has-keit*! Hear, O Israel![74] Today you have become the people of the Lord your God.'" (Deuteronomy 27:9). Jeffrey Tigay notes that "this is the first time that the appeal to hear is preceded by a call for silence, teaching us that absolute concentration is required at the awesome moment when Israel becomes the people of God."[75]

Not only is the call for silence unusual, but the word used here in the Hebrew, *has-keit*, is unique to this one place in Hebrew Scriptures. Thus, many attempts have been made to understand this word, whose meaning can continue to guide us today in ensuring we remain God's people. The first comes from the sound of the word: *has-keit*. With the hiss of the first syllable and the harsh consonants of the second syllable, it sounds like a teacher's command to "hush up and look up here." That's what RaSHI concluded in the 11th century. Using a very early Aramaic translation of the Torah, RaSHI translates *has-keit* as "pay attention."[76]

Another attempt to understand this word comes from splitting the one word *has-keit* into two by its syllables. For example, the sages of the *Talmud* suggest that *has* means "hush," while *keit* means "shatter." Likewise, the Tanchuma translates *has* as "hush," but understands *keit* as "form small groups and incline your hearts to words of Torah."[77] Putting these together, one could read *has-keit* as meaning "hush; shatter your hearts to hear words of Torah."

---

[74] This is the same word that begins our declaration of faith, speaking to the Oneness of God; Deut. 6:4.
[75] Jeffrey Tigay. *The JPS Torah Commentary: Deuteronomy*. The Jewish Publication Society: Philadelphia, 2003.
[76] RaSHI commentary on Deuteronomy 27:9.
[77] *Midrash Tanchuma* on Ki Tavo.

What an odd suggestion, right? For we are accustomed to thinking of Torah as something that heals not hurts, something that brings wholeness not brokenness to our lives. But like all good teachers, there is a method to Moses' madness. Because more than being quiet, Moses needed his class – the people of Israel – to take these words of Torah to heart. And, as strange as it may sound, a shattered heart makes that possible. As the Chasidic Rabbi, Menachem Mendel of Kotsk, taught: "There is nothing more whole than a shattered heart," for then the heart is open and receptive to the power of the Eternal.

So, *has-keit*/silence! And, let us *shema Yisrael*/hear, O Israel… the shatter (as opposed to the "shush"): the shattering of our isolation, so that we may connect with community, the shattering of our firm and impenetrable hearts, so that we may open ourselves to the tender love of God. Thereby, as it was with our ancestors, we too today can affirm with all of our hearts, with all of our souls and with all of our might that now and forevermore God is indeed our God and we are and will remain God's loving people.

Ki Tavo // When You Come Into
Bite 2 – *The Slow Pursuit of Happiness*

Access Hollywood. Entertainment Tonight. TMZ. These shows are just a portion of the media blitz on our nation's celebrities; a blitz reinforced most visibly by an array of tabloid magazines which fill the ranks of check-out counters around the world, firing off inflammatory headlines as we stand helplessly in line. So, whether we like it or not, our brains are often scarred from this 24-hour celebrity coverage, especially when the chase of fame ends up in flames. Which, brings up the age-old-question: "Why do so many individuals, who appear to be on the fast track of life headed towards success, often end up finishing dead last?"

In this Torah portion of *Ki Tavo*, we are provided with one possible explanation. It is stated in Deuteronomy 28:2: "All these blessings shall come upon you and take affect if you just heed the word of the Lord your God." It seems to be a fast acting solution embraced as of late by many celebrities as they turn to *kabbalah* (Jewish mysticism) in order to avoid the typical snares of the Hollywood lifestyle. However, nothing about this Biblical verse from Deuteronomy is intended to be understood as 'fast.'

Although the first half of the verse states, "all these blessings shall come upon you and take effect," it is not simply as the second half of the verse implies about "heeding the word of God." In order to truly receive the blessings God has intended for our lives, we read in the Hebrew that "all these blessings shall *hi-si-gu-cha*," which means they must literally "overtake" us. By understanding better the original intention of God's word through the Hebrew, we are provided with a valuable lesson. We learn that sometimes in the pursuit of happiness we maintain a pace that is counterproductive, outrunning the blessings which given the chance would have overtaken us.

Now, for those of us from the good-ol' South, this concern for sustaining a pace that is faster than we need and quicker than we can handle, may appear irrelevant. Not only are we miles from the same track these celebrities circle around at neck-breaking speeds, we are also in a place which boasts of a pace that is slower than that which exists in the rest of the United States. For example, in a heated exchange about life in the South on City-Data.com, a resident of South Carolina wrote: "Yes, there is a slower pace to life in the south – but we LIKE it that way. We enjoy taking time to 'smell the roses' and not live a 'dog-eat-dog' existence." But, before we throw caution totally into the wind, let me say these two little words: fast and food.

And, it's not just fast food which threatens our healthy pace through life. We have moved into an era where "I'll have that ready in a minute" is one minute too long; where speed-limits are merely suggestions; and where, according to Louis Tully from the movie *Ghostbusters*, we "play '20 Minute Workout' [tapes] at high-speed so it takes only ten minutes to get a really good workout."[78] I suppose this mode of living is apt for a species which calls itself "the Human RACE." As if numbers were affixed on our backs and endorsements on our sleeves, we hurriedly circle around the race track of life, deluding ourselves into thinking that we are actually getting somewhere because we happen to make a little more money, have a little nicer car, a slightly bigger house, and slightly newer technology (which, by the way, seems to be the 'pace-car' no one can ever really catch up to). But, at what cost?

By chasing after these false-measures of success, we may not realize that we just outran life's true blessings: the beauty of nature beheld in a gaze not a glance, the treasure of friendship found in long hugs not quick handshakes, and the love of family nurtured in moments not minutes. These are life's true mile-markers on the road towards success, which sadly cannot overtake us if we don't slow down. But, that is not the worst of it. As we learn from the tragic stories of some celebrities, by moving at such high speeds we actually become less aware and thus more prone to accidents on the road of life. Acknowledging the correlation between our pace in life and the blessing of peace we feel in life, the book of Proverbs stated long ago: "A slow and steady man will receive many blessings, but one in a hurry…will not go unscathed."[79]

It seems, therefore, in light of our traditions that the pursuit of happiness should not really be a pursuit at all. Rather, it could be said, that the Jewish pursuit of happiness is literally a walk in the park. Fittingly, Adventure Rabbi Jamie Korngold wrote in her new book, *God in the Wilderness*: "We become aware [in the fullest sense of that word] by slowing down and waking up to the world around us… [For] when we slow down, we have the opportunity to meet the Divine…and [thus be] embraced by a sense of belonging, of oneness,

---

[78] Dan Aykroyd and Harold Ramis. *Ghostbusters*. Columbia Pictures: 1984.
[79] Proverbs 28:20

and of peace." In other words, when we slow down, we keep pace with God. And, in doing so, we allow God's blessings to catch up and overtake us.

As we approach the High Holy Days, may we heed the subtle caution sign found in *Ki Tavo*. That way we may begin the New Year on a steadier and more secure pace. For, as the 6th century Greek fabulist Aesop reminds us in his famous tale *The Tortoise and the Hare*, it is not necessarily the fastest that will cross the finish line of success first. Rather, it is most likely to be the "slow and steady who wins that race."

Ki Tavo // When You Come Into
Bite 3 – *Judaism: A Slow Revelation*

"Who lives in a pineapple under the sea? *Spongebob Squarepants!*
Absorbent and yellow and porous is he? *Spongebob Squarepants!*"[80]
Who's been put through the ringer by psychology? *Spongebob Squarepants!*

Yes, according to a 2011 study in *The Journal of Pediatrics*, "just nine minutes of viewing a fast-paced television cartoon – like *Spongebob* – had immediate negative effects on the ability of four-year-olds to learn."[81] Responding to the study, producers of *Spongebob* stated, that's because "*Spongebob* is not meant to educate four-year-olds. It's entertainment for those six years of age or older."[82] That distinction comes as little relief to child psychologist Dr. Dmitri Christakis, who believes the results "will only add to the growing concern that we are over-stimulating developing brains," compromising our children's abilities to think and understand.[83]

Among that group of concerned citizens would likely have been our illustrious teacher, Moses. Because, as it is written in this Torah portion of *Ki Tavo*, in their march towards the promised land "Moses summoned all Israel and said to them: 'You have seen all that the Lord did before your very eyes in the land of Egypt, to Pharaoh and all his courtiers and to his whole country. These wondrous feats, these prodigious signs and marvels [which happened in quick succession, one after another], you saw with your own eyes.'" Yet, as we would say in the South "bless your heart," for even though you saw all this, states the Bible, "to this day, the Lord has not given you a mind to understand, eyes to see, or ears to hear." (Deuteronomy 29:1-3)

---

[80] Pat Pinney. "Spongebob Squarepants Theme Song." Hank Smith Music:1997.
[81] Courtney Hutchison. "Watching Spongebob Squarepants Makes Preschoolers Slower Thinkers, Study Finds." *ABC News*: Medical Unit, 12 September 2011. According to the study, there was nothing wrong with the subject or content of the cartoon, but the problem resided in the frantic pacing of its scenes, which occurred on average every 11 seconds (compared to other cartoons which had a scene change every 30 seconds on average). As a result, children who watched Spongebob were often left wound-up and unable to concentrate. http://abcnews.go.com/Health/Wellness/watching-spongebob-makes-preschoolers-slower-thinkers-study-finds/story?id=14482447
[82] Ibid.
[83] Ibid.

Strange, no? For the Bible seems to imply that the people of Israel saw but did not really see, heard but did not really hear, understood but did not really understand. So, the sage MaHaRaL teaches these verses "do not mean that the people were not endowed with intellect or the faculties of vision and hearing. Rather," like the fast-paced action on Spongebob, "witnessing these signs [in such quick succession] overwhelmed these faculties so that they could not understand the loving-kindness of the *Kadosh Barech Hu*, the Holy Blessed One," which was behind all those acts. And, as a consequence, "the people of Israel were not able to cleave to God."[84] Therefore, to truly comprehend and cleave to the Divine depths which reside behind all that we see, hear, touch and smell, the curtain of holiness must be revealed... but slowly.

Even with the caveat of 'slowly,' some will resist the unveiling all together with such protest as "pay no attention to that man behind the curtain."[85] For there is a sense that what exists behind the heavenly curtain is a trade secret, delicate nuances of the Divine craft which make for awe. And – like a magic trick – if revealed, it is believed not only will the admiration for the Divine Craftsman be threatened, so will the indelible meaning that moment of awe was meant to make. While a valid concern, it's one we – in Judaism – cannot embrace. For, a state of unknowingness is in no way aided by the words "pay no attention;" nor is it helped by unveiling everything so quickly. For in doing so, suggests the study, the developing mind gets overwhelmed and cannot – to use the famous quote – "handle the Truth!"[86]

Therefore, it seems only logical that a solution to a state of unknowingness resides somewhere in the middle: permitting the heavenly curtain of Truth to be lifted, but in a gradual fashion as to allow the developing person in both mind and heart, in both body and soul, to process the information. This principle has been applied, for example, in the education curriculum of the ISJL. The curriculum is spiraled, meaning that when the students revisit concepts or ideas, they will do it with an increased level of sophistication and with a new experience attached to it. This makes sure that every moment is an opportunity for greater learning. For example, when learning about *tzedakah* (charity):

> A child may begin with a sensory experience like constructing a *tzedakah* box and fund-raising for the poor. In middle school, the value of *tzedakah* is explored in greater depth through examining RaMBaM's ladder of *tzedakah*. So that, by the time High School arrives, students are applying the value of *tzedakah* in their daily lives by designing social justice projects for their communities.

---

[84] Judah Loew ben Bezalel, (c. 1520 – 1609) is widely known to scholars of Judaism as the MaHaRaL, for the Hebrew acronym "*Moreinu ha-Rav Loew* // Our Teacher, Rabbi Loew." Rabbi Loew was an important Talmudic scholar, Jewish mystic, and philosopher who served as a leading rabbi in the city of Prague in Bohemia for most of his life. His best known scholarship may be his super-commentary on RaSHI's Torah commentary, called the *Gur Aryeh al HaTorah*, from which this teaching was derived.

[85] *The Wizard of Oz*. Metro-Goldwyn-Mayer: 1939.

[86] Aaron Sorkin. *A Few Good Men*. Columbia Pictures: 1992.

Truly, from this and other examples of an orderly progress of revelation, the developing person is able to adequately process the ever-increasing amount of information, so that we can earn what "*Adonai lo natan* // what God did not [initially] give" us. And that was, as we were told from our portion, "a mind to understand;" what the Hebrew calls a "*lev da'at*," literally "a heart of knowledge." For, beyond obtaining understanding of a teaching, the Bible is acknowledging (through this gradual system) that we are meant to develop a passion for the teaching as well. For, it is by this passion, that our collective journey continues; a journey that behooves us to keep on unveiling the loving-kindness of the Holy Blessed One that resides behind all that we see, hear, taste and feel *l'at l'at* (slowly, slowly). For, therein resides an opportunity to cleave more closely to God and one another.

> Who redeemed the people from slavery? *Ka-dosh Bar-chu.*
> His knowledge and wisdom revealed slowly? *Ka-dosh Bar-chu.*
> Who charged us then to raise the lowly? *Ka-dosh Bar-chu.*

Double Portion 8 & 9:
Nitzavim-Vayeilech // Stand Still-Go Forth
Torah Portion: Deuteronomy 29:9-31:30

"YOU STAND THIS DAY, ALL OF YOU, BEFORE THE LORD YOUR GOD…" As well, they stand before Moses, hearing him ratify the Eternal Covenant mentioned at the very end of the previous portion. Everyone is included in this ceremony, states the portion, "even those who are not with [them] there that day." (Deuteronomy 29:14)

Even then, Moses acknowledged, "there is some man or woman, some clan or tribe, whose heart is turning away from the Lord our God." (Deuteronomy 29:17). Clearly, entering the land is not the completion of the Israelite journey, just another stage of development. Thus, Moses tempers his despair with hope, telling the people: "The Lord your God will restore your fortunes and take you back in love." (Deuteronomy 30:3)

The way back, indicates Moses, is through the laws of God. There is no excuse for not following them, as they are neither in Heaven nor across the sea. Rather they are so very close: on the lips and in the heart of the people. The great difficulty, he acknowledges, is having the choice to follow them.

After this, "MOSES WENT AND SPOKE TO THE PEOPLE." He walked through the camp to bid the children of Israel his final *adieu*. Moses teaches them the commandment of *hakhel*: the once in seven years gathering of the entire nation to hear the king read certain passages from the Torah. After God addresses Moses and Joshua in the Tent of Meeting, he commands them to copy over the Torah and to continue teaching it to the Jewish people.

The double-portion concludes with Moses' concern that the Jewish people will stray from the Torah after his death. In response, he writes a poem as a witness of what transpired before, so as not to repeat the mistakes of the past.

Nitzavim-Vayeilech // Stand Still-Go Forth
Bite 1 – *A Mature Mind: A Precondition to a Mature Life*

Maturity. When, exactly, is it determined? Is it at the age of thirteen, when one becomes a Bar or Bat Mitzvah, assuming the adult responsibilities of the commandments? Is it at the age of sixteen, when one becomes old enough to properly and (God willing) safely manage a motor vehicle? Is it at the age of eighteen, when one graduates from high school, setting out on his/her own? Or, is maturity not so much reached as it is achieved through experience, like receiving one's first paycheck and thereupon (to the relief of a great many parents) paying one's own bills? Or, maybe it's when we get married and have children of our own? Still, maybe maturity is only achieved when we experience the finite nature of human life and have to deal with death? I ask, because today it seems that we each maintain a different standard of maturity.

Anyone, who has ever had even the briefest of experiences with Torah, will know well that the Israelites were no different, as varying levels of maturity as well as immaturity were recorded throughout their journey from slavery in Egypt to anticipated freedom in the Promised Land. And now, standing/*nitzavim* on that land's border in this double Torah portion of *Nitzavim-Vayeilech*, God finally presents the people with a standard of maturity to *vayeilech*/move forward. As that standard is written in the book of Deuteronomy, "You stand here this day, all of you, before the Lord your God…to enter into the Covenant… This Covenant, with its sanctions, I make not with you alone, but with those who are standing here with us this day before the Lord our God and with all those who are not with us here this day." (Deuteronomy 29:9-14)

Critical is the timing of this covenantal ceremony, comments RaSHI, for "this day was the day of Moses' death."[87] As such, the people stood poised for a transition from their adolescent desert wanderings (so closely guided by Moses) to assuming the adult responsibilities of establishing a home spiritually as much as physically in the Promised Land (without him). Therefore, there was a pronounced need for a standard of maturity to guide the Israelite society forward. Yet, unlike today, our scholars conclude that maturity for the people of Israel would be less determined by age or experience and more so by a particular mindset. That is to say, there is a maturity of the mind articulated in these brief verses mentioned above that can help us act more responsibly in the world.

This mental preconditioning begins with those, whom the Bible states, "were standing there that day." Think about it for a moment. What must our ancestors have felt knowing the decision they were about to make would last well beyond their lifetimes? Probably, pride. After all, is that not the aspiration of human life, to see our actions reverberate blessings for generations to come? Yet accompanying that portion of pride was likely a large side of paranoia. As

---

[87] RaSHI commentary to Deuteronomy 29:9

any grandparent or parent will tell you, knowing that the decision you make today will affect your children tomorrow or the next day or someday thereafter, causes one to rethink and reexamine the variant choices to no end. But, psychologists affirm, within that mental awareness there is maturity. For, in considering how our actions may affect others, allows us – as the knight in *Indiana Jones and the Last Crusade* stated – to "choose [more] wisely."[88]

Nevertheless, on occasion, even the most thoughtful decisions will provoke resentment amongst those "not there that day." Because, in obligating a later generation to a previous decision, there is a feeling that their subsequent free-will is being stinted, subverted, or even outright squandered. This state of acrimony defines not just the state of Israel back then, but most states today. For how many times have you heard some unhappy individual pray to have been born at some other time, in some other place? And, it's not just here where discontentment reigns. Countless aspects of our lives have little to no personal input: what physical qualities we would inherit, what natural skills we would possess, where and how we would be educated. Yet, according to Rabbi Kushner, the second step towards "maturity consists in accepting those conditions as the facts of life."[89] For in accepting what is, we can better use our time to choose what will be.

As we can hear, both steps – accepting certain facts as unchangeable and future action as causal – may help us make more mature and responsible decisions in the here and now. And to be clear, it's not just with the one we read about at the end of this Torah portion, which states that God "puts before us this day life and death, blessing and curse," suggesting, encouraging, beseeching that we "choose life."[90] This mental acuity is an essential precondition for all the choices presented to us in the course of life, whether small (like deciding between hamburgers and hotdogs) or big, like deciding: which friends to associate with, which career to pursue, which school to attend, which person to marry. For, there is little hope to answer and thus act more maturely in these and countless other decision-making moments in life without first thinking maturely. As the Dalai Lama once stated:

> Take care of your thoughts, because they become your actions. Take care of your actions, because they become your habits. Take care of your habits, because they form your character. Take care of your character, because it shapes your life.[91]

The time has come in our Jewish year to give concentrated effort to do just that: shape our lives. For like our Israelite ancestors, we too stand in a moment of transition, poised/*nitzavim* to *vayeilech*/move forward towards a more mature and blessed year than the one before. Therefore, let us take a cue from this Torah portion, by first acquiring a mature mind that accepts the things we

---

[88] Jeffrey Boam. *Indiana Jones and the Last Crusade*. Lucasfilm Ltd. and Paramount Pictures: 1989.
[89] Harold Kushner. *Etz Hayim: Torah and Commentary*. Rabbinical Assembly: New York, 2001. p. 1166
[90] Deuteronomy 30:19
[91] Articulated by the Dalai Lama while in dialogue with the Brazilian theologian Leonardo Boff in 2010.

cannot change as well as appreciates that which we can change as a force on the lives of others. For, in this awareness, we are blessed with an opportunity to act more maturely no matter how old we may be, no matter what situation we may be facing. Because, as our sages have taught, maturity is not a condition of age or experience. It's a condition of the mind, one we pray to obtain in the contemplative celebration of our New Year.

Nitzavim-Vayeilech // Stand Still-Go Forth
Bite 2 – *Setting Down our Burdens of Sin*

Once, a wise and compassionate rabbi arrived in a small town, just days prior to the High Holy Day season. As the word spread of his arrival, the townspeople quickly assembled to seek counsel with this rabbi, who was renowned for giving the most accurate advice in seeking atonement. One particular woman, however, could not go. It's not that she didn't want to go. In her heart, she truly did. She desired very much to see the wise and compassionate Rabbi, and to receive his counsel on how to deal with a very large and terrible mistake she had made that year.

But, she felt that she could not go, at least not alone, for the burden she carried from that one mistake was too heavy. So, she asked a friend to accompany her. "I don't need to go!" protested the friend. "Sure I made some mistakes this past year. But they were all so small. Insignificant. In fact, they hardly amount to anything at all." "I understand," responded the first woman. "But, it would mean a lot to me if you could come and support me as I carry this large burden before the Rabbi in order to get his advice." Agreeing, the two women went off together to see the Rabbi.

"Yes," said the Rabbi, welcoming them in. "How can I help you?" "Well, rabbi..." started the first lady, "I caused a great sin during this past year and it caused a lot of grief and trouble for my people. I am deeply sorry for what I have done, but I do not know exactly what to do to make up for it. Honestly, I am afraid that I will never be able to achieve atonement." After listening intently to every word the woman had spoken, the Rabbi tilted his head slightly to the right and saw the women's friend, who had stood behind her... way behind her. So far back, in fact, that she had hoped – with the Rabbi's poor eye sight and her fortunate color choice in her clothing that day, which matched the color on the wallpaper – that she may go unnoticed, blending into the wall. But, her hopes were smashed when the rabbi asked: "And, you?"

"Uh...who?... me?" responded the friend. "Yes," said the Rabbi. "What transgression have you made this year that I can help you with." "Oh no, Rabbi," responded the friend. "You don't understand.

Look, it's not that I haven't transgressed this year. I have…many times. Oh, but don't get me wrong, they were little ones. You know, a little one here… and a little one there; nothing to worry about though. I came here just to provide some support for my friend."

"No worries, huh," thought the Rabbi. "Listen," he continued, speaking to the first lady, "I have a way to help you. But, first, I must ask you both to do one thing for me. You, with the large sin, I want you to go and bring back to me one large rock. And you, who say that you made only very small transgressions this year, I want you to bring back to me one small rock for every transgression you made." So, the two women went off to do as the Rabbi had asked.

When they returned, the woman with the large sin slowly made her way into the rabbi's room, placing a very large and very heavy boulder at his feet. Her friend, still not understanding the rabbi's reason for including her in the task, entered the rabbi's room nonetheless with her own burden, a sack – now large and heavy – with small stones, one for each transgression she had made over the past year. This too she placed at the rabbi's feet. Taking a long look at what was brought before him, the rabbi instructed: "Now that you have brought these to me, I want you to put them back."

"Back?" exclaimed the woman with all the small stones in disbelief. "Yes, back," said the rabbi, cautioning the women: "They must be placed back exactly from where you found them." While the first woman grinned with a sense of relief, the second woman with all the small stones shouted: "That's impossible! Rabbi, how could I return each and every one of these small stones back exactly from where I took them?" "Ah-cha!" the rabbi said, "You cannot. But, try, you should nevertheless!"

As we approach the High Holy Days, we acknowledge that in this past year we have likely made both types of mistakes: the large ones as well as the small. And with ease, I am sure, we can – to this day – recall the large ones. We can remember, with amazing clarity, the details: *where* it happened, *when* it happened, with *whom* it happened, *how* it happened, and even *why* it happened. Details, honestly, that we would like to forget. But, because they weighed so heavy upon our souls at that time, the imprint that mistake has made seems to have lasted a lifetime.

The same, however, cannot be said for our smaller mistakes, whose imprint appears to fade more rapidly over time. In fact, even in the course of this year, a plethora of these smaller mistakes have likely been glazed over… forgotten… dismissed, as we consider them merely to be par for the course of life, the expected imperfections in a life that is so often imperfect. Think about it: how many times did we lose our temper with a co-worker or a family member and not say I am sorry; how many times did we make a promise to a friend that was never fulfilled; how many times did we witness an injustice but not protest against it; how many times did we pass a stranger on the street and not acknowledge his/her existence with a simple hello; how many times was the extended hand of help, ignored; how many times was the phone-call, the text, the e-mail never returned? However small we may consider these mistakes, the story teaches us, they are of no lesser weight. For if they go unacknowledged, they too will become a heavy burden on the path towards perfection: equal in weight to one large one, but even more difficult to replace.

Perfection, at least from a Jewish perspective, is not a life without mistakes. Rather, perfection is a process in achieving wholeness, or more aptly stated for this time before the High Holy Days, a process in achieving 'at-one-ment,' made through an exact accounting of and holding ourselves accountable for our mistakes. May we, as *Nitzvaim-Vayeilech* states, not "walk with a stubbornness of heart," acting as if we carry no sinful burden (Deuteronomy 29:18). Rather, as it advises, "let us do [proper] *t'shuvah*: opening our hearts in repentance as we return to the ways of our Lord." (Deuteronomy 30:2) In this way, we pray, we may continue on a path towards perfection in the new year!

Nitzavim-Vayeilech // Stand Still-Go Forth
Bite 3 – *An Oxymoronic Guide to the Days of Awe*

An accurate estimate of our current history is one of consistent chaos. The once safe bet of the stock market has us in cold sweats and silently screaming, 'good grief,' especially after a detailed summary of our accounts shows constant change. As a result, we have abundant poverty, gas tanks half full, and irate patients. To act naturally seems like the only choice, for those who consider this old news. To others, however, this is no minor crisis, but the beginnings of a great depression. To avoid this situation, may I suggest a farewell reception, as we depart on a working vacation for some serious fun? Please, stand down! I can see that I'm clearly misunderstood. It's not that I'm a kosher ham, nor even a clever fool. I am simply a recent graduate student who enjoys from time to time a good oxymoron.

After all, is it not intriguing how two words, with separate and incongruent meanings, can come together in a tenuous harmony to provide one valuable message! The title of this double portion is a perfect example: *Nitzavim-Vayeilech*, meaning, "Stand Still; Go Forth." This double-talk should not be confused with the endowed speech of a fork-tongued politician, who panders to both sides of a diverse audience. As if, for example, it was expected that both (a) those who wish to 'stand' in synagogue during the High Holy Days as well as (b) those who wish to 'go forth' beyond its walls would hear support for their cause in the solitary utterance of *nitzavim-vayeilech*, 'stand still; go forth.'

It is for this reason that we are not to equate God to a politician, whose words may be manipulated at will for the sake of the audience's agenda. Rather, God is our Teacher. And, as God's students, it is our responsibility to hear out the entire lesson. Even so, we are left to question: "How are we to make sense of an oxymoron like 'stand still, go forth?'" I speculate these words were brought together, intentionally to be puzzling, in order to grab our attention. For contained within this tenuous connection is a guide for the Days of Awe, which can facilitate a meaningful summation of one year and a successful initiation of another.

Like an assemble-it-yourself piece of furniture, the first step in understanding the guide is to layout its respective parts: "*nitzavim*/stand still" and "*vayeilech*/go forth." In the context of this Torah portion, *nitzavim* describes the stance taken by the Israelites as they stood before Moses to hear his final oration. This, however, is not the only time the Israelites took such a stance. In the book of Exodus it states, "Moses let the people out of the camp towards God and they *nitzavim*/stood at the foot of the mountain." (19:17) In another passage from the book of Exodus, God commands the people: "Be ready by morning. For, in the morning, you will come up to Mt. Sinai and *nitzavim*/stand there before Me." (34:2)

While *nitzavim* is typically translated as 'stood,' (as it is above), the contexts of these verses suggest that its meaning extends beyond the physical. As Professor Joseph Edelheit proposes, "*nitzav* [is used to] suggest an act of will, a physical statement of *hineini* – 'Here I am, prepared to respond to your call.'"[92] I suppose, had the intention been only to communicate a physical stance, it is likely that the Biblical author would have used the generic Hebrew word for 'stand:' *omeid*. Instead, *nitzavim* is used to convey an important first step in these Days of Awe. Instead of throwing a large celebration as we do on the secular New Year, we are guided to create an inner stillness, where we can stand firm, ready to affirm our relationship with God, with each other, with ourselves. But, again, this is only step one.

Once we have taken the preparatory stance of *nitzavim,* we are then ready to truly and successfully *vayeilech*, "go forth" (the second step in the oxymoronic guide to the Days of Awe). In its contexts, *vayeilech* refers to Moses' actions as he "went forth to be among his kinfolk to witness their hard labor," (Exodus 2:11) as well as when, in his final days, he *vayeilech*/went forth from his place to be among the people, preparing them for their promised future (Deuteronomy 31:1). It could be said that a similar journey was undertaken by Abraham, as God told him to "*lech*/go forth from [his] native land," redirecting the course of our history forever.[93] Whenever we read such accounts of *vayeilech* or any formulations of its shared Semitic root (*hey-lamed-chaf*), it is not to be understood as a haphazard journey, as if the sojourner was a pinball bounced around at the will of the many forces surrounding him/her. Rather, from its contexts, we understand that *vayeilech*/go forth initiates a journey of purpose which will bring about significant change.

---

[92] Elaine Rise Glickman, ed. *Living Torah: Selections from Seven Years of Torat Chayim.* p.400
[93] Genesis 12:1

For us, these Days of Awe are a journey. And, like Moses and Abraham, it shall be for us a journey of significant change as we come closer to God, to each other, and to ourselves. Yet, before we even begin, we take a cue from the title of our double portion and *nitzavim*/stand still. We stand still in order to know what we stand for. Then, and only then, can we successfully *vayeilech*/go forth into the world, maneuvering through life's many obstacles. Now, it is true. The incongruity of "standing still and going forth" is initially jarring. Yet, we cannot choose to pacify this abrasive conjunction by picking one part over the other. In order to truly deal with this oxymoron we must follow both steps. In doing so, may we meaningfully end one year and successfully begin another. *L'shanah Tovah Tikateivu*. Happy New Year and may we all be written in the book of Life for health and blessing!

ROSH HASHANAH:

Beth Kander's "Apples & Honey (Bourbon)" Challah Bread Puddin'

Ingredients (The Bread Pudding):
10 cups of challah (approximately 1 big loaf, torn into chunks)
1 cup milk   1 can (12 oz.) of evaporated milk
1 cup half-and-half   8 eggs (beaten)
½ cup granulated sugar   ½ cup butter
½ cup honey   1 tsp. vanilla extract
1 teaspoon cinnamon   2 teaspoon baking powder
Dash of salt
2 cups of peeled, chopped apples

Ingredients (The Sauce):
½ cup sugar
½ cup light corn syrup
¼ cup butter
¼ cup honey bourbon

First, preheat oven to 350 degrees. Lightly grease a 9"x13" baking dish. Place the challah chunks in a large mixing bowl. In a different bowl, mix together milk, evaporated milk, half and half, eggs, sugar, butter, honey, vanilla, cinnamon, baking powder & salt. When thoroughly combined, pour mixture over challah chunks. Let it sit for about 10 minutes so the challah can absorb all the deliciousness. Then, add the apples, and spoon everything into the baking dish. Bake for approximately 35-45 minutes, until the bread pudding is a beautiful light golden color. Remove from oven and let cool 5 minutes before serving.

While the bread pudding is cooling, make the sauce! Just combine sugar, corn syrup, and butter in a small saucepan over medium heat. Bring to a simmer; cook for about a minute, stirring it constantly. Remove from heat; stir in the honey bourbon.

Immediately drizzle one tablespoon of sauce over each serving of bread pudding. ENJOY! (If you're traveling with the dish, you can either bring the sauce and re-heat there, or go ahead and drizzle it over the whole bread pudding – it won't be as gooey-and-fresh, but will coat the dish nicely and still be delicious when eaten.)

Portion 10:
Ha-azinu // Give Ear
Torah Portion: Deuteronomy 32:1-52

"GIVE EAR, O HEAVENS, LET ME SPEAK; LET THE EARTH HEAR THE WORDS I UTTER!" This is the last portion of Torah that is read during a weekly Shabbat service. It consists almost entirely of a poem, summarizing the themes reminiscent throughout the five books of Moses: God's righteousness and compassion, and the corruption and irritableness of the people, even since the time of the Tower of Babel.

Recalling this history, studded with human frailty, transgression and ineptitude, reinforces the greatness and generosity of God, as there were many justifiable moments for God to destroy humanity but, instead, the world was spared and the Jewish people lived on. The portion further clarifies that God did not destroy the Jewish people by the hand of an invading army because that nation might have inaccurately taken credit for the demise of the nation of Israel.

The Israelites' misery is correlated with their actions, actions which are chronicled and often cyclical (you would think after this long they would have learned better!). As not to end on a negative note, once again we read of hope. God has the ability to eventually forgive the transgressions of the Israelites and instead focus the Divine wrath against those who seek to destroy Israel. In that way, the Israelites may feel assured to keep on working on their own perfection.

Speaking of the future, the portion ends with Moses and his successor Joshua passing the poem unto the children of Israel with a warning to heed this ever important message. As Joshua will take over the helm of Israelite leadership, God once again reminds Moses of his instructions to climb Mount Nebo, where he will view the land of Israel from afar, but never enter it.

Ha-azinu // Give Ear
Bite 1 – *Our Words are Money*

Whether it's at a conference, a convention or a collective meeting of the minds, there always seems to be those individuals, who apparently have a persistent need to have their voices heard. We know these individuals well, because when they speak, sadly, their words are often met by silent groans of "not again;" which, by the way, only provokes those individuals further, as they plead to have their words heard. For this time, they emphasize, "It is *really* important!"[94]

In his repeated attempts to get the Israelites to hear words of the Divine, Moses may have been similarly provoked. Because, at the end of his life, in this Torah portion of *Ha-azinu*, Moses pleads: "Give ear, O Heavens; let me speak! Let the earth hear the words of my beak! May my discourse come down like rain, my speech distill as dew; like showers on grass whereupon herbs produce. For, it is the Name of the Lord I proclaim; give to God great fame!"[95]

After forty years of frustration, Moses seems to have finally lost it… or, perhaps, found a better way to get his point across: a poem![96] I'm betting on the latter. Not because a poem necessarily engages more than prose. Rather, this lyrical medium worked precisely because – as the case above demonstrates – people tend to listen more the less one speaks. Or, as my homiletics teacher Rabbi Ken Ehrlich put it, "The ears will hear only what the butt will stand to listen to."[97]

Yet some stand in protest of that assertion, defending a tradition that has encouraged our people to offer countless commentaries on any number of issues, whether welcomed or not. And, it's a tradition not unique to the Jewish community. Pervasive is the claim that speaking up is a productive way to legitimize one's place within and one's perspective on a particular issue. Through offering countless words at the community altar, we say: "I am here. I count. I matter."

---

[94] This contemporary scenario may also help us understand more fully the message behind *The Boy Who Cried Wolf*. Though often his demise is summarized in his lies, in light of this scenario we can see that there may be an additional lesson to teach: words, in general, have value. And, if we choose to speak at unnecessary times for unnecessary reasons, the value of our words decreases to a point where and when they are worth absolutely nothing.

[95] My translation to Deuteronomy 32:1-3. To be fair, I took a little liberty with the Hebrew, in order to over-emphasize the poetic form of these verses through rhyme.

[96] The Bible actually ascribes three poems to Moses. One of them is Psalm 90. And, the others are in the Torah itself: the Song of the Sea (Ex. 15) and the Song of Return (Deut. 32). Together, these Torah poems are the bookends to the Wilderness experience. The back poetic bookend, this Song of Return, warns, instructs and gives hope as the people stand poised to enter the Promised Land. As well, it is typical of Biblical poetry as each verse consists of at least two lines that create parallels of meaning.

[97] Rabbi Ken Ehrlich is the immediate past dean of the Hebrew Union College – Jewish Institute of Religion, Cincinnati Campus and director of Homiletics.

But, that's exactly why others say this tradition of words should be closely guarded.[98] Because, in the need to express the "I" within community, an abundant offering of words may actually be counterproductive, leading – as the case above proves – one to be discounted or discredited. Plato concluded as much in his observation of the Republic's debates: "Wise men speak because they have something to say; fools, because they [merely] have [a need] to say something."[99]

So, even when well-intended this devaluation can occur. Why? Because our words, to quote the movie *Swingers*, are "money."[100] And, like the Federal Reserve, it's within our power to produce an endless supply. But if we do, whether for good or bad, we risk the value of each word – like each bill – becoming less. Therefore, to retain the value of our speech, we must strike a balance between not speaking at all and speaking too much. For, therein, our words retain their worth.

Surely, the rabbis of old understood this. For, historically, they delivered publically only two sermons. One was given on *Shabbat HaGadol* (the Great Sabbath) to prepare the people for the coming festival of Passover. The other occurred, and still occurs, on the weekend of *Shabbat Shuvah* (the Sabbath of Return). Because, as Moses discovered, we – the people of Israel – can often do a lot more with less, returning us – we pray – to the ever-resourceful words of God.

Ha-azinu // Give Ear
Bite 2 – *"To Boldly Go Where No One Has Gone Before"*

After assigning an art project, an instructor briefly leaves his classroom to retrieve the paper he had forgotten in the supply closet. Upon his return, he noticed that one of his young pupils had not waited for the paper. Instead, this pupil had found another medium upon which to begin his masterpiece. "Michelangelo!" yelled the instructor. "Why did you paint on the wall?" The young Michelangelo replied: "Because it needed a little something. Don't you think? I mean, the wall just seemed so empty."

It is, after all, within our nature to create in, and in the case of Michelangelo, on the empty spaces of our lives. In this Torah portion of *Ha-azinu* we begin to understand where this creative drive comes from as we read in Deuteronomy 32:10: "God found him (referring to Israel) in a desert region, in an empty place, a howling waste." Although there appears to be very little that is

---

[98] One such guard that tradition places on our speech is *LaShon Hara*. Though it literally translates into "to speak evil," the sages did not interpret such value limitedly, restricting only negative speech. They included even positive remarks about particular individuals/subjects when the subject of such words was not present.

[99] Quoted in Larry Chang's *Wisdom for the Soul: Five Millennia of Prescriptions for Spiritual Healing*. Gnosophia Pub.: Washington, DC, 2006. p. 480

[100] Jon Favreau. *Swingers*. Miramax Films: 1996.

extraordinary about this poetic verse from the English translation, the Hebrew contains a very rare and important Biblical word: *tohu*, meaning "empty."

Modern commentator, Richard Elliot Friedman, notes: "This word has not occurred since its mention at the very beginning of Torah: 'the earth had been empty (*tohu*) and unformed (*v'vohu*)' (Genesis 1:2). Now," continues Friedman, "Israel's environment in the wilderness is pictured comparably to the condition of the universe prior to the acts of creation."[101] It is not a coincidence that *tohu* appears in the first and last portions read on regular Sabbaths. This word is written particularly in these two places, I speculate, to teach us that just as God began Torah by creating the world from emptiness, we – at its end – must be similarly inspired, continuing God's work of creation in the empty spaces in our lives.

I think it is fair to say that as a species we have pursued our Divine drive of creativity boldly, going, in the words of Star-Trek, "where no man (or woman) has gone before." Interestingly, Dwayne Day from *The Space Review* points out that this fictional mission statement may have come from a real initiative to explore the emptiness of space.[102] In a 1958 White House document, meant to garner support for a national space program in the wake of the Sputnik flight, it is written: there is "a compelling urge in man to explore and to discover; a thrust of curiosity that leads men to try to go where no one has gone before."[103]

This statement is particularly true for the Jewish people, who – it may be argued – have disproportionately gone where no one has gone before. As Mark Twain put it, "If statistics are right, the Jews constitute but one percent of the human race. It suggests a nebulous dim puff of stardust lost in the blaze of the Milky Way. Properly the Jew ought hardly to be heard of, but he is heard of, has always been heard of. He is as prominent on the planet as any other people and his contributions to the world's list of great names in literature, science, art, music, finance, medicine, and abstruse learning are also way out of proportion to the weakness of his numbers… He could be vain of himself [for utilizing and filling in this emptiness], and be excused for it." But, we do not entertain such vanity.

Or, at least we should not, for all of us have realized that our explorations, despite the best of intentions, have caused unforeseen consequences. Some of these consequences have been productive. For example, while making white wine at the end of the first millennium C.E., the Benedictine monks accidently created a carbonation process within the bottle. The unplanned result… champagne! Other consequences, admittedly, are downright tragic. For example, when Christopher Columbus "discovered" the New World, his voyage initiated an enormous exchange (known as the Columbian Exchange) between the Eastern and Western hemispheres. While the exchange of plants

---

[101] Richard Elliot Friedman. *Commentary on the Torah*, p. 668
[102] "Boldly Going: Star Trek and Spaceflight," 2005
[103] "Introduction to Outer Space," March 1958

and animals proved very helpful, it was the unforeseen and unseen transfer of communicable diseases which devastated the indigenous populations in America. It has been estimated that the ensuing epidemic of small pox alone may have killed up to 90% of some Native American societies.

At these moments, when our imaginative faculties get the better of our rational faculties, causing outcomes we fail to see, we may be inclined to go back to the drawing board and erase what was written. This impulse is understandable. After all, seeing that there may have been a mistake in the creation of human beings, even God attempts to wash the slate clean with a flood. We can hear the Divine's frustration in Genesis:

> "The Lord saw how great the wickedness of people on earth could be, and how every plan devised by their minds was nothing but evil all the time. And, the Lord regretted having made human beings on the earth, and God's heart was saddened. The Lord said, 'I will blot out from the earth the people whom I created – them together with beast, creeping things, and birds of the sky; for I regret that I made them.'"[104]

But as God understood, and as we all understand, the slate can never be totally wiped clean. Some dust always remains on the chalk board; some paint can never be completely removed from the wall.

And, that is not only okay. That is the point. For our faith teaches us in the book of Psalms that when these unforeseen consequences occur as a by-product of our creative pursuits we must "be ever mindful of them and not attempt to blot them out," (Psalm 109:14). For these stains on our record, these indelible marks on our soul serve a purpose. They act as signs of caution, which if heeded, help us steer all our Divine drives, creativity included, towards more productive ends. For it is human to err and then be inclined to give up. It is all-together Divine to continue in the face of errors, as we learn from the mistakes of our past in order to create a better future.

Certainly Michelangelo understood this message well, for he did not give up on his ambitions in the face of the stern reprimand from his instructor. Instead, being ever mindful of the reproach, he found a more appropriate wall upon which to display his Divine creativity: the Sistine Chapel. May we, too, at this moment of introspection and reflection be human enough to realize we are not all-together perfect. We too have erred. Nonetheless, let us not give up on our dreams. For when we take our creativity and make it a reality we act divinely, bringing a measure of fulfillment and wholeness to the *tohu*, the emptiness, which remains in our world.

---

[104] Genesis 6:5-7

Ha-azinu // Give Ear
Bite 3 – *Finding Renewal in Days of Old*

With the High Holy Days behind us, we look ahead to a year still in its infancy. The newness of the year matches the sense of renewal in our souls, fresh-scrubbed and fully atoned following our spiritual exertions. It is time to move forward, to embrace the future and all the opportunity that it offers. Yet here we read in *Ha-azinu, zakhor yamot olam*—"Remember the days of old, consider the years of ages past." (Deuteronomy 32:7) Jewish tradition, it often seems, consists of a constant negotiation between memory and future longings, a managing of the tension between looking backward and moving forward.

On the one hand, we've always been a people who boldly forge ahead. We were born in transit; we have remained in transit. When the Temple was destroyed, Rabbinic Judaism emerged, pulling from Torah the *Mishnah*, which inspired the *Gemara*, which influenced the medieval codes of *Halachah* (Jewish law) and the still-growing tradition of *Responsa*: a living, breathing, much-debated statement of values that should guide our conduct. We Jews work and yearn for the arrival of the messianic age, a time when all the world will be at peace, a future point that endlessly beckons: "*Lech-l'cha!*" Get going! Keep moving!

And, so, we do. In Babylon and Spain, we established towering institutions of Jewish culture. When fortune's wheel turned and Spain expelled the Jews, we rebuilt in Europe and beyond. When pogroms swept Europe, and then the Holocaust, we left again for America and Palestine (later Israel). Wherever we went, again and again, we recreated our food, language, music, and literature. In recent centuries, Judaism has given birth to Movements: Orthodoxy, Reform, Conservative, Reconstructionist, Renewal, and more: communities who continually seek new expressions of our ancient values, who embrace to varying degrees scientific and cultural progress even as we cling to our Torah.

On the other hand (speaking of Torah), Judaism is a tradition of memory. "*Zachor et yom ha-Shabbat*," the Torah teaches each of us, "remember the Sabbath day:" the very first one, that seventh day of creation; and every Sabbath of your lifetime, which recalls the original. Remember who created you, who led you out of Egypt. Remember Egypt, the origin of our social justice consciousness to this day. Remember Sinai, where all of us stood, not-yet born right beside the born, for the gift of Torah itself. Together, we remember our departed loved ones on *Yizkor*, and at the end of every service. All of our holiday celebrations and many of our rituals are deeply rooted in historical and mythical memory. We invoke the memory of Abraham, Isaac and Jacob, Sarah, Rebecca, Rachel and Leah in our prayers. And, week after week, year after year, we read the Torah, all the old stories, lest we forget. Remember where you come from! Judaism exhorts us. Remember who you have been!

And, so, we do. We read the Torah, recount *midrash*, recite prayers, observe holidays, in ways our ancestors did. Yes, the Temple is gone and, sure, melodies and recipes change; but the lamb shank on the seder plate still represents the Paschal sacrifice, which itself represented the lamb described in Exodus, whose blood marked the doorposts, staying the Angel of Death from their doorsteps. In our seder we recite words of Torah, and chant blessings recorded in the *Talmud*. Sure, we put cotton on our sukkah; they likely used corn stalks, palm fronds, olive branches, or grape vines. But cotton bolls or grape leaves, a sukkah is a sukkah: reminiscent of the Israelite wandering in the wilderness, reminiscent of our ancestors' long nights harvesting in the fields, representing the same lessons of the fragility of material possessions by contrast with the durability of love and friendship, the strength we gain from each other and from God. Each year we are older, perhaps wiser, certainly different, but the Torah, our love for Torah and *am Yisrael*, the Jewish people, remains at the center.

Perhaps the paradox is best contained and illuminated by the line from Lamentations, much repeated during the Ten Days just ended: *hashiveinu adonai elohecha, ve-nashuva*—"return us, Adonai our God, to you and we shall return, renew us as in days of old."[105] As Jews, we move forward by going backward, returning to our origin. When we repent from sin, we make *t'shuvah*, we return—to God, to our best selves. When we immerse in the *mikvah*, we don't imagine that we are being "born again;" rather, we are being washed clean, restored to our original purity. And yet, the *mikvah* does not wash away our wisdom, born of experience, carried in memory. For us, moving ahead and looking back are not mutually exclusive; rather, our history and our spiritual inheritance serve as the foundation upon which we build a better future.

"Remember the days of old, consider the years of ages past," Moses exhorts the people. In the next moment, he is gone, and the children of Israel are on the move again. As they cross the Jordan, an uncertain future awaits them; but a knowledge of their past, as solid as Mount Sinai, bears them onward.

---

[105] Lamentations 5:21.

Portion 11:
V'zot Habrachah // This is the Blessing
Torah Portion: Deuteronomy 33:1-34:12

"THIS IS THE BLESSING WITH WHICH MOSES, THE MAN OF GOD, BADE THE ISRAELITES FAREWELL." As the first book of Torah ended with Jacob blessings his 12 sons, so does the last book end with the father of the Israel nation delivering a blessing to each of its 12 tribes.

According to the *midrash*, Moses was intentional about ending the Torah this way. It imagines Moses beseeching God, saying, "All my life I have scolded this people. At the end of my life, let me leave them with a blessing." (*Midrash P'titrat Moshe*) And he does so brilliantly, stating an uplifting word to each and every one... save the tribe of Shimon. It's not that he gave them a "bad" blessing, as Jacob had done. Rather, they don't get mentioned at all. The Rabbis have two theories regarding this omission. They postulate that either the tribe of Shimon was being punished for its culpability in worshipping the Golden Calf or that the tribe was virtually non-existent, as many of its members had been absorbed into the tribe of Judah.

Moses' final words reassure the Israelites that despite impending suffering, God will guide and protect them. Moses ascends the mountain and God shows him all that will happen to the Israelite people until the end of days. Moses receives the "Divine Kiss" and dies there, atop the nondescript Mount Nebo. "Moses was 120 years old when he died; his eyes were undimmed and his vigor unabated. And, the Israelites bewailed Moses in the steppes of Moab for thirty days. When the period of wailing and mourning came to an end, Joshua son of Nun was filled with the spirit of wisdom." With that, the next chapter of our story continues.

Chazak, chazak, v'nitchazeik!
From strength to strength, we are strengthened!

Index